D0119499

The Doc: My Story

The Doc: My Story
Hallowed Be Thy Game

Tommy Docherty

headline

First published in 2006
by HEADLINE PUBLISHING GROUP

1

Cataloguing in Publication Data is available from the British Library

10-digit ISBN: 0 7553 1554 5
13-digit ISBN: 978 0 7553 1554 3

Typeset in Plantin by Palimpsest Book Production Limited,
Grangemouth, Stirlingshire

Printed and bound in Great Britain by
Mackays of Chatham plc, Chatham, Kent

Headline's policy is to use papers that are natural, renewable and recyclable
products and made from wood grown in sustainable forests. The logging
and manufacturing processes are expected to conform to the environmental
regulations of the country of origin.

HEADLINE PUBLISHING GROUP
A division of Hodder Headline
338 Euston Road
London NW1 3BH

www.headline.co.uk
www.hodderheadline.com

My autobiography is dedicated to Mary –
simply the best!

ACKNOWLEDGEMENTS

We would like to thank the following who by way of recollection, access to memorabilia or friendship have helped significantly in the creation of this book: Julian Alexander and all at Lucas Alexander Whitley; Barclays Bank plc in particular John Lowe; Ken and Jean Bolam; Frank Blunstone; Chelsea FC; Phil Dann; Ron Harris; all at Headline in particular David Wilson and Wendy McCance; Lou Macari; Toni and Charley Morrell – simply great; Lawrie McMenemy; Arthur Montford; Jack Rollin; Ian St John; John Turnock; Steve and Deb Waterall.

I would like to express my sincere thanks to my good pal Les Scott who worked with me on my autobiography. As the likes of Stanley Matthews, George Best, Jimmy Greaves and Gordon Banks discovered when Les helped them write their respective autobiographies, his knowledge of football is phenomenal and, as a football writer, he is up there with the all time best. Thanks Les, what I initially saw as an awesome task turned out to be smooth, easy and – fun!

For Lauren and Ruby – shine on!

To Jane Morrell (LW), for giving what was believed never existed.

Tommy Docherty, 2006

Contents

1

I BELONG TO GLASGOW

I knew Jimmy Johnstone was a great winger, but until I had him under my charge I didn't know just how great a footballer he was. It was October 1971 and I was conducting my first training session since my appointment as manager of Scotland. It had been four years since 'Jinky' had played a key role in Celtic winning the European Cup and, in the course of that 1966–67 season, help the greatest team ever to have graced Scottish football score over 200 goals in competitive matches. Having been a manager in England for ten years, I well knew the capabilities and idiosyncratic ways of the Anglo-Scots. My knowledge of the home-based Scots was good, but nowhere near as detailed as it was for the players with English clubs such as Billy Bremner, Archie Gemmill, Asa Hartford, George Graham, Peter Lorimer, Willie Morgan and Martin Buchan.

The general feeling was that Jimmy Johnstone had never produced his club form at international level. (How many Scots can one say that about?) More to the point, the word was Jimmy had passed his peak. For the greater part of his ten years as a player with Celtic – six as a member of the Scotland national squad – Jimmy had been a paradox. In essence he was an orthodox right-winger, but such were his imperious and impish skills his career had been a continuous exasperation and affront to the conventional; to the sober, hardworking artisans of the game and, above all, to officialdom. On and off the field he was always incalculable and often outrageous. As a player Jimmy was an eccentric, erratic genius, a gifted individualist; a showman who drew the crowds, entertained and astonished them, and sent them home with the feeling that football had indeed a place in the best of all possible worlds.

Jimmy had an impish streak. When he caught himself being orthodox a perverse impulse took hold of him. To be conventional for a full ninety minutes was beyond him. Having produced a masterly show of the winger's art that even Stanley Matthews or Tom Finney would have found hard to equal, and, satisfied Celtic were in the driving seat with the game won, he would then decide to amuse himself. One of my predecessors as Scotland manager, Andy Beattie, who combined his duties with that of being manager of Kilmarnock, once held a fullscale practice match of Scotland players at his home ground of Rugby Park. For reasons known only to him, not only did Andy not include Jimmy Johnstone in the twenty-two for the match, he told Jimmy to don a linesman's uniform and run a line – implying that on recent form that was all Jimmy was good for. Jimmy flatly refused to be a linesman for his team-mates and spent the entire afternoon sitting watching the practice game from the empty grandstand.

Some weeks later Jimmy returned to Rugby Park with Celtic. Celtic wiped the floor with Kilmarnock that day, winning 6–0, with Jimmy helping himself to a hat-trick and setting up the other three goals. With the score at 5–0 and with two goals to his name, Jimmy set off from the half-way line on a characteristic jinking run which took him past five Kilmarnock players before rounding goalkeeper Campbell Forsyth, and side-footing the ball into an empty net. As soon as he saw the ball cross the line Jimmy took off again and made a bee-line for the Kilmarnock dugout where a now-forlorn Andy Beattie was seated.

'Hey, Andy,' shouted Jimmy, jerking a thumb over his shoulder in the direction of the goal where he had just planted the ball. 'Not bad for a bloody linesman, eh?'

Brilliant as he was on that day, after such a show of cheek his international career appeared dead and buried. Beattie and his successors were wary of Jinky, thinking him more trouble than he was worth. But when I became Scotland manager, I wanted to resurrect that career. When I announced Jimmy Johnstone was to be part of my first Scotland squad for the European Championship qualifier against Portugal in October 1971, there was no shortage of people to tell me I had made a mistake: 'He's lost his appetite for the game,' I was told by a top Scottish football writer. 'Jimmy's not interested any more,' said another, adding, 'Including him in your squad is your one mistake. He'll screw it up for you.'

I have always trusted my own judgement in matters of football – that might not come as a surprise to many – especially where the relative merits of players are concerned. I firmly believed Jimmy was still a great player, though I was well aware that an up-and-coming talent at Celtic had assumed his mantle at Parkhead. Lou Macari had emerged as a player of sublime quality and had become the firm favourite of the Celtic faithful. In addition, the performances of a teenage forward by the name of Kenny Dalglish had everyone describing him as a star in the making. As the first practice match with my squad got underway, I was supremely confident of achieving success with the team. What's more, I was certain I could handle wee Jinky. He was my sort of player and I firmly believed I could get him fired up again, so that he would be intrinsic to my success. We were both from the Gorbals in Glasgow, so I felt we had a certain affinity. More importantly, I felt I was his type of manager: a no-nonsense, straight-talking manager who, like his boss at Celtic, Jock Stein, lived and breathed football and encouraged flair players to express their talent.

It was not without some pride that I got my first session with the Scotland team underway. However, the practice match I'd planned was only twenty minutes old when I decided to abandon it. The news soon got around and in no time the press were knocking on my door.

'Why did you abandon the first practice match after only twenty minutes? Word is, it was all because of Jimmy Johnstone.'

'That's right,' I said.

Mumbling beset the room, some of which was audible to me.

'Knew Jimmy'd be trouble.'

'Doc thought he could handle him.'

'Told you, Jinky's not hungry any more.'

It was then that a reporter from the Scottish *Sun* piped up. 'So, what was it with Jimmy, Tommy?'

'We'd been playing for twenty minutes when, because of Jimmy Johnstone, I decided it was pointless carrying on,' I informed the press boys.

'Why?'

'Nobody could get the ball off him!'

I was involved in football as a player and manager for forty-five years. To me football has always been more than a game, not something one simply 'takes up' like squash or golf. It is akin to religion, the players its disciples, the supporters its congregation. I have been fortunate enough to encounter some of the greatest exponents of the game, Jimmy Johnstone being but one. It was also my privilege to pit my wits against some of the greatest managers, men such as Matt Busby, Bill Shankly, Jock Stein, Brian Clough, Bob Paisley, Alf Ramsey, Bill Nicholson and Don Revie, who occupy a lofty plateau in football. For me, reaching somewhere near that level involved a long, often arduous, sometimes controversial, journey. It was a journey that began in my native city of Glasgow.

I was born Thomas Henderson Docherty, in the Gorbals district of Glasgow in 1928. The 1930s was a tough decade in British history and to be brought up in the Gorbals was arguably the harshest upbringing of all. Life for the Dochertys was hard, a constant battle for survival made all the more difficult when my father, Thomas senior, died when I was only nine years old. Poverty and hardship went virtually unnoticed in an area of the city so deprived, where illness and malnutrition were a constant threat to family life. The Gorbals was not only impoverished and socially deprived. In the 1930s it was also home to the notorious razor gangs. The Gorbals was a multicultural melting pot of people who had come from the Highlands, Ireland and Eastern Europe to seek work in the iron, locomotive and brewing industries. There were some 10,000 Jews in the area, over 150 Jewish shops, two synagogues and a Jewish school. When more Jewish people came to the area after fleeing Nazi Germany, it was not unusual to hear Yiddish spoken amidst the bustle on Crown Street or Cumberland Street. Each community spawned its own razor gangs who, having established their turf, often resorted to extreme violence to protect it.

As a boy growing up in the area I never came into contact with these vicious criminals, but it is no secret that many of them operated extortion rackets and preyed on the poor and vulnerable. Many was the young man walking home from a night out who had the fear of God put in him when stopped by a gang asking, 'Who are ye, an' where dae ye stay?'

There is a tendency for some former Gorbals folk of the 1930s and '40s to look back on such days with misty-eyed sentimentality. I'm not one of them. I've heard people bemoan the loss of community spirit in the area. Whilst it is true there was a strong sense of that back then, there was also grinding poverty, exploitation and the ever-present threat of violence. Happily the razor gangs have long gone, as has much of the deprivation I knew as a boy, and the second regeneration is proceeding apace. But for me, I bless the day my mother, sisters and myself were liberated from the area and the poverty that shackled our lives. No human being should have to live in the conditions that we endured during my early childhood. The name Glasgow derives from the Celtic word *Glascu*, which loosely translates as 'the dear, green place'. In the 1930s there was precious little greenery to the Gorbals and I should imagine the area, once described as one of the worst slums in Europe, endeared itself to very few people.

Glasgow may well have been a dear, green place at one time in history, but the industrialisation changed the place beyond recognition. Due to the wide and navigable Clyde, Glasgow had been a major trading port since the fifteenth century. The Industrial Revolution, however, literally transformed Glasgow as a city. One of the necessities for steam power was coal. The abundant seams of the Lanarkshire coalfields fuelled the industries that sprang up alongside the river, industries that were worked by cheap labour from the Highlands and those fleeing the Irish potato famine of the 1840s.

As Glasgow's industry and trade boomed so did its population, from 77,000 in 1801, to over 700,000 in 1901 and nigh on a million come the 1930s. (The city's population is actually less now, some 620,000.) In the mid-Victorian age, tenement blocks were built in an attempt to cope with the choking influxes of people. The tenements offered accommodation that was basic in the extreme. Many families occupied but a single room which had no running water or sanitation; the sole source of heat and cooking was the 'range'. Come the late 1920s these buildings were dilapidated and it was into one of these tenements that I was born.

We lived in what was known as a 'single end', which, as the name implies, was a single room in an 1850s tenement block that contained some dozen similar homes. Though my mother gave birth to a daughter shortly after my father's death, for much of my young childhood my parents Thomas and Georgina, my younger sister Margaret and I all slept in one bed. To refer to it as a bed is misleading. It was in fact a plank of wood that inserted into a slot in the wall which my mother covered with a mattress and blankets. There was one hand-basin in a corner of the room and our daily ablutions were performed there, except on Fridays when my father would bring an old tin bath up from the yard and laboriously fill it with kettles of boiling water. Filling the tin bath with water from the kettle was no easy matter, so the entire family took it in turns to bathe in the same water. My mother first, then my father, my sister and finally me.

Being the fourth occupant of the same water, I must have emerged little cleaner than when I got in.

I never really got to know what sort of man my father was. He worked impossibly long hours at Stewarts & Lloyds iron foundry and my abiding memory of him was that he never enjoyed good health. I should imagine this was the combined result of him living in a cramped, damp room and working in a foundry where there was scant regard for health and safety. My father was not a man given to showing emotion or affection for his children. It was not just the tenements that were Victorian; looking back now the Victorian age seemed to over-hang into the 1930s. Irrespective of how poor a family might be, men considered themselves to be the head of the family. To display love and affection would have been seen as a sign of weakness. Men saw their role as being providers of a roof, food for the table and coal in the hearth. But often the weekly wage would be spent in the pub on a Friday and Saturday night, leaving the mother to provide for the family for the rest of the week from her even more meagre wage. I can't recall my father ever doing this, though he did drink a lot which is why Mother had to supplement my father's wage by working as a charlady.

I never really connected with my father. Gorbals men never seemed to spend any 'quality time' with their children. Children were to be seen and not heard, and were certainly not to be indulged even by means of play; another throwback to the Victorian age. My father never took me to the cinema – the 'pictures' we used to call it. We never went for walks, visited museums or played football down in the backyard. We never had a holiday either. This was normal in the Gorbals where children played on their own, happy to keep their distance from fathers who might give them a clip round the ear for simply being around. I consider myself fortunate in one respect – in that my father, unlike some men in that tenement block, never beat us children for minor indiscretions, nor came home rolling drunk ready to take issue with my mother.

There is a story of King George V visiting the homes of mining families in the Lanarkshire coalfields just after the First World War. The king was appalled at the living conditions of these mining folk as their homes had no running water, sanitation or electricity. The only means of sanitation was a single outside privy, which was communal and shared with up to six other families. The squalor in which his subjects lived came as a shock to King George V who told one miner, 'No person in this great country of ours should have to tolerate such appalling living conditions.' The king went on to inform the miner that as soon as he returned to London he would summon the Prime Minister, and demand immediate action to be taken to improve the dreadful living conditions of Lanarkshire mining folk. As the king continued his walk-about reporters rushed up to the miner to ask what the king had said to him. The miner repeated the king's words, which prompted one reporter to ask, 'When did you first realise you lived in such terrible conditions?' 'Aboot a minute ago,' replied the miner, 'when His Majesty the King telt me.' Similarly, it was only in my early teens, when we moved to Shettleston, that I came to realise the deprivation of my formative years.

I was nine years old when my father finally lost the fight to keep himself alive. Following his death, Mum took to cleaning early in the morning as well as the evening. Mother had little alternative: as four months after the death of my father, she gave birth to my sister Mary. Having arranged for a neighbour to 'check on the bairns', my mother would rise at around 4.30 a.m., report to work at five and return to us children at around seven so that we could have breakfast and, in the case of Margaret and me, get ready for school.

Occasionally my mother cleaned offices, but in the main she did the homes of middle-management people who lived in the 'well-to-do' part of the Gorbals, or in nearby Queen's Park. Quite often my mother would return from these houses with food that the owners, rather than throw away, would let her have.

These windfall provisions supplemented my regular diet, such as it was. A staple meal in the Docherty home was 'mince 'n' tatties' which, as the name implies, comprised mince and potatoes and whatever cheap vegetable was in season such as carrot. I can never recall eating a beef or lamb roast. We simply couldn't afford such cuts of meat.

The clothes my sisters and I wore were second-hand, bought for pennies at local jumble sales or off the stalls at the Barrowland market. I can't ever recall having new clothes. My trousers were patched, my jumpers and socks darned, and any fraying on my shirts was systematically stitched by my mother. My clothes were second-hand but always clean and ironed. Every morning my mother would check that I had washed properly, that my hair was clean and combed, and shoes polished in readiness for school. For all the deprivation we experienced, Mother maintained standards.

Our clothes were washed once a week in the 'steamie', a large Victorian wash house some hundred yards from our home. It was there that the women folk of the Gorbals met, with their children, to do the weekly wash – a labour-intensive affair. Clothes were washed in a large aluminium tub and pounded with a wooden 'dolly'. The 'dolly' was about three feet long with handles at the top which women would twist and turn to manipulate clothes to and fro. The washed clothes were then put through a mangle, which comprised two heavy rubber rollers which squeezed out excess water and deposited it into the tub below. The rubber rollers were turned manually by cranking the mangle handle; in the days of large cotton sheets and heavy woollen blankets, it was arduous work.

The steamie was not only a place to wash clothes, it served as a social meeting point. It was here that I learned about the community in which I lived. The women all knew each other. They talked of the trials and tribulations of their families. Listening in, I became acquainted with the history of illnesses, operations, marriages, loves unfulfilled, deaths and the idiosyncratic ways and characters of Gorbals folk. Invariably these people were male and, as such, were always afforded the suffix of 'man' – the schoolboard man, the cruelty man, the polis-man, rent man, gas man, insurance man and ragman. Of all these people the only one that appealed to me as a boy was the ragman.

The ragman would signal his entry into our street with a blast on a bugle which brought all us children running from our homes. In exchange for rags, old ornaments or unwanted domestic appliances, the ragman would give us children a toy or a goldfish. It was as if Santa Claus visited our street every week. Occasionally the ragman would also give us hand-me-down clothes from another neighbourhood. Domestic appliances would be mended and then resold, or if beyond repair they were sold for scrap. The ragman fulfilled an important function in our community, like some peripatetic swapshop of the 1930s.

Another business that thrived in the Gorbals was the pawn-broker, of which I can recall some six shops in total. There appeared to be no stigma attached to going to a pawnbroker's, just about every family I knew did it, often every week. Visits to the pawnbroker were not confined to adults. More often than not parents sent their children to pawn items. After my father's death Mother found it hard to bring up her children on her meagre wages. My weekly visits to the pawnbroker's with the mantel clock were usually on a Wednesday. When Mother was paid on a Friday evening I would return to reclaim the clock, paying the pawnbroker the original price of half a crown plus sixpence (2.5p) interest.

Once I was in the shop when a young girl handed over a size-able package wrapped in brown paper. Like me she was a regular, the package she pawned every week was her father's only suit. The pawnbroker handed over the money and stored the parcel with all the other suits. I remember the girl making her lips disappear as she handed over her parcel. As we left the shop together her father was waiting outside. He took the couple of bob off the girl and, in all probability, headed straight for the nearest pub. As the girl and I walked along the street together I remarked that her father must be doing all right as, seemingly, he had bought a second suit.

'Away wi' ye, he only has the one suit. The one he's wearing,' said the girl.

'But I thought you just pawned his suit,' I remarked.

'Ach, no,' said the girl. 'After months o' pawning the same suit, the 'broker stopped opening the parcel. So now we just wrap an old bed sheet in brown paper.'

For me, as for all children, rich or poor, Christmas was a very special time. On Christmas Eve I would accompany my mother and sisters to midnight mass, only for us to return to church the following day. I would wake on a Christmas morning to find an old sock hanging from my bed that looked as if it contained a leg bearing the worst varicose veins imaginable. I was bursting with excitement as I opened the wrapping paper, carefully folding it and putting it away for my mother to reuse the next year. There would be an orange, an apple, perhaps a colouring book and crayons, and a book to read, the latter usually a classic adapted for children, such as *Treasure Island* or *The Count of Monte Cristo*. Even as a small boy I knew how difficult it was for Mother to provide Christmas presents for my sisters and me so, meagre as these gifts were, I was always grateful for whatever was in my stocking.

My mother, like most Gorbals women, saved up for Christmas by putting away a shilling or so every week into the 'Christmas Club'. The club was run from a local shop, and must have been a moneyspinner for the proprietor, who for about ten months kept a record of the weekly payments and, come December, would inform each woman how much she had to spend in his shop on presents and food for her family. Not only was the shopkeeper assured of the custom at Christmas, I assume he also earned a tidy amount in interest from the club funds on deposit at the building society or bank. So it was that even at Christmas, and by virtue of someone seeming to provide a helping hand, Gorbals folk were subject to a deft form of exploitation.

My best Christmas presents were football-related. Mother couldn't afford a leather caseball, but I might receive a small rubber ball, or perhaps a pair of football shorts, something of a misnomer as they would hang down below my knees for me to 'grow in to'. Every couple of years I would be given a pair of second-hand football boots bought from the Barrowland market; Mother would polish and dubbin them, and wash the laces so they appeared as new. She would also have a new set of leather studs inserted in the soles at the local cobblers. As with the shorts, the boots were always at least two sizes too big. To make them fit I wore two or three pairs of socks. As my feet grew, I simply shed a pair of socks as a snake would a skin.

I was eleven years old when war was declared. Fearful that Glasgow was to be heavily bombed, many families in the Gorbals were evacuated, ours included. My mother, my sisters and I travelled by train to Stirling then by bus to Bridge of Allan. We had been informed that on arrival we would stay with a local family until it was safe to return to Glasgow. This was the first time I had ever travelled outside the city and even though we were at war the journey was a source of wonder to me. My initial excitement, however, quickly evaporated when we arrived in Stirling and discovered our boarding arrangements. Probably because no Bridge of Allan household could accommodate a woman and three children, we were informed that we were to be split up. My mother and younger sister were billeted with one family, whilst my other sister and I were allocated to another. This arrangement was wholly unacceptable to my mother. To our relief, she announced she was taking us back home to Glasgow.

'If we're tae be bombed and die, at least we'll die in our ain hame,' Mother told the well-meaning Evacuation committee, at which point we gathered up our belongings and walked back to

Stirling. It was late in the evening and on arriving at the station we discovered to our dismay we had missed the last train to Glasgow. Undeterred, Mother entered into discussions with a taxi driver, the result of which was we travelled back home in his cab. I have no idea how much that trip cost, but I remember Mother saying it cost her almost every penny she had. Like the rest of us, she felt it was money well spent. We subsequently saw the first stages of the war in our 'ain hame', happy that we had stayed together as a family. As it was to turn out, the Gorbals did not suffer heavy bombing, certainly not as much as the areas that contained the shipyards.

My mother couldn't afford to take Margaret, Mary and me to the theatre, even to the annual pantomime, so the wireless provided my only means of entertainment. I loved hearing comedians such as Sid Field, who did a marvellous routine explaining golf to a beginner; the Crazy Gang, featuring Bud Flanagan and Chesney Allen; George Formby, and Leslie Sarony. Of course the acts that appealed to me most were Scottish. It was a rare treat to hear Will Fyffe on the radio, the man who wrote the classic song 'I Belong to Glasgow', which to this day remains synonymous with the city.

The acts we children heard on the wireless inspired us to perform our own impromptu neighbourhood shows. The 'Backcourt Parade' was once a feature of Gorbals life and took place on Saturday evenings during the summer. Every tenement block spawned its own version where children would sing songs, perform comedy (usually 'stolen' from acts heard on the wireless) and dance routines. A group of us would decide after Saturday tea that we were going to 'do a show', the precursor to much arguing over what was going to be in and who was going to do what.

I might tell a few jokes, or else sing. I usually sang Al Jolson numbers or songs I had heard around the streets in praise of Celtic. One in particular I can remember to this day, sung to the tune of 'The Lambeth Walk':

Any time you're Lambeth way
Any evening, any day
You'll find the Bhoys
Doing the Celtic walk;
Tuohy, McGonagle; that Delaney,
On the field he's brainy,
Take a look at McDonald; Divers . . . Murphy;
They've got Rangers on their toes,
They've put four past Dawson's nose,
That's just the Bhoys,
Doing the Celtic walk!

The reference to Dawson was to Jim Dawson the Rangers goal-keeper of the day. McDonald and Divers were Celtic stalwarts. Malcolm McDonald was Celtic's centre-half who, unusually for a player in such a position, was only 5ft 9in tall. What McDonald lacked in inches, however, he more than made up for with immaculate timing, which enabled him to compete in the air with the tallest of centre-forwards. John Divers was an inside-forward who joined Celtic from Renfrew Juniors. He was a good all-round sportsman, an accomplished cricketer, golfer and tennis player.

Parents and relatives would hang out of the windows of their homes to watch these shows which, as the name suggests, took place down in the backyard of the tenement block. We children carried on performing these shows even with the advent of the war, although the content did change, becoming very patriotic and anti-Nazi. For all its militaristic tone, the 'Backcourt Parade' still served as a momentary diversion from the worries of the war for many. They certainly did for me.

My family would not see out the duration of the war in the Gorbals. We lived for a short time in a house in Gallowgate before moving to one of the new council houses in Shettleston and boasted not only an inside toilet but also a sitting room, three bedrooms and a kitchen. We had never known such undreamed-of luxury. I attended St Mark's school and though never a distinguished scholar, I did comparatively well and was never a source of trouble. A scamp, yes, but I was never a disruptive pupil. I learned to read and write, do arithmetic, memorised my times-tables, was familiar with the Bible and had a basic grasp of history and geography. I enjoyed reading the books I borrowed from school or the local library, and was fanatical about football. From early childhood I'd had two dreams in life: to remove my mother and sisters from poverty and provide them with a better quality of life; and to become a footballer.

In Glasgow at the time for a boy of my background, there were two routes of escape: football or boxing. Though I had always been able to look after myself, I just didn't have it in me to want to knock the living daylights out of anybody. It was always football for me. Besides which I have never been totally convinced of boxing's image as the ultra-macho sport – they always seem to be talking about belts, purses and rings.

I had been brought up a Catholic and Parkhead, the home of Celtic, was not too far from our home. My mother could never afford the price of admission to Celtic games, but on a Saturday afternoon I would walk to Parkhead twenty minutes before the end of the game – about the time when the exit gates were opened. As soon as I saw part of a gate open, I was through and on to the terracing to enjoy, free of charge, the last quarter of the game. Sometimes, for big matches such as those against Rangers or Hearts, I would arrive at the ground just before the kick-off. I would hang around outside and listen to the noise of the crowd, which was always a good guide to how the game was going and what the score was. It was amazing how many folk did this in those days. Admission to the terraces was only a shilling (5p) but still beyond the means of many.

Celtic had a very good team in the late 1930s – they won the Scottish League Championship in 1936 and 1938 and the Scottish FA Cup in 1937. My heroes were right-back Bobby

Hogg, inside-forward Gerry McAlton and Jimmy Delaney who was equally devastating at outside-right or inside-right. Jimmy Delaney was the dazzling star in the Celtic constellation. Delaney's clubs included Manchester United, Derry and Cork City and he has the unique distinction of having won English, Scottish and Northern Ireland FA Cup winners' medals as well as an FAI FA Cup runners-up medal when at Cork.

The success of Celtic owed much to manager Willie Maley who, unbelievable as it may seem nowadays, was manager for forty-three years from 1897 to 1940. During Maley's long tenure at Parkhead, Celtic won thirty major trophies, not bad for someone who, when he took over the post during the reign of Queen Victoria, told the press, 'I am only here as manager until the club find someone more suited to the post.' I was twelve years old when Maley finally gave way to 'someone more suitable'. In 1940 Jimmy McStay took over and lasted the duration of the war, during which competitive football was suspended.

In 1945 Jimmy McGrory succeeded McStay as manager. McGrory was already a Celtic legend having scored a club record 395 League goals; to put McGrory's tally into perspective, it considerably outranks the scoring record of Henrik Larsson (174 League goals from a Celtic career total of 242) and that of those two great strikers Bobby Lennox (167) and Stevie Chalmers (138) who formed such a devastating partnership in the 1960s. I was excited about his appointment at the time, but little did I realise that three years later McGrory would have a huge role to play in how my life was going to develop.

Another boyhood hero of mine was a man few Glaswegians may now recall. Jimmy McGrath, thin, with wild grey hair and crumpled clothes, worked in a local factory but lived for football. He set himself up as an unofficial scout for the Glasgow clubs and was always on the lookout for promising youngsters. Celtic, Rangers, Patrick Thistle, Clyde and Third Lanark all had players who had been recommended to them by Jimmy McGrath, but he wouldn't accept a penny for spotting an unpolished gem. He enjoyed the satisfaction of seeing a youngster he had recommended sign professional forms and make the first team at one of the Glasgow clubs, his own judgement of a young player endorsed.

I first met Jimmy when still at school. He had been watching me play for the school team and he came up and offered to take me to see Third Lanark play Celtic at Cathkin Park. He showed me the dressing room and introduced me to the 'Thirds' players. An unbelievably kind man, he took me and other boys to several matches and kept an eye on me generally. When he heard how my mother was struggling to bring up my sisters and me, he even turned up on our doorstep with a parcel of clothes.

Amongst the many Jimmy McGrath discoveries was Jimmy Mason, a legendary figure at Third Lanark. Wartime excepted, Jimmy Mason gave seventeen years of unbroken service to the 'Thirds' and was capped seven times by Scotland. Sadly, the Second World War robbed him of his prime years. Following Jimmy McGrath's recommendation, Mason joined Third Lanark in 1936 and although his sublime skill was at once apparent he had no time to impress nationally before war broke out. When official football recommenced the character of the game had changed in Scotland. The demand was for a power-type of play and three years passed before Mason's real class was truly recognised – the Scottish selectors took a lot of impressing in those days. Arguably his best ever game for Scotland was against England at Wembley in 1949 when he partnered Willie Waddell on the right wing, and made the Rangers man play as he had never played before. That day Mason scored the first of Scotland's three goals in what was a famous 3–1 victory over the 'auld enemy'. Amongst the near 100,000 crowd was Jimmy McGrath, looking down at the boy he spotted playing parks football, running rings around England.

Our home in Shettleston was even nearer to Parkhead than the one in the Gorbals, which only sharpened my desire to be a footballer. While I had a Catholic upbringing I never indulged

in the bigotry that existed between certain sections of Celtic and
Ranger supporters. When I later signed for the local junior side
in Shettleston I bumped into an old pal of mine who told me
he had read in the paper that I was playing for Shettleston and
asked the religion of my team-mates. I told him I didn't know,
and what's more, that I didn't care. He looked at me with total
disbelief, then I eyeballed him and he thought better of pursuing
that line of conversation. The truth was that from the day I
signed for Shettleston until the day I left the club I never knew
the religion of my team-mates because it was not an issue that
concerned me. The Gorbals was a cosmopolitan area of Glasgow,
with Catholics (many of whom had originally come from
Ireland), Protestants (many originally from the Highlands), a
large Jewish population and a great cross-section of people
whose parents or grandparents had arrived from Eastern Europe
and followed various Christian doctrines. This cultural melting
pot touched, and, in many ways, shaped my early life every day.
I lived cheek by jowl with people of other races and religions;
tolerance of one another was fostered by the one thing we all
had in common – extreme poverty.

I played for the St Mark's school football team on a Saturday
morning. The teacher in charge of football was Mr Lewin who,
on a Friday afternoon, would enter our classroom with a handful
of football shirts and simply throw them to the boys he had
picked to play for the school team. Even at the age of ten I
understood that Mr Lewin saw his involvement with the school
football team as something to be endured rather than enjoyed.
That said, St Mark's had a decent team. Our centre-half was a
boy called Willie Toner who would later enjoy a fruitful career
with Kilmarnock and win two caps for Scotland.

In addition to playing for my school I also trained at every
given opportunity. Even in those early days I was a bit of a fitness
fanatic, an aspect of the game I would carry not only into my
days as a professional footballer, but also into my managerial
career. When I lived in the Gorbals I would kick a football about

with my pals at any given opportunity. As there was no proper football pitch we played in the street, at night under the illumination of a gas lamp. Most kids would chip in a halfpenny or a farthing (a quarter of an old penny) to buy a football which cost around sixpence. There were any number of kids in the Gorbals who did the same and such groups were known as 'tannerba footballers'. We would kick the ball about day and night, until the time came when it literally fell apart. If there was no money to buy another, we would play with an old tennis ball, or even a ball made up of crushed newspaper held together with elastic bands. No doubt kids of today would not be enamoured at the thought of playing 'fitba' with a bald tennis ball, but I'm convinced it helped hone my ball skills. In my days as a manager invariably I would be able to spot the players who had played football with a tennis ball when young, as opposed to those who hadn't.

As I turned twelve the opportunities to watch Celtic became fewer as Saturday afternoons were spent playing for St Paul's Boys' Guild, a youth team run by a local priest, Father Joseph Connolly. Rarely a day went by without Father Connolly dropping in to see us. 'One day,' I told my mother, 'when I start work I am going to give my first wage to Father Connolly in thanks for all the help he has given us, so that he can use it to help those less fortunate than ourselves.' It was a very proud moment in my life when I eventually did just that, all £1.5s.9d (£1.29p) of it. Father Connolly had one simple rule about playing for St Paul's Boys' Club. You were not allowed to play unless you attended holy communion on a Sunday morning and made confession on a Saturday night. Attending church was not a problem to me, but so keen was I to play football regularly I diligently went to confession every week, even when I felt I had nothing to confess.

Being in the St Paul's team involved travelling around Glasgow to play other youth organisations. Again this was a revelation to me as, even at the age of twelve, I had not seen much of Glasgow other than the immediate areas in which I had lived. The team travelled around the city in a little bus driven by Father Connolly, who always saved a seat for my mother so she could come and watch me play.

I remember an old saying: 'The Clyde made the Glasgow and Glasgow made the Clyde.' This was certainly true of the Glasgow of the 1930s and early '40s I knew in my youth. The river was a hive of industry. In addition to world-famous shipyards, the Clyde was alive with shipping of all shapes and sizes. Away from the river itself and the noise of shipbuilding and vessels coming and going, the sound of the city was that of human chatter punctuated by trams, in those days painted with broad bands the colour of Neapolitan ice cream. The trams hissed like ganders as they made their predetermined, unalterable route around the city. There would be a sudden sharp clangour of bells, the asthmatic cough of a steam locomotive clearing its throat on the road to Carlisle and, ultimately, London. And the people of Glasgow trading, shopping, nattering, and heading home, some to flats in Pollokshaws; others to the relative grandeur of the prim Victorian homes of Queen's Park with their hidden back gardens the size of a parks football pitch; others to the squalor of the Gorbals. Others would patronise the many bars of the city until the last Neopolitan ice took their swaying bodies home to Partick, Maryhill or Bridgeton.

The most amazing thing about Glasgow then was its size: over a million people squeezed into an area not as big as Newcastle-upon-Tyne, a compression that created a feeling of immensity. There were miles of wide main streets of a certain grim and solid quality; shops as fine as any in London's West End; clubs as stuffy and exclusive as any in Pall Mall; and a block from all this would be 'shawlie wives' queuing for jugs of animal blood to make black puddings to combat anaemia in their children. This meeting of extremes was another characteristic of Glasgow. Splendid riches and abject poverty seen in such close proximity made a contrast that was, I am sure, sharper than anywhere else in Britain.

We Glaswegians are industrious, hard-working, cosmopolitan, humour-loving, generous of spirit, forthright to the point of occasionally being aggressive in our views, respectful of others, lovers of culture, the history and traditions of our native land, yet with a rough, hard edge to us; and last, but not least, totally fanatical about football. Football to me is not simply a game to pass the time. It is a religion. Anyone who has been to a Celtic–Rangers match will have felt the impact of that, particularly so in years gone by when the Catholic–Protestant rivalry on the terraces often erupted into violence. Happily there is a much healthier atmosphere at Old Firm matches these days, though the rivalry is still intense.

When I was young, religion seemed to dominate every aspect of Glasgow life. The first question to be asked at a job interview was, 'Which school did you go to?' This was simply to discern whether you were Protestant or Catholic. Many companies employed Protestants only, others only Catholics. Give the wrong answer to the opening question at an interview and there was no way the job would be yours, irrespective of your qualifications and experience. Again, happily, largely thanks to anti-discrimination legislation, this seems to have all but disappeared from modern Glasgow living. In the 1960s under the management of the great Jock Stein (a Protestant), Celtic relaxed their 'Catholic only' policy in recruiting players. Rangers, however, continued to sign only Protestants. The 'Gers were finally dragged into the twentieth century as late as the 1980s when Graeme Souness took over as manager, on condition he be allowed to sign whoever he wanted, irrespective of their race or religion. When he signed Mo Johnston, a Catholic, the old mould was finally broken. Nowadays with so many foreign players in the ranks of both teams religion is not an issue at either club, though no doubt there are still supporters for whom integration does not rest easy.

For many years Celtic had a turnstile reserved for the use of Catholic priests only. They were given free admission not only because of their standing in the community, but also because they would often recommend to the Celtic manager any lad of exceptional talent who played for their church or youth club teams. Many was the time a Celtic supporter unable to get a ticket for a big cup tie would don a dog collar and announce to the gateman he was 'Father So-and-So' – though being good Catholics, I'm sure they confessed their sin come Sunday.

The priests also had their own football team, as did the Protestant ministers, and the meeting of the two spawned any amount of good tales and jokes. One such story that did the rounds in the 1960s concerned an important cup match between the Catholic priests and the Protestant ministers. The story goes that one day prior to the game, the manager of the team of Protestant ministers rang Ibrox and spoke to Rangers manager Scot Symon. The minister explained his team had an important cup match against the priests who, for a number of years, had always managed to beat his team. Just once, he said, he would love to put one over on the priests. The minister proceeded to ask the Rangers boss if he would allow two of his best players, Eric Caldow and Ralph Brand, to play for his team under the guise of being Protestant ministers themselves. Understandably, Symon was a little taken aback at this request and questioned the ethics of it.

'Minister, is it not a little dishonest to pass off two Rangers players as members of your church?'

'Oh, it'll only be a one-off,' said the minister. 'Our team has not beaten the priests for years. No one will ever know.'

Not wanting Protestants to suffer defeat at the hands of Catholics yet again, Scot Symon agreed to allow Caldow and Brand to turn out for the ministers. The match was duly played and, curious to know the result, Symon rang the Protestant minister to ask if Eric Caldow and Ralph Brand had been of use to his team.

'They were magnificent,' replied the Minister. 'What marvellous footballers those two boys are. From the kick-off they took control and proceeded to run the game.'

'How did you get on?' asked Symon.

'Lost 4–1,' replied the minister.

'Lost 4–1!' said Symon, incredulously. 'How could you have lost 4–1? Caldow and Brand are Scottish internationals.'

'That's as may be,' replied the minister. 'But what you forget is, Fathers Jimmy Johnstone and Bobby Lennox are also marvellous players.'

As a schoolboy I harboured the dream that one day I would be good enough to play for my beloved Celtic, though in truth I was never a teenage prodigy. There were better footballers than me in the teams I represented but football, like growing up, is all about development. Though there was no way of knowing it at the time, my ability as a footballer was to develop apace, whilst the ability of some of those boys I considered my football superiors never advanced.

I left school at the age of fourteen knowing that I had to get a job – hopefully one that would allow me to play football on a Saturday afternoon. After a chequered career working in a pottery and a bakery, I got a job as a window cleaner, which was fine until on the third day I discovered I suffered from vertigo. My next job was in a factory until my skin reacted badly to the chemicals used there. I came out in red blotches and had trouble breathing. After three weeks at the Shettleston Bottle Works I realised the long hours and shift work was not conducive to playing football and training. I walked out yet again – I'd had five jobs in a matter of two months. Finally I at last found work I liked, this time as a van boy delivering bread. I enjoyed getting out and about and the hours fitted with my football commitments.

It was round about this period that I came to the attention of local non-league club Shettleston Juniors. The club asked me to sign for them and I jumped at the chance of playing at a higher grade of football than at St Paul's. To my amazement and delight, Shettleston Juniors gave me a £3 signing-on fee and agreed to pay me expenses of £1 a week plus an occasional share of the gate money when the team posted good results and decent attendances. To be paid for playing football was a dream come true. When the Shettleston manager told me this, I didn't hear his words clearly due to the sound of angels singing.

I worked as a delivery boy for the bakery and played football for Shettleston Juniors until 1946 when at the age of eighteen I was called up for National Service. I joined the Highland Light Infantry (HLI) but in my first few months of service still managed to turn out for Shettleston thanks to weekend passes. National Service is much maligned, but I think it proved the making of me. I learned self-discipline, I was given responsibility and responded well to it. Life in the army broadened my mind and my horizons, and offered me a hitherto unknown sense of purpose – and plenty of opportunity to play football at a decent standard. Of course, it was no bed of roses; after some six weeks of basic training with the HLI, I found myself serving in that troubled corner of the world called Palestine.

2

ONE OF THE BHOYS

Join the army and see the world, so they say, and so it proved for me. And the first part of the world I saw was Whittington Barracks in Lichfield, which was the first time I had ever left Scotland. I spent six weeks in Staffordshire, mainly 'square bashing', before being transferred to Edinburgh and assigned to the First Battalion Highland Light Infantry with whom I commenced my training proper.

I was to spend three months stationed in Edinburgh and it was there I learned the basics needed to fulfil my two years as an infantry soldier. One of the first things I learned was the history of the HLI which, within a matter of weeks, became a source of great pride to me. I was told that the origins of the HLI were that of the County Regiment of Lanarkshire, an honour it shared along with the Cameronians. In the late nineteenth century the headquarters of the regiment was in Hamilton, but switched to Edinburgh in 1946.

The First Battalion HLI was formed in 1881 (it lasted until 1959) and its history was illustrious, seeing action in some of the most prominent conflicts in British history, for instance at Waterloo (1815) and in the Crimea (1855). The regiment had also distinguished itself in the First World War, particularly at the Battle of Flanders, and in north-west Europe during the Second World War. In addition to being told the history of this fine regiment, I was immersed in its traditions and ethos. I enjoyed the camaraderie of my fellow conscripts, the life of a soldier and the fact that I was now a part of a famous regiment. I felt I had a purpose and army life induced in me a sense of belonging.

Discipline was never a problem to me. If anything it helped me a great deal. I had always been at pains to keep myself fit. At Shettleston Juniors when not training with the team, I would often turn up at the ground to train on my own, and my personal fitness regime continued in the army – the difference being the facilities were much better! Army life not only helped me become fitter, I also became healthier and stronger. Service food was much maligned at the time, but for a lad who had come from my background, army catering provided me with a healthier and more varied diet.

I also learned how to take responsibility, whether working alone or in a group. When working alone I realised that I was not conducting a task completely alone, that I was part of a unit whose success depended on every member doing his job. When given responsibility within a group, however small, I was taught leadership is action not position. I also learned that my training and newfound self-discipline could one day save my life. It was ingrained in me that my training had a purpose and should I ever find myself in a life-threatening situation, either when alone or in a group, to remember my training and act accordingly. The mantra was: 'If you find yourself in a sticky position and start to brick it, remember your training – do what you've been trained to do!' Within just a few months I would owe my life to such advice.

After three months in Edinburgh I was given two weeks' leave, after which the battalion boarded a ship at Southampton bound for Palestine, which was occupied by we British. Though talks were in process regarding the formation of an independent state for Jewish people, we were seen by some Jews who lived there as 'occupiers' of their nation; it was a volatile and dangerous situation, with various groups waging violence against the British, Arab civilians, and United Nations personnel.

Our ship took us to Port Said in Egypt where we spent three days before moving on to Casanoh Barracks in Cairo. We spent four weeks in Cairo but, to my delight, in that time I managed to play six games of football. No sooner had the HLI arrived in Cairo than Regimental Sergeant Major Gaffey formed an HLI Battalion football team which was to play a series of matches in Cairo, not only to maintain battalion morale but also keep relations sweet with the locals. Further matches followed when we left Cairo for Port Fayd, and later during our tour of duty in Palestine where we played in Padres Hana and Jerusalem. RSM Gaffey had some quality football talent to work with. At various times our team boasted Arthur Rowley, who went on to enjoy a highly productive career with Leicester City, Fulham and Shrewsbury Town. Arthur's career tally of 434 Football League goals still stands as a record today, one, I believe, that will never be surpassed; Doctor Adam Little who was a wing-half for Rangers; Jock Neave who played for a number of Scottish teams including Third Lanark; and Jaz Nibloe who in addition to playing for Grimsby Town also played rugby for Selkirk. The other player I would like to mention is my pal Gordon West. Although Westy never became a professional footballer, his grandson has made a decent fist of it – the lad being none other than David Beckham. (You know what they say, Westy – talent skips a generation!)

Of course army life was not all about sport, there was the serious business of soldiering to be done. To say a tour of duty in Palestine was edgy is putting it mildly. For the first and only time in my life, I was aware of being in the presence of people some of whom wanted to kill me. Their hatred of me was nothing personal, more the result of the task I was undertaking, the uniform I wore and what various Zionist groups believed it stood for. All through the Second World War the groups (the Haganah, the Irgun and the Lehi) suspended their activities against the

British so as not to distract from the fight against Nazi Germany. When it became clear that the Nazis were to be defeated, hostilities were resumed. In 1944 Lord Moyne, a British minister, was assassinated in Cairo, and the activities of the three main groups continued apace, culminating in what was arguably the most horrific atrocity of all.

The King David Hotel in Jerusalem was constructed from locally quarried pink sandstone in 1931, and was, as it is now, one of the most renowned hotels in the world. Little wonder the British government and army had chosen it as the administrative headquarters. On 26 July 1946 I was on guard duty outside when there was an almighty bomb explosion that rocked the building to its foundations. As chance would have it, I was on the other side of the hotel from where the bomb was detonated. There but for the grace of God . . . Having got over the initial shock of the explosion but with adrenalin still pumping around my body, I called on all my training – all three months of it. I quickly found a niche in a wall across from the hotel to shelter from possible sniper fire and, having established communication with my fellow guards, from there viewed the immediate vicinity for signs of any 'hostiles'. Assured, as best we could given the circumstances, that we were clear, we then decided some would stay to hold the area, whilst another group, of which I was one, would go round to the front to ascertain the damage and assist those in need.

It is inappropriate to go into detail here as to what confronted us when we eventually reached the front of the hotel that day. Suffice it to say, amongst the choking clouds of smoke and dust we discovered carnage, much of it human, of the most unimaginable sort. Army training does not prepare you for what I encountered when I went into the building to offer help. The first person I encountered was a man, his face and arms lacerated by shards of glass. I led him outside and across the road to a safe assembly point. He was suffering from shock and screaming. I sat him down on the pavement and joined my colleagues in looking for more survivors, every one of them shocked, dazed, trembling, screaming. Sirens were wailing as help arrived, the sound of the sirens oddly accentuating the horror, panic and sheer hell of it all.

A total of ninety-one people died as a result of that bomb, some of them British soldiers, nearly all of whom were mates of mine. Believe me, when you have witnessed the things I did that day, nothing the game of football will throw at you can ever chasten or unduly upset you. In the wake of the bombing, as is often the case, there were conflicting accounts of what had happened. The Irgun group, who admitted planting the device, claimed they had made three telephone warnings in 'good time' urging the hotel to be evacuated. The British authorities said they received no such warning. For their part Irgun counter-claimed by saying the British had received a warning but chose to ignore it, thus sacrificing lives in an attempt to turn world opinion against Irgun and other Zionist 'freedom fighters'. It is not for me to suggest which side was giving a true account of events at the time. However, to this day I do not find it credible that, had it received a telephone call warning of an imminent bombing, the King David Hotel would not take the appropriate action and immediately evacuate the building.

On another occasion our barracks in Jerusalem were strafed by machine-gun fire. We returned fire before going in search of those who had attacked us, only to find the perpetrators had disappeared into the night. And so it went on. Following my tour of duty, Count Bernadotte, who had been sent to Palestine as a mediator, was shot dead by members of Lehi in 1948. I remember thinking then when a representative of the UN, bent on mediating between the two sides, is assassinated, what hope for peace can there be?

I completed my National Service on 27 July 1948. During my two years with the Highland Light Infantry I had risen from private to become Sergeant Docherty. At first I declined to accept my sergeant's stripes as they were awarded only a matter of days before I was due to be demobbed. I thought, 'What is the point?' The army, however, believed otherwise. On the day I was demobbed I was told that the army would like me to make a career in the service, and should I consider applying for Officers' School, my application would be looked favourably upon. I not only felt flattered and proud, I was filled with a great sense of achievement. For the first time in my life I was presented with a real opportunity to make something of myself. If the army saw in me the possibility of becoming an officer, they obviously believed I had qualities that could benefit others – qualities that, prior to joining the HLI, I had been unaware of. This endorsement gave me confidence in my own abilities for the first time. I was one month short of my twentieth birthday, still young enough, I believed, to pursue whatever career I chose in life. But while the prospect of an army career was not unappealing, there was another career I dearly wanted to pursue. I didn't know if I was good enough or possessed the talent to make a success in football; all I knew was that I had to give it a try.

I would not have to wait long to discover if football was going to be the career for me – just twenty-four hours. As I journeyed back to Glasgow I hatched a plan to write to a number of clubs asking for a trial. I reasoned that should all come to nothing, given my service record with the HLI, the army would have me back and the opportunity of applying for Officers' School may still be open to me. A good plan, but I never did write those letters. I had no need to.

As I turned the corner of our street in Shettleston, suitcase in hand, I was surprised to see a number of cars parked outside our house. It was rare to see a single car in our street let alone four, and the fact these were parked by our place set my heart racing. Once indoors I hugged and kissed my mother and sisters but my welcome home was brief. My mother told me that she had four representatives from football clubs sat in the lounge. (I can only think that my army pal Dr Adam Little, who had good connections in football, must have recommended me.) There was Harry Potts from Burnley, Cliff Britton from Everton, a Manchester United scout whose name escapes me, and Jimmy McGrory, the secretary/manager of Celtic. I spoke to each in turn whilst the other three took tea with Mum in the kitchen. I listened intently to what each had to say out of respect and politeness but, in truth, my mind was already made up. As soon as I had seen Jimmy McGrory of Celtic, there was only ever going to be one club for me.

I arranged with Jimmy to meet him at Parkhead the next day where we could discuss terms and I would sign the necessary forms to make my dream of being a Celtic player come true. That night I lay in bed thinking life really had begun for me. I had behind me two successful years in the army during which I had acquired all manner of practical and personal skills. Now I was home and about to begin a career in football with Celtic. Life was just great.

I have to say some of the lustre of signing for Celtic became badly tarnished when Jimmy McGrory told me that, initially, I would begin at Parkhead as a part-time professional player. I had been hoping to be full-time; nevertheless, I was delighted to accept terms of £10 a week in the winter and £8 in the close season, plus winning bonuses. Even when deducting the board and lodging I was going to pay my mother, pocket money for my sisters, and putting away a few pounds in a savings account, I would still be left with more than enough to sustain my weekly needs.

Part-time training at Celtic took place on a Tuesday and Thursday evening, which left me with every day of the week in which to occupy myself. So I went out in search of work. I soon found a job in what, in those days, was referred to as a departmental sports and sporting goods shop. With my army record, my background in sport and the fact that I was now a Celtic player, the owner of the shop jumped at the chance of employing me as a counter sales assistant. O'Connoll's Sports Shop was situated in Renfield Street and for all it traded under a name of Irish origin it was, in fact, owned by a lovely Jewish family – yet another example of the cosmopolitan nature of Glasgow at that time.

The fact that I trained with other part-timers and amateur players two evenings a week meant I only saw the regular first team players on the occasional Saturday. However, I still had to pinch myself that I was now part of the same club I supported as a boy, and was rubbing shoulders with players like John Bower, Alec Boden, Conrad Capler, John McGrory, Joe Baillie, Willie Gallacher, Willie Miller and Willie McPhail whom I had cheered on from the terraces the previous season when home on army leave.

Having been at the club only a matter of weeks I never expected to be selected for Celtic's opening fixture of the 1948–49 season at home to Morton – and I wasn't. I was picked for the reserves, where I played most of my football throughout my first five months at the club. In that period, however, I did make four first team appearances – and the first of those was a belter. But it is time to say that the majority of my football up to Christmas was for the reserves.

At the time the Scottish League had three divisions, A, B and C. Divisions A and B were really what Scottish football was about, as Division C comprised part-time clubs such as Brechin City, Montrose, Forfar Athletic, the now defunct Edinburgh City and the reserve teams of such clubs as Airdrieonians, St Johnstone, Raith Rovers, Dundee United, Dunfermline Athletic Kilmarnock and Queen's Park whose second team played under the name of Queen's Park Strollers, which to me suggested a form of animated recreation rather than top-flight football. The standard of football in this division was not as high as the Scottish Division A Reserve League in which Celtic competed along with the reserve teams of clubs such as Rangers, Hearts, Hibernian, Aberdeen, Dundee, Motherwell, Clyde and St Mirren. I have fond memories of my early days of playing for Celtic reserves. Probably because I was still somewhat star-struck and everything was new to me, I actually relished a trip to play Dundee or Motherwell reserves.

In these pre-Beeching days the Scottish rail system was largely still intact, but Celtic reserves usually travelled by motor coach. Though my military service had taken me to Egypt and Palestine I had, up to this point, seen little of my own country bar my home city and Edinburgh. Playing for Celtic reserves enabled me to visit places I had never before seen – the flesh-pots of Dumfries, Kirkcaldy, Methil and Falkirk, all reached by coach.

My team-mates in the Celtic reserves included Willie Gallacher, the son of Patsy Gallacher, who won League Championship and FA Cup winners' medals with Sunderland in the 1930s; Jimmy Sirrel, who went on to play for Brighton, Bradford Park Avenue and Aldershot and later managed several clubs, including Notts County with whom he enjoyed promotion to the First Division in 1981. Another was Bobby Collins, who was later to enjoy a fruitful career with Everton, and with Don Revie's Leeds United where he formed a formidable midfield with Billy Bremner and Johnny Giles.

I always felt my best position was at right-half but I played outside-right, inside-right and centre-half for the reserves. Wherever I played I always contrived to give my best. I was so happy to be playing for the club, I would have played anywhere they asked me – apart from in goal perhaps, not being the tallest of players.

Attendances at Parkhead for reserve team matches were in the region of 2–2,500. Quite a number of Celtic fans travelled to see the first team play away and those who didn't often went to see one of the other Glasgow teams who were at home that day, such as Third Lanark, Partick Thistle, Clyde, or Queen's Park, though never, of course, Rangers. It was a different matter when Celtic reserves went on the road. Like Rangers' second eleven Celtic reserves often drew healthy crowds at places such as Hearts, Hibernian, Dundee and Motherwell. When we played away to East Fife or Queen of the South reserves we occasionally drew a larger crowd than had been at the previous week's first team home match. By far the largest crowd when I played for the reserves was on a Friday night at Aberdeen. When I ran from the tunnel I was amazed to see nigh on 20,000 inside Pittodrie.

That 20,000 attendance, however, was dwarfed by the crowd that came to see me make my debut for the first team on 21 August 1948. The fixture was a nondescript league match for a Celtic debutant – home to Rangers.

The night before the big game I found sleep difficult. It was one of those nights we have all had, where you keep telling yourself you must go to sleep, but you can't because your mind is so active. Like most people I have a little routine where sleep is concerned. I settle down in a particular position, only to turn over when I feel I am ready for sleep. I must have done that routine a dozen times, yet sleep was still not forthcoming. I looked at the clock. When I saw how late it was, it made me even more anxious. I kept telling myself, 'If I don't get to sleep soon, I'll be in no fit state to play tomorrow – later today!' I couldn't get comfortable. The blankets tickled. When I turned on my 'favourite' side the bed covers didn't lie right across my back. There was a draught. Then there was a noise in the house that was too brief and inconsistent for me to work out where it was coming from. The pillow was too hot so I flipped it over in order for my face to lie on the cool side. The pillow was too flat. All manner of minor irritations conspired to rob me of my rest. I did eventually fall asleep, but by then it must have been well after 2 a.m.

When I arrived at Parkhead, the first person to greet me was goalkeeper Willie Miller.

'Hello, Tommy, son. Trust ye slept well afore yer big day?'

'Aye, no bother, Willie. But I bet the fans hardly slept a wink in the excitement of seeing me play,' I replied.

I had been selected to play outside-right. Though it was not my favoured position I felt I could do a job on the wing and though I didn't cover myself in glory, I felt I contributed to the game. It being my debut I was just happy to get through the ninety minutes without making a costly mistake. But mistakes were made in our defence: Rangers won the match 1–0 and went on not only to win the championship that season, but also the Scottish Cup and League Cup as well. Rangers' 'treble' was a remarkable achievement. The manager was Bill Struth who, following this success, was dubbed 'God Struth' by Rangers' supporters.

What I remember most about my debut is the vitriol I was subjected to by certain sections of the visiting supporters. Although in the minority in the 50,000 packed inside Parkhead, being on the wing, I was within earshot of those Rangers fans in the paddocks. When I touched the ball for the very first time I did so to shouts of 'Awa' hame ye Fenian bastard' and worse. The resentment and hatred so evident amongst rival supporters of the Auld Firm was, however, noticeable by its absence amongst the players after the game.

Once washed and changed both sets of players enjoyed a drink together. I had a friendly chat with Rangers players Ian McColl, Willie Waddell and Willie Woodburn who, knowing it had been my debut, offered me kind words of encouragement. I never found the hatred that existed between various factions of supporters ever transmitted itself to players. Obviously there was keen rivalry on the pitch, especially in big derby matches, but in my experience it was never more than just that. This has much to do with the empathy all players feel for one another. They know their career in the game is relatively short. The anxieties and concerns a footballer feels are common to all. A player knows he is only as good as his last game; a good run of form can suddenly and inexplicably turn into a bad patch; a simple turn may result in a debilitating injury that sidelines him for months, or may even end his career. The simple truth is that professional footballers always maintain respect for one another.

In total I played nine first-team league matches for Celtic in the 1948–49 season, plus a couple in the Glasgow Charity Cup, and managed three goals. In those eleven games I played two at outside-right, four at inside-right, once each at centre-half and inside-left and three games in my favoured position of right-half. Manager Jimmy McGrory began to share my view that I was best employed in that role, though this was to pose me problems as far as establishing myself in the first team was concerned. Celtic's regular right-half was Bobby Evans, who had made that position his own not only at Parkhead but also in the Scotland team. Bobby was a fine ball-playing wing-half who with his tousled red hair cut an unmistakeable figure on the pitch. Bobby was very comfortable on the ball, cool, immaculate and when in possession always appeared to have time. He had originally joined Celtic as an inside-forward, but his eagerness for work and a tendency to drop deep in search of the ball led to his successful conversion as a right-half. Now that Jimmy McGrory had decided my best position was right-half I knew my opportunities to play first-team football would be limited as there was no way a player of the calibre of Bobby Evans would ever be dropped.

Celtic finished sixth in Division A which, though disappointing, was in fact an improvement on the previous season when the club had finished twelfth, collecting only twenty-five points from thirty games. Rangers pipped Dundee to the title by a single point with Hibernian, East Fife and Falkirk all finishing above Celtic.

One thing that always strikes me when I look back to my playing days is the familiarity that the players and the fans had back then. That is certainly not true now, for players or managers, not that you'd know that from the tabloids, which have a tendency to refer to David Beckham as 'Becks', Rio Ferdinand as 'Rio', or Sir Alex Ferguson as 'Fergie'. Yet this familiarity is surely at odds with the minimal (if any) contact top players and managers now have with fans. Supporters are no longer allowed to watch Manchester United at their training ground. In the past, on match days players arriving at a ground allowed fans to get an autograph and have a few words with their heroes. All that is gone, particularly where many Premiership clubs are concerned. Nowadays many clubs ensure supporters are kept well away from teams arriving at their stadium. Same applies to the national squad. The England bus is bedecked with signage signifying it is transporting the England football team, yet its darkened windows prevent anyone seeing the players inside.

Clubs have become very canny when it comes to seducing supporters. Chief executives and club PR departments are forever telling the fans 'this is your club', yet the reality is somewhat different. In addition to buying the latest kits, supporters are encouraged to take out club credit cards, insurance and even book their holidays through their football club, as a way of showing club loyalty. Yet the same fans are kept at a distance from their heroes at all times, and banned from the club training ground. The press are also complicit in perpetuating the myth of close contact between fans and players. The truth, now, is that the ordinary supporter simply cannot relate to Wayne Rooney or David Beckham and their lifestyle, the way they related to, say, Jimmy Greaves or Bobby Moore. When I was manager of Chelsea and living in the Cockfosters area of London, my nextdoor neighbour was a regular at Stamford Bridge whilst the chap across the road was a Chelsea season ticket holder. Managers and players lived cheek by jowl with the supporters of their club. They knew one another, spoke about the team and the club, all of which fostered an understanding. That just doesn't exist today – regardless of what someone might think after having read about the superstars in the newspapers.

And while I am on about the papers, let me pick up on nicknames. As opposed to the media-given ones of today's stars, the nicknames given to players back in the 1950s and '60s came from supporters. Take, for example, the East Fife trio of Charlie 'Cannonball' Fleming, 'Square Jaw' Aitken and 'Bomber' Brown who helped their club finish above Celtic in my debut season (yes, I know, it shows how much the game has changed – unthinkable now). These were genuine examples of players given terrace nicknames by which they eventually became known nationally. There was the 'Clown Prince' Len Shackleton, 'Wor Jackie' Milburn, 'Commando' Lishman (Arsenal), 'Iron Tackle' Sherwood (Cardiff City), Stan 'Master Blaster' Mortensen (Blackpool), and Willie 'Warpath' Redpath (Motherwell) – sobriquets that appear to have jumped straight from the pages of adventure comics such as *Hotspur* and *Rover*. These players were revered as comic-book heroes, and their nicknames reflected the adventurous way they played the game. Such affectionate invention could come only from the terraces, not a sub-editor's desk at some national newspaper.

The 1949–50 season began with the group matches of the Scottish League Cup. Celtic were drawn in a group that contained Rangers, St Mirren and Aberdeen, and we opened our campaign with a home match against all-conquering Rangers; Bobby Evans played in his customary position of right-half, whilst I got the new season underway in what was now my customary position, as Bobby's understudy in the Celtic reserves. By now it had become increasingly apparent that if I was to play regular first-team football and carve a career out of the game, I had to move on from my beloved Celtic. This thought preoccupied me in the opening months of the 1949–50 season, though I did nothing to change my situation and for a very good reason.

In October 1948 I had met the girl of my dreams in Girvan, a small town situated on the Firth of Clyde some twenty miles south-west of Ayr. In 1948 Girvan was little more than a village whose population grew appreciably in the summer months as it proved a popular holiday destination for Glasgow folk. The town was also popular with Celtic directors, which is why the players often stayed there either prior to an important game, or for a few days' training to break normal routine. We always stayed at the Shelbourne Hotel and it was there that I met Agnes, who was a friend of the hotelier's daughter. It was, for me at any rate, love at first sight. I had never set eyes upon such a beautiful girl, nor one with the personality to match. Agnes was vibrant, had a keen wit and her conversation never failed to enthral me. We hit it off straight away. In my spare time we would meet and go for walks during which she introduced me to not only her friends, but Girvan itself. Every house in which she had attended a party and every street which contained a memory of her became shrine-like to me. I actually began to envy these houses and streets for having shared a part of her life that had been denied to me. Up to this point in my life I had never had a regular girlfriend. Agnes and I began what in those days was referred to as 'courting steady'. On my return to Glasgow I wrote to her whenever I could, as she did me. Occasionally there was the bonus of a phone call, but as we had no telephone at home, such calls were conducted on my part in public callboxes which in those days could be something of an adventure in itself.

Public telephone boxes had two buttons designated 'A' and 'B'. To make a call you first inserted your money, usually a couple of pennies, dialled the number, then on hearing the person at the other end answer, pressed button 'A'. The pressing of this button was supposedly to connect you, though this function had more than a hint of hit and miss about it. Many was the time I heard Agnes say 'Hello' only to press button 'A' and, instead of picking up the conversation, was treated to the sound of my money falling into the machine followed by the continuously frustrating sound of 'bip-bip-bip-bip-bip-bip' as the connection failed. When such a situation occurred (which believe me was often) you had to press button 'B' in order to retrieve your money. Invariably the pressing of button 'B' resulted in nothing happening at all, which only served to increase your frustration as not only had you been unable to make your call, but you had lost your money as well. Those of us who attempted

to make calls on these instruments will rarely be heard grum-
bling about mobile phones.

Immediately after playing for Celtic on a Saturday, I would
head by train for Girvan to see Agnes, returning to Glasgow on
the Sunday evening. It was a slow journey, especially the return
to Glasgow which, having spent some twenty-four hours in the
company of Agnes, seemed to me to last twice as long. Yet,
despite the distance between us and the brief periods we spent
together, our love flourished. Little over a year after we first met,
Agnes and I decided we had had enough of spending so much
time apart, so we set a date to be married.

The fact that I was due to marry put me in a tizzy as far as
my career at Celtic was concerned. In thinking of my responsibilities to Agnes and the possibility of a family, I was torn
between staying in the reserves at Celtic or trying to advance
my career elsewhere. At Partick Thistle or Third Lanark I might
enjoy regular first-team football, but not earn as much as Celtic
were paying me. Agnes and I set a date for our wedding in
December but, four weeks prior to that, a phone call to the
sports shop solved my career quandary for me.

On the other end of the line was Celtic manager Jimmy
McGrory who informed me that Jim Taylor, the chairman of
Preston North End and a fellow director, Bob Smith, were travelling up to see me and that I should report to the ground that
afternoon. It was obvious to me that the purpose of Jim Taylor's
visit was to sign me. It was the first inkling I'd had that any
club, let alone one from south of the border, had a serious
interest in me and I spent the remainder of the morning at work
on tenterhooks. I rang Agnes to put her in the picture. I was
anxious to hear her reaction to the possibility of a move away
from Scotland. To my delight she told me she would travel with
me to the ends of the earth. 'Fortunately that won't be necessary,' I informed her, 'we're only talking Preston.'

It transpired that Preston's Scottish scout Johnny Kerr had
been tracking my performances for Celtic reserves and, following

a succession of favourable reports, the Preston manager Bill Scott and the Deepdale board had decided to sign me. The fee was set at £4,000 which, though not hefty for the time, was a not inconsiderable sum to pay for a reserve with limited first-team experience. Only later did I find out that Jimmy McGrory was under pressure to sell fringe players in order to generate funds to strengthen the Celtic first team. It had been eleven years since Celtic had last won the Scottish League title and twelve years since the Scottish Cup had last been in the Parkhead trophy room, albeit both competitions had been suspended during the war. Rangers' post-war domination of the domestic game was beginning to irk. Celtic's failure to mount a serious challenge not only to Rangers but also Dundee, Hibernian and East Fife prompted the board to have a clear-out.

Today it might take anything up to six weeks to finalise the details and paperwork of a player's transfer. In addition to salary and bonuses, medical care, a home, schools should the player have children, there are matters such as image rights, endorsement rights and all manner of commercial details that need agreement. In 1949 it was all very different. If a club wanted to sell, that was it; the player himself had very little say in the matter.

Having got over the initial surprise of Preston's interest, I quickly decided that a move away from Celtic would further my career. I knew very little about English football at the time, and even less about Preston North End other than they had recently been relegated from Division One. I knew they were a decent sized club who enjoyed good attendances, and from what Mr Taylor told me came across as being an ambitious club that might match my own ambitions.

Apart from anything else the notion of trying my hand in English football appealed to me greatly, and so it was that around Guy Fawkes' Day 1949 I became a Preston North End player. I felt it was a good move for me. Little did I know at the time, it would turn out to be a great one.

3

GROUND CONTROL TO MAJOR TOM

With our marriage pending, I arranged with Preston for Agnes and me to move into a club house for which we paid a rent of 25 shillings (£1.25p). Given that I was earning £10 a week, the same as my part-time wage at Celtic, this left Agnes and me more than enough to live on and the opportunity to save for a deposit for a home that in time would truly be our own.

In the 1940s it was unheard of for young couples to co-habit until they were married, so during my first month I lived alone in the house, with Agnes an occasional visitor. During her visits we shopped for furniture and household items, she selected the décor for the house and I did my best to put her ideas into practice. I am not by any stretch of the imagination a practical man. I can change an electric plug and that's about it. The evenings I spent alone at the house I gave painting and decorating my best shot. It's a good job I wasn't a striker. My best shot wasn't up to much. Agnes and I were married in Girvan on 27 December 1949. When I carried her across the threshold the house hardly appeared a show home, but at least I had made it presentable. Following our marriage, it was Agnes's touch that turned that house into a home.

At the time I joined the club, Preston North End were in a period of transition. Bill Scott had been appointed manager following the club's relegation the previous season, when the team had been selected by a committee of directors and club officials, a situation which had pertained in all but two seasons since 1931. I have travelled the world and walked through many a city park but have yet to see a statue to a committee. Limited though my experience was at the time, I was glad the club had given up on this way of picking the team. My time in the army had taught me the value of good leadership and that it came from individual not collective responsibility. Bill Scott was a Geordie who, in keeping with just about every manager of the time, was not a great tactician. But he did have an eye for a good player and adhered to the football adage that signing good players made the job of the manager easy, as you don't have to tell good players what to do – they know.

Bill believed the current Preston team was not good enough to gain promotion back to the First Division so he set about creating a team he believed could not only win Division Two, but sustain the club in the top flight. It transpired that Bill signed me primarily as a replacement for the great Bill Shankly who had retired the previous season. Bill Scott told me he believed I could emulate Shanks's authority on and off the pitch, his tough tackling and ball-winning, and that I shared Shankly's infectious enthusiasm for the game. I would like to believe he was right on every count. That would be some compliment.

Bill's plan was to create a strong, well-balanced half-back line that would form the backbone to the team. A few weeks after my arrival he signed another Glasgow lad, Willie Forbes from Wolverhampton Wanderers for £18,000. Some months later Bill signed the man who would complete the half-back line, centre-half Joe Marston. Eddie Quigley joined us from Sheffield Wednesday for a fee of £26,500 which was a record at the time – evidence of the club's ambition that Mr Taylor had referred to when signing me from Celtic. Of the new signings Joe Marston was the most unusual in that he came over from Australia. He was spotted playing for the Sydney club Leichhardt by a chap called Percy Sewell who had emigrated there. Percy was something of a Jimmy McGrath in that he was not connected to any club, but loved watching football at all levels and often recommended a young player who had impressed him. Joe Marston impressed Percy enough for him to get in contact with the Blackpool manager Joe Smith. Having sung the praises of his latest discovery Percy asked Joe Smith if Blackpool would pay for Marston to come over to Bloomfield Road for a trial. Smith, however, said he was well blessed with defenders and declined Percy's recommendation. I dare say the cost of the passage from Australia was also a stumbling block, as Smith and his Blackpool board had a reputation for financial prudence.

Undaunted, Percy Sewell contacted Bill Scott who brought Joe to Deepdale for a two-month trial. Joe impressed everyone, was offered a contract and within weeks was playing in the first team at right-back. However, he failed to make his mark in that position and came in for some flak from supporters and press alike. One reporter cruelly suggested Preston fans should club together to pay for Joe's fare back to Australia so he could ply his trade there. But Joe had a thick skin and a keen wit, and took such criticism in his stride. 'I don't agree with what this guy says about me,' he responded, 'but I would fight to the death for the right of anybody to shut him up!'

As so often in football one man's tragedy can prove to be another's opportunity. In 1950–51 our regular centre-half Harry Mattinson broke his leg playing against Huddersfield Town in a fourth-round FA Cup match at Deepdale. Bill Scott replaced Harry with Joe Marston and Joe never looked back. Having struggled to make any sort of impact at right-back, he immediately looked at home at centre-half. I am sure some older Preston fans would agree that Joe, along with Willie Forbes and me, at last formed the half-back line Bill Scott had yearned to create.

Such were Joe's performances for Preston he was an ever present in the side from 1950 to 1954 and clocked up 200 senior appearances during his time with the club. He returned to Australia in 1954 with his very pretty wife and two gorgeous daughters, both blondes. This was somewhat unusual, as both Joe and his wife had dark hair. As I was one of the few players in the dressing room with blond hair, whenever Joe brought his daughters down to the ground the likes of Charlie Wayman and Willie Forbes would impishly nod and offer me knowing looks! As if.

Although on signing for Preston I became a full-time professional, initially I was disappointed to find myself playing reserve team football during my first two months at the club. I had hoped to go straight into the first team but Bill Scott felt a period in the reserves would enable me to adjust, not only to full-time training, but the speed and tempo of the English game which was much quicker than in Scotland.

I didn't find the transition from part-time to full-time training difficult. As I have said I was always a fitness fanatic, training on my own at every given opportunity. I felt my level of fitness was on a par with those players who had always enjoyed the benefit of training every day. But it is one thing to be fit, quite another to be match fit. Of course, I was keen to show everyone that I was capable of playing in the first eleven and I was given that opportunity on Christmas Eve 1949 against Leeds United.

I had made my Celtic bow in the unaccustomed position of outside-right, and so it was I made my debut for Preston in an unaccustomed position. Having played, I believe, quite well at right-half for the reserves, I was chosen to play outside-left at Leeds! The game resulted in a 3–1 victory for the home side, and while I did my best, I failed to pull up any trees on the left wing. As with my Celtic debut I did, however, manage to get through the game without making a serious mistake. I then flirted with first-team football while continuing to appear for the reserves until Bill Scott selected me for an FA Cup third-round replay against Watford.

Preston had secured a 2–2 draw at Vicarage Road at the first attempt. We were expected to dispatch Watford, then in the Third Division (South), with some ease at Deepdale, but in the FA Cup anything is possible. I was deputising on the right-wing for Tom Finney who was injured. From Tom's point of view it was a good one to miss. Watford upset the odds by beating us by the only goal of the game. It is a strange phenomenon of football that the disappointment a player feels when his team have lost an important game is tempered if he himself has had a good game. Though I was disappointed we had gone out of the FA Cup at home to a Third Division side, albeit a good one challenging for promotion, I was pleased with my own performance. The *Lancashire Evening Post* had given me a polite but cool write-up following my debut at Leeds, probably because they knew I had played out of position, but according to the same newspaper I was one of the few players to emerge with any credit from the replay against Watford. Soon afterwards Bill Scott chose me at right-half. I felt comfortable in my chosen position and went on to make a further sixteen appearances for the first team that season. My initial season as a Preston player saw us finish sixth in Division Two. Our tally of 45 points was well adrift of Tottenham Hotspur who with 61 points were runaway champions.

The annual Scotland–England match at Hampden Park had more than national pride and the destination of the Home International Championship at stake. It had been decided that the winners and runners-up in the Home International Championship would automatically qualify for the World Cup finals in Brazil that summer. Though the first World Cup had taken place in 1930 none of the home countries had participated in the competition in Uruguay. Following the Second World War all four home nations rejoined FIFA, and to mark the occasion world football's governing body had generously offered two places in the World Cup finals.

British football institutions at the time were very pompous and insular, nowhere more so than the Scottish Football Association. The SFA announced they would only deign to send a team to compete in the World Cup should Scotland win the Home International Championship. With Wales and Northern

Ireland out of the frame, the annual meeting between the two nations took on an extra dimension. England won the match with a goal from Chelsea's Roy Bentley and despite subsequent pleas from Scotland skipper George Young, the SFA did not relent and Scotland did not travel to the World Cup. The pomposity and narrow-mindedness of the Scottish FA denied players the honour of representing their country in a great tournament.

England did participate in the 1950 World Cup finals though few of the English players would have thanked their FA for taking part. England finished runners-up in their group but that masks what was a disastrous World Cup for them. Having beaten Chile 2–0 in Rio de Janeiro, England then suffered the most humiliating defeat in their history when beaten 1–0 by the USA. The USA team comprised part-time and amateur players and the fact they defeated an England side that contained the likes of Alf Ramsey (Spurs), Billy Wright (Wolves), Stan Mortensen (Blackpool), Roy Bentley (Chelsea), Wilf Mannion (Middlesbrough) and Tom Finney was regarded as one of the biggest sports upsets ever. England called upon the services of Stan Matthews in the final group match against Spain but even he in tandem on either wing with Finney couldn't prevent England going down by the only goal of the game.

The saddest aspect to England's World Cup was that nothing was learned from it. Finney and Matthews had been mightily impressed by the technique of the South American players, especially the Brazilians. England, too, had talented players but the team did not possess the organisation of Brazil, Uruguay, Spain and Yugoslavia for instance. Stan was so impressed by the lightweight strips and boots worn by the South Americans that he bought a couple of pairs of the boots and, once back in England, paid a company in Yorkshire to produce bespoke pairs that were even lighter, for him to wear when playing for Blackpool.

With England out of the World Cup and heading home, Finney and Matthews asked the permission of the FA to stay

on in Brazil to see what further they could learn. That permission was not granted and both were ordered to fly home with
the England party. Not a single English journalist stayed on
following England's exit. The 1950 World Cup proceeded and
developments in the rapidly changing world game took place
whilst English heads blithely turned the other way.

England's dismal showing on the global stage apart, the hot
topic of conversation in the Preston dressing room as we
prepared for the 1950–51 season was the 'Bogota Affair', which
coincided with the World Cup and took the spotlight off
England's humiliating experiences. During the close season Neil
Franklin, who had been England's regular centre-half prior to
the World Cup, and his Stoke City team-mate George
Mountford, left the English game and signed for the Colombian
team Santa Fé. It was rare for English players to move to a
continental club, let alone one in South America. Accordingly
Franklin and Mountford hit the headlines. The opportunity
came because Colombia's professional clubs had broken away
from their national football association and FIFA, and formed
a 'rebel' league. Franklin and Mountford went to Colombia
because they had been offered signing-on fees of £3,400 each
plus £170 per match, plus free accommodation and a home help
thrown in for good measure. The maximum wage in England
was £14, so the temptation was plain to see. At the time rumours
were rife as to how much they were to receive. Once Franklin
and Mountford had blazed the trail, a number of other players
were keen to follow. Bill Higgins of Everton signed for another
Bogota club, Millonarios, as did Roy Flavell of Hearts. Another
star name to go to Colombia was Charlie Mitten, who had been
Manchester United's second leading goalscorer the previous
season. Mitten joined Franklin and Mountford at Santa Fé but
two of his United team-mates, Henry Cockburn and John Aston,
having visited Bogota, turned down the offers they were made,
as did Swansea's Roy Paul and Jack Hedley of Everton. In the
event this was to prove a wise move on their part. The prom-

ised money was never forthcoming. Colombia was a very unstable country (nothing new there then) and a 6.30 p.m. curfew added to the anxieties of the British players and their families. I spoke to Neil Franklin after he arrived back in England. Neil said he only received a single week's wages and his signing-on fee never materialised. To add further misery to his sad tale, once back at home Neil found himself not only out of favour but in many ways ostracised by Stoke City and the FA. He never played for Stoke or England again. After being out of the game for a time he signed for Hull City, but what had been a fine career at the highest level of the game was by then in rapid decline. Neil failed to recapture the sublime form he had shown prior to his Colombian sojourn, and his final days as a player were spent in non-league football.

The 'Bogota Affair' was used by some of the game's officials and club directors as a cautionary tale for players against accepting lucrative offers from abroad. Some even cited the affair as evidence of what could happen should players seek to increase the maximum wage or, heaven forbid, move to have it scrapped altogether. The reaction of players in general to the Bogota Affair played into the hands of FA officials and club chairmen keen to carry on dictating terms and conditions to footballers. As teams prepared for the 1950–51 season, the general mood amongst players appeared to be, 'We're not badly paid, don't make waves, we could end up worse off.' So for eleven years, no one did.

Like every one of my fellow professionals, I was subject to the maximum wage. In reality players received two wages. A winter wage, paid during the actual playing season; and a summer one, which was a retainer paid during the close-season. In 1950 the maximum winter wage was raised from £12 to £14 per week, and the summer retainer from £8 to £10. As Preston's centre-forward Charlie Wayman said in 1950 after having signed from Southampton, 'You can name your own salary in this business. I'm going to call mine Arthur.'

In 1953 £14 per week was far in excess of what the average

man or woman earned, but it has to be said that the vast majority of players at the time were not paid the maximum wage. That was reserved for a team's star players such as Matthews, Wright, Milburn, Ramsey and, in the case of Preston North End, Tom Finney. In 1951–52, for Preston's return to the First Division, I was on £10 a week in the winter, two pounds below the maximum wage; and I dare say, at the time, there were regular first-team players who were on less than that. This was a golden period in English football as far as attendances were concerned: in 1951–52 just under 40 million spectators attended Football League matches; in the four seasons prior to this the number had exceeded 40 million with a record 41,271,414 watching league games in 1948–49. In 1952–53 the number of spectators who watched games in the First Division was 16,050,278. That is over three million more than watched Premiership matches in 2004–05.

At the time, Preston were enjoying attendances of between 30–35,000. The admission price for an adult standing on the terrace was 1s.6d (7.5p). Accepting that children paid less and the away team received a share of the receipts, it is still fair to say that for a 40,000 crowd at Deepdale, the club would realise receipts of £3,000. Preston had thirty-eight professional players on the staff in 1952. If we consider the average wage paid was £12, which I should imagine is on the high side, it makes the total outlay on players' salaries £456. The differential between match receipts of £3,000 and that of players' wages (£456) is £2,544, but I guess you could have worked that out for yourselves. After additional costs such as entertainment tax, overheads, contributions to each player's pension fund, wages to administration staff and a police bill (which in those days would have been a nominal amount as few policemen were in attendance at matches), the profits made by a top club such as Preston North End were still sizeable. Consider how much profit was generated in the course of a season and we are talking a hefty sum. Where did all that money go? Not to the players or on ground improvements and better facilities for supporters, that's for sure. The majority of Football League grounds in the 1950s had changed little, if at all, since the Edwardian era.

The maximum wage was, as the High Court would decide in 1961, an infringement of a player's labour rights. As was the contract a player had with a club that tied him for life, or until such time as the club felt he was no longer of use to them. The usual three-year contract did offer some security, of course, but when the time was up, you had to await that most dreaded of letters. At the end of every season the manager would publicise his 'retained list', namely, those players whose contracts were up and who were to be offered renewals. A player not to be kept on would discover his fate by way of a letter issued by the manager three weeks before the end of the season. A player didn't have to read the letter to know if he was being retained by the club or not. He only had to look at the colour of the wording. Players who were not being retained received letters typed in red!

If the maximum wage had a beneficial effect other than generating healthy profits for clubs it was that it enabled provincial clubs such as Preston, Sunderland, Middlesbrough and Blackpool to compete on a level playing field with the big city clubs when it came to signing players. Tom Finney was on the maximum wage with us, as was Wilf Mannion at Middlesbrough and Stan Matthews at Blackpool. It was pointless any one of those players moving to a bigger club such as Arsenal, Spurs, Wolves or Manchester United because they wouldn't be paid any more, and in fact they might have been worse off financially as the cost of living in London was far higher than in the north of England. So clubs such as Preston or Blackpool retained the services of international class players, or, in the case of Finney and Matthews, world class.

As Preston prepared for the opening game of the 1950–51 season at home to Manchester City, the feeling in the dressing room was that this could be our year. We were quietly confident that promotion to the First Division could be achieved as Bill Scott had assembled what we believed was a formidable team. But that optimism soon evaporated as we made a poor start and by mid-September we were stuck in mid-table, but a 2–0 success against Grimsby Town rekindled our early confidence. The Grimsby match proved to be the beginning of a sequence of eighteen matches up to the end of December in which we were defeated only three times. The crowded Christmas and Easter programmes were crunch times for teams battling to win promotion or avoid relegation. It amuses me when I hear managers or players bemoan the number of matches they have to play over those periods. Four games in nine days, as it was for most Premiership clubs over the 2005 festive period, is a small price to pay for the salaries and lifestyles afforded to them, and is popular with the most important people connected with the game – the supporters. The two things which entice people out of their homes over the Christmas period, whatever the weather, are football and the sales.

Preston had four matches over a period of seven days during the 1950 festive period. We began with a 1–1 draw at home to Coventry City on 23 December, and the following day we travelled to London for a Christmas Day match against Queens Park Rangers. The game kicked off at 11 a.m. and resulted in our best away performance of the season. It had been our home form that had sustained us in the promotion race, but that Christmas morning we recorded a 4–1 victory at Loftus Road. Immediately after the game we took the train back to Preston – there was a rail service on Christmas Day in those days, part of what appears now to be an anachronistic policy of wanting to serve the public irrespective of weather or time of year. Also on board that train – in another carriage – were the QPR players, as the 'return' fixture was to take place at Deepdale on Boxing Day.

QPR proved sterner opposition the second time around, but a 1–0 victory followed by a 2–0 win at Cardiff City four days later confirmed our status as genuine promotion contenders. The win at Cardiff was especially pleasing as they had been among the front runners in the promotion race. We started the game confidently and proceeded to boss it throughout. As the *Daily Sketch* reported, 'Preston have, for some weeks, been gaining a head of steam. At a bitterly cold Ninian Park . . . Preston, prompted and probed by the mercurial Finney, took command from the start and after the half-time interval picked up the same script.'

With Manchester City and Cardiff City hot on our heels we maintained our good form up to and including the crucial Easter period, when the men were sorted out from the boys, with three matches in four days. On the Saturday a Deepdale crowd of 39,122 saw us beat near neighbours Blackburn Rovers 3–0. What I remember about this match is spectators spilling over the perimeter wall and having to watch the game from the cinder track. That wouldn't be allowed today, but I can't remember a single fan encroaching on the pitch during the game. Success in the local derby was followed by a 3–2 home win over Leicester City on Easter Monday before another bumper attendance of 37,581. The following day we completed what for us was the perfect Easter when we travelled to Filbert Street and won by the same score as the previous day. My old army pal Arthur Rowley was on fine form netting both Leicester goals, but goals from Ken Horton, Angus Morrison and Bobby Beattie established us on top of Division Two. A few weeks later promotion and the championship were secured in our final home match of the season when Hull City were beaten by the only goal of the game. Come the final day of the season, with the Division Two championship in the bag, we were not too bothered about a 2–0 defeat at Doncaster Rovers.

Preston's championship success was very much a team effort, but I must make special mention of the efforts of manager Bill Scott and the peerless talent of Tom Finney. Bill hailed from

Willington Quay, close enough to Newcastle-upon-Tyne to qualify as a Geordie. As a young teenager in the early 1920s he made a name for himself in local non-league football, winning a Sunderland Shipowners' Cup medal. He was signed by Middlesbrough as an inside-forward in 1927, and spent five years on Teesside before moving to Brentford. He stayed almost fifteen years with the Bees, the highlight of which was a five-goal haul against Barnsley in 1934. He was appointed manager of Preston in 1949 and remained with the club until 1953 when he was succeeded by Scot Symon.

One of Bill Scott's strengths as a manager was his organisation. As I have previously said he was no great tactician, but he introduced good players and welded them into a formidable, well-balanced outfit. Every member of the team had a job to do and did it to the best of his ability. Left-half Willie Forbes did a holding job in midfield but he was more than just a stopper. Willie was an all-action player with a formidable tackle, an explosive shot and the necessary vision and distribution to be regarded as a classy playmaker. He never knew the meaning of defeat and his stamina enabled him to battle right through to the end of a game, even when the pitch resembled molasses. Centre-half Joe Marston was what was then referred to as a 'great pivot'. He was a terrific ball-winner but not a great passer of the ball. But he didn't need to be. He simply pushed the ball a couple of yards to me or Willie (I always tried to be there in support) and we did what we had to do – give the ball to Tom Finney.

One of Bill Scott's most astute signings was Charlie Wayman who scored twenty-nine goals for Preston that season. Charlie was a County Durham lad who began his career with Newcastle United and made a name for himself by scoring thirty league goals in Newcastle's promotion season of 1947–48. Southampton tempted him south and he continued to find the back of the net with regularity, scoring thirty-two goals to finish as the leading scorer in Division Two. Bill Scott did a deal with Southampton for Charlie, which comprised cash and Eddie Brown leaving

Deepdale for The Dell. It was a masterstroke as Charlie's goals played a key role in our championship success. Now I have known plenty of forwards who have clocked up a good haul of goals by scoring them when a game was won. More often than not, this type of forward rarely scores when his team really need him to do so, when a game is really tight. Charlie Wayman was not that sort of player; he scored any amount of match-winning goals for Preston. The same can be said of Ken Horton whose twenty-two league goals in 1950–51 was also a key factor in our success. With two such prolific lads up front, record signing Eddie Quigley found it hard to hold down a regular place in the team after recovering from a bout of flu. Eddie scored nine goals in twenty appearances during our promotion season. That itself is indicative of the form of Wayman and Horton, and yet he still managed to average just under a goal every other game. If he were playing today and boasting such a record, he'd be hailed as a superstar.

In all Preston used a total of eighteen players in the 1950–51 season, the lowest of any league club. I was an ever-present along with Willie Forbes and Angus Morrison. Joe Horton missed only five matches and Tom Finney would have played more than his final tally of thirty-four had it not been for England and other representative games. Of the eighteen players used Harry Anders played six games and Eddie Brown and Fred Ramscar five, on each occasion due to injuries. Had it not have been for those injuries we would have called upon the services of only fifteen players. Those statistics are testimony to the consistency we showed following our poor start to the season, when from late September onwards, Bill Scott only had need to change the team when his hand was forced. Then again, the players were not to be found hanging about in the treatment room and for one simple reason. Even if we did have an injury, we kept quiet about it, fearing that should we miss a game, the team were playing so well we might not get back in the side. Nothing hurts when you win.

What Bill Scott and his trainer Jimmy Milne (father of

Gordon) insisted upon was that Preston kept it simple. We gained a reputation for being the 'aristocrats' of the English game, yet Bill had us playing a deft blend of English and Scottish styles which matured over the years like good whisky. From the Scottish game he liked the artistic, ball-playing schemers whose vision opened up opposing defences, whilst the aspects of the English game he incorporated were fitness, physical prowess and ball-winning. Above all, Bill Scott preached that football was a simple game. He never gave complicated team talks and was rarely negative; every word I ever received from Bill was constructive.

Bill had that keen Geordie sense of humour and was a ready wit. He was a very amiable man, as was the Blackburn manager of the day, Jackie Bestall, but for some reason, probably intense local rivalry, the pair never hit it off. As Bill once told the Preston players, 'I'll never forget the first time I met Bestall . . . and don't think I haven't tried.' During one game a supporter spent much of the match heckling Bill from behind the dugout. The supporter kept up the tirade into the second half of the match until Bill, fed up with having his management of the team questioned in such a way, stood up and with a downward gesture of both palms indicated the fan should 'keep it down'.

'I pays me money, so I'll give thee a piece of my mind,' the fan shouted.

'That's very generous of you,' Bill shouted back, 'especially as you have so little to spare.'

The crowd in the paddock doubled up with laughter.

There is one member of Bill's backroom staff I have not mentioned and that is the physio and masseur, Des Coupe. Des was a super physio for the time, his talent all the more remarkable for the fact he was blinded during the Second World War. Yet Des would 'watch' a game and not miss a trick. Somebody would sit beside him and give a detailed running commentary of the game, and that, combined with his own knowledge of the way things were done, would give Des an uncannily accurate picture of what was happening. So accurate and detailed was his recollection of matches, if someone couldn't properly remember a particular incident we would say, 'Go and ask Des.' I never met a man more cheerful and confident than Des Coupe. Whenever I thought of him and his disability it used to make me feel ashamed when I grumbled about a minor knock picked up in a game. Des would welcome the Preston players at his home for treatment any hour of the day or night, Sundays included. He had a tremendous sense of humour and would often disconcert us players by making light of his blindness. Once he came into the dressing room and said to Bob Beattie, 'I have a bone to pick with you, Bob. I challenged you to a game of darts last week and I won.'

'So, what's your problem?' asked Bob in all innocence.

'You didn't tell me,' said Des before bursting out into laughter.

My lasting memory of Des is of him doing two laps around the perimeter track at Deepdale holding the hand of full-back Willie Cunningham. And all the time he was smiling as if it was the happiest day in his life and he didn't have a care in the world.

Preston's Second Division Championship team of 1950–51 was very much that – a team. But it boasted one player who was truly world class. Tom Finney had already given Preston supporters ample evidence of his enormous talent prior to our promotion season. He was an established England international, but such is his modesty, he always came across as being 'just one of the lads' in the dressing room.

Of all the footballers I have taken the field with, the greatest was Tom Finney, a player whose abundant skills were matched only by his sportsmanship and gentlemanly conduct both on and off the field. Like Stanley Matthews, Tom Finney has the proud record of never having been booked or sent off during his career. In the 1950s going to a match at Preston was a ritual for many working folk. I didn't have a car at the time, so I caught a tram up the hill from the town centre to the ground on match days and would sit amongst the fans chatting about the prospects

of the game ahead. I didn't delude myself. They weren't coming
to see me. They had come to the home of their hero, Tom Finney.
I can think of no other footballer who played for his club in a
Wembley Cup final and who then had to wait the five war years
before making his league debut for the same club. It was not
until 1946, after being demobbed, that he finally played his first
official league match for Preston. Such was his talent, less than
a month later he made his international debut for England at
outside-left against Northern Ireland, the first of his seventy-six
caps.

In an era when footballers wore shorts that contained enough
material to rig an East India tea clipper and were shod in heavy
boots with bulging toe-caps, Tom improvised his considerable
array of skills up and down a thousand muddy touchlines. He
was brilliant on either wing and was a fine centre-forward, as
his career tally of 187 goals testifies. Tom could also play in the
centre of midfield, where his considerable skills and incisive football brain ensured he masterminded many a game. Tom was
without doubt the dominant force in the Preston team in which
I played. He took all the corners, the free-kicks, throw-ins and
penalties. He was so devoted to Preston North End I used to
say to him, 'You'd take the money on the turnstiles if they'd let
you.'

I remember in the 1960s once taking Chelsea to play
Liverpool at Anfield. I was sitting in the Anfield boot room with
Bill Shankly, Bob Paisley and Joe Fagan when a knot of press
lads knocked on the door asking for post-match comment. One
of the scribes had noticed Tom Finney in the press box (he was
working at the time for the *News of the World*) and had the
temerity to ask Bill Shankly if Finney would have been strong
enough to cope in the modern game. Shankly suddenly stood
up and with a characteristic Cagneyesque hitching of the shoulders turned on the doubter with a jabbing finger. 'Tommy
Finney was grisly strong, son,' said Shanks, letting the syllables
curdle with disbelief. 'Tommy could run for a week. What a foot-

ball brain. His passing was so sharp and precise it could open tin cans. Tommy Finney is a genius of a player. Could he cope with the modern game? Jesus Christ, son, if Tommy Finney had been playing for the Doc today, I'd have had four men marking him at the kick-in.'

Bill Scott would sometimes refer to us, his players, as 'soldiers on a quest for glory'. In that case Tommy Finney was our major. Bill had few words to say before a game other than, 'Lads, play the ball across the ground, and make sure it goes to Tom.' If I ever misjudged the weight of a pass it never bothered him. He would take any speed of pass at any height and have the ball under control in one swift movement. Having controlled an awkward ball with his thigh or chest with a defender breathing down his neck, then laid it off, he would never turn and berate me. If he said anything at all, it was, 'If you can, try and play to my feet, Tom.'

It was rare, but as the 'Bogota Affair' had shown, not unknown for English players to be lured by lucrative offers from abroad. In the late fifties another great, John Charles, was to leave Leeds United for a highly successful sojourn in Italy with Juventus, but Tom was perhaps the first English player to receive an offer from Italy. In 1952, Palermo offered Tom a £10,000 signing-on fee, a salary of £130 a month, plus bonuses, a villa and a car. Even the ultra-loyal Tom was tempted by such an offer. Tom went to see the Preston chairman who soon disabused his star player of any such idea: 'Tha'll play for us, or tha'll play for nobody.' As far as Tom was concerned it was a case of Hobson's Choice: he either played for Preston or his professional career was over – such was the power of the club that held a player's registration.

Few people remember that following his retirement from Preston, Tom played a single game for the Northern Ireland club Distillery. George Eastham senior (whose son George, a member of the 1966 England squad, had been used as a test case by the PFA in their High Court battle to abolish the maximum wage) coaxed Tom into playing for Distillery in their European Cup match against mighty Benfica. Tom only agreed to play in the first leg at Windsor Park and his performance that night enabled the gallant part-timers to secure a 3–3 draw. Tom was voted 'Man of the Match' – he was forty-one.

In his early days Tom favoured the left-wing berth, but in time switched to the right where he was to make his name in the game. Tom had, in fact, turned down an offer of joining the Preston groundstaff at the age of fifteen in preference to learning the plumbing trade, which he later used to build a profitable business, one that is still thriving today. His early international opportunity came because his good friend Stan Matthews was injured. But when, two months later, Matthews was fit again, England overlooked him and retained Tom for a game against Wales, a decision that caused heated debate amongst supporters as to who was the better player. Since Tom proved to be equally brilliant when playing at outside-left, the selectors were to have their cake and eat it – Matthews on one wing, Finney on the other.

Tom's genius as a footballer is known and respected throughout the world, as is his unassuming demeanour, sportsmanship, grace and dignity. What is not so well known is his marvellous sense of humour. In 1959 England played Northern Ireland at Windsor Park in what was to be Tom's seventy-fifth and penultimate game for his country. Making his England debut that day was a very nervous Wilf McGuinness of Manchester United. From kick-off to final whistle Tom nursed young Wilf through the game, talking incessantly to him about when to drop back, go forward, when to release the ball and to whom. Recognising the help he had been given by the maestro, Wilf made a point of going up to Tom at the end and thanking him. 'I owe you,' said Wilf. 'If there is anything I can ever do for you Tom, you only have to say.'

'Be at my works at eight in the morning,' replied Tom, with characteristic humour. 'I have two lads off sick and I have a bathroom to fit.'

The mark of his versatility as a player is that he played in every forward position for Preston and in 76 international appearances he won 40 caps at outside-right, 32 at outside-left, three as a centre-forward and one at inside-left. He scored a record 187 goals in 433 League matches between 1946 and 1960 and, I dare say, created twice as many. He was voted Footballer of the Year in 1954 and 1957, awarded the OBE in 1961, a CBE in 1992, and later knighted and deservedly so.

His final game for his beloved Preston was against Luton Town in 1960. That momentous afternoon is indelibly printed in the minds of all who were present. Before the start of the game, all twenty-two players and the match officials formed a circle on the pitch and joined the crowd in singing 'Auld Lang Syne'. Immediately after the game he was introduced by a well-meaning club official who described him as 'a great man'. Modest to a fault, Tom replied 'There are no great men, only men.' He concluded his speech of heartfelt thanks by saying, 'Whatever you do in life, give of your best. As I discovered to my delight, for some, it may be better than you dared hope.'

To my mind, great words from a truly great player.

4

PROUD PRESTON

During the summer of 1951 the FA announced a ban on the televising of FA Cup matches, with the exception of brief highlights of the final which could be broadcast at a later date. At the time still relatively few households had TV sets, but the FA still took a firm line: the Cup final was to be filmed only as a news item, which meant showing about one minute of the game in cinemas as part of the Pâthé News weekly news round-up. For most people this was the only source of news in pictures, and contained a precious snatch of the previous week's most important football match. For a player or fan starved of televised football, these weekly vignettes offered a brief, teasing insight into matches elsewhere. But the FA considered the prospect of televised football a 'menace' that would have a detrimental effect on attendances.

Preston regained their First Division feet at the first time of asking. We finished seventh in 1951–52 which everyone at the club believed more than satisfactory. After two early wins, two defeats and a draw we took our inconsistent form to local rivals Blackpool for the eagerly awaited derby match. Blackpool were one of the best teams in the division and FA Cup finalists the previous season. The added ingredient to this derby was the opportunity to see Tom Finney and Stan Matthews in action on the same pitch. At the time both were great crowd-pullers: they could put as much as 10,000 on the gate, so with both appearing in this game, the ground was full ninety minutes before kick-off. Blackpool had a star-studded team. In addition to the England trio of Matthews, Stan Mortensen and Harry Johnston, there was Jackie Mudie, Bill Perry, goalkeeper George Farm and the recently signed Ernie Taylor. On the day Tom Finney stole the headlines from Stan Matthews by producing a superb perform-ance, whilst up front Charlie Wayman proved he could score goals at the highest level. Blackpool were beaten 3–1, a result which confirmed to me that Preston were back in the top flight to stay.

I was enjoying life as a First Division footballer. I was playing better with every game I played, but I was still surprised to be called up for Scotland in the Home International against Wales later that month. I knew my mother would read of my selection in the newspapers and be very proud, as was Agnes. To be chosen for my country was a huge honour for me. I was thrilled at the prospect of pulling on the famous dark blue jersey and playing at Hampden Park for the very first time. I had come a long way from Celtic reserves, though I knew I still had a lot more to learn.

The game against Wales took place on 14 November, I can still rattle off the teams to this day: Scotland: Jimmy Cowan (Morton); George Young, Sammy Cox (both Rangers); Tommy Docherty (Preston North End), Willie Woodburn (Rangers), Alex Forbes (Arsenal); Willie Waddell (Rangers), Harry Orr (Morton), Lawrie Reilly (Hibernian), Billy Steel (Dundee) and Billy Liddell (Liverpool). Wales: Bill Shortt (Plymouth Argyle); Walley Barnes (Arsenal), Alf Sherwood (Cardiff City); Roy Paul (Manchester City), Ray Daniel (Arsenal), Ron Burgess (Tottenham Hotspur); Billy Foulkes (Newcastle United), Billy Morris (Burnley), Trevor Ford (Sunderland), Ivor Allchurch (Swansea Town), Roy Clarke (Manchester City).

I was expecting a tough game as three weeks earlier Wales had held England to a 1–1 draw, and so it proved. A Hampden Park crowd of 71,272 saw Ivor Allchurch score the only goal of the game to give Wales a memorable victory and two points that would subsequently help them top the Home International

Championship. Personally I felt I did OK against Wales, though the result was a hammer blow to Scotland who had won the Home International Championship the previous season. J. L. McCormack writing in the *Glasgow Evening Times*, said of my debut, 'Docherty, the debutant, offered ample evidence that he could have a solid international career ahead of him.' I took heart from those words but particularly those of my team-mates who, having helped me through the game, afterwards were generous in their appreciation of my efforts. I travelled back by rail to Lancashire in the company of Liverpool's Billy Liddell, as players were expected to make their own way to and from Home International matches – and it wasn't a first-class carriage, I can tell you! I had played against Billy at club level, of course, but this was my first opportunity to get to know the man. On the journey he offered me nothing but encouragement. I knew I had done all right against Wales but still felt I needed reassurance from someone who would be honest with me. Billy laid my anxieties to rest, telling me that he had no doubt I would be making further appearances for Scotland.

I respected Billy Liddell as a footballer and a man. He was tall, upright and strong, and possessed the courage to go in where it hurt. He would chase any lost cause and, as I knew from experience, no defender could ever feel comfortable when he had the ball at his feet. In the fifties good players did not fade away as quickly as they seem to now. Billy carried on playing until he was forty, and such was his influence on the pitch when Liverpool were struggling in the mid-fifties, Reds fans often referred to the team as Liddellpool. He never reacted or retaliated and was booked only once in his career, including the war period, lasting twenty-two years, during which he played in 537 matches and scored 229 goals for Liverpool. Perhaps the most baffling thing about Billy Liddell is that throughout his entire career he remained a part-time professional and supplemented his income from Liverpool by qualifying as an accountant. He won 28 caps for Scotland to add to his unofficial eight wartime internationals.

In December I was selected to play for a United Kingdom XI against Wales in Cardiff in a match to celebrate the 75th anniversary of the Welsh FA. Coming so soon after my debut for Scotland, this gave me the feeling that I had finally arrived in English football. At the time there was a belief amongst Anglo-Scots, that the Scottish FA preferred to pick Scottish-based players and English-based players only if they had to. So I was relieved to have caught the selectors' eye from south of the border.

A healthy crowd of 35,000 saw Wales triumph 3–2, with the Welsh goals coming from Ivor Allchurch who netted twice, and Trevor Ford. My team-mates in the United Kingdom XI included goalkeeper Jimmy Cowan (Morton), George Young (Rangers), Billy Wright (Wolves), Gordon Smith (Hibernian), Nat Lofthouse (Bolton Wanderers) and Alf McMichael (Newcastle United) – all quality players. But as we were sent out without any game plan or tactics, the final result had a certain inevitability about it. That said, I suppose we delivered exactly the sort of game and result the Welsh FA had hoped for – a flag-waving win for Wales on what was an auspicious occasion for Welsh football. I received £10 for playing in the game, together with my rail fare. I was also issued with a form to complete for what were termed 'necessary expenses in the course of travelling to and from the venue'. I dutifully noted the cost of a modest meal I had enjoyed on the train when travelling back to Preston. The reply I received from the Welsh FA brought a wry smile to my face. As we players had been provided with a buffet following the match at Ninian Park, my meal on the train was considered to be 'an unnecessary expense'.

Yet, as the 1951–52 season drew to a close I was disappointed to be omitted for the annual Home International against England and the close-season tour of the Continent. On their summer tour Scotland opted for Celtic's Bobby Evans and Jimmy Scoular of Portsmouth as options for right-half. They even had Ian McColl of Rangers on stand-by should anything happen to either Evans or Scoular. I was out of the mix, but determined to continue my progress the following season to such an extent the selectors would not be able to ignore me. I never received an explanation for my omission, then again I never expected to. The system by which the SFA picked the national team was often as much a mystery as the function of the human appendix.

Christmas games were special to players and supporters alike. A home game on Boxing Day made for a real Christmas holiday, and was more attractive to supporters than a Christmas Day fixture, though the latter was well attended. But attendance at a game on Christmas Day could lead to strained relations between man and wife. I sometimes imagined what Agnes might have had to say if football had not been my job and I had been a supporter, on a Christmas morning turning to her and saying, 'I'll leave you to get on with the kids and the Christmas dinner, love, I'm off to the match.'

As a teenager everything appeared different to me at Parkhead on Boxing Day. On the terraces hipflasks flashed like camera bulbs, while the distinctive aroma of miniature cigars joined the normal fug of Woodbines and Senior Service. Supporters appeared to rustle in their new clothes. The match programme would contain a seasonal greeting to the supporters from the club directors, players and staff printed in gothic type within a thick black border more like a Victorian funeral notice. But it was not only supporters and club directors who adopted a different countenance at Christmas. The players seemed to be affected too. As a boy I imagined this was because, like the rest of us, they had been imbued with the magic of Christmas. Only in my mid-teens did it dawn on me that it might have had some-thing to do with the change in the licensing hours over the festive period. Those players recruited to the services during the war were naturally not keen to spend their precious leave guesting for their local team on Christmas Day. Understandably the vast majority wanted to spend Christmas with their family, not running around on a football pitch. Those who did turn out, however, were often called upon at the last minute and were seen to be the worse for wear.

At a Boxing Day game at Parkhead one of the opposing team's players was looking decidedly lethargic around the pitch. During the second half he valiantly gave chase after a Celtic forward. However, the goalkeeper managed to push the resultant shot away for a corner. As players gathered in the penalty area, to await the corner-kick, the breathless player rested his hands on his knees. Those present believed he was just catching his breath, but suddenly his whole body shook and he retched violently before discharging the most monstrous Technicolor yawn. The trainer was quickly summoned from the bench and at first threw a bucket of water over the former contents of the player's stomach, before eventually covering the incriminating evidence with sawdust. Next day a press report stated that the player had 'suffered a stomach disorder, the result of him having partaken of wholesome family food at Christmas when normally used to army ration'. I dare say there are still folk around in Glasgow today who would describe a pint of 'heavy' as wholesome food.

As I've already described, teams would play one another twice at Christmas. In 1951 Preston made the short trip to Burnley on Christmas Day with the return fixture taking place at Deepdale on New Year's Day. Curiously, when two teams meet twice over Christmas, neither side will win both matches. Having enjoyed a comfortable 2–0 win at Burnley on Christmas Day, a week later we contrived to lose 2–1 at home to the same team.

Following the festive programme we embarked upon a poor run of results in the New Year, only to find form again in the final third of the season. Preston's last game, a 4–0 home win over Liverpool, secured that seventh-place finish and confirmed our newfound status as a top ten First Division club. Charlie Wayman finished the season with 24 league goals to his name, while Tom Finney (13) and Angus Morrison (12) struck some telling blows from the wings, both in the making and taking of goals. The valuable inside-forward play of Bob Beattie and Ken Horton was supplemented by Bobby Foster, who was signed that season from Chesterfield, and 'Die' Lewis who cost what was then a sizeable £15,000 fee from Gillingham. Joe Marston proved a formidable barrier at centre-half whereas the position of left-half was filled with distinction first by Willie Forbes, then by Joe Dunn, yet another Scot, who came from Clyde. Full-back duties fell in the main to Willie Cunningham, the manager's namesake, Bill Scott, and Joe Walton. Jimmy Gooch turned in some fine performances in goal until giving way to Malcolm Newlands, who returned to the side after a sixteen-month lay-off due to injury. Willie Cunningham, Angus Morrison, Joe Marston and I were ever-presents, while five players missed only a handful of matches. Having this core of nine players who were regulars clearly helped us to maintain consistent form over the course of the season. The only blip was in the New Year when a sequence of poor results in the League was coupled with an ignominious exit in the third round of the FA Cup when we were beaten 2–0 by Bristol Rovers of the Third Division (South).

As the 1952–53 season was about to get underway the national newspapers did not fancy Preston for the title which, given this was only our second season back in the top flight, was fair enough. What irked me, however, was that some believed Preston had been a surprise success the previous year but that now we would be found out and candidates for relegation. Not for the first time so-called 'informed' football writers got it completely wrong. Our first three matches all ended in 1–1 draws. We dominated and created enough chances to have won handsomely against Liverpool in our opening game and, in the course of events, our profligacy was to cost us dear. The next two games were home wins, but uncharacteristic sloppy defending saw us go down 4–3 at Newcastle United – another game we should have won. This was followed by a disappointing goalless draw against a struggling Stoke City side, and a 3–2 defeat at home to Cardiff City. Once again we had dominated proceedings but contrived to miss a hatful of chances, while Cardiff crafted three goals from only four scoring attempts.

From a possible sixteen points we had collected eight, which saw Preston occupying a satisfactory tenth position. Come autumn any hopes of Preston winning the title appeared little more than a pipe dream. By mid-November we found ourselves in the bottom half of the table when we entertained Sunderland who had championship aspirations of their own. They were lying second, a point behind Wolves but with a game in hand. Few fancied our chances, although we were encouraged by the absence through injury of Sunderland's Welsh international (and Glamorgan cricketer) Trevor Ford, the second leading goalscorer in the First Division; his place was to be taken by Dickie Davis, himself no mean scorer, but with due respect not in the class of Ford.

Sunderland, for all their talent, like Len Shackleton, George 'Square Jaw' Aitken, Tommy Wright and Willie Watson (a double England international at both football and cricket), and their lofty status in Division One, proved no match for us in the first-half. After only twelve minutes we went ahead through Charlie Wayman. Nine minutes later Angus Morrison added a second. Tom Finney's skilful repertoire of long and short passes probed ceaselessly into the Sunderland defence. One such pass found 'Die' Lewis who fired through a thicket of defenders to make it 3–0. We were coasting, but two minutes before the break, Len Shackleton decided to produce a little bit of his magic. He latched on to the ball just outside the penalty box, beat two of our defenders in the space of a hearthrug, then audaciously flicked the ball over the shoulder of Joe Marston. We were caught pushing out of our penalty area. Dickie Davis had timed his run to perfection and slipped the ball past George Thompson to give his side hope.

In the second period our play was riddled with anxiety. It was almost as if, having established a 3–1 lead against a top club, subconsciously we began to question how we had managed it. Sunderland pressed forward but we repelled them until twenty minutes from the end. Once again, when under pressure, we failed to clear our lines and Harry Kirtley made us pay. Sensing they might get something from a game that at one stage appeared lost, Sunderland went for all-out attack. The final quarter was nerve-jangling for our supporters, though at no point did we stoop to hacking and whacking the ball to all corners of Deepdale – that was not the Preston style. We continued to play purist football in order to deny Sunderland possession and, in the end, it paid off. It was a close run thing, but the fact we had beaten a team with genuine title hopes was a great fillip to our confidence. Indeed, proved to be the turning point in our season.

The following Saturday we won 2–0 away at table-topping Wolves, and come the Christmas holiday programme had risen to seventh in the table. Christmas time was especially fruitful for us. For a change we had no fixture on Christmas Day. Manchester City were thrashed 6–2 at Deepdale on Boxing Day and, after a comfortable 4–2 victory in the local derby against Blackpool on 1 January and a home win against Middlesbrough two days later, by mid-January we were up to fifth, only three points behind leaders Sunderland but with two games in hand. Our indifferent form at the start of the season appeared but a distant memory.

A diversion from the League programme was our pairing against Wolverhampton Wanderers in the third round of the FA Cup. Wolves were a powerful force in the First Division with a penchant for attacking football, a reputation further enhanced by the fact they had scored 47 goals from 24 league games. On the day, however, it was Preston who were to find the back of the net with regularity. A 5–2 victory took us into round four where we were drawn at home to Tottenham Hotspur. In what was a typical blood-and-thunder Cup tie we shared four goals, but our hopes of progression were scuppered in the replay at White Hart Lane when a late goal gave Spurs victory. Though disappointed I don't think any of the players were despondent. We all felt we had manoeuvred into a position in the League that afforded us a genuine crack at winning the championship and, to a man, we all decided we were going for it.

On 14 February we played host to Sheffield Wednesday. It is a game I will never forget, for it was the day tragedy befell one of the most gifted young centre-forwards of the post-war era. Sheffield-born Derek Dooley was a prolific goalscorer who in October 1951 began a sequence of eleven matches in which the raw-boned twenty-year-old was to score twenty goals. That season he really hit the headlines, scoring 47 goals in 30 matches during Sheffield Wednesday's promotion season from Division Two.

Derek was a majestic-looking young man, tall, broad-shouldered, with legs like bags of concrete. He was hugely strong if perhaps a little cumbersome and unpolished at times, but his presence in a penalty area created panic amongst defenders. Following Sheffield Wednesday's promotion those who doubted his ability to score goals in the top flight were quickly silenced. When he arrived at Deepdale with his team-mates on a bitterly cold 14 February 1953, he had scored 16 goals in 28 League games.

The Deepdale pitch was particularly icy – these days the game would not have gone ahead; how many times I have wished that had been the case that day. During the course of the game Derek Dooley sprinted after a 50–50 ball. Our goalkeeper, George Thompson, never one to shirk a challenge, came racing out of goal, flung himself forward at the ball and Derek careered into him. There was no malicious intent from either player, but the challenge resulted in Derek breaking a leg. We went on to win the game 1–0, our joy tempered by what we believed to be a cruel but straightforward fracture of Derek's leg.

Derek was taken to Preston Royal Infirmary. A couple of days later as he prepared to be discharged and coming to terms with the notion of having to miss the rest of the season and face a long haul to regain his fitness, it was discovered that gangrene had set in. In order to save his life doctors informed him they had no alternative but to amputate his leg. (Only towards the end of the decade were footballers given tetanus injections when they sustained injuries that involved broken bones or open wounds.) The whole of British and Irish football mourned the loss to the game of this rising young star. When I visited him in hospital I struggled to find the right words to say. In such tragic circumstances everything that came into my head appeared pithy or trite.

Happily the story of Derek Dooley is one of triumph over adversity. He began working in administration at Sheffield Wednesday before moving into their commercial department. In 1971 he was appointed manager at the club, but was sacked on Boxing Day 1973. Supporters of both Sheffield clubs were outraged at the insensitivity of the timing of his sacking, and said that the Wednesday board should have found him another job within the club. However, Derek did find alternative employment, and soon. He was taken on by local rivals Sheffield United and worked in their commercial department, rising to chief executive before becoming the club's chairman, a post he holds to this day. In 2002 Derek was awarded the MBE and later an honorary degree by Sheffield Hallam University for 'having campaigned, educated, inspired and supported the wider community'. I don't think I need add to those words.

As we entered the Easter holiday programme things were getting tight at the top of the League. On Good Friday, having drawn 2–2 with Burnley, we had 44 points and were top of Division One, but only three points separated the top seven sides: it was anybody's Championship. Just before we travelled to Sunderland for our Easter Saturday fixture, we learned that manager Bill Scott was to retire from football, and the board had appointed Scot Symon as his replacement. Symon was a former Rangers player who had proved his worth as a manager in Scotland with East Fife. I was sad about this: Bill Scott was always respected by the players – he was scrupulously fair, always positive and had brought some fine players to the club. For all our success in the League, though, Bill had gradually become more of a figurehead at the club than team manager: it was Jimmy Milne who ran the show behind the scenes as far as the training, coaching and organisation of the team was concerned. Some weeks Bill's only involvement was to pick the side – and usually it picked itself. That said, Bill Scott was popular with the lads; we thought that our ideal retirement present to him should be the First Division championship.

Up at Sunderland, when we heard their team we knew they planned to take the game to us with their dangerous forwards Ford, Shackleton and Dickie Davis all playing. What transpired was a cut-and-thrust game of football with metaphorical blows traded from the very start. At half-time but for some good defending from both sides the scoreline could have been 3–3, as opposed to 1–1. The second half was played in similar vein, we got our noses in front and I thought we were set to return home with both points; but late in the game Sunderland's John McSeveney tried his luck when cutting in from the left and it paid off. McSeveney's shot ricocheted off a forest of Preston legs and past George Thompson before nestling into the far corner of the net.

A draw was a fair result, but with the race for the title hotting up, we could ill afford to drop too many points, if any at all, if we were going achieve our aim of winning the title. By that stage of the season, no sooner had we come off the pitch than someone would ask for the Arsenal result and how Charlton Athletic and Wolves had got on. At the request of the rest of the players Tom Finney and I would then sit down with paper and pencil and work out positions at the top of the table, including goals for and against and the mystery of goal average. For a lad whose education ended at fifteen years of age, I developed a surprising mastery of long division as we worked out goal average to the last decimal point. Goal difference is a piece of cake!

We completed the Easter holiday programme with a hard-fought 2–1 win over Burnley on Bank Holiday Monday. Our elation, however, was somewhat tempered when we heard Arsenal, Charlton, Wolves and West Brom had also won. Now we were a point behind Wolves with two games in hand, and we had two more than Arsenal who had played one fewer game than us. Everyone now realised this was going to be the closest title race in history and would go down to the last kick of the season. We were also sure that our clash with Arsenal at Deepdale was crucial to our title hopes. It was essential that we produced a victory in what was our penultimate game of the season.

Deepdale was heaving with 40,000 crammed inside and an estimated 10,000 locked out. Arsenal gave it everything they had, but we produced our best performance of the season to win 2–0 and go top of the table. It was a terrific result from our point of view, but Arsenal did have that game in hand. I insisted that it was better to have points on the board than a game in hand. I don't know if that eased the lads' anxieties, but I thought if I keep saying it often enough, it might make me feel better.

We completed the season with a hard-fought 1–0 win over lowly Derby County, a result that condemned them to relegation. As the news of other results filtered through, it was clear that with their final game to play, against Burnley, Arsenal had the title in their grasp. We had given it our best shot; after a poor start to the campaign the team had galvanished and produced some excellent results and terrific performances. Arsenal were due to play Burnley at Highbury the following Friday night: anything less than a victory for Arsenal would make Preston champions of Division One. This made for an agonising wait for everyone connected with Preston North End. Of course Burnley would apply themselves to the match as they would any League game. I knew their professionalism would not allow them to take it lightly. Many of their players were personal friends: Jimmy Adamson, Tommy Cummings, Brian Pilkington, Billy Elliott, Reg Attwell and Jimmy McIlroy. I also knew Arsenal would be brimming with confidence. With their superior goal average, a victory over Burnley would give them the title. But I lived in hope.

I spent the Friday evening trying to find the running score on the wireless, but even for a game of such importance the normal radio schedule was not to be interrupted. When not twiddling with the dials on the wireless, I made several phone calls to Walter Pilkington, the Preston match reporter of the *Evening Post* who had gone into his office to monitor events from Highbury via the wires. Poor Walter, he must have taken dozens of calls that night. All my Preston team-mates and, as it later transpired, a good number of supporters too had the same idea. Initially the news was good: Burnley took the lead after only three minutes. My joy, however, was short lived, as Alex Forbes, who rarely scored, soon equalised for Arsenal. Doug Lishman and Jimmy Logie added further goals to give Arsenal a 3–1 advantage at half-time. As the second half progressed I began coming to terms with the prospect of the title going to Arsenal, only for my hopes to rise again when Burnley pulled the score back to 3–2. Those final few minutes as Burnley went on the attack in an attempt to salvage something from the game were sheer agony for me. I willed them to score an equaliser, but Arsenal, well marshalled by skipper Joe Mercer, held out for the result they wanted and we didn't need.

To say I was downcast is putting it mildly. After experiencing so much tension and having no positive outlet for such, I was gripped by a mild form of depression which took a couple of days to lift. At first I kept running through my mind all the games at the start of the season which we should have won but didn't. I kept telling myself if only I had done this, or that, if only so and so hadn't snatched at that goalscoring opportunity. After a few days of such ruminating I gave it up as a bad job, coming to terms with the fact we had finished as runners-up in the closest title race in years, with Preston and Arsenal finishing with identical results – 21 wins, 12 draws and 9 defeats. Arsenal clinched the title from us on goal average, their 1.51 being marginally better than our 1.41, a difference of 0.10. It was to be some time before I wanted to see a pencil and paper again. But I had to be philosophical about us having gone so close in a season packed with excitement.

In early November 1952 I received a letter from Park Gardens in Glasgow, the headquarters of the Scottish FA informing me I had been chosen to play for Scotland 'B' against France 'B' in Toulouse later that month. Neither England nor Scotland had an Under-23 team at the time. When a player was chosen for a 'B' international it was widely thought that he was knocking on the door of the full international team. Needless to say I was determined that I should be heard to be knocking very loudly. But when I got home after a dreary goalless game, I scanned the newspapers for a report of the game, but the only mention of the match was the scoreline. Obviously Fleet Street editors did not deem a Scotland 'B' match worthy of sending a reporter to France to cover! However, it was a different matter for my next 'B' international, against England 'B' at Easter Road. One day, I hoped, I might again be called up by Scotland at full international level.

The game ended in a 2–2 draw, and I received a very favourable press for my general play and in particular how I'd handled Arsenal's Doug Lishman. I must have impressed the Scottish selectors too. Within a few weeks I received yet another letter from Park Gardens, this time to inform me of my inclusion in the full international team to play England at Wembley for what would be my second cap.

England versus Scotland is the oldest fixture in the international calendar, the meeting of the 'Auld Enemies'. It was the most eagerly anticipated game for both nations and with so much national pride at stake, such fixtures were always keenly contested

and drew capacity crowds to both Wembley and Hampden Park.
English supporters feel strongly about a match between England
and Scotland whether it be football or rugby. But for a Scot this
annual fixture seemed to seep into his being and become a part
of his instinct. Whilst the emotional response of an English
supporter to a game against Scotland would last only for the
duration of the matchday itself, for a Scot it lasted from the
moment one match ended until the next encounter. Within a
week or so of the Hampden encounter, thousands of Scots would
begin saving a shilling or two bob a week to fund their trip to
Wembley the following year. Courtesy of 30,000 fans bedecked
in tartan bonnets, some wearing kilts, many carrying yellow flags
depicting the rampant red lion, Scotland was transported to
London every two years – and not for the sightseeing.

This was my first appearance at Wembley and just to step on
to its famous turf thrilled me. When the two teams walked from
the tunnel the stadium immediately filled with a cacophony of
noise, an alarming, volatile sound that sent a shiver through my
body. The terraces undulated. We passed the Band of the Royal
Marines as they exited. The music they played and the accom-
paniment they offered to the community singing were to tunes
steeped in tradition and laudatory of the old British Empire.
That day the Marines played 'Festival of Empire', 'Heart of
Oak', 'The British Grenadiers' and 'Rule Britannia'. Great
Britain was no longer the world power it had once been, as I
had witnessed for myself in Palestine. The playing of these tunes
and songs at Wembley appeared an attempt on the part of the
FA – very much a part of the establishment – to promote the
illusion that the Empire was still strong.

In the dressing room I read in the match programme that I
was 'one of the finest constructive wing-halves in the country'
(did my mother write the copy?) and that I'd received an offer
to sign for Aston Villa but declined it. This was the first time I'd
heard of it! The England team lined up as follows: Gil Merrick
(Birmingham City); Alf Ramsey (Spurs), Lionel Smith

(Arsenal); Billy Wright (Wolves), Malcolm 'Mountain' Barrass (Bolton), Jimmy Dickinson (Portsmouth); Tom Finney (Preston), Ivor Broadis (Manchester City), Nat Lofthouse (Bolton Wanderers), Redfern Froggatt (Sheffield Wednesday), Jack Froggatt (Portsmouth). This was the Scotland team that day: George Farm (Blackpool); George Young, Sammy Cox (both Rangers); Tommy Docherty (Preston North End), Frank Brennan (Newcastle United), Doug Cowie (Dundee); Tommy Wright (Sunderland), Bobby Johnstone, Lawrie Reilly (both Hibernian), Billy Steel (Dundee), Billy Liddell (Liverpool).

Ivor Broadis gave England the lead which they held until half-time. I thought Scotland unlucky to be trailing at the interval as we had produced some fine football which forced England into some desperate defending at times. Tom Finney, of course, was a constant threat, as was Nat Lofthouse. The second half was even more of an open game. At the time the Wembley pitch was laid with Cumberland turf, which was very springy and soft underfoot and made legs tire as matches wore on. There were certainly some tired legs out there in the final quarter of this game which led to some uncharacteristic mistakes on the part of both teams. As far as goals were concerned the day belonged to Broadis and Lawrie Reilly. Lawrie equalised Broadis's effort of the first half only for the Manchester City player to add a second. Scotland kept on battling and taking the game to England and our efforts were rewarded when Reilly scored a deserved equaliser. The draw was all the more creditable as we had played for much of the second half with only ten men after Sammy Cox was carried off on a stretcher following a collision with Finney and Broadis.

The result meant Scotland remained unbeaten at Wembley since the end of the war. I still have the programme from the game. It is a treasured possession. I had a taste once more for international football; I didn't want it to be my last. And I certainly wanted to experience that unique Wembley thrill again.

5

WHEN MY SHIP CAME IN I WAS AT THE AIRPORT

The 1953–54 season began with the new manager in place at Preston. James Scotland Symon, known to everyone as Scot, had actually arrived at the club in late March, which allowed him to familiarise himself with the players by the time Preston reported back for pre-season training. A player for Dundee, Portsmouth and Rangers, Scot Symon was a good all-round sportsman who had the distinction of representing Scotland at both football and cricket, an accomplishment shared almost fifty years later by Andy Goram. When his playing days ended he became manager of East Fife and was to lead this unfashionable club to the most productive and successful period in its history. He obviously had an eye for a good player having brought Allan Brown, 'Cannonball' Fleming and 'Square Jaw' Aitken to the club, all of whom went on to enjoy fruitful careers in the English First Division.

I liked Scot Symon from the off. He was fair, honest, showed respect for every player, proved himself good at man management and was always positive in his talks to the team. He was not, however, a great tactician. Nor did we often see him out on the training field. As was the case when Bill Scott was manager, when it came to our training and tactics, and highlighting weaknesses in the opposition, this all came from trainer Jimmy Milne, whose football nous was quickly recognised and respected by Symon.

Half of the Preston players were Scottish and our contacts north of the border were forever informing us that Symon had taken on the manager's job at Deepdale only until the Rangers job became vacant. The word was the Rangers manager, Bill Struth, was ready to retire from the game and the Ibrox directors had already sounded out Symon as his successor. In the event the word was to be proved correct. Scot Symon stayed but one season at Deepdale, but what a season it turned out to be.

We failed to produce the scintillating league form of the previous season, stuttering through the fixture list and finishing eleventh in Division One. The team remained much the same as in the previous season, though because of injuries we used twenty-five players. Injury prevented me from playing any more than 26 league matches, and a troublesome groin restricted Tom Finney to 23 appearances though such was his form in those games he was voted Footballer of the Year. That wily predator Charlie Wayman scored 25 goals in 34 league matches, one of those being the two hundredth goal of his career.

Curiously the 1953–54 season began on a Wednesday – the only time in the history of English football this has ever happened. The reason was that the Football League had, for the first time, agreed a deal with the BBC for a live TV broadcast of the 1954 FA Cup final. The Football League were concerned a live broadcast of the Cup final would seriously affect attendances at league matches originally scheduled for that day. The problem was that the Football League had published the fixtures for the season prior to negotiating the deal with the BBC and so, in their wisdom they brought forward (by an entire season!) the fixtures designated for the Cup final day to the Wednesday preceding 22 August, the original date set for the opening of the season. The famous Blackpool-Bolton Wanderers final of 1953 was the last FA Cup final to take place on the same day as a full programme of Football League fixtures.

Perhaps the fact Preston's League form was so patchy enabled us to apply ourselves fully to the FA Cup. As with every FA

Cup, the story of the 1953–54 competition began with part-timers and amateurs invading the nation's living rooms via the newspapers and the wireless as the vast majority of homes were still without televisions, and enjoying their fifteen minutes of fame and harbouring hopes of giant killing.

I remember a photograph in the newspaper of Great Yarmouth supporters constructing makeshift terracing at their ground from fish boxes. Such a Heath Robinson construction would never be tolerated today. But it was 1953 and it was the Cup, and everyone admired Yarmouth's ingenuity. Their endeavour was richly rewarded when Great Yarmouth caused the shock of round one by beating Crystal Palace 1–0, only to go out of the competition in the next game, beaten 5–2 at Barrow.

In the third round it was the eccentricity of one supporter that captured the imagination of the press. A sixty-year-old Notts County fan, Gordon Wood, hit the headlines for cycling all the way to Everton to watch his team narrowly lose by the odd goal in three. The newspapers reported Mr Wood had not missed a Notts County away match for over two years and that he made every trip on his bicycle – a staggering total of over 10,000 miles, including a recent 500-mile round trip to Plymouth Argyle. When arriving at his destination he simply parked his bicycle, unlocked, beside the turnstile, and always returned to find his bike exactly where he had left it.

Preston's Cup run began with a 2–0 victory at Derby County which earned us a trip to Lincoln City in round four. Another 2–0 success resulted in a home tie against Ipswich Town. At the time Ipswich were in the lower reaches of Division Three (South) and the match turned out to be a bit of a canter for us, 6–1. Next we encountered our toughest opponents to date, in Leicester City. Every time I played against them in a Preston shirt, Leicester proved a very difficult team to beat. When we met them in round six, Leicester were top of the Second Division. As ever, they gave us one hell of a battle.

The tie took place at Filbert Street where a capacity crowd of 40,065 were witness to an open, fluid game of football. Angus Morrison put us ahead and it appeared we were bound for the semi-finals, but Leicester's characteristic tenacity then came to the fore. With only minutes remaining Leicester full-back Ron Jackson chipped a free-kick over the defensive wall and Deepdale beckoned both teams.

The attendance for the replay was 38,130 and North End fans were treated to yet another pulsating Cup match. Leicester were on fire from the start. Goals from Peter Small and my old army pal Arthur Rowley gave them a 2–0 lead. Our interest in the Cup looked decidedly dim but we showed Leicester that we too had plenty of mettle. When Willie Cunningham floated a free-kick into their penalty area, the ball was headed back where it came from and there were Charlie Wayman to give us hope. There were only some seven minutes remaining, so we threw caution to the wind and piled men forward. Yet another free-kick was won outside the box. Once again Willie Cunningham floated the ball into the penalty area, again the ball was headed back, only this time it was Angus Morrison who latched on to it to volley a great equaliser. The tie went to extra time, both teams hit the post but nothing would separate us, so a second replay at a neutral venue it was. We travelled to Hillsborough where the tie produced its highest attendance – 44,558. Ironically, Sheffield Wednesday were waiting to meet the winners in the semi-final. On the day we proved just too good for Leicester. Goals from Jimmy Baxter, Bobby Foster and Tom Finney saw us safely through with the Leicester consolation goal coming from, you've guessed it, Arthur Rowley.

Semi-final matches are notoriously fraught affairs, often not producing the most entertaining football. With Wembley just a step away play is usually riddled with tension and nerves and our match against Sheffield Wednesday at Maine Road was far from a classic. The players, however, accomplished the job we were sent out to do – win, which we did 2–0. Yet our semi-final appeared to pass the neutrals by relatively unnoticed. This was because the imagination of both press and public had been taken by the Cup heroics of Port Vale from the Third Division (North).

Vale had an exceptional team at the time. They won the Third Division (North) title by a country mile. They could score goals, but their greatest strength was their defence which was well marshalled by centre-half Tommy Cheadle and England 'B' goal-keeper Ray King. Vale conceded only 21 goals all season which was unheard of (the previous season, we had conceded 60!). In reaching the semi-finals Vale accounted for two First Division sides in Cardiff City and Cup-holders Blackpool. Could they become the first Division Three club to reach an FA Cup final?

Port Vale met West Bromwich Albion at Villa Park. With the score at 1–1 and the game deep into the second half, West Brom were awarded a penalty. The Vale players remonstrated with the referee believing the offence had taken place outside the penalty area, which a newsreel film of the incident appeared to confirm. Vale's protests fell on deaf ears, however, and up stepped the former Port Vale player, Ronnie Allen, to score from the spot. If they felt they were hard done by, worse was to follow. Minutes from the end Vale's Albert Leake scored what looked to be an equaliser, only for his effort to be ruled offside. Again, film of the incident seemed to indicate Leake was onside when the ball was played to him. It was very hard on Port Vale whose surviving players, to this day, believe they were diddled out of reaching an FA Cup final.

Following our semi-final victory, the town of Preston appeared to undergo a metamorphosis. Those who had never set foot inside Deepdale were gripped by Cup fever simply because their town was the focus of national attention and they wanted to do it proud. As the final drew closer, shops were adorned in blue and white, with photographs of me and my team-mates. Blue and white bunting fluttered above the streets, 'Good Luck Preston' signs hung from lampposts. Then there was the frenetic scramble for tickets.

The capacity at Wembley was 100,000 and each club received from the FA a ticket allocation of 12,000. Preston's average home attendance was 28,000, which meant some 16,000 of our regular supporters were going to be very disappointed. The allocation of tickets to the finalists was always a highly emotive matter. With just 24,000 headed for the clubs, it meant tickets were going, well, I don't know where. The system of distributing tickets was unfair, unjust, a sham and open to widespread abuse. Earlier in the season the Sunderland chairman, E. W. Ditchburn, proposed at the Football League's annual meeting that each finalist should receive up to 26,000. The allocation would then rise on a sliding scale over five years to 40,000. In his address Ditchburn attacked the allocation of 43,000 tickets to amateur organisations, and questioned giving tickets to politicians, foreign embassies and senior members of the armed forces and civil service. Not surprisingly every aspect of Ditchburn's resolution failed; his subsequent application to join the FA Cup Organising Committee was also unsuccessful. Seemingly such sedition was not to be tolerated by the FA or Football League.

The bookies made Preston favourites for the final. Following their semi-final victory over Port Vale, West Brom's form dipped, which cost them the championship to Wolves, the first in their 66-year history. We, on the other hand, were flying. As we came off the pitch following our 6–2 victory at White Hart Lane, Spurs captain, Ron Burgess said, 'Why don't you collect the cup while you're down here? The way you're playing no one will beat you, the club might as well save on train fares.'

No team in the country was playing the pure, fluid, passing football of Preston, what the *Daily Sketch* described as 'ice-cold footballing brilliance'. In the event, the *Sketch*'s preview couldn't have been more wrong.

With the burden of expectation weighing heavy on our shoulders, we travelled down to London on the Wednesday morning. At the time I felt this was a mistake. Footballers are creatures of routine. For an away match in London we would usually travel on the Friday, do some light training in the afternoon and finish off with a game of six-a-side. After tea we would catch an early film at a local cinema, then it was back to the hotel and bed. But for this match we stewed for three days at a hotel in Weybridge. We didn't train or even go for a run. I'd soon finished reading my book, Raymond Chandler's *The High Window*; there was no television in the hotel, not even a wireless in the rooms, and so once the morning papers had been read the players just sat around, killing time from one meal to the next. The arrival of the laundry van on the drive was an event of major interest, and immediately following lunch the topic of conversation would invariably centre around what would be on the menu for dinner. The tedium was broken by a visit to the cinema on the Thursday evening where we saw William Holden star in *Stalag 17*, the irony not being lost on any of the players.

As the monotony increased, the tension built up in every one of us. There was nothing to take our minds off the final. I think we all knew the atmosphere was wrong. We should have stuck to our normal preparation for an away match. We felt bored and irritated, it did not bode well.

It was significant that West Brom did not make the same mistake. They arrived at their hotel early on the Friday afternoon, after having undergone light training back in Birmingham in the morning. News of their arrival in London served only to compound our listlessness. Whether it be true or not, we imagined the West Brom players had all been having a good time training and spending time with their families before coming to London.

On the day of the final itself it was decided the team should not arrive at Wembley until late, a decision taken, we were told, to offset nerves. So the tedium of that hotel was prolonged. When we finally walked out to the team coach we felt like William Holden escaping from his POW camp.

We arrived at Wembley only thirty-five minutes before kick-off. We had no time to go out on to the pitch to soak up the atmosphere. We grabbed a cup of tea as we changed before settling down to hear Scot Symon's team talk. He was unhelpfully laconic: 'Let them [West Brom] do the worrying. Just play normally.' He offered a few words to Charlie Wayman and Willie Forbes, told me to get forward when I could, and that was about it before he handed over to Jimmy Milne. Jimmy had only just begun his talk when the buzzer rang, the signal for us to leave the dressing room and line up in the tunnel. Although we felt positive and confident, the extra edge to our mental attitude, that should have been there, was missing.

When the referee signalled both teams should proceed down the tunnel to the pitch, my heart was racing. The brightness of a May day appeared in sharp contrast to the dim light of the long Wembley tunnel. As soon as the crowd saw the teams striding on to the emerald green turf, Wembley resounded to the bedlam of 100,000 voices as rattles whirled, flags waved, handkerchiefs fluttered and caps careered from side to side above heads. We wheeled to the right, heading towards the area in front of the Royal Box where the teams were to be presented to the Queen Mother.

Tom Finney escorted the Queen Mother down our line, introducing each player in turn. H.R.H. extended a gloved hand wished each one good luck. As she passed on down the line I drank in the scene, trying to absorb every detail in case this was to be my only Cup final. In front of the Royal Box was a flower bed that would have put a seed catalogue to shame. In the midst of it, incongruously, the newsreel cameras were recording the moment for posterity. Behind each goal was a crescent of fresh sawdust, the reason for which I never did find out. I looked to the far end terrace which heaved with humanity, then across to the South Stand whose seats rose higher and higher, their top tiers lost beneath the overlap of the stand.

Preston North End lined up as follows: George Thompson; Willie Cunningham, Joe Walton; Tommy Docherty, Joe Marston, Willie Forbes; Tom Finney, Bob Foster, Charlie Wayman, Jimmy Baxter, Angus Morrison. The West Brom team was: Jim Sanders; Joe Kennedy, Len Millard; Jimmy Dudley, Jimmy Dugdale, Ray

Barlow; Frank 'Speedy' Griffin, Reg Ryan, Ronnie Allen, Johnny Nicholls, George Lee.

Preston were at full strength which meant disappointment for players such as Bill Scott, Joe Dunn, Dennis Hatsell and Harry Mattinson all of whom had come into the side at one point or other during the season and done a great job. For West Brom Joe Kennedy, usually a centre-half, deputised for Stan Rickarby, whilst Jim Sanders kept goal in place of Norman Heath who was suffering from a spinal injury and watched the game on television in a Birmingham hospital.

Scot Symon had told us to 'just play normally' but this is just what we could not do. Instead, our football had none of its normal fluency and incisiveness. It was strained, fitful and in attempting to rectify the matter, we tried too hard. The natural easiness which we normally applied to matches was absent. After an opening twenty minutes in which both teams cautiously sounded one another out, we suddenly found ourselves a goal down. Right-back Willie Cunningham tried to find Tom Finney with a raking ball down our right-hand side. The ball hit the West Brom winger, George Lee, rebounded past Willie and Lee took it on towards goal and tried his luck. His shot flashed across the face of the goal and appeared to be heading for a throw-in on the far side but, from seemingly out of nowhere, up popped Ronnie Allen unmarked just beyond the far post and simply passed the ball into our gaping net. My stomach turned cartwheels, my eyes studied the turf as the West Brom players whooped in celebration.

We were chasing the game – but not for long. Straight from the restart Tom Finney played the ball to me and I made ground down our right. I glanced up to see outside-left Angus Morrison cutting in from the wing and drove the ball into the space between the penalty spot and the edge of the area. Angus rose high above Joe Kennedy and timed his header to perfection. The ball sailed over Jim Sanders who had been caught in no-man's land and we were level. I saw the crowd undulate en masse then, a split second later, a noise like someone ripping up lino in heaven assaulted my ears. I took to my toes to join my team-mates in congratulating Angus.

During the half-time interval Scot Symon and Jimmy Milne told us we had yet to demonstrate the quality football we were noted for producing. 'Get out there and play them off the park,' Jimmy told us. Well, we got out there at least. In the early stages of the second half we showed a glimpse of our fluid, passing football. An eight-player move concluded with Jimmy Baxter slipping the ball through to that bundle of fiery endeavour Charlie Wayman, which immediately prompted the West Brom defence to raise an arm to appeal for offside. I have to be honest and say that when Jimmy Baxter passed the ball I thought Charlie looked to be offside. The linesman on the right touchline, however, was perfectly placed and kept his flag down. So Charlie rightly continued, carrying the ball deep into West Brom territory before cutting across to the left and flashing past the flailing Jim Sanders as if he were standing at a bus stop. Charlie took the ball on a few yards before applying the conclusive touch. Having been the recipients of some good fortune in the semi-final, the West Brom players were incensed and directed their frustration towards referee Arthur Luty. But the goal stood.

However, West Brom's play took on an added fervour as if they believed consummate effort might wipe the impact of this setback from their consciousness. Minutes later left-half Ray Barlow came through with the ball at his feet and when he reached our penalty area I committed myself to the tackle. Ray had actually overrun the ball when I executed the challenge but he regained control just as I slid under him. Ray went over my right shoulder, his knee caught me on the way, and I froze as I heard the shrill blast of the ref's whistle. Once again the babble of argument was heard on the Wembley pitch, and I dare say amongst half the spectators present.

Only three penalties had ever been awarded in Wembley Cup finals. Ronnie Allen's contained both drama and farce. When he placed the ball it rolled into a dip in the middle of the penalty spot. He moved it forwards, then back to the rear lip of the spot which prompted Willie Cunningham to protest. Allen once again picked up the ball, attempted to stamp the ground flat, failed, and moved the ball back again into the depression. While this was happening, their goalie Jim Sanders had his back to the incident, his hands wrapped around his left-hand post as he offered a prayer. At last Allen planted the ball towards the bottom right corner, George Thompson at full stretch got his fingertips to it but could do no more. The ball had just enough pace to squeeze inside the post.

It looked as if the final was to go to extra time, but Allen's penalty proved the turning point. Ominously West Brom grew stronger. With only two minutes of the game remaining Joe Kennedy touched off the movement that was to determine our fate. He switched the ball to Reg Ryan, whose chipped pass gave Frank 'Speedy' Griffin the beating of Joe Marston on the outside. Ryan hit a shot that would have normally been meat and drink to George Thompson, but the ball went under his body and the cold voice of reason pressed home the truth: we had lost. Rarely could Wembley basking in May Day sunshine have appeared so dismal. When the final whistle sounded, the Preston supporters' bleakness and suffering was palpable. After receiving my runners-up medal I sat in the dressing room feeling utterly devastated, both my body and mind as empty. I always hated to lose, but this was disappointment as never before.

An FA Cup final with five goals and two comebacks sounds riveting but, in truth, it was a disappointing final in which neither side, particularly Preston, played to anywhere like full potential. The newspapers looked for conclusive photographic evidence that Charlie Wayman was offside when he received the pass that led to our second goal. Similarly proof was sought, and debate ensued, regarding my challenge on Ray Barlow which resulted in the penalty. Referee Arthur Luty was either chastised, or given top marks for being spot on. Incidentally, Luty went on to become one of the nation's favourite referees, highly respected by managers, players and supporters alike and did not retire from officiating until the mid-sixties.

I felt sorry for myself but just as sorry for Tom Finney. He was singled out for some harsh criticism, as if he had committed a heinous crime. One reporter said without hesitation or qualification that Finney had let Preston down, whilst Sunday's *Empire News* ran with 'Finney's Wembley Washout'. The truth of it was, Tom simply had an off day, but then none of us were at our best. Had it not been for his efforts, Preston would not have got to Wembley anyway. At the time football writers were much more scathing of bad performances than they tend to be today.

The Preston post-final dinner took place at the Savoy Hotel. Our wives accompanied us and each received a gift at what was a lavish do. From all accounts we received far better treatment than did the West Brom lads. The occasion was sumptuous, if somewhat subdued. Music was provided by the Carroll Gibbons Orchestra who could knock out a good tune, the cabaret by Norman Wisdom, Petula Clark and Al Read. All three went down well, though I couldn't help feeling they would have gone down better with the FA Cup in the room.

Even my favourite comic Al Read failed to lift my mood; a downcast feeling that was to be accentuated when we returned to Preston on the Monday. Thousands lined the streets and massed outside Preston Town Hall, cheerful and loyal as ever even in defeat. Their generosity only made us feel that we had let them all down. And for Tom Finney, it was worse for him than any of us, as he was a local lad and totally devoted to the town and its people. I later discovered this feeling of guilt was common amongst just about every footballer who had played on the losing side in a Cup final. I once talked to Duncan Edwards about it after Manchester United had lost to Aston Villa in the 1957 final. Duncan said: 'I think we all felt a lump in our throats as the Manchester people welcomed us back. They couldn't have been kinder had we brought the Cup with us. All the players vowed to win it next year for those supporters. That is what glory is all about.' Tragically for that particular Manchester United team there was not to be a next year. Munich intervened.

★

I knew I had to put the Wembley disappointment quickly behind me – and for one very good reason. I had received one of those infamous, impersonal letters from the SFA informing me I was in the squad for the 1954 World Cup finals in Switzerland. As I had been overlooked for every Scotland international of the season, including the 'B' internationals I can only assume my club form won me a call-up. It was turning out to be quite a season: an FA Cup final followed by the World Cup.

Although England had recently been trounced by Hungary, British football was still held in some esteem by FIFA who designated two home countries would compete in the World Cup finals by virtue of being champions (England) and runners-up (Scotland) in the Home International Championship. Both countries' preparations to the World Cup did not bode well. England were at first buoyed by a 4–2 victory over Scotland at Hampden Park in May but later that month lost 1–0 to Yugoslavia in Belgrade. A week later, and for the second time in six months, Hungary wrote another chapter in the record book at England's expense when they beat them 7–1 in Budapest, following that 6–3 humiliation at Wembley. It was England's biggest defeat in 90 years of international football. Having been beaten by England, Scotland had nothing to crow about, but we did salvage some prestige by beating Norway 1–0 at Hampden Park. I was chosen to play at right-half in this game and was flabbergasted, though delighted, to be told by manager Andy Beattie I was to captain the team. Captaining Scotland had always been a dream for me – what player wouldn't feel like that? When I led the players out on to the pitch the rampant lion on my shirt badge was bulging with pride. Behind me was a new-look Scotland team that contained five debutants: goalkeeper Fred Martin (Aberdeen), my Preston team-mate Willie Cunningham, Jock Aird (Burnley), Jim Davidson (Partick Thistle) and Paddy Buckley (Aberdeen). Considering all these new faces, the 1–0 success was a satisfactory result, although, our performance did nothing to inspire a meagre Hampden crowd of 25,000. I, at least, had the satisfaction of helping to set up our goal. Following a free kick from Hibs's Bobby Johnstone I managed to flick the ball on with my head for George Hamilton (Aberdeen) to rise above the Norwegian defence and head home. At least Scotland had won in my first game as captain of my country.

A fortnight later Scotland flew out to Oslo for the return. Once again I was appointed captain of a side that showed four changes: Celtic's Bobby Evans was replaced at left-half by Doug Cowie (Dundee), whilst upfront Johnny McKenzie (Partick Thistle) took over from Johnstone at outside-right, Jackie Henderson (Portsmouth) replaced Buckley at centre-forward, and Celtic's Neil Mochan, winning his first cap, took over at outside-left from Willie Ormond. The game, played before a capacity crowd of 24,000, ended 1–1, though I feel with better finishing we would have won this one too. Having taken a first-half lead through Johnny McKenzie, Norway's late equaliser was farcical. George Hamilton, back to help out in defence, mis-hit an intended clearance straight to Kure. The ball hit the Norwegian left-winger in the face, rebounded to Fred Martin who was so surprised he could not react quickly enough when the ball hit him square in the chest and then fell back into the path of Kure, who prodded the ball into the net.

I was rested for Scotland's final match of our World Cup preparations, a 2–1 victory over Finland in Helsinki. Here I use the term 'preparations' loosely. The Finland match was an opportunity for the Scottish selectors to give an outing to those who were members of the World Cup squad but who had not played in the previous two matches. Well, that's what I thought. The SFA selection committee, who held sway on team matters and who only 'consulted' manager Andy Beattie, obviously had other ideas. With only Finland to play before we began our World Cup campaign, the selectors introduced another four new caps: goalkeeper Jack Anderson (Leicester City), Alex Wilson (Portsmouth), Davie Mathers (Partick Thistle) and Willie Fernie

(Celtic) – that made a total of nine debutants in three matches. Consequently we went off to Switzerland not knowing our best team.

When the Scotland squad arrived in Zurich, my Preston team-mate Willie Cunningham was not hopeful of being chosen for our opening match against Austria. With only three caps to his name, Willie felt his lack of international experience would count against him when the selectors came to choosing the team. I tried to reassure him that he had done well in his two recent games and that in any case he was guaranteed to play. I told him, 'There are only thirteen players in the squad and that includes seven forwards.' Unbelievably we had travelled to the World Cup with a squad of thirteen, two of whom, manager Andy Beattie confided in me, were only there on stand-by should injuries occur to the selectors' preferred eleven – which, by the way, Andy Beattie, was not yet privy too. After all, he was only the manager!

The day before the game, Willie emerged from the room where the selectors were meeting to pick the team, his face looking forlorn. I heaved a sigh and thought about what I might say to comfort him. But he had been picked to play against Austria. It was something else.

'It's a difficult one, Tommy,' said Willie, his eyes not meeting mine.

'Go on, spit it out.'

'They've replaced you as captain,' he said hesitantly.

I was dumbfounded. I thought I had done a good job as captain; the newspapers certainly thought so. I was ready to lead Scotland in the World Cup. Now, without any consultation, I had been replaced as skipper.

'Well, never mind,' I heard myself saying. 'At least you're in the team, that's the main thing. Go on, give me a laugh, who've they appointed captain?'

'Me,' said Willie somewhat embarrassed.

Part of me was genuinely delighted for Willie, but he had

played in only three internationals and it had been little over three weeks since he had made his debut. Now he was to captain us in the World Cup. I couldn't be upset for my own situation because Willie was a grand lad and good friend. Still, I should not have been surprised, I'd been given the captaincy on my fourth appearance for Scotland. Rather than being joyful at his appointment, Willie simply felt embarrassed. He knew, as I did, that he was inexperienced at international level and that he hardly knew some of the players.

'Do the job to the best of your ability and you will be fine. You have my full support, and I'm sure the rest of the lads will back you . . . skipper.'

He offered me a wincing smile.

'Come on, be happy for yourself. If you want to be happy for a short time, become captain of Scotland. If you want to be happy for longer, fall in love,' I said.

'What if you want to be happy for ever?' he asked.

'Take up gardening.'

I prepared for what was to be my first World Cup feeling certain of three things: that I was now good enough to play at the highest level; that playing for my country was always a matter of great pride to me; and that Scotland would not win the World Cup. If I was to enjoy my career as an international player, I realised I simply had to live with the pomposity of the Scottish selectors and their Quixotic policies.

One evening Willie, Allan Brown (Blackpool), Doug Cowie (Dundee) and myself were sitting enjoying the evening sunshine when two of the SFA blazer brigade approached us. After exchanging small talk, conversation turned to our forthcoming game against Austria.

'I've seen Austria play on three occasions. Let me give you boys some advice about the Austrian players,' ventured one official. All four of us listened intently. 'When you take to the field, remember this word, "dexterity". The Austrian players are very

. . . dexterous,' he said, straining the syllables. 'Keep that in mind, and you'll no go far wrong.'

The SFA blazer gave us a knowing nod, before he and his pal walked on, leaving us bemused. Having seen Austria play three times, was this the sum total of his observations?

Having thought the matter over I eventually came to the conclusion that his words were intended not to help but to re-inforce status. I imagined, as the two toddled away, him smirking as he turned to his colleague to say, '"Dexterity". That will have those boys reaching for the nearest dictionary.' I found myself shaking my head at such pretentiousness.

Against Austria we fielded a very inexperienced team; with my six caps I felt a comparative veteran. Austria were one of the best teams in the world at the time, with plenty of experience. They played a style that was not dissimilar to Hungary's with a deep-lying centre-forward, Dienst, and an inside-forward, Schleger, prompting from midfield. They, together with Hanappi and Ocwirk were outstanding players. But what we lacked in the way of knowledge of one another's play, tactics and cohesion, we more than made up for by our application. Every player gave his all and the newspapers agreed we were very unlucky to lose by the only goal of the game.

The following day, Andy Beattie announced his resignation as Scotland manager. He had only taken up the post in February, becoming the first Scotland manager, but four months in the job was obviously too much for him. For him to have resigned after our first World Cup match, and after what had been a heartening performance, speaks volumes for his frustration and angst. He told me he was totally fed up with the way the Scottish FA ran the show. In particular the fact we arrived for a World Cup with only eleven players and two designated as 'stand-bys'. 'There are more SFA officials here than players. It's a nonsense,' said Andy, and he was right.

When Andy departed an SFA official suggested to him that walking out on Scotland would seriously damage his chances of getting another manager's job. 'Aye, maybe,' said Andy, 'but with my experience, if not as a manager, I'll get some sort of job in the game.'

'What makes you so sure?' asked the official.

'I'm very dexterous!' replied Andy.

When a team loses its first game in a World Cup it is vital not to lose the second. This was particularly so in this campaign because while there were four teams in each group, they only played two matches, not three. In their wisdom FIFA decided that each group would contain two seeded teams but that they were not to meet, which was tough on the Czechs, and tough on Scotland. Our second match was against Uruguay, and this was, indeed, a big ask for us as the South Americans, like Austria, were considered to be one of the best teams in the world. Just how good Uruguay were, we found out in Basle on 19 June.

They tore us apart. We were 2–0 down at half-time, and any hope we had of staging a recovery disappeared when Uruguay upped the ante in the second half. Even the team kits represented a clash of football styles, of the old against the new. Scotland wore heavy cotton, button collar, long sleeve shirts; baggy shorts and thick woollen socks, the staple kit of every British team. Uruguay wore short-sleeved V-neck cotton shirts; skimpy black shorts, lightweight cotton socks, and lightweight boots cut below the ankle. We were shod in boots that contained a metal plate in the sole and bulging toe-caps. Thus ended Scotland's World Cup, when the SFA tried to conquer the best with a squad of just eleven players, half with four caps or less, and then, without a word or a reason, stripped another player of the captaincy.

Uruguay's dynamic left-winger Borges netted a hat-trick and there were two goals each for Miguez and Abbadie to complete the 7–0 rout. The game was played under a blazing sun and Willie Cunningham had spent the entire game puffing and panting trying to catch Borges. After the game we sat forlorn in the dressing room marvelling at the skill and athleticism of the Uruguayan players. England, meanwhile, progressed to the quarter-finals before they too capitulated to Uruguay. Their 4–2 defeat was comparatively respectable, but as Stan Matthews later told me, 'We were always chasing the game. It could have been eight.'

Hungary confirmed favouritism by beating South Korea 9–0 and West Germany, another much fancied team, 8–3. The German manager Sepp Herberger rested eight players against the Hungarians and the ploy appeared to backfire when West Germany finished third in their group behind Turkey. I could never understand why Hungary played West Germany, as both had been seeded and, as was the case in the respective groups containing Scotland and England, the seeded teams were supposed to have been kept apart. Goal average counted for nothing and because Turkey and West Germany finished level on points, they met in a play-off match. On this occasion Herberger was taking no chances; he fielded a full-strength side and the Germans coasted home 7–2. This was hard on Turkey; if goal average had been taken into consideration they would have progressed to the quarter-finals.

In the semi-finals Hungary overcame Uruguay and West Germany enjoyed a comfortable 6–1 victory over Austria. For the final Ferenc Puskas insisted on turning out for Hungary, even though he was carrying an injury picked up when playing against the Germans at the group stage. Hungary seemed to be coasting when they took a 2–0 lead, but as we were so often to see down the years, German resolve is formidable. West Germany got one back within a minute and drawing strength from this gradually asserted themselves. They were level at half-time and in the second period Rahn turned the game on its head when he made it 3–2. It was a crazy turnaround after having lost the group match 8–3, but now they were world champions.

Like many of my team-mates I was never paid for playing for Scotland in the 1954 World Cup. Before the tournament began the SFA informed the players we would receive a £15 fee per match or opt to keep our shirt. I kept the shirts, which I later donated to charitable causes.

The day after the Uruguay defeat, I gave an interview for the Scottish *Daily Express*. At one point the reporter suggested it had been a great season for me. 'You played in an FA Cup final at Wembley. You were made captain of your country and have now played in the World Cup. You must feel your ship has come in,' he suggested.

'Aye,' I replied, 'just my luck I was at the airport.'

The performances of both England and Scotland only served to emphasise how far British football had fallen behind the rest of the world. England's defeats by Hungary and the lame performance in the World Cup. Now it was accepted that the domestic game had stood still for far too long. Scotland too came under fire from its press critics. Alec Young in the Scottish *Daily Mail* wrote, 'Scottish football is now light years behind that of Hungary, Uruguay and newly crowned world champions, West Germany. As for the way the Scottish Football Association conducted affairs for this World Cup, it would make a good Whitehall farce.'

I was sure the SFA and the English FA still didn't fully grasp the magnitude of what had happened. They appeared to consider the World Cup as something of a gimmick, a tournament that still played second fiddle to our domestic competitions. In the *FA Yearbook*, thirteen pages were devoted to the reports of Home International Championship matches and other internationals involving the home nations, whereas coverage of the entire World Cup finals was limited to two pages. Even amateur football was given more coverage than the World Cup. There was no hint of official concern. The ostriches had buried their heads in the sand. However, many in the game, myself included, were convinced that change was inevitable. What's more, we were ready to welcome change. I decided I wanted to be at the forefront of such changes that were to take place in British football.

6

MUD, SWEAT AND FEARS

Following the World Cup I had the idea of opening a business. Immediately after the war the quality of food in restaurants and cafés was poor. Just about every town contained at least one government-owned café, which were notorious for their often deplorable catering, hygiene and service, and where the food was overcooked and unappetising. Family cafés were invariably of the 'greasy spoon' variety. It occurred to me that a neat, clean, welcoming café that served simple, but tasty, wholesome food could be a good business. One day I mentioned this to Joe Dunn, the Preston half-back. Joe didn't say much at the time, but a few days later he collared me after training and asked if I was serious. I told him I was; he told me he thought the idea was a good one, that he'd thought the matter over, had a 'few quid' in the bank and was interested in becoming business partners. We found some suitable premises in Cannon Street, not far from Deepdale and had the place refurbished, decorated and equipped. Our wives chose the décor and furnishings, we hired an excellent cook, appointed a manager and an assistant and the Olympic Café was open for business.

The café proved to be a good little business. If we weren't required to return to Deepdale for extra training, Joe and I would lend a hand in the afternoons. In busy periods we helped prepare sandwiches and even did a little baking. In the main, however, we served meals to customers, many of whom were Preston supporters who wanted to chat to us about the club. This was great PR for the café. I enjoyed my time as co-owner of the Olympic and learned a lot from the venture; not least, life is too short to stuff a small tomato. The café gained a good reputation for morning coffee, lunches and snacks, so we decided to stay open a little later and provide meals for people on the way to the cinema or theatre. This subsequently opened up a new market for us. Many visiting teams would call in for a light meal on a Friday evening. When word of this got round, every other Friday would see a knot of autograph-hunting schoolboys hanging about outside. Spurs and Chelsea in particular were regular visitors.

I had the initial idea for the business with one eye on my future. At the time I didn't know what I wanted to do in life once my playing days were over. I saw the café, as did Joe, as a possible job after football. Joe and I were by no means unique in looking ahead in this manner. Tom Finney had a thriving plumbing business; Stan Matthews had a hotel in Blackpool; Harry Johnston (Blackpool) owned a newsagents; Stan Mortensen (also Blackpool) and Walley Barnes (Arsenal) owned sports shops; Ted Ditchburn ran a grocery shop not far from White Hart Lane and Harry Kirtley (Cardiff City) had an electrical business. Joe Dunn and I were partners for six years until I eventually sold him my share of the café. Joe was a super guy and fine half-back who Preston signed from Clyde for the bargain price of £1,500 in 1951. He played his final game for Preston against Sheffield Wednesday in 1961, by which time he had accumulated 224 league appearances, most of which were clocked up during his final five years at a club he served as well as he served light lunches.

The rumour about Bill Struth's retirement from Rangers was correct: following Preston's appearance in the FA Cup final, Scot Symon left the club to become manager of the Glasgow team. Symon's replacement was Frank Hill, who began his managerial career as player-manager of Crewe Alexandra before taking over at Burnley in 1948. During his six years at Turf Moor Hill did a solid job without pulling up any trees, though he did sign Jimmy McIlroy, one of the finest inside-forwards ever to grace British football.

By previous standards the 1954–55 season was disappointing for Preston, though it certainly sustained interest until the end. We finished just below half-way, though only five points ahead of Leicester City, who were relegated along with Sheffield Wednesday. Curiously, Preston finished only twelve points adrift of Chelsea who, in their jubilee year, clinched the championship in what was the most competitive Division One in living memory. Chelsea won the title with the lowest points tally (52) ever recorded by a championship side.

On the international front, the season brought the same combination of initial excitement and subsequent disappointment that I had felt in playing for Scotland in the World Cup. I was chosen to play for Scotland in the Home International against Wales at Ninian Park in mid-October, with our second match, against Northern Ireland, a fortnight later. (The 'big one' against England was the finale to the domestic season, which gave the championship a rather fractured appearance.)

A capacity crowd of 60,000 saw Aberdeen's Paddy Buckley head a spectacular goal late in the game to give Scotland victory. Before the match I consoled Willie Cunningham who, like me, only found out he was no longer the captain when it was announced that Rangers' George Young was to be skipper. Three weeks later when the selectors announced the team for our game against Northern Ireland, I wasn't in it. Neither was Willie. The other omission from the team that had beaten Wales was inside-right Harry Yorston who had made his first and only appearance for Scotland that day. Given that the newspapers had been complimentary about my performance at Ninian Park, that we had kept a clean sheet, and that my subsequent performances for Preston had been good, I felt hard done by. But I was not surprised that no one rang from the SFA to explain my omission. That was normal.

In the event Scotland were lucky to draw 2–2 against the Irish. Leading 2–1, Northern Ireland were effectively reduced to ten men when Danny Blanchflower sustained an injury that, in the days before substitutes, rendered him little more than a passenger for the rest of the game. It had been a very disappointing Scotland performance and the press made no bones about saying so. The Scottish selection committee came in for some awful stick which, it was said, prompted one of the more memorable quotes from SFA President Harry Swan, 'Assistant heads will roll!'

Players' heads certainly rolled for the next game against Hungary in December: no fewer than eight changes from the team that had drawn against Northern Ireland. My Deepdale team-mate Willie Cunningham returned as right-back and captain and, to my delight, I was named at right-half.

To allow for the black-and-white newsreel cameras to identify the teams, Scotland's shirts, unusually, had white sleeves. Hungary may well have failed in their quest to win the World Cup but they were still the team everyone wanted to see. On a bleak December afternoon a Hampden crowd of 113,146 saw a 4–2 victory for Hungary and a Scottish performance that exceeded all expectations. This was not the walkover the press and many supporters had expected.

I remember it being a bitterly cold day. There had been light snow early on but the pitch had been protected from the worst of the overnight frost by tons of straw which, a couple of hours before kick-off, had been heaped around the perimeter of the pitch. On a difficult surface Hungary sometimes displayed the classic close-passing movements upon which their greatness had been built, but for long periods they were thrown out of their stride by Scotland's vigorous tackling and lancing thrusts into their opponents' half. Before the game we had decided that our only hope of containing Puskas and Co. was to get to the ball first, or, failing that, harass the Hungarians into making errors. From the kick-off Hungary had the lions' share of the play but the goal that gave them the lead after twenty minutes was a lucky one. Our left-back, Harry

Haddock of Clyde, making his international debut, deflected a shot from Bozsik past Fred Martin, who had appeared to have the shot covered. It was disappointing to go behind to such a goal, and five minutes later Hungary increased their lead when Hidegkuti ran clean through an untenanted central defence. Two minutes before half-time we pulled one back when I slipped the ball through to Bobby Johnstone who in turn found Tommy Ring. Hope sprang eternal but hardly had the cheers died down when, straight from the restart, Hungary swept down the pitch and restored their two-goal advantage through Sandor.

Finding themselves 3–1 down to Hungary at half-time many a team would have folded, but not Scotland on this day. Willie Cunningham and I spent most of the interval geeing-up our team-mates. 'Leave Puskas to me, I'll sort him out,' I heard myself saying, though I had no idea how.

In the second period I knew my job was to stick as close as I could to Puskas and 'get a foot in' – easier said than done against such a player but I did manage to deny him the ball often. He proved to be as mercurial a talent and as difficult to play against as his reputation suggested. If the ball was played anywhere near him, it was his; his first touch was instant and perfect. He was a master at screening the ball and although he looked a little portly even then, he used every part of his body to full effect. Puskas's anticipation and reading of the game was uncanny, he seemed to know what a team-mate was going to do with the ball before the thought occurred to him. When he received the ball he would turn his back to me. When I came around to his side he would then twist and turn, an arm would come out to fend me off. If not an arm, he would use a shoulder or his backside. All I could do was to constantly reposition myself, harass and hustle the man until he inadvertently offered me a glimpse of the ball, where-upon I'd attempt to get a toe on it and hopefully knock it away. His passes were beautifully accurate and weighted to perfection. His power was in his left, though like most players of the time, he was good on either foot. One thing I noticed about Puskas was how he always held his head high when the ball was at his feet. Not once did I ever see him look down to see where that ball was, which enabled him to assess the movements of team-mates and opponents alike. He was more than just a stylish creator; I found him quite aggressive. He gave as good as he got, and for all he looked a tad out of shape, he was not without pace. Mindful of my words at half-time, I resolutely stuck to my task. I remember one moment when he harnessed the infamous Hampden swirl to his advantage. With the outside of his foot Puskas curled the ball past Willie Cunningham only for it to finish up some three yards on the inside of Willie for Fenyvesi to run on to. It was, indeed, magical stuff.

The second half was only ten minutes old when Bobby Johnstone (Hibernian) met a perfectly flighted free-kick from Partick's Johnny McKenzie and headed past Farago. The ground erupted once more and urged on by the famous roar we took the game to Hungary. Twice Hibernian's Lawrie Reilly went desperately close to giving the Hampden crowd what they yearned for. Farago made a brave block when McKenzie, six yards from goal, got what looked like a conclusive touch to a low, hard centre from Tommy Ring. Johnstone fizzed a shot past the post, and I had a drive tipped over by Farago. A minute from time Hungary broke out of defence and a typically flowing movement ended with Kocsis putting the result beyond doubt.

A 4–2 defeat it may have been, but Scotland's performance was widely seen as a moral victory in light of England's two humiliating maulings at the hands of the Hungarians. While not good enough to win, we did compete extremely well against the best football team in the world. So it was all the more galling and, indeed, bewildering when in Scotland's next international we were beaten out of sight.

Following the heroics against Hungary, Scotland – it grieves me to say this – contrived to reach a new low when beaten 7–2 at Wembley in April 1955. It was Scotland's record defeat in the Home International Championship and equalled our own record victory against England way back in 1878. The day belonged entirely to England, in particular to Stanley Matthews, Dennis Wilshaw and a young player making his international debut that day, Duncan Edwards. Scotland were out-gunned in almost every department. At the age of 40 it is doubtful whether Stan had ever been greater, whilst Wilshaw, the Wolves inside-left, entered the record books courtesy of his four goals. They stole the headlines but the player who caught my eye was Edwards. I had of course come across Duncan before in the First Division, but against Scotland that day he belied his youth by producing a powerhouse display in the England midfield.

The influence of the Hungarians was evident as the England team took to the pitch, if not for their style of play, then for their style of kit. While Scotland wore the traditional, heavy, collared and buttoned shirt, albeit with short sleeves, England wore lightweight V-neck cotton shirts with short sleeves, the first time they had worn this style of strip. England signalled their intent by taking the lead in less than a minute. Frank Blunstone (Chelsea) centred, Fred Martin flapped when challenged by Nat Lofthouse, as many goalkeepers of the time did, and Wilshaw was there to pick up the pieces. Harry Haddock was a plucky little full-back, but try as he might he just couldn't contain Matthews. The old maestro was conjuring up his past, and with less than half an hour played we found ourselves 4–1 down.

The second-half was practically all Matthews and Wilshaw, the latter hitting three to take his tally for the game to four and England's to seven. Six minutes from time Scotland were awarded a free-kick some thirty yards from goal. I elected to take it and thought, 'What the hell, I'll try and give our supporters at least one memory of the day to cherish.' I saw a gap to the left of Bert Williams and went for it. I powered the drive and, not being known for my goalscoring, it was a rare moment of sweetness when I saw that ball balloon the net.

A month later the Scottish selectors once again said, 'All change!' I was included in the squad for the home game against

Portugal, but didn't get a shirt, short sleeved or otherwise. The selectors again made eight changes to the team that had succumbed to England but had put up such a spirited perform-ance against Hungary. Yet again Willie Cunningham lost his place and the captaincy, whilst Harry Haddock who'd been given such a roasting by Matthews retained his place in the team. Scotland triumphed 3–0 over Portugal in a match played in almost inces-sant rain. I watched from the stands but to be honest the margin of victory was flattering, Scotland were made to look cumbersome.

Later in May I joined the Scotland party at Prestwick airport, as we set off on a tour of the Continent that was to include a tough programme of matches against Yugoslavia, Austria and Hungary. The squad included some relatively new faces to the international scene: Bobby Collins (Celtic) and Alex Parker (Falkirk), both of whom would later join Everton, goalkeepers Tommy Younger (Hibernian) and Bill Brown (Dundee and later Spurs) and Andy Kerr (Partick Thistle), as well as experienced internationals such as George Young, Bobby Evans, Billy Liddell, Doug Cowie, Lawrie Reilly and Gordon Smith (Hibernian) and, I suppose, me.

Given our result against England and the fact the team had not performed well in beating Portugal, even the most ardent Scottish supporter feared the worst. But Scotland were yet again to prove the doubters wrong. Once more, my participation was limited to that of an observer in the stand when Scotland opened the tour against Yugoslavia in Belgrade. The match ended 2–2 which was a very good result for Scotland as Yugoslavia had a decent team, and were particularly effective on home soil. Though itching to play, I have to be honest and say Scotland played so well as a team against Yugoslavia, I wasn't expecting any changes for our next match against Austria in Vienna.

We travelled back to our hotel by coach and as I was leaving the bus one of the SFA selectors turned to me and said, 'You'll be playing against Austria.' I was completely taken aback. The Yugoslavia game was barely over and, as far as I could see, there could have been no discussion between selectors on the journey.

Though keen to play, I was sure no one deserved to be dropped from the side that had done so well against the Yugoslavs. The same selector also told Bill Brown that he would be replacing Tommy Younger in goal. The newspapers somehow got hold of the story about Bill, and as it was set to be his international debut, gave it ample column space. When the team to play Austria was announced, sure enough, I was in for Bobby Evans who switched to centre-half in place of the injured George Young; Doug Cowie replaced Tommy Cumming (Hearts) at left-half, Archie Robertson (Clyde) took over from Tommy Gemmell at inside-left and Andy Kerr made his debut in place of Harry Haddock, all which made for five changes. The notable absentee was Bill Brown. Tommy Younger kept his place in goal, the reason for which, I am sure, was all down to the press having run with the story of Bill's debut before it had been officially announced.

In Vienna we enjoyed an even greater triumph, beating Austria 4–1 with goals from Robertson, Smith, Liddell and Reilly. We took the lead as early as the first minute and from there asserted our authority. In front of a capacity crowd of 60,000 it was Scotland's first victory over Austria, and went some way to avenging our defeat in the World Cup.

We moved on to Hungary with confidence and spirits high, though not for one moment underestimating the task that lay before us. Once again I was pitched against Ferenc Puskas and as at Hampden, I did my level best to stick to him like bark on a tree. I managed to keep 'getting a foot in' and as the first half progressed on a surface made treacherous by heavy rain, I could sense Puskas becoming frustrated with events. We were putting up a tremendous fight, defending in depth and breaking to good effect. Three minutes before half-time the unbelievable happened. I received the ball from Andy Kerr and made progress before feeding it through to Gordon Smith who hit the accelerator and left two Hungarian defenders in his wake before hitting a low drive past Danka. As we celebrated Gordon's goal

I joked, 'Now you've gone and done it, you've upset them.' Little did I know at the time the truth of those words.

In the second half Hungary took the option of playing one of their substitutes. Though the idea had never been adopted in British football, home international teams had the option of naming two substitutes when playing on the Continent. The Scottish FA, in their wisdom, never chose that option. Farago replaced Danka in goal but the telling substitution proved to be that of Palotas for Sandor on the right wing. Hungary began the second period like a whirlwind. They appeared a different side, more like the Hungary that had won everyone's admiration. I stuck grimly to my task of shadowing Puskas but he had an added edge to his play. He would feint to go one way, only to go the other.

Learning from the relative success I'd enjoyed in the first period, he didn't hang on to the ball in the second half – now it was all one touch football from him.

Hungary had found an appetite for the game and it paid off. When Hidegkuti cut in from the right to shoot past Tommy Younger I saw some heads drop. I clapped my hands together and shouted encouragement but I sensed the confidence draining from one or two of our lads. Minutes later Kocsis added a second and Hungary appeared to relax a little. That was our cue to take the game to them and twice Billy Liddell hit the woodwork. Ten minutes later a bout of pressure from the home side ended with Fenyvesi making it 3–1. To compound our misery and add to his frustration, fifteen minutes from time Liddell put a spot kick wide. Yet again Scotland received plaudits in the wake of a defeat, though given our performances against Hungary I do feel that this time the praise was justified. On a personal note I felt I had done my standing as an international no harm at all as a result of my battles with Puskas. In his autobiography Puskas was to say, 'We were surprised at how hard and tough the Scotland players were . . . They were not "technical" players at all, but had real heart and gave it everything. They gave us two very hard games and in Tom Docherty, I was confronted with a man who played me very well. He was dogged in his pursuit of me. I found it difficult to settle into my normal rhythm and play the ball as I pleased.'

All these years on, I'll settle for that.

Football was now very much a world game, and change was well and truly underway, albeit a little slowly within our own shores. Football had become a melting pot of new ideas. Allow substitutes, if only in the FA Cup final; set the players free from contracts that bind them to a club for life; have more seats in grounds; standardise playing pitches; reconstitute the Football League; employ full-time referees; lift the ban on amateur players playing on a Sunday; don't blame TV for falling gates; improve the technical ability of our players; institute better training programmes, some geared to the needs of the individual; make all clubs have a specialist tactician in addition to the manager; ensure floodlights are installed in all clubs by 1960; help develop the new European competitions. In time most of these ideas were to be implemented. British football was standing still no longer.

Not all people, however, were willing to embrace progress. There was the little matter of the Football Association and Football League, for whom change seemed to be anathema. The 1955–56 season saw the inaugural European Champions Clubs' Cup get under way. As reigning champions Chelsea accepted an invitation to take part, and were subsequently drawn against Swedish side Djurgardens. Following pressure from the Football League and the FA, however, Chelsea withdrew their application. One FA official described the European Cup as, 'a gimmick that will never catch on', whilst the League were at pains to point out that 'nothing should distract Chelsea from defending their title' adding, 'The First Division of the Football League is still Europe's premier club competition.' *Plus ça change.*

The season proved another taxing one for Preston. We finished fourth from bottom, only a point above the relegation places –

our worst performance since I had joined the club. It was to be Frank Hill's last season in charge at Deepdale. He was only at Preston for two years, but it felt much longer. I quite liked Frank as a person. He was a colourful character with a tremendous sense of humour, which he needed after that season. In my opinion, however, Frank was not as good a manager as Scot Symon or Bill Scott and this showed in Preston's results and in the haphazard way we often approached matches.

The season had begun in sensational fashion when we travelled to Everton, played them off the park and won 4–0. The key to our success that day was the partnership forged by Tom Finney and the club's big signing of the summer, Tommy Thompson, who joined from Aston Villa for a fee of £27,000. The pair tore Everton apart and would go on to terrorise defences until 1960. I remember this day well. In front of a Goodison Park crowd of 54,357 Tommy Thompson had the ball in the net within two minutes of the start. Preston supporters, of course, had their Finney but I think they were a bit greedy and also yearned for a free-scoring centre-forward. They were able to have their cake and eat it when Tommy arrived at the club. Frank Hill encouraged us to take the game to opponents which is all very well, but as a manager you must also make provision for defending. When we scored a goal Frank urged us to throw caution to the wind and go for a second. That's why we ended up losing a lot of matches that season 3–2!

Come January we were hoping for a good run in the FA Cup to add some real interest to what had been a disappointing season but was about to get worse. In the third round we travelled to West Ham who were wandering aimlessly up and down the bottom half of Division Two, but we ended up being well beaten 5–2. There were inquests, and Preston fans wrote to the *Evening Post*, wanting to know why their team was losing so many matches. The answer was simple. We were conceding too many goals. One thing I was aware of during that poor season was that I was taking a greater interest in the tactical and technical aspects of football and wanted to develop my knowledge of this side of the game.

The Preston chairman, Mr Buck, and his co-directors were far from happy with the events of the season. The previous campaign was mediocre enough but we had got worse. It was felt the team needed fresh impetus and the best way to accomplish that was a change of manager. As a consequence, Frank Hill left the club at the end of the season. Always a character, on his final day he thanked us players for our effort and support, and left us with these final words – 'Remember lads, if football directors are too old to do it to their wives, they'll do it to the manager. Adios, boys!' A few weeks later it was announced his replacement was to be Cliff Britton. He was, for a time, credited with reviving the fortunes of the club but I never got on with him – and I was far from being the only Preston player in this respect.

During 1955–56 I once again received the honour of representing a Great Britain XI, this time against the Rest of Europe in a match at Windsor Park to commemorate the jubilee of the Irish Football Association. The Great Britain team consisted of fifteen players as it was agreed beforehand that substitutes would be allowed as an experiment. The GB squad included players such as Stan Matthews, Billy Liddell, Danny Blanchflower (Spurs), Jack Kelsey (Arsenal), Don Revie (Manchester City), Peter Sillett (Chelsea), Roger Byrne (Manchester United), John Charles (Leeds) and Jimmy McIlroy (Burnley). The Rest Of Europe fielded a strong side that included goalkeeper Buffon (Italy), Ocwirk (Austria), Boskov and Vukas (Yugoslavia), Sorensen (Italy) and the great French trio of Kopa, Vincent and Jonquet. The ROE side proved just too strong, winning 4–1 with Vukas hitting a hat-trick. After the game Danny Blanchflower and I were talking about the changes that needed to take place in British football. Danny said that this game showed 'how far we have to go before we even catch up, never mind overtake the best the Continent has to offer. Problem is, we got people who run this game and the only thing they like about the modern world, is its dentistry.'

I may have been considered good enough to be selected for

a Great Britain team but not for my country. I spent this season in the international wilderness. I found it perplexing to say the least. My Scotland team-mates and the press believed I had done well the previous season; true, Preston had struggled but my club form had been good. I began to fear for my international future. Willie Cunningham, himself subjected to many a strange decision by the selectors, offered me hope: 'Just keep on producing those performances and you'll be back for Scotland. And when you eventually do get back, knowing those selectors, they'll probably make you captain.'

Many a true word spoken in jest.

The 1956–57 season turned out to be as good a one for Preston as the previous one had been bad. We found consistency, tightened up considerably in defence, had organisation and shape to our play, all the while playing the sort of purist football Preston was noted for. We were to enjoy two terrific seasons under Cliff Britton when, yet again, we just failed to go the whole mile and win the championship. Though never popular in the dressing room, Britton not only got the first team playing wonderful football again, he instigated a fine youth policy which, during his time at the club, would see Preston reach the FA Youth Cup final. Yet it should not be overlooked that our trainer, Jimmy Milne, played a major role in all this. It was he who restored authority in the dressing room and out on the training field.

Cliff Britton played for Bristol City and Everton where he won an FA Cup winners' medal in 1933. He won nine caps for England, forming a formidable half-back line with Stan Cullis (Wolves) and Joe Mercer. After the war he became manager of Burnley and guided them to promotion to Division One and the FA Cup final. He returned to Everton as manager in 1948 where he earned a reputation as a strict disciplinarian. When once asked by a reporter from the *Liverpool Echo* to name his ideal team, Britton replied, 'Eleven teetotallers'. In 1950–51 Everton had 'enjoyed' a run of nine games without a victory and were eventually relegated to

Division Two. Relegation from the top flight was not a sackable offence in those days, so Britton got to keep his job as manager. After three seasons in Division Two he led Everton to promotion, but was forever at loggerheads with the club directors, who Britton complained were not investing in the team. After selling Everton's talisman, Dave Hickson, a transfer that went down with Evertonians like a parachute with a hole in it, Britton left the club in 1956 only to be offered the vacant manager's job at Preston.

Cliff Britton was a complex character. He was indeed a strict disciplinarian, never appeared to relax, and his man-management skills left much to be desired. We were all good, enthusiastic, responsible pros at Preston. No previous manager checked up on players to make sure they were at home at night. No previous manager had any cause to carpet players and remind them of their responsibilities to club and team-mates, and no manager ever had a go at Tom Finney; Cliff Britton did all of these. He was as hard as a fireside poker without its occasional warmth. He left all the day-to-day training to Jimmy Milne, thank heavens, but would often watch us being put through our paces whilst picking his nose. One day he stepped onto the training pitch to give us a pep talk, which ended with him saying to Tom Finney, 'You know, you would be a much better player if you trained harder.' We were all slack-jawed. Apart from being a truly world-class player, Tom was one of the hardest trainers at the club. It is often cited that Britton's masterstroke in his first season at the club was to switch Tom Finney from outside-right to centre-forward. He scored 23 goals in 1956–57 but let me remind you, the previous season Tom had scored 17 from out on the wing: he was such a brilliant talent he could have scored goals from any position in the forward line – and did! I don't hold with the Britton 'masterstroke' theory. It first cropped up in the newspapers during the season and I have my suspicions as to who first suggested it to the press boys, albeit in a veiled way.

One other change to the team that proved significant was the establishment of Fred Else in goal. Fred had been in and out of the team but in this season made the number one spot his own and was an ever-present. He was a fine keeper who possessed an astute sense of positioning and electric reflexes. Fred was popular in the dressing room and with the Preston fans but, sadly, not with the England selectors. Fred was a snappy dresser. For away games he always wore a fashionable suit which, on one occasion, drew a snide comment from a rather overweight autograph-hunter outside Highbury who appeared to take exception to the cut of Fred's Italian-style two-piece.

'I wouldn't be seen dead in that suit,' said the chubby Arsenal fan.

'You'd have to be dead for six months before it would fit you,' retorted Fred. Touché!

We opened the 1956–57 season with four consecutive defeats. It was looking grim and Preston were rooted to the foot of the table. Suddenly we found our feet beating Cardiff City 6–0 at Deepdale. To prove this was no case of a dead cat bouncing, we then went down to Arsenal and returned with both points. The two Tommys, Finney and Thompson were now forging a lethal striking partnership, ably supported by Sammy Taylor (12 goals) and Jimmy Baxter (9). Sammy had signed from Falkirk for a fee of £8,500 at the end of 1954–55 in a deal which saw the Preston board agree to a curious bonus in his contract: the club agreed to stage a friendly match under the new floodlights for his benefit. In the previous season, Sammy's outings with the first team had been restricted to fifteen appearances because he was competing for a place on the wing with either Tom Finney or Angus Morrison. When Cliff Britton moved Tom to centre-forward, Sammy gained his favoured right-wing berth.

As the season developed we quickly put our nightmare start behind us and settled down into a fine run. Our home form had been particularly disappointing in the previous season, but this time we lost only twice at Deepdale. We enjoyed some outstanding results: Arsenal were beaten 3–0 and Portsmouth

7–1. If our away form had been better I am sure we would have pushed champions-elect Manchester United even closer and, perhaps, have been champions ourselves. As it was, Preston were to finish third on goal difference behind Tottenham Hotspur, eight points adrift of United. In the third round of the FA Cup we were paired with our old rivals Sheffield Wednesday in a tie that went to a second replay. Having been held to a goalless draw at Deepdale the two sides again could not be separated at Hillsborough, the game ending 2–2 after extra time but I was left wondering why we had made such a meal of it when we breezed the third 5–1. We then travelled to Bristol Rovers and found little discomfort in winning 4–1. That set up a cracking fifth-round tie at Deepdale against Arsenal.

I remember the tie pretty well. The game was a sell-out with 39,608 at Deepdale which included some 3,000 Arsenal fans. The Londoners were easily the best supported team away from home in those days and I recall the majority of those Gunners fans arriving on football specials from Euston, whilst the remainder endured what in pre-motorway Britain was a ten-hour coach trip from London. Supporters of both teams were so desperate to see the game, tickets were being exchanged for petrol ration cards. Though not many people owned a car, petrol was in short supply due to the Suez Crisis of the previous year. Prior to the game, Cliff Britton gave an interview for television and the press. It was rare to have television previewing a game and Cliff found the presence of a TV camera prompted him to adopt an affected accent and vocabulary hitherto alien to him. Said Cliff, when asked to predict the result, 'One doesn't like to estimate how a football game will go, but suffice it to say, we shall strive our hardest to keep Preston in the Cup.' Jolly good show, Cliff. But strive our hardest we did.

The Deepdale pitch was lightly covered in snow but was very heavy underneath. We got off to the worst possible start. In the opening minute David Herd tried his luck with an angled shot. Joe Dunn stuck out a leg and the ball was diverted past a stranded Fred Else. Joe never settled and ten minutes later, when trying to clear his lines, he missed the ball completely, only succeeding in kicking Willie Cunningham on the knee-cap. Willie was in some pain. His knee blew up like a balloon but he had no alternative but to carry, or rather limp, on.

Arsenal were in the ascendancy but against the run of play we suddenly broke from defence. I pushed the ball behind a square-looking Arsenal rearguard and Tom Finney did the rest. If our equaliser shook Arsenal they didn't let it show. The Gunners poured forward. Danny Clapton restored their lead and just before the break David Herd, who once had the distinction of playing in the same Stockport County team as his father, David Senior, made it 3–1.

We had a monumental task on our hands but we took to the field for the second half determined to take the game to Arsenal. The pitch was by now cutting up badly. It was heavy going, especially through the middle, so our plan was to not go that way. A great cross from Les Dagger was converted by Tom Finney who minutes later hit a shot of such ferocity against the Arsenal bar it reverberated like a tuning fork. We gave it our all and eventually our pressure brought dividends. Tommy Thompson latched on to a through ball and hit a goal-bound pile-driver that was travelling at such speed it was a wonder Arsenal keeper Con Sullivan didn't catch pneumonia from the draught the ball created as it sped past him. Six goals had been shared in a blood and thunder Cup tie.

We travelled down to Highbury for an afternoon replay on the following Tuesday, but that didn't stop a bumper crowd of 61,451 packing Highbury. What they saw was another keenly contested tie, only this time Arsenal squeezed home by the odd goal in three.

After being overlooked by Scotland for the autumn Home Internationals against Wales and Northern Ireland, I was recalled for the match against Yugoslavia at Hampden Park on 21

November. The SFA's letter said, that 'those resident in the south' were to 'make their own travel arrangements to arrive in the North British Hotel, Edinburgh by twelve noon on the day of the game.' Lunch was to be at '12.15 p.m. prompt' (Cliff Britton would have approved of the precise timing) and 'any player who requires hotel accommodation must notify headquarters at once'. The final two words of that sentence being underlined in heavy black type. Happily, jerseys, shorts and stockings were to be supplied by the SFA, though players 'must bring their own boots, soap and towel'. Players were to receive a £15 match fee (seemingly they wanted the shirts back) and, on application, two complimentary match tickets which curiously, had to be 'disposed of before the match and not after it'. Finally under the terse heading, 'Dispersal', I was informed that, 'Dinner will be served at the North British Hotel at 6.15 p.m. prompt, after which players will disperse.' It was good to be back, especially in such warm company.

Goals from Blackpool's Jackie Mudie and Sammy Baird gave Scotland a morale-boosting 2–0 victory over Yugoslavia. George Young continued as centre-half and captain but the Scotland team was beginning to have a new look to it. Amongst my team-mates that day were John Hewie (Charlton Athletic), Alex Parker (Falkirk) and Alex Scott (Rangers and later Everton). We received good press for this victory. Tommy Pearson wrote in the Scottish *Daily Mail*, 'Docherty caught the eye. His ball winning skills and intelligent use of the ball fortified Scotland. On the evidence of his performance against a talented Yugoslav side, Docherty must surely be in line for a regular Scotland place.' I appreciated Tommy's words, but I'd had too many dealings with the SFA to ever take for granted that I could ever be a fixture in the Scotland team.

There was to be no close-season as such for me. Scotland embarked upon a busy summer schedule of matches that included the final game of the Home Championship against England at Wembley, a match against world champions West Germany, and World Cup qualifiers against Spain (home and away) and Switzerland. It proved to be a wonderful summer for Scottish football though it began on a disappointing note with defeat against the 'auld enemy'.

The game was only a minute old when Stan Matthews lost his footing on the Wembley turf. Tommy Ring was on to the loose ball in a flash and raced unchallenged into the England penalty area where he slipped the ball past the oncoming Alan Hodgkinson. A dream start for us, certainly, but a nightmare for Hodgkinson: on his international debut, his first touch of the ball was to pick it out of the net. Rather than trying to protect our lead, we laid siege to Hodgkinson's goal. We bossed the midfield, had the feel of the game and could have added to our tally but for some fine goalkeeping from Hodgy. England were so rattled, so much on the defensive, that we knew we had the game in our pockets if we could keep them like that.

We came in at half-time in buoyant mood but it was during the interval that a decision was made that was to cost Scotland the game and, arguably, George Young's international career.

If ever a reporter asked a member of the SFA about Scotland's tactics, he would be given the reply, 'Oh, George Young looks after those.' As a centre-half, or right-back, George was a very fine player indeed. He hailed from Falkirk and joined Rangers in 1941 where he was to win every domestic honour the Scottish game has to offer. Having played for Scotland in unofficial wartime internationals, George went on to win 53 post-war caps, 48 times as captain. He remained loyal to Rangers throughout his career and when his playing days ended he tried management with Third Lanark, before concentrating on his business interests that included running a hotel and writing a newspaper column.

George was a man of imposing physique who cut a readily recognisable figure on the pitch. Dominant in the air and possessing a devastating tackle, he used the ball well and, when the occasion demanded, could kick it further than anyone I can remember. He was as hard as a pine-knot and not a man given to trying to get in touch with his feminine side. I have a snapshot in one of my photo albums. It shows the Scotland players in jovial mood before our World Cup qualifier against Switzerland that summer. We are in a square in Basle, all walking towards the camera. I am in the centre of the group with Alex Parker, Tommy Ring, Andy Kerr, Tommy Younger and George. We are laughing and linking arms as we walk. Tommy Younger has linked to George's right arm, but you can tell from the dour expression on George's face he feels decidedly uncomfortable with such frivolous, unmanly companionship.

George Young somehow gained a reputation for being an astute tactician. He was of the old, steady-as-a-rock school who saw the game simply as eleven men against eleven – and never in my experience offered an assessment of the strengths and, more importantly, weaknesses of opponents. True to his type and background, should Scotland take a one-goal lead George would say, 'Now they've got to get two to win. So let's hang on to what we've got.' I never agreed with this tactic, such as it was. During the half-time interval at Wembley, George told the team that if we shut up shop England would become frustrated and we would hold our lead and win the game. He asked that Ian McColl and myself play much deeper in the second period, a request both Ian and I took umbrage with. George also asked inside-forwards Jackie Mudie and Willie Fernie to play much deeper and for Tommy Ring to get back more to help John Hewie contain Matthews. Ian McColl and I were the most vociferous protesters, but George was having none of it. Reminding us he was the captain and in charge of tactics, he asked us in his haughty way to respect his position and not usurp his authority. Ian and I acceded to that request but as the team took to the field for the second half, I knew we had made a big mistake.

Sure enough England took advantage of Scotland now playing very deep and laid siege to our goal. Ronnie Clayton and Duncan Edwards started to do what Ian and I had done in the first half – take control of the midfield. In acres of space they began spraying passes to Matthews and Grainger on the England flanks. During one of the many England forays deep into our half of the field, Tom Finney turned to me and said, 'It'll only be a matter of time, Tommy.' He was right.

Just after the hour mark Derek Kevan equalised for England, after which the English team produced more of the same. It was one-way traffic. Scotland fought a valiant rearguard action and for a time I did think we were going to get away with a draw. Five minutes from time, however, Duncan Edwards sped ominously through the middle, looked up, then looked down and with the minimum of back-lift hit a blistering shot from twenty-five yards that all but ripped the net from the stanchion. George's tactics went out of the window as Scotland poured forward in search of an equaliser – and we very nearly got it. I thought we had. Alex Scott and I combined on the right, the ball was played deep into the England penalty area. Lawrie Reilly challenged for the ball with Alan Hodgkinson. As a result of Lawrie's aerial challenge the England keeper dropped the ball, and there was Willie Fernie to bundle it home. The 40,000 Scottish supporters went berserk but their joy was short-lived. The referee ruled Hodgkinson had both feet off the ground when the challenge was made and promptly disallowed the goal. Wembley resounded to a volley of catcalls and booing from its Tartan contingent.

Four weeks later, Scotland defeated Spain 4–2 at Hampden Park to get our World Cup qualifying campaign off to a great start. It was a fine all-round performance and a personal triumph for Blackpool's Jackie Mudie who hit a hat-trick, our other goal coming from a John Hewie penalty. Next we met Switzerland in another World Cup qualifying match, in the St Jakob's Stadium in Basle. The Swiss had already taken a point off Spain, and a win for Scotland would take us three points clear at the top of the group – those were the days. There was a farcical situation before the game when it was discovered that Scotland's dark blue shirts were deemed unsuitable. The game was being transmitted to most parts of the Continent by Eurovision with the second half broadcast live back in Scotland. As this was black and white tele-

ged three with neighbourhood
ls in the tenement backyard.
hat's me, front right, getting in
me practice for the day Rubik
vents his cube.

With pals from the HLI. Seated next
to me is Willie McPhail who was later
to become a team-mate at Celtic.

Paul's Boys Guild, I am seated centre front. To qualify for selection players
d to attend confession – I was so keen to play, I went along even when I
dn't have anything to confess! Honest I didn't.

When Chelsea played a friendly in Glasgow I returned to my old home in the Gorbals – I wasn't aware of anything having changed!

With my mum in 1976 enjoying a drin to celebrate the wedding anniversary of Agnes and me.

ake the field for my Preston home debut, the response of the press can be
uged by the reaction of the photographer on the right.

om Finney, the greatest player and
e greatest man I ever played with.

In the kitchen of the Olympic Café.
Many opposing teams visited prior to
playing at Deepdale. Jimmy Greaves
once called me 'The Elizabeth David
of fifties football'.

Being presented to H.M. Queen Mother prior to the 1954 FA Cup final against West Brom. As you will note, it is difficult to shake hands with royalty when protocol states they extend a flattened hand.

Preston's equaliser in the final. Third left, in the background, my cross is met by Angus Morrison in Tommy Lawton-style. But it wasn't to be enough.

On tour with Preston in Switzerland. Tom Finney, Joe Marston and I lean from the carriage window.

I sign for Arsenal watched by manager George Swindin, secretary Bob Walls and Preston manager Cliff Britton who, just in case the pen I was using ran out of ink, has reserves in his top pocket.

oe Marston, me and Bill Scott in Switzerland (again) during a Preston close-season tour.

n action for Arsenal against my old club Preston at Deepdale. I was going for he ball, honest!

Spending quality time with daughter Cath after breaking my leg whilst playing for Arsenal. During my time out of the game this was not the only type of reading I did – I was studying hard to be a coach.

NEWS CHRONICLE

Walter Winterbottom's FA Coaching School at Lilleshall. Walter is seated centre front, Jimmy Adamson fifth left. This particular 'class' includes Bob Paisley, Dave Sexton, Peter Taylor, Bert Johnson, Jimmy Andrews, Frank O'Farrell, Phil Woosnam, Billy Bingham and me (rear third right).

'orld Cup 1954, Scotland
Uruguay. The clock
dicates eight minutes
ayed and the score goalless;
they had stopped the game
en we would have been
1 right.

Tommy Younger demonstrates safe hands,
Hungary v Scotland, 1955, in Budapest.
Puskas would later say I was one of the most
difficult defenders he ever encountered –
that'll do for me!

'ith Scotland team-mates in Austria, 1955. I am seventh left; fifth from right
George Young seemingly uncomfortable with linking arms and 'bonding'.

GEORGE OUTRAM

Prior to Spain v Scotland, 1957. Eric Caldow and Bobby Collins take evasive action as goalkeeper Tommy Younger takes exception to my comment about him being like a crocus – 'Only coming out once a year and then only briefly'.

World Cup, 1958. Taking the sun at the team hotel with Alex Parker, Bobby Evans, Dave Mackay, Jimmy Murray and Sammy Baird. No WAGS present – except for me!

Posing with the Glums. I still maintain this was a very good Scotland team. Included are Martin Buchan, Alan Rough, Jimmy Johnstone, Billy Bremner, Asa Hartford, John O'Hare and front row, second right, a very young Kenny Dalglish.

vision the red shirts of the home side were not easily distinguish-
able from Scotland's dark blue. The problem was, we had not
brought an alternative strip. The officials were in a quandary as
to what should be done, then one member of the Swiss FA
suggested we borrow Switzerland's second strip of white shirts
with a red trim. It must surely be the only time in the history of
Scottish football that a team have taken to the pitch for an international wearing another country's shirt.

We found ourselves a goal down after twelve minutes and
struggling to inject any fluency into our play due to the
deplorable weather and the treacherous nature of the pitch. Ten
minutes from the interval Jackie Mudie put us back in the game
when he met a Gordon Smith corner and glanced a header wide
of Parlier in the Swiss goal. No doubt to the relief of those
watching at home, in the second half Scotland were rewarded
for being more adventurous when Bobby Collins slid in at the
far post to meet another Smith corner. It hadn't been a vintage
Scotland performance by any stretch of the imagination, but it
was another two points towards the finals in Sweden; besides,
we were reserving the vintage stuff for our next match against
world champions West Germany.

With George Young declared unfit and replaced by Bobby
Evans, to my delight I was appointed captain. Scotland's result
in Stuttgart was the shock of the season. Rather than approaching
a match against the powerful Germans with appropriate modesty,
we fancied our chances. We had been playing well, and against
West Germany we played even better. Two goals from Bobby
Collins and one from Jackie Mudie gave Scotland a famous
victory and their captain tremendous satisfaction and pride.

The Scotland squad was in a very happy frame of mind when
we arrived in Spain for the final leg of our tour. We stayed at
the Hotel Felipe II in El Estoril where, the Sunday night before
our World Cup qualifier, we were to have dinner, during which
the team selection would be announced. It wasn't my idea of
how to do things before an important World Cup match, not in

the dining room of a hotel between the pudding and the coffee and biscuits, but that was the SFA for you.

Everyone was on tenterhooks to hear his own name, but also that of a fit-again George Young for what was meant to be his swansong for Scotland.

The names were read in the same agonisingly slow and deliberate way that the identity of the city that has won the right to stage the Olympics is announced – every syllable stretched to breaking point; pregnant pauses between every word; each name pondered upon for a few seconds as if the person reading has trouble discerning the writing. Every attempt to make a drama of the situation succeeded only in creating cringe-inducing melodrama. After what seemed like an hour we finally reached the central defence. The chairman of selectors gazed about the room as if his attention had suddenly been drawn by a querulous fly, before readdressing the business in hand. Milking the moment dry, Sir George Graham, to everyone's irritation, then repeated the position – 'Cen-tre . . . half . . . Evans.'

The room immediately began to hum with voices. The key drama over, Sir George continued to announce the team but with a greater sense of urgency. Such was the chattering across tables, nobody could hear him. Gordon Smith, who obviously hadn't heard who had been nominated to play at outside-right, was manically asking around his table, 'Who did he say for outside-right? Am I playing?'

I looked across to George Young. He was doing his best to appear expressionless and unconcerned, but I could see his eyes darting here and there. Bobby Collins said something to him. George pursed his lips and nodded his head to one side, a laconic gesture suggesting 'That's the way it goes', but I could see the big man was upset. I had learned very early in my career there is no room for sentiment in football, but I did feel for him at that moment. George had enjoyed a great career as a Scotland player, the best. But the new chairman of selectors Sir George Graham was looking to the future. I had a lot of respect for the selectors in making such a choice. It was a tough call but for once they were positive. They made a decision that was unpopular with many, deposing of a player who was idolised in Scotland. It would have been easy to have included George in the team to play Spain. George was hoping our last match of the tour would be his last game too. Had he been picked to play against the Spaniards he could have taken his bow, gratefully accepting the plaudits that were certain to have come his way. Scottish supporters would have waxed sentimental over his departure, and thanked the selectors for a last chance to remember him. The Scottish selectors were not thinking about George, however. In my opinion they had in their minds the future of Scottish football.

Far from bowing out gracefully, grateful that he'd had such a wonderful career as a Scotland player, George harboured a grievance about the way he had been treated. George was of the mind he'd been badly done to. Maybe after so many years of unswerving loyalty he believed the selectors owed it to him to play him one last time. Whatever, George made it known he was not happy. He thought it wrong of me to have assumed the captaincy immediately after it was announced. As soon as I learned of my reappointment, I had right away started the job of being captain. I devised tactics and met the players to discuss them. George reckoned me a trifle hasty in assuming command, telling me I should have waited until the match. I, on the other hand, saw no point in waiting.

George made it plain that he felt the selectors should have at least taken him to one side and had a quiet word with him about his omission from the team. I suppose he had a point but, as I have indicated, the selectors never made contact of any sort with a player who had been left out of the team. In not speaking to George beforehand, the selectors had indicated that no player was being singled out for preferential treatment.

As the SFA were not given to talking about such matters, the newspapers were quick to tell George's side of the story. From being cock-a-hoop following our results thus far in the World Cup and against West Germany, the mood in the camp changed. I was sure Machiavellian deeds were afoot and my suspicions were further aroused when the Scotland team left to board the coach that would take us to the Bernabeu Stadium. As we walked across the car park to the bus a selector, who looked after what passed for PR in those days, asked if I could get the players together for a photograph. There was no problem until I approached George and his Rangers team-mate Ian McColl, who had also been omitted from the team. Both refused my request for them to come and join the group. After some discussion and diplomatic coercion on my part, Ian McColl changed his mind and decided to join the group. George offered me a few well-chosen words and walked off. The photograph of the squad was taken without him.

It would be good to have said that following such a hiatus we went out and accounted for Spain. We didn't. Spain had a comfortable 4–1 win. Scotland were handicapped by the fact we played the second half with ten men following an injury to Dave Mackay, who was making his debut. The pre-match atmosphere in the camp didn't help matters either, but I don't want to make excuses. Spain were worthy winners.

One of the press reports of the following day made me smile. It was reported that at half-time George Young had come into the dressing room to 'give the Scotland players a tactical talk and try and salvage something from the wreckage of the first-half performance'. This was untrue, George never came anywhere near our dressing room at any time before, during or after the game. The selector whose job it was to organise press interviews and photographs had nothing on George when it came to generating PR.

The George Young affair apart, the Scotland party travelled home happily enough. We knew we only had to get a result against Switzerland to qualify for the World Cup finals; what's more, we knew we had the beating of them. What I didn't know, however, was that in just over a year, I would be moving on from Preston.

7

FROM INFANTRYMAN TO GUNNER

As I joined my Preston team-mates for pre-season training in the summer of 1957, I was keenly anticipating the coming campaign. Though I hadn't warmed to Cliff Britton and his style of management, Preston had a super team and I was confident we would do well. I was captain of Scotland who stood a very good chance of qualifying for the World Cup finals in Sweden. Family life was great and the café was doing well. It was a joyous time in my life. Yet, no matter how well things appear to be going, problems and heartache are but a step away.

We began the season with a 2–1 win at Nottingham Forest, but three defeats and two victories in our next five matches gave no indication we were about to mount a serious challenge for the championship. Following a 2–0 defeat at Manchester City in mid-September we suddenly found our form. Spurs were beaten 3–1 at Deepdale, we gained revenge for our defeat at Maine Road by hammering Manchester City 6–1 and we continued to post good results throughout the remainder of the season. We were almost invincible at Deepdale, losing only one match, albeit a key one against Wolves, but 18 victories on home soil was a club record. In 21 home matches we conceded only 14 goals, the lowest in the entire Football League. With the striking partnership of Tom Finney and Tommy Thompson in their pomp we were far from defensive though, scoring 100 goals, only three less than Wolverhampton Wanderers who gained the reputation for being the most free-scoring team of the post-war era. It was a terrific season for the club, but again we had to settle for the runners-up spot. Wolves clinched the title by five points and proved their championship mettle by beating us both home and away.

What was one of the more memorable football seasons both north and south of the border – with goals galore and results like the 7–6 thriller between Huddersfield Town and Charlton Athletic with Charlton clinching victory with the final kick of the game after trailing 5–1 and down to ten men; or Hearts running away with the Scottish league, scoring 132 goals in the process – was also beset with tragedy.

Manchester United, in particular their manager Matt Busby, had won their battle with the Football League and FA for the right to compete in the European Cup. Following a match in Belgrade, the aeroplane carrying the United party crashed when taking off at Munich. Over half the forty people on board lost their lives. The United players who perished were all known to me, if not personal friends – Roger Byrne, Geoff Bent, Eddie Colman, Mark Jones, David Pegg, Tommy Taylor, Billy Whelan and Duncan Edwards who hung on for two weeks in a Munich hospital before succumbing to his injuries. The United players who survived were Bobby Charlton, Dennis Viollet, Ken Morgans, Bill Foulkes, Harry Gregg, Johnny Berry and Jackie Blanchflower, though the latter two never played competitive football again. Matt Busby spent a month in a Munich hospital before being released.

Under the guidance of assistant manager Jimmy Murphy, who missed the trip because he was fulfilling his duties as manager of Wales, United rebuilt. Amazingly they reached the FA Cup final only to be beaten by near neighbours Bolton Wanderers. Given the tragedy that had befallen the club the whole nation wanted to see United win at Wembley, but there is no room for sentiment in football, not even in such heartbreaking circumstances. Bolton triumphed 2–0 with both goals being scored by

Nat Lofthouse. The success of Manchester United, however, was their triumph over tragedy and adversity.

By this time I was beginning to take a greater interest in football in general, in particular the tactical side. I made a concerted effort to familiarise myself with the new training methods that had come in as the game went global. From talking to opponents when on Scotland duty I realised that continental training was more varied, aimed at toning every muscle in the body. The training of the Austrian players involved a lot of work with the ball, their routines seemed more interesting and designed to keep boredom at bay. Playing twice against Hungary provided an opportunity to observe their ball skills and technique at close quarters, sometimes very close. Players like Puskas, Kocsis and Hidegkuti had been very impressive, all the more for the fact these weren't tricks performed on the training ground but in the heat of battle.

When I first began my career as a player, the ball was almost of secondary importance in training. Now managers and trainers were realising the folly of starving players of the ball in midweek in the hope it would make them hungry for it on a Saturday. I began to compile files containing ideas on what I called 'TPT' – technique, physical training and tactics – and noting my own tactical ideas. For example, when the centre-half pushes upfield in support of the forwards and moves, say, into the inside-left position, then the left-half fills the gap in the middle and the forward nearest to the attacking centre-half drops back to left-half. I came up with all manner of variations on this: if the centre-half pushes deep into the opponents' half of the field, then the centre-forward drops behind him as cover, and so on. I knew, of course, that chatting to the Austrians and Hungarians plus my own ideas on training and tactics was not enough if I wanted to pursue a coaching career. It was during 1958 I heard about England manager Walter Winterbottom's series of coaching schools at Lilleshall, the end product of which would be an officially recognised coaching qualification. Though I still had a number of years left in me as a player, I decided to find out more, as an officially recognised FA coaching badge could open doors to me.

Scotland did not fare too well in the Home Internationals, drawing against both Northern Ireland and Wales before being comprehensively beaten 4–0 by England at Hampden. The Northern Ireland game in Belfast I remember well and for good reason. The Irish played a system not dissimilar to 4-4-2, with the two front men playing off each other, Rangers' Billy Simpson taking on a secondary attacking role to Bill McAdams (Manchester City). As captain I was responsible for Scotland's tactics and any changes to play that were to be conducted during the course of the game. Given that we were faced with two centre-forwards, I reckoned it would be in the interest of the team if I changed my style from that of an attacking wing-half to a more defensive role. This tactic worked well – I moved across to pick up Billy Simpson and the threat of the twin centre-forward was nullified. On the boat back to England I fell into conversation with the Northern Ireland skipper, Danny Blanchflower, a shrewd man who possessed a considerable knowledge of football. Danny said how my decision to play more defensively and track Simpson had rendered redundant his tactic of playing two centre-forwards. Danny had hoped Bobby Evans would have been isolated in the centre with two men to mark, but my positioning ensured that never happened. On the face of it then, a job well done although word reached me that the Scottish selectors were unhappy with me for not playing my normal attacking game. It was a common problem for players, and indeed the England manager Walter Winterbottom, for tactics that proved effective not to be realised or understood by selection committees. The fact that players were always at the whim of selectors who had no deep knowledge of the game, invariably led to players even of the quality of Matthews and Finney having an erratic international career.

Scotland's next match was the crucial World Cup qualifier

against Switzerland that would decide whether we were going to Sweden. Knowing the SFA's propensity for knee-jerk reactions in team selection, I was relieved to learn I had kept my place and the captaincy for the game.

Switzerland had shown they were adept at fluid, penetrating play but it was Scotland who struck the first blow. Back to my attacking game, the first half was 15 minutes old when I slotted a pass through the Swiss defence for Clyde's Archie Robertson to run on to and slide the ball under the body of their keeper Parlier. The game see-sawed and with the score at 2–2 and only minutes remaining came the controversy. Following a goalmouth scramble in which I managed to clear off the line, the ball was played long to Alex Scott who immediately took off in the direction of the opposition goal. Those Swiss defenders near him, rather than giving chase, raised an arm to appeal for offside. As a good pro Alex did the right thing: hearing no whistle he kept on going and planted the ball in the net. The Swiss players were furious and surrounded the English referee Reg Leafe who waved away their protests. It was a tight decision but the goal stood and Scotland joined England, Wales and Northern Ireland for the first and, to date, only time all four home nations qualified for the finals of a World Cup.

As the domestic season in England drew to a close I was on tenterhooks waiting to hear if I was to be included in the World Cup squad. Eventually an envelope bearing the SFA crest dropped through my letter box. As soon as I saw it on the mat, a broad grin swept across my face – the SFA wouldn't be writing to me to say I hadn't been picked.

Scotland were due to play two warm-up games before arriving in Sweden: against Hungary at Hampden and Poland in Warsaw. I was very keen to play in at least one of these games as I wanted to reinforce in the minds of the selectors I would do a job for Scotland as captain in the World Cup. The dates for those two games, 7 May and 1 June, coincided with Preston's end-of-season tour of South Africa. Initially there didn't appear to be a problem with this and I wasn't concerned at all – until Cliff Britton intervened.

Cliff told me club came before country: not only would I miss Scotland's warm-up matches, but also the World Cup finals themselves. I don't often swear (honest) but I made an exception on this occasion. Initially I tried to be diplomatic, thinking it was no good flying off the handle, and that reason would win the day. Not a bit of it. I was very cross with Cliff Britton's intransigence, especially as there was a precedent. In the past other players, Tom Finney being one, had been allowed to miss or leave an overseas tour in order for them to play for their country. Why not me? I had several more conversations with Britton and even had a word with Preston chairman, Mr Buck and his vice-chairman Mr Ingram. Buck and Ingram were sympathetic to my case, but informed me it was a team matter and as such they could not interfere. Without actually undermining Britton's authority as manager, I had thought the pair of them might have had a quiet word in his ear. But their failure to intervene left me with no alternative but to go back to the negotiating table with Britton, only he wasn't in the mood to play. As things stood at that time, I was contracted to Preston North End for life. Or so they thought.

I contacted the SFA to explain to Sir George Graham that due to club commitments I would be unavailable for selection for the games against Hungary and Poland, but could join the Scotland squad thereafter for the World Cup. Frustratingly, when I joined the Preston party for the tour of South Africa I wasn't even selected for the first two games. I promptly informed Cliff Britton I wanted a transfer. I'll never know whether I would have played in the remaining two matches of the tour – by then I'd packed my bags and was on my way to Sweden.

I needn't have bothered. I arrived in Sweden as the captain of Scotland but come our first match against Yugoslavia in Vasteraas, I wasn't even in the team. Eddie Turnbull (Hibs) played right-half, Bobby Evans at centre-half and the left berth went to Doug Cowie. The match ended 1–1, not the best of starts, but at least Scotland didn't lose. The same could not be said of our second game, against Paraguay in Norrkoping. Paraguay were hardly in the class of Brazil or Argentina and it was a game Scotland were expected to win. It didn't turn out that way, a 3–2 defeat virtually ending our hopes of progressing to the quarter-finals. What slim chance Scotland had was finally extinguished when in the final group match we lost 2–1 to France in Orebro.

I was not happy to see Scotland exit, neither was I happy that my contribution to our cause was limited to watching from the stands. I watched a lot of games during that World Cup. For whatever reason, I was given the job of compiling reports on Paraguay and France. Having seen the French hammer Paraguay 7–3, I submitted my report on what I perceived to be the strengths and weaknesses of both teams. It was never used, and I should be surprised if it was ever opened.

All players were given passes that allowed them admission to the terraces. I saw as many matches as I could, not purely as a means of entertainment, but as part of my ongoing football education. I knew there would be new tactical formations on show, and players displaying techniques I had never come across before. At first some of the Scotland squad came with me to games, but when I could find no takers, I attended matches on my own.

I don't think the England team had come to terms with the tragic loss of Duncan Edwards, Roger Byrne and Tommy Taylor in Munich. All three were key to England's hopes of doing well in the World Cup; bereft of their talent, England never looked to be serious challengers. Arguably in the toughest group of all, England opened with a 2–2 draw against USSR but Tom Finney picked up an injury and was to take no further part in the tournament. They did well to hold Brazil to a goalless draw but also drew against Austria. Brazil won the group with England and USSR level on points and with identical goal difference. The two teams met in a play-off. The press were demanding the inclusion of Bobby Charlton but the England selectors opted for Derek Kevan, a good player but not in Bobby's class. The Soviets scored the only goal of the game though England were a tad unfortunate to exit as they had been the better team for lengthy spells.

Wales and Northern Ireland both made it to the quarter-finals via play-off games. Northern Ireland, managed by Peter Doherty, did well to beat Czechoslovakia before succumbing to France, while Wales did even better in beating Hungary. The Welsh, denied the services of John Charles through injury, put up a terrific performance in their quarter-final against Brazil only to lose by the only goal of the game.

However, it was Brazil's World Cup. I saw all their matches from the quarter-final on. I was impressed by the way their players displayed complete mastery of the ball and was much taken with their midfield general, Didi, and, of course, 17-year-old Pelé who burst onto the world scene that summer. Even at such a tender age Pelé's relationship with the ball was totally different to anyone else I had seen. He seemed to see or sense everything that mattered on the field. Even then he was immensely forceful, athletic and resilient. I loved the way he passed the ball. Like Puskas, Pelé displayed great vision and imagination and, as he proved with his six goals against Wales, France and Sweden, his finishing was devastating with either foot. In defeating host nation Sweden 5–2, Brazil became the first team to win the World Cup outside their own continent and won many friends when, on their lap of honour, they carried the Swedish flag.

During the World Cup I met a man who set me thinking about the importance of mental fitness in football. Of course I already knew a player had to take to the field in a very positive frame of mind, otherwise the game was up before he'd kicked the ball. But a chance meeting started me thinking that there was much more to having the right mental attitude than simply geeing oneself up.

I met this man while sitting outside a café in Stockholm. He was a tall, distinguished looking guy who spoke quite good English. He told me his name was Carvalhaes and that he was a professor from Brazil. He worked with various teams in his home country with a view to developing players' mental attributes. He argued that the psychological make-up of each player was important in developing attitudes and, because we are all different, he had to address the individual needs of each player. 'In England,' he said, 'all players are treated the same, yes? They do the same training, but what is good for a full-back is not good for a goalkeeper. How can one type of training be of benefit to all? Training must be done to the needs of the individual, likewise, developing the right psychology.'

He told me that on the morning of a match he blindfolded players and asked them to do a series of drawings – of horizontal and vertical lines, circles and steps. I have to say I was sceptical at first. As he continued, however, it all started to make some sense. The professor said he could tell whether a player was in a state of anxiety, too tense or lacking in confidence from the way the line he had drawn deviated to the right or left, above or below. Those who he found to be too emotional, or not mentally tuned for the task ahead, were not selected. Those who were on the borderline had a session with him during which he would talk, about their individual strengths and the need to be totally focused. Whilst I didn't think British football was quite ready for such radical ideas, I did believe there was a lot in what Professor Carvalhaes told me, particularly relating to the importance of total focus and the right attitude, and the need to tailor training, physical and mental, to individuals. I made a mental note to find out as much as I could about sports psychology.

Following their success in the World Cup and their lap of honour with the Swedish flag, the Brazil players offered one final wave of goodbye to the crowd before heading towards the tunnel where a knot of ecstatic Brazilian backroom staff tearfully greeted them. As I watched this I glimpsed one member of the backroom staff in particular. Two Brazilian players, Orlando and Vava, made straight for this man and embraced him. It was Professor Carvalhaes.

When I joined my Preston team-mates for pre-season training I confirmed my desire to leave the club. I had spent nine years at Deepdale and, up to the last month or so, had loved every minute. I had a very good relationship with the supporters and liked the town. Saying I wanted to leave did not come easy, but I'd had my fill of Cliff Britton and felt a new challenge would be good for my career.

By asking for a move I would forfeit a percentage of any transfer fee, which might amount to a considerable sacrifice. Matt Busby made no secret of his interest and felt I could do a job for him at Manchester United, whilst less than a year before Everton had put in a bid of £18,000 only for the Preston board to turn it down flat. Even though the maximum wage was now £17 a week in the winter, I was not so financially comfortable that I could easily forfeit a percentage of a transfer fee, but my desire to move to pastures new was so acute, it was a case of Hobson's choice.

Perhaps my chance meeting with Professor Carvalhaes had something to do with this, but during pre-season training I began to think about Cliff Britton's insistence on my going on a jolly at the expense of representing my country in a World Cup, then not even playing me once when I was out there in South Africa. I began to wonder what might have induced this vindictiveness. Perhaps the fact I was loud on the pitch did not go down too well with him. Maybe my increasing interest in and knowledge of tactics and training methods made him feel ill at ease, vulnerable even? Or maybe he just thought I was a cocky little so-and-so who needed taking down a peg or two.

I am certain the Preston board did not want me to leave the club; perhaps they made their feelings known to the manager. I say this because in the weeks leading up to the start of the 1958–59 season he took me aside several times and said, 'Are you absolutely certain you want to leave?' – not, you notice, 'Don't go, your future is here.' Even if he had it would have made not one iota of difference. I am extremely stubborn when I feel I have been wronged. Eventually I was told to train alone, and in practice games my place was taken by Jimmy Milne's son Gordon, who was playing his first season as a professional and went on to succeed me in the team. Gordon enjoyed a fine career, later becoming a key player in Bill Shankly's Liverpool team of the 1960s and a member of England's 1966 World Cup-winning squad.

After watching our opening game of the season against Arsenal from the stand, Cliff Britton asked again, 'This is the last time, do you still want to leave? You can change your mind if you like.' I told him my mind was made up.

'Right,' he said. 'There is somebody in my office who wants to talk to you.'

That somebody turned out to be the new Arsenal manager George Swindin, who told me he was keen to make me his first signing and that I would be an ideal replacement for Joe Mercer. Arsenal were, even then, a famous name throughout the world. They had a rich tradition and history and a reputation for doing everything right. I was as keen to sign for the Gunners as Swindin was to sign me. Even so, I asked him for forty-eight hours so that I would discuss the move with Agnes. Like a serviceman's wife, she knew my profession meant we could be moved at any time. In the event Agnes was excited at the prospect of a new life in London. Having decided the move south was what we wanted we broke the news to the children who thought it a great adventure which, in truth, it was.

My team-mates were sad to see me leave, but realised it was a good move for me. Tom Finney wished me the best of luck, adding, 'I suppose I'll just have to work out those goal averages on my own now!' The transfer fee was £28,000 which was good business for Preston, who had paid Celtic £4,000 and had nine years' good service out of me. George Swindin didn't waste any time in introducing me to the Arsenal fans: the following Tuesday I made my debut in a 3–0 win over Burnley.

I was mightily impressed with the set-up at Arsenal. The first time I walked through the main entrance I felt I had stepped into a place of football reverence. The marble entrance hall was lavish, with a red artillery gun set in the floor, the *pièce de résistance* being the Jacob Epstein bust of legendary manager Herbert Chapman set within an arched niche. To me this famous hall was indicative of the style and dignity that made Highbury and the club itself so special. Behind this imposing entrance were five storeys containing offices, lounges for guests and players, the boardroom, a gym, a restaurant and, a rarity in the 1950s, heated dressing rooms. Out on the pitch I marvelled at Highbury's East Stand with its clean straight lines, the two tiers of seating leading down to the paddock terracing. Highbury's art deco style set the stadium apart from any other ground in British football, Wembley included.

I quickly settled in at Arsenal and made friends with my new team-mates. The squad included goalkeepers Jack Kelsey and Jim Standen. The latter, who was also a county cricketer with Worcestershire, went on to gain an FA Cup winners' medal with West Ham United in 1964 (they beat Preston) and the following year, a European Cup-Winners' Cup medal. When his playing days came to an end Jim Standen emigrated to the USA where he worked in real estate. Jim's West Ham days are still very precious to him, particularly that FA Cup win – he has a personal car registration which reads 'WHU 64'.

Dennis Evans, Len Wills and Billy McCullough competed for the positions of full-back, whilst alongside me in the middle of defence were either Dave Bowen, Bill Dodgin or Vic Groves to whose number was added Mel Charles, brother of John, who joined in March 1959 from Swansea Town. The forward line consisted of players such as Jackie Henderson who I knew well from the Scotland squad, Len Julians, Gordon Nutt, Jimmy

Bloomfield, David Herd, Danny Clapton, Gerry Ward and Joe Haverty. Arsenal had a good team as we proved by finishing third in the First Division that season. Manchester United were runners-up, a remarkable achievement given the tragedy of Munich, whilst the champions were Wolves for a second successive season. Preston finished in the bottom half of the table – the start of a decline that would result in their relegation in 1961.

Not long after my debut against Burnley, I was faced with a North London derby against Tottenham Hotspur. I felt I was playing well and I knew George Swindin was pleased with my efforts because he told me so. Yet the Arsenal fans were reserving judgement, they hadn't warmed to me in the way I'd hoped. That was all to change when Spurs arrived at Highbury.

As soon as Arsenal took to the pitch, I sensed the air of expectancy in the capacity crowd of 65,000. It was an unusually warm and sunny day for mid-September and on the packed terraces men were in shirtsleeves and women in rayon blouses. Spurs had finished second and third in the previous two seasons whereas Arsenal had become the butt of the critics. This season it was different. Part of my job that day was to mark Tommy Harmer out of the game and, according to my team-mates and the press, I did that right enough. Harmer and Danny Blanchflower pulled the strings in the Spurs team and if Arsenal were to continue our good run, it was important we didn't let Spurs settle and dictate proceedings.

We dominated the early exchanges, but surprisingly it took us as long as 40 minutes to take the lead. Following a terrific run and cross from Danny Clapton, Gordon Nutt's miscued volley hit the back of the net anyway. Soon after half-time David Herd scored from 20 yards to extinguish Spurs' spirited reply and what little flame of hope was left was snuffed out imperiously ten minutes later when Herd, from even further out, hammered a fierce drive into the roof of the net.

Believe it or not I was a vociferous player on the pitch. In quiet moments of a match I would clap my hands and gee up my team-mates, or I'd shout instructions to push up or drop back. Seemingly some sections of the Highbury crowd had taken exception to this. On more than one occasion I heard shouts of 'Shut it Docherty. Get on with ya own game' or 'Pipe down loudmouth'. Such calls never bothered me and certainly did not deter me from advising team-mates as I thought fit. Following my performance against Spurs, however, the catcalling aimed in my direction ceased. I imagine my style of play – a blend of the combative and creative – endeared me to the Arsenal faithful. Whatever, after that game against Spurs I was to enjoy a fine rapport with Gunners fans.

Following the deep disappointment of having been on the side-lines for the duration of the World Cup finals the previous summer, I was recalled by new Scotland boss Matt Busby and the Scottish selectors in October for the Home International against Wales at Ninian Park. I played at left-half and alongside me at centre-half was my old pal from St Paul's School football team, Willie Toner, then with Kilmarnock. My fellow Arsenal players David Herd and Jackie Henderson also played in a new-look Scotland team that included goalkeeper Bill Brown (Dundee and later Spurs), Dave Mackay, Graham Leggat (Fulham), Eric Caldow, Pat Grant (Hibernian) and a spindly blond-haired teenager from Huddersfield Town called Denis Law who, at 18 years and 236 days, became Scotland's youngest international. It was a team that proved far too strong for Wales, Leggat, Collins and Law scoring to give Scotland a comfortable victory.

Three weeks later I was in the Scotland team that drew 2–2 with Northern Ireland at Hampden. On the face of it that sounds a disappointing result, but under the management of Peter Doherty and the coaching of skipper Danny Blanchflower, Northern Ireland had developed into a good team. Some weeks earlier they had drawn 3–3 with England and apparently should have won that game.

In November 1958 I was flattered that Matt Busby thought

enough of my knowledge of the game to ask me to compile a report on England in their match against the Welsh at Villa Park. I felt I had a foot on the management ladder. So I joined a crowd of 41,581 to see a 2–2 draw. Playing for England at outside right was my Arsenal team-mate Danny Clapton, whilst in goal for Wales was Jack Kelsey. All three of us had informed Arsenal that we would be available to play a prestigious floodlit friendly against Juventus in the evening, so as soon as the game at Villa Park was over I was sitting in the car park with my engine running. The car was a green Morris Traveller commonly known as a 'shooting-break' – not that I have ever been into shooting except on a football field. No sooner had Jack and Danny emerged from the foyer than we were on our way to London. We arrived at Highbury half an hour before the kick-off time of 7.30, and would have arrived earlier but such was the interest in this game the streets around N5 were stiff with traffic.

To me it shows how much football has changed over the decades that two players took part in a major international match in the afternoon then, in the evening, played against Juventus. But in those days players were not treated as capital assets on a balance sheet, so there were no great financial implications in the event of one sustaining an injury. Also there were fewer international players on a club's books then, and directors and managers were very happy for their players to represent their countries as it was seen to improve the status and standing of the club. Besides, players loved playing football so much they were willing to commit to two games in a day.

Danny, Jack and I were keen to play against Juventus because such a friendly was considered to have great importance. In 1958 there was the European Cup but that competition was only open to champions. The Inter Cities Fairs Cup (later UEFA Cup) was cumbersome in its organisation in that the initial competition did not take place during a single season but spanned three seasons, from 1955 to 1958. The pace of life was indeed slower back then. Initially the competition was only open to cities which had staged a European industrial fair, England's entrants being Birmingham City and a representative London XI. So it was a rare opportunity for supporters to see their club take on top continental opposition.

Floodlit matches were also a big attraction as they were still a novelty, as evidenced by the fact England had played Wales at Villa Park in the afternoon. Hitherto teams from overseas were rare visitors to these shores, but the 1950s saw a burgeoning of commercial air traffic which allowed teams from overseas to pay a midweek visit. Supporters were also keen to see their team play a top side from the Continent, as the quest to prove British football had developed since 1953 and was no longer second-rate gathered momentum. And don't forget there was very little football on television. The only way people could see the top teams in action was to attend their games. Little wonder then that 51,107 people turned up to see Arsenal take on the star-studded Juventus team featuring Giampiero Boniperti, Gino Stacchini, Umberto Columbo, Omar Sivori and the great John Charles, but Arsenal did our little bit to restore pride in British football with a 3–1 win.

Agnes and our three children Michael, Catherine and Tommy had settled in to our new home in Ashurst Road, Cockfosters. Life was great. The children were happy in their new schools and enjoying the new experiences London life had to offer. Agnes and the children made new friends quickly; I have often heard it said that London people, which is what we now were, are unsociable and distant, but happily we never found that to be the case. Agnes and I were happy and stimulated by the new life we were creating.

Come January, Arsenal were lying second in the table and on course for the championship and a tilt at the FA Cup. We had a tough game at Bury in round three squeezing through with the only goal of a game played on a snow-covered pitch. Colchester United proved just as difficult to dispense with. After a 2–2 draw at Layer Road, and before a Highbury crowd of

62,000, we won the replay 4–0 and it would have been more but for some fine goalkeeping from Percy Ames. It was in round five that we came unstuck, losing 3–0 to Sheffield United after a 2–2 draw at Highbury. This was my first match back as I was serving a suspension following a silly incident at the end of our game at Luton Town on Boxing Day. After two successive home defeats Arsenal desperately needed a result at Kenilworth Road to keep in touch with table-topping Wolves. We lost 6–3. Looking back I suppose I was very frustrated at losing to a side who were struggling near the foot of the table. I felt that referee Ken Stokes had made a series of poor decisions throughout the game that favoured the home side, and as we left the pitch made no bones about telling him so. Ken reported me for using foul and abusive language, a charge I strenuously denied at my subsequent hearing. The three-man Football Association commission, however, found me guilty. I was upset with their verdict but when they announced my punishment I was livid. I was given a two-week ban, fined £50, which amounted to three weeks wages, and had my wages docked for the duration of my suspension. I was shocked by the punishment meted to me. It was the first time in my ten years in English football that I had ever been in trouble. I felt the punishment to be grossly excessive and that I had been very badly done by. Moreover, with my ambition to eventually coach or manage one day, I didn't want to gain a reputation as a troublemaker.

My last match before my suspension was in Arsenal's 4–1 derby win at Spurs. This was a terrific result for Arsenal as Len Julians was sent off early in the second half for kicking out at Bill Dodge, while David Herd picked up an injury that rendered him a virtual passenger out on the wing. The newspapers were very complimentary about Arsenal's performance and mine in particular. The *Daily Express* said I was like 'a sergeant in the charge of the Light Brigade', which, given its historical significance, I wasn't sure was a compliment or not. The *Daily Sketch* said, 'Docherty gave another outstanding exhibition of half-back play and is quickly becoming a folk hero with the Arsenal faithful.' I put that one in my scrapbook.

With nine matches of the 1958–59 season remaining there were four clubs in with a real chance of winning the title, Wolves, Arsenal, Manchester United and Bolton Wanderers. Our hopes of landing the title were to evaporate during a disastrous end of season for us. With ten matches remaining we travelled to Molineux for what the newspapers termed a 'fourpointer'. We knew that if we didn't get a result at Molineux it wasn't the end of our title hopes, but a crushing 6–1 defeat seemed to destroy confidence. That, and a series of injuries to key players, was to cost us dear. We were never the same team following that defeat, and of our remaining nine games we only managed three victories.

It was very disappointing to capitulate in the run-in but, in the general scheme of things, it had been a good season for Arsenal. Third was a great improvement on the previous season and there was an air of confidence about the club which I was told had been absent in recent years. The balance of power in North London was shifting back to Highbury.

Spurs, however, hadn't let the grass grow under their feet. In late October when they languished near the foot of the table, they appointed former player Bill Nicholson as manager in succession to Jimmy Anderson. For Nicholson's first game in charge against Everton, he immediately recalled Tommy Harmer, who had fallen out of favour with Anderson. It proved to be the most sensational start to any managerial career. Spurs annihilated Everton 10–4. Most newspapers agreed it was going to be hard for Bill Nicholson to maintain his incredible start, but he was already thinking long-term. The rise and success of Tottenham Hotspur under Nicholson and his cerebral captain Danny Blanchflower was to create English football history, in so doing putting paid to Arsenal's hopes of once again establishing themselves as the leading club in the country.

★

Nottingham Forest won the FA Cup by beating Luton Town 2–1, but the headlines in the newspapers were devoted to the so-called 'Wembley Jinx' which was said to have struck again. Forest's outside-right Roy Dwight, the uncle of Elton John, was carried off with a broken leg after only half an hour of the final. Dwight's injury added to the catalogue of injuries sustained in FA Cup finals at Wembley in the fifties. The following season Blackburn's Dave Whelan (now chairman of Wigan Athletic) broke his leg when playing against Wolves; in 1960–61 it was the turn of Leicester City's Len Chalmers. Prior to the Forest–Luton final, serious injuries had occurred to players in just about every Cup final: three Arsenal players in 1952; Bolton's Eric Bell (1953); Jimmy Meadows in 1955 (Manchester City); Bert Trautmann (Manchester City) who courageously played on with a broken neck in 1956; and Manchester United's Ray Wood in 1957. Imaginative reporters had a field day, spiritualists and clairvoyants were consulted, and it was even suggested that in 1950 a gypsy, turned away from Wembley when trying to sell clothes pegs, put a curse on the stadium.

I put the 'jinx' down to two things. First, the pitch, which was formed of Cumberland turf. I found it very soft and springy, almost moss-like underfoot. The softness made legs tire quicker than normal and tired legs are vulnerable to injury. The 'danger' was further enhanced by the fact that Cumberland turf did not allow for the best footing, especially when wet. The unfamiliarity of players to Wembley's grass led to all manner of collisions. Secondly, being an FA Cup final, players tended to pull out all the stops, stretching for the ball and committing themselves to challenges they might not normally make in a league match. Such a combination was bound to result in injuries. Oh, that and the spurned gypsy . . .

Indicative of the times was the composition of the England team that beat USSR 5–0 at Wembley in 1958, which included goalkeeper Colin McDonald (Burnley), Graham Shaw (Sheffield United), Johnny Haynes (Fulham), Bobby Charlton (Manchester United) and Tom Finney, who had all come through from the junior ranks of their respective clubs. Not one player in the England team had cost a transfer fee.

In the summer of 1959 England embarked upon what proved to be a very disappointing tour of South America, the only highlight of which was the introduction of Jimmy Greaves on the international scene. He made his England debut in the 4–1 defeat against Peru and, true to form, he scored. Jimmy's inclusion in the England tour party shows once again just how different attitudes were to players in this era. Nobody in authority was too concerned about the well-being of footballers. The day before the party departed for South America from Heathrow, Jimmy Greaves and Jimmy Armfield played for England Under 23s in Italy. Following the game they and manager Walter Winterbottom, who managed both England teams as well as being the FA's Head of Coaching, travelled by train to Geneva. From Geneva they flew to Heathrow to join the party for the flight to South America. The trio had no time to nip home for a change of clothes. It was simply expected of them that they were happy to fly off to South America straight away. That players of the time were treated little better than serfs by those in authority was further exemplified when the two Jimmys grabbed a cup of tea. Jimmy Greaves bought a cake to eat with his cuppa and was just about to take a bite when Sir Stanley Rous walked by, accompanied by other mandarins from the FA. Noticing Jim with his cake Rous backtracked and confronted him.

'Greaves, put that cake down this instant,' ordered Rous. 'You will be fed on the plane.'

Seemingly in the mind of Rous, Jimmy and his England teammates would not be dining on the plane, nor would they be having a meal. They were to be fed, as one would sustain an animal.

Whenever I heard things like that I made my mind up that should I ever become a coach or manager I would treat the players under my charge with more respect. I had been brought up to believe that in order for others to respect you, you must first display respect to them. This was an attitude I was to carry through my entire career as a manager. I was to have my differences with several players, which sometimes were acute and led to harsh words from both parties, but at no time would I ever have anything but respect for my players.

Scotland's close season programme consisted of matches against West Germany, Holland and Portugal. To my disappointment I wasn't chosen for any of these games. It appeared Scotland's quest to give new blood its chance was gaining momentum, which was fair enough. The majority of names in the Scotland squad that summer were very much about the future – John White (Falkirk, later Spurs), Duncan MacKay and Bertie Auld (Celtic), Alex Scott, Bobby Collins, Eric Caldow, Alex Young and Dave Mackay. But it has to be said the goalkeeper blooded for those summer matches was 34-year-old George Farm (Blackpool) – Scotland were finding it difficult to produce a young goalkeeper of international class, a problem that was to dog the nation for some years.

So I spent the summer with Agnes and the children. With one eye on the future I began a course to qualify as a fully fledged FA coach. At the time the qualification involved three stages, Preliminary, Intermediate and Full. Each stage involved taking coaching sessions on the training field, course work which led to a final practical session and written exam. As proof of qualification each successful student received an official certificate together with a cloth badge bearing the crest of the Football Association and denoting the level at which he had qualified. That summer I received my Preliminary FA Coaching Badge, I was on my way, though at this point my destination as yet unknown.

8

I CAN MANAGE

In the summer of 1959 Arsenal boasted something many First Division clubs did not have – a coach. The coach in question had been appointed by George Swindin and had played his football with Brentford and Bradford Park Avenue. Like most of his generation his best years as a footballer had been lost to the war. When his days as a player eventually came to an end in the early fifties he got a job coaching the Oxford University football team. From Oxford he moved to the top amateur club Wealdstone where he had gained a reputation as a great tactician, and an advocate of purist football where the ball was passed out of defence rather than simply kicked. George Swindin was very much taken with the fellow and following his appointment gave the coach full responsibility for all the Arsenal training and tactics. There was even talk of Walter Winterbottom giving him a coaching role with England Under 23s. I wasn't surprised to hear this. I had been impressed with his ideas and methods, and he'd proved to be a really likeable guy who had formed a good relationship with the Arsenal players. His name, by the way, was Ron Greenwood.

At the time English football was a melting pot of ideas, some borrowed, some new. I was pursuing my quest to become an FA coach and Ron's arrival at Highbury only served to further my desire to qualify and learn more about new training methods, tactics and game plans. I had several absorbing conversations with Ron, and the more I learned the more I realised how much there was to learn.

British football was undergoing a renaissance and I wanted to be at the heart of this change. I had been a player in top-flight football for nearly twelve seasons. I was 31 and believed I still had at least a couple of years left at the top. But I didn't want to carry on playing in the lower divisions. Some players do that because they simply love playing and want their career to last as long as possible. Others know their career is drawing to a close and drop down a standard because they don't know what else they can do for a living. In either case that's fine, but it didn't suit me. I wanted to end my playing days at the top and, as for later on in life, I was beginning to have a firm idea of what I wanted my future to be.

The betting was that five teams would be involved in the race for the 1959–60 First Division title – Wolves, Manchester United, Spurs, West Bromwich Albion and Arsenal. Rarely do the bookies get it wrong, though they did on this occasion. Burnley were very talented but few believed they would mount a serious and sustained challenge, but that's exactly what Harry Potts's unfancied side contrived to do. What's more, they maintained their momentum until the very last day of the season when they overtook Wolves and topped the table for the first time – when it mattered.

I began the new season with my usual enthusiasm and application. It would be an exaggeration to say Arsenal came out of the starting blocks like a rocket; more like a jumping cracker, explosive in fits and starts. After six matches we were seventh in the table with seven points, a good platform on which to begin a serious tilt at the title. The newspapers felt I was playing as well as ever. Following our 1–0 success at Bolton, the *Sunday People* reported, 'Docherty had another fine game, as befits a player who is now the complete wing-half.' I wouldn't have gone that far but I thought I was doing a job for my team. Any complacency I felt was to end abruptly, however, when Preston North End visited Highbury in mid-October.

I was eagerly anticipating the arrival of my old team-mates. I had yet to return to Deepdale with Arsenal. I didn't enter the game thinking I had anything to prove to anyone. I had no grudge against Preston; on the contrary, I loved the club. It had, after all, been my decision to leave Deepdale. I had nothing against manager Cliff Britton either, though I had never warmed to the man or his methods. I remember prior to my leaving Preston, Walter Pilkington, who reported on PNE for the *Evening Post*, approached Tom Finney and me for a quote on Cliff Britton.

'How's he doing?' asked Walter.

'Cliff? Oh, he's doing his best,' said Tom.

Walter Pilkington offered Tom a knowing nod. Tom was always the model of diplomacy, so Walter knew he had to read between the lines of such a seemingly innocuous reply.

'And what is your opinion of Britton, Tommy?' Walter asked me.

'He's a twat.'

'True as I believe that to be, I think I'll run with Tom,' said Walter, nodding in Finney's direction.

As I turned away, Frank O'Farrell looked up from tying a bootlace. 'Don't beat about the bush, Tommy,' he said. 'Tell it the way it is.'

Arsenal's game against Preston was only 20 minutes old when I attempted to cut out a cross from the Preston right. Centre-half Bill Dodgin moved up to meet the cross as well. Bill and I were both moving at some speed, but I just managed to get a boot to the ball when Bill clattered in to me. I had one foot off the ground and Bill's momentum carried him through and I fell awkwardly, turning my ankle as I did so. If there was a cracking noise I didn't hear it. A seering pain shot from my ankle up my leg and I feared the worst.

You can always tell when a player is really injured. He doesn't roll about on the grass, he lies still, which is what I did. The first person at my side was my old friend and colleague Tom

Finney. Tom was a highly experienced player who had seen more than his share of bad injuries on a football field. He asked if I was OK but I could tell by the concerned look on his face what he thought. The Arsenal physio, Bertie Mee, was summoned and Jimmy Milne ran from the Preston dugout to offer assistance. When the opposition trainer lends a hand, it's always a bad sign. Bertie and Jimmy inspected my ankle and summoned a stretcher. When you sustain a bad break a terrible sickly feeling wells in your stomach, probably something to do with adrenalin and shock. You also feel annoyed: if only moments before you had done something ever so slightly different, you would be on your feet as normal with the game unfolding about you. As I was carried from the pitch the Highbury crowd spontaneously broke into a round of sympathetic applause.

I was taken to hospital where my leg was put in plaster. My ankle was broken but as the match reporters of the Sundays rang for a last-minute update on my situation before their final deadlines, I found myself telling them I would be fit to play in two months. In the event I was out for a little longer. The weeks I spent at home were a time for reflection and introspection. Such an injury at this stage of my career made me seriously contemplate my future. I definitely wanted to stay in football and decided that once I had fully qualified as an FA coach I would put out feelers.

I wanted to stay in the game because it was all I knew really. I had sold my interest in the Olympic café to Joe Dunn but had no desire to go into catering as a second career. Since childhood it had always been football for me and my hunger for the game had not diminished one bit. As I sat at home with my leg up, to pass the time I took a greater interest in the game with a view to my future. I still felt it was too early to make any concrete plans, but I felt positive in assessing the scene as I saw it. I looked at the potential of just about every club in England and Scotland with a view to their being possible employers. It was wishful thinking on my part – I was yet to qualify as a coach

– but it helped pass the time and I felt better for having thought about my future.

It was whilst I was recuperating at home that a monumental change occurred regarding the England team. In October 1959 Walter Winterbottom chose an England team for the first time. Winterbottom had been England manager since 1948 but had always struggled to wrench selection from the FA Selection Committee. Latterly Winterbottom had offered advice to the committee as to who should be picked for England, but in October he persuaded the FA to allow him to pick a team of outstanding young players for the international against Sweden at Wembley. Winterbottom's plan was to blood such young ones with the purpose of developing a team over a four-year cycle with a view to winning the World Cup, a policy he hoped would continue into the future. The England team that faced Sweden included Trevor Smith (Birmingham City), Ron Flowers (Wolves), John Connelly (Burnley), Jimmy Greaves (Chelsea), Bobby Charlton (Manchester United), Tony Allen (Stoke City), Brian Clough and Eddie Holliday (both Middlesbrough), the latter three from Second Division clubs. It was the youngest team ever to be fielded by England, no fewer than eight players being under the age of 21.

Unfortunately England lost the game 3–2, only their second defeat against continental opposition on home soil. The FA were not best pleased. For the following game against Northern Ireland, selection reverted to the committee with Winterbottom in an advisory role. I don't think Walter ever got over the retrograde step taken by the FA. When Alf Ramsey took over in 1963 he accepted the England job on two conditions, the same plan set out by Walter: first, that he would be solely responsible for selection of the England team, and second, that he be allowed to develop the team over four-year cycles with a view to World Cups and that such development be free from FA interference.

The mark of how correct Walter Winterbottom's thinking was can be gauged by the fact that six of his young England squad who played in the Sweden game – Flowers, Connelly, Greaves and Charlton, plus reserves George Eastham (Newcastle United) and Ron Springett (Sheffield Wednesday) – were members of England's World Cup winning squad almost seven years later.

I was absorbing every new idea that emerged. Not all were feasible; some which did display foresight were doomed to fail due to the myopia of many club directors and those charged with running the game. Once such doomed idea to emerge whilst I was sidelined was a plan to restructure the Football League into five divisions of 20 clubs each together with a rejigging of non-league football into six regions. That failed to meet the approval of the club chairmen but League Secretary Alan Hardaker's idea for a League Cup was agreed.

With so much reform in the air and new opportunities in the offing it was a very exciting time in football, yet there I was confined to my armchair with a broken ankle. I started to compile a file on training methods and tactics. I was very keen to construct schemes for training that had a series of aims and objectives rather than simply exercises to keep players fit. Tactical formations often change on a match-to-match basis, but I started compiling notes that detailed new formations, or adaptations of existing ones. More league clubs began to use 4-4-2 and 4-2-4 formations. Blackpool had adopted a variation of 4-4-2 when they won the FA Cup in 1953 and in Italy the *catenaccio* system of defence, though far from producing fluid entertaining football, was proving highly effective. *Catenaccio* ('bolt' in Italian) was really nothing new. It was an adaptation of a highly defensive system based on a 4-4-2 formation which denied opponents scoring opportunities by defending the 'scoring space', that is in and around the penalty area, and adopting man-to-man marking supported by a sweeper. *Catenaccio* would never go down well with British players or supporters, but watered down versions of it were beginning to emerge as early as 1959. Joe Mercer, who I had been brought to Highbury to replace, had since become manager of Sheffield United. Joe had them playing a sweeper system with Joe Shaw behind a back four of Cec Coldwell, Tommy Hoyland, Gerry Summers and Graham Shaw. The system proved very effective, particularly at Bramall Lane where, during the first five months of the previous season and for 17 games in all, United conceded only seven goals, and this in a season that saw a post-war record number of goals scored in the league. I had noticed when watching Sheffield United that it was Joe Shaw's job to assess where opponents were making attacks and seal off any gaps he found in the back four. He was never assigned to mark a player, except at corners when he would pick up the player breaking from deep into a scoring position.

With time to dwell on such matters I gave some thought to Sheffield United's system. Arsenal had played United the previous season in the fifth round of the FA Cup. During that match I had noticed the United right-back, Cec Coldwell, did not cover the centre-half as well as left-back Graham Shaw. I made a note that should I encounter the Blades again, I would make a point of suggesting the ball be played towards the right of their defence into the space in front and out of reach of goalkeeper Alan Hodgkinson and behind Coldwell and Hoyland. I also made a note to the effect that any attacks down the United left would draw sweeper Joe Shaw out of the middle whereby the plan would be to thread the ball through to the inside-left position. In order for this to work and create opportunities for forwards, the ball from the right would have to be a 'quality' ball that was out of Hodgkinson's reach but not too far out as to allow the back four to clear. I wrote the words 'diagonal ball' in capital letters.

It wasn't rocket science nor was it mind-boggling football tactics, but I felt a degree of satisfaction in having passed the time by devising a strategy to counteract Sheffield United's sweeper system. I remember thinking, 'How come I've thought of this?' I wondered at the thought process that led me to arrive at my solution. I was confident the strategy would expose

Sheffield United and cause them problems yet, at the same time, a part of me was saying, 'No one else appears to have worked this out. Am I really spot-on with my thinking?' Indeed, was this the right way forward for me in the years to come? I had no real plan of what I would do when my playing days were over – and so when an opportunity did come my way, literally out of the blue, it owed much to spontaneity and luck.

My prediction of playing regularly again within two months proved over-optimistic. I had a couple of run-outs but I was cautious about declaring my fitness too early. When a player has been sidelined for some time, his natural inclination is to play again as soon as possible. Invariably he gets through his first game back without much of a problem. What often happens, however, is in his second match he doesn't perform quite as well and come the third he appears out of sorts. People are confused, wondering why he did so well in his return match and not the others. There is talk of him not being the same player since his injury and doubts are cast about his long-term future. This scenario comes about because while the player is not fully match fit in his first game, adrenalin gets him through. In his second match the buzz of being back has been diluted a little; come the third it is diluted even more and he finds it hard to keep up with the pace and the demands of ninety minutes of robust football.

I was as keen as mustard to be playing again but aware that I needed a few games in the reserves as a period of adjustment. Those games under my belt, George Swindin came up to me and asked, 'How are you fixed?' I told him I was fit and raring to go. So when Arsenal made the short trip to Fulham on 18 April I was delighted to be running out alongside my team-mates. Fulham occupied a mid-table position in the First Division, with Arsenal two places below them. It had not been the season all connected with the club had hoped for, and a

3–0 defeat at Craven Cottage further emphasised what most knew. Arsenal had been well off the pace for much of the season.

I liked George Swindin, he was a good guy but by now out of step with the revolution that was taking place in English football. I guess he knew that too which is why he had brought Ron Greenwood to Highbury. In the dressing room prior to the game against Fulham, George had said little to the team other than general comments such as 'Keep it going' and 'Play your normal game'. When we found ourselves trailing at half-time George never said anything constructive during the interval. I was assigned to mark Johnny Haynes and believed I'd done a decent job of keeping him quiet – no mean task. The right-wing pairing of Johnny Key and Graham Leggat was causing us problems; Leggat, usually a left-winger, using his pace to run from deep. George Swindin never remarked on the pair at all. Self-appraisal is no guarantee of merit I know, but I sat in the dressing room at Craven Cottage looking at George and thinking, 'I could do your job, I can manage.'

Remember what I was saying about luck playing a part in one's destiny? The concluding part to my coaching course took place in the wake of a football match that changed the way everyone on that course, and a good many other people as well, thought about football. The European Cup final saw Real Madrid beat Eintracht Frankfurt in front of 127,621 enthralled and enchanted fans at Hampden Park. In the two-legged semi-finals Frankfurt had put twelve goals past Rangers, thought to be one of the best teams in Britain at the time. Frankfurt were indeed a good team, but Real Madrid were in a totally different class again.

Prompted by Alfredo Di Stefano and buoyed by Puskas, Real produced a breathtaking display of attacking football and clinical finishing the like of which no one had seen before – not even from Hungary in 1953. Real's performance showed individual skill was still of great importance, but it was even more effective when harnessed as collective skill. In Di Stefano, Puskas and Gento, Real possessed three of the greatest individual football talents in the world, but above all they were team players. Real's performance that night was the greatest performance by a club team I had ever seen. I think I knew then that Real were so outstandingly brilliant no club team would ever emulate them, but at least we all now knew what was possible in football. As Jimmy Greaves later described Real's performance, 'It was like discovering Shakespeare, Picasso and the Beatles for the first time and all on the same night. A stunningly formative experience from which we knew there was no going back.'

Real Madrid's performance was the subject of much conversation at Lilleshall, the consensus being no one had seen the like of it before. As one of my fellow students, my pal from Preston Frank O'Farrell said, 'If that is what playing top-class foreign opposition is all about, we still have a long, long way to go.'

I still have the photograph of those of us who qualified as coaches at Lilleshall that summer. It is the composition of the class which proves interesting now. Included amongst my fellow students are Frank O'Farrell, Bob Paisley, Malcolm Allison, Billy Bingham (later to manage Everton and Northern Ireland), Peter Taylor (of Clough and Taylor fame), Dave Sexton (later to manage Chelsea, Manchester United and work for the FA as a coach), Les Cocker (assistant to Don Revie at Leeds United and Alf Ramsey with England), Tony Barton (coach of Aston Villa and later manager when they won the European Cup), Bert Johnson (coach at Leicester City), Phil Woosnam (later a key figure in the development of soccer in the USA), Malcolm Musgrove (coach at several clubs including West Ham and Leicester City) and Harry Evans (assistant to Bill Nicholson at Spurs). As managers or coaches all were to play a key role in the development of English football in the sixties and seventies. In the cases of Paisley, Allison and Taylor their influence was to be of great significance.

★

Following my qualification as an FA coach I combined my career at Arsenal with coaching Barnet, who, having heard of my qualification simply rang and asked if I would be interested in coaching their players two nights per week. Barnet were then a top amateur club in the Athenian League. They trained on Tuesday and Thursday nights which rarely coincided with a midweek match for Arsenal. I wasn't paid by Barnet but that didn't matter – I was out on the pitch training players and putting my ideas into practice.

One evening in January 1961, I learned that the *Daily Mail* was to run a story the following day which claimed I was going to ask George Swindin for permission to apply for the vacant job as coach at Chelsea. This was all news to me – I didn't even know Chelsea wanted a coach. Apparently the Chelsea board had been sounding out Walter Winterbottom for his opinion on coaches who might be available. Walter said Jimmy Adamson and Tommy Docherty. With Jimmy heavily involved on the playing side with Burnley who were still in the European Cup, that left me. The following morning after training I had a meeting with George Swindin who gave me permission to apply for the vacancy at Chelsea. That afternoon I sat down with some Basildon Bond and wrote my letter of application.

In less than a week I was in the Chelsea boardroom attending the interview for what I had been informed was the position of player-coach. I was always one to speak my mind, and at the board interview I was no different. At one point chairman Joe Mears informed me the board were considering offering the post to Vic Buckingham, the former West Bromwich Albion player who was coaching Ajax, but they had heard that he was keen to return to the UK.

'If you appoint him, it'll not be a coach you'll be needing, it'll be a hearse,' I told them, not bothering to hide my light under a bushel.

The board passed my letter of application amongst them and nodded approvingly. I heard one mutter, 'Very confident', another, 'Cocky'.

The vice-chairman Mr Pratt looked up. 'Is there anything you're not good at?' he asked.

'Failure,' I replied.

'You have obviously played against Chelsea,' said Mr Withey, another director. 'What did you think of our defence?'

'A jellyfish has more shape,' I told him, 'and by comparison is more solid. I know what's wrong and I can put it right.'

There was an awkward silence and I wondered if I had been too frank. It was Joe Mears who broke the ice.

'Appreciate your honesty. I know nothing about football,' he said, and then waved his hand towards his fellow directors. 'And this lot know a damn sight less.'

The talk turned to my family. I told them I was happily married and had three children.

'Three children, and did you and Mrs Docherty plan to have three children?' asked Mr Pratt, now showing signs of living up to his name.

'Yes,' I informed him. 'We wanted three children, so if one turns out to be a genius the other two can support him, and Agnes and me.'

Towards the end of the interview Mr Mears asked what, at the time, I thought a curious question seeing as I was there to be interviewed as a possible coach.

'Do you have ambitions to manage, Mr Docherty?'

'Yes.'

'Why do you want to be a football manager?' Mears asked.

'If you ask, you will never know; and if you know, you need never ask,' I told him. He sat back in his chair, looked straight at me and smiled.

That evening I received a telephone call from Joe Mears who told me the job was mine. 'When can you start?' he asked.

Whether it was my broken ankle, or my growing interest in coaching, perhaps a combination of both, but in the weeks preceding my application for the job at Chelsea I was aware I had lost some of my enthusiasm for playing. I know some players who have reached the end of their careers and become managers or coaches because they believe it to be the next best thing to actually playing. I wasn't like that. Over the past year I had turned more and more towards the idea of coaching, and eventually to becoming a manager. Indeed, a few weeks before the Chelsea job came up, George Swindin had taken me aside and told me he had received an offer for me from Blackpool. If I had still maintained my burning passion to play I might have given serious consideration to the move, but in my heart of hearts I knew the old desire was no longer there and turned it down.

As it was, one morning in mid-February I steered my shooting-break not to N5, but to SW6 to begin my first day as Chelsea's new player-coach. I was filled with optimism and enthusiasm at the thought of starting my new career. In a bag in the back of my car was all the kit I felt I would need for my new post. Like a diligent schoolboy who brings order to his pencil case and satchel the night before a new school year, I had sorted and cleaned every item of kit. My boots were polished and dubbined; in these days before training shoes, my 'baseball boots' had been washed and relaced; I'd bought pens, paper and files, and systematically filed all my ideas for training and coaching.

The first person I saw when entering the Bridge was secretary John Battersby, who wished me good morning and good luck. I introduced myself to the office staff who told me that manager Ted Drake was waiting to see me. Then the trainer Jack Oxberry introduced himself, saying he thought this season would be his last. 'I have a garden and tomatoes that are waiting for me,' he said. 'I like to grow my own, you see.' I reminded him of the golden rule of gardening: 'Nothing ever turns out to look like it does on the seed packet.'

People were laughing as they attended to their work. The atmosphere appeared less formal, less stuffy even, than at Highbury. I was going to like life at Chelsea. I had a bounce in my step as I made my way to the manager's office. It may well have been February, but I felt full of the joys of spring.

I knocked on Ted Drake's door, and found him doing some filing. With a wave of a hand he indicated I should take a seat.

'Good morning, Ted. I'm ready and raring to go,' I said brightly.

'I didn't want you here,' he told me. 'You weren't my choice. I wanted Vic Buckingham.' He had a winning way with words, did Ted.

I set to work with the players straight away. I also started to assess the situation at the club, the playing staff, their training routines, tactics (of which there were none to speak of) and the abilities, character and mood of the other back-room staff. Chelsea were going through a tough time. In the lower reaches of the First Division, they had the previous month been knocked out of the FA Cup at Stamford Bridge by Crewe Alexandra. I sensed that the manner of their defeat had irked.

Chelsea had a defence like a sieve. On the plus side however, in Jimmy Greaves the club possessed a player who, though not yet 21, had already proved himself the greatest goalscorer in Europe, arguably the world. Another plus was that the club had some excellent youngsters on their books. Under youth team manager Dickie Foss, Chelsea had won the FA Youth Cup for two successive seasons. The youngsters who had come through from the junior ranks included Greaves, Peter Bonetti, Ken Shellito, Alan Harris, Barry Bridges, Mick Harrison, Mel Scott, Micky Block and Bobby Tambling. A quick assessment of the current youth team indicated another batch of quality young-sters would be knocking on the door soon – Terry Venables, Ron Harris, Bert Murray, Gordon Bolland, Cliff Huxford, John Dunn and Colin Shaw.

Amongst the senior pros were goalkeeper Reg Matthews, brothers Peter and John Sillett, Frank Blunstone, Peter Brabrook, Ron Tindall – who missed the beginning and end of each season as he also played cricket for Surrey – John Mortimore, Sylvan Anderton, and an old pal from my days in the Scotland team and the man who unwittingly instigated my departure from Celtic – Bobby Evans.

In the previous season Chelsea had scored in excess of 76 goals but conceded 91. Results in the season thus far were following a similar pattern. Manchester City had been beaten 6–3, West Bromwich Albion 7–1 and Blackburn Rovers 5–2, in addition to three four-goal victories and a creditable 3–3 draw with Wolves. The team had only managed to keep a clean sheet once, a 2–0 victory at Preston of all places. Recently they had suffered some smarting defeats, 3–1 away to West Ham and, in late December, back-to-back six-goal defeats to Manchester United and Wolves. You didn't have to possess an in-depth knowledge of football and tactics to see where the main problem lay, so in my first week I set to work tightening the defence and midfield.

New brooms sweep clean, so they say and I did my best to be as spic and span as possible. Though Ted Drake selected the team he was rarely seen on the training field and seemed to spend all the time in his office. I did chat to him about team matters before my first match as coach, at home to Blackpool, but doubt whether my advice was taken on board.

The game ended up a 2–2 draw and although we put in a credible performance, I'd seen enough to know there were serious problems. Another draw followed, away at Everton, before our first defeat since I had joined the club, at Sheffield Wednesday when an Alan Finney goal settled matters, though I was more happy with how the team applied itself to this game than in the previous two matches. The next four outings were pleasing, but what the *Daily Sketch* described as being Chelsea's 'Jekyll and Hyde' nature emerged once again. Birmingham City were beaten 3–2 at home, but what appeared a decent 4–4 draw at reigning champions Burnley made me believe the balance of the team was wrong. In truth the 4–4 draw was achieved against Burnley reserves: faced with the prospect of a European Cup quarter-final and an FA Cup semi-final against Spurs, manager

Harry Potts had rested ten first-team players. It was a completely calculated risk for Rule 23 of the Football League clearly states, 'Each club shall play its full strength in all league matches, unless some satisfactory reason is given.' Reserve team or not Burnley held us to a draw but they paid a heavy price for it, a record fine of £1,000.

With Jimmy Greaves and Bobby Tambling on fire, each scoring two goals, we should have won the match at Turf Moor, but the old problem of poor defending returned to haunt us. Two of the Burnley goals were scored by Andy Lochhead. I was sitting in the dugout but I reckon I was the nearest Chelsea man to Lochhead when he netted his double. On Monday it was back to the drawing board.

We then drew 1–1 with Preston at Stamford Bridge before travelling up to Newcastle United where we gained the result of the season – a 6–1 victory. Jimmy Greaves scored four times to take his season's tally to 35 league goals and was to finish with 41 from 40 appearances. On the journey home Ted Drake said to me, 'I think that result is ample evidence that we have turned the corner.' 'Turned the corner?' I said. 'I don't think we've even started to walk down the street yet.' Ted sat back with a look of surprise, but I was to be proved right. There was a humorous footnote to this match. The bias and loyalty of local football papers was never more apparent than in the *Newcastle Chronicle*'s headline: 'Magpies In Seven-goal Thriller'.

Jekyll and Hyde came and went through swing doors up until the end of the season. A 4–2 defeat at Spurs was followed by a 6–1 victory over Cardiff City, and so it went on, until the final day of the season when Nottingham Forest were beaten 4–3 at Stamford Bridge, all four of our goals coming from, who else, Jimmy Greaves, playing his final match for Chelsea. Earlier in the year Chelsea had negotiated an option deal that would take Jimmy to AC Milan at the end of the season. Jim didn't want to go to Italy and tried to get out of the deal but to no avail. Ironically the contracts that bound a player to a club for life, unless the club in question wanted to get rid of him, would soon be declared null and void. Such contracts, and the maximum wage which had been a significant factor in Jimmy initially agreeing to go to Milan, were declared by a High Court judge as an infringement of players' labour rights. The court case had been brought by the PFA against the Football League and the clubs, the main protagonists being PFA chairman Jimmy Hill and secretary Cliff Lloyd, a former solicitor. Had the case come to court some six months earlier, Jimmy Greaves would possibly have remained a Chelsea player.

Jimmy had become fed up with playing in a team that regularly scored goals only to concede with equal regularity at the other end. He had turned 21 in February and the burden of shouldering such responsibility for one so young was beginning to tell on him. He was discontented and once told me, 'I'm happy with your training, I like the club, and I love scoring goals for Chelsea, but I just feel I'm helping bail out a sinking ship.' Morever, Chelsea were strapped for cash and needed the £80,000 Milan were willing to pay for him. Ultimately, though, he pleaded with the club to find some way of getting him out of the deal and the board told him they would see what could be done. Jimmy was due to fly to Milan to tie up the deal so the club hired a Rumpole-type lawyer, R. I. Lewis, to fly out with him. The board told Jimmy that R. I. Lewis had been hired to do all he could to get him out of the deal. Jimmy went to Italy feeling a bit better about matters but his heart sank when, after a meeting with Milan officials that Jimmy was not allowed to attend, Lewis told him there had been nothing he could do. Milan had taken up the option on Jimmy, he was now their player. It was only in the late 1990s Jimmy found out the truth behind the lawyer's visit to Milan. Far from going there to try and get Jimmy out of the deal, Mr Lewis had been hired by Chelsea to ensure it went through.

Jimmy and I got on well together and have remained very good friends to this day. If matters had been left to me I am sure I could have persuaded him to stay at Stamford Bridge. Jim is an intelligent guy and I like to think if he'd heard about the plans I had for the team and the club, he would not have sought to move on. Contrary to what some might think, Jimmy was a good trainer and applied himself fully to all that was asked of him, unlike some of the players I inherited. I had plans to cut out the dead wood and rebuild the team should I be given that authority. But the timing was all wrong. I couldn't talk to Jimmy because I was only the coach and just finding my feet at the club. To this day I maintain if Jimmy Greaves had stayed at Stamford Bridge and been a part of the team I was to create, Chelsea would have dominated English football in the 1960s. Jimmy is without doubt the greatest goalscorer I ever encountered in the 41 years I was involved in football as a player and manager. Including cup games, internationals and other representative matches, his career tally stands at a record 491 goals. A remarkable feat when you consider he retired at the relatively early age of 32. I doubt Jimmy's record will ever be broken.

Chelsea finished the 1960–61 season just below mid-table, one place below Arsenal. The season belonged to Spurs who became the first team in the twentieth century to win the League and Cup double. In so doing, Bill Nicholson's team, so ably skippered and coached by Danny Blanchflower, created several records. Spurs dropped only one point in their first 16 matches and began the season with 11 successive victories. They collected 66 points, equalling Arsenal's record set in 1930–31. They had the most wins (31) in the history of the First Division. They had the most away wins in a season – 16. They had double victories over 11 clubs, thus equalling the record set by Manchester United (1956–57) and Wolves (1958–59). They reached 50 points in 29 matches. They equalled Arsenal's away record of 33 points. Spurs played 49 League and Cup matches but only used 17 players, three of whom played two matches or less. They were watched by a record number of 2,550,683 spectators. It was a fantastic achievement and if that wasn't enough, in the coming season they signed Jimmy Greaves after his brief, unhappy stint at AC Milan.

During the summer of 1961 I worked hard with the players I had at my disposal, some of whom, if it had been up to me, I wouldn't have allowed within a mile of Stamford Bridge. Ted Drake was a reclusive figure as far as training and coaching was concerned, as I said spending most of his time in the office. He spent months desperately looking for a replacement for Jimmy. I could have saved him the bother: there was no one in British football who came anywhere near Jimmy in the goalscoring stakes.

I tried to help Ted in his quest to sign a quality inside-forward. I'd hear from my old pals in the Arsenal team that George Eastham, who had been signed from Newcastle United, was in dispute with the club over terms. I rang George and had a long chat with him about coming to Chelsea, and felt I was on the point of landing him. Eventually Arsenal offered him a new contract with improved terms and he decided to stay at Highbury. It was beginning to look as though time was running out for Ted. He'd had a great playing career with Arsenal in the 1930s, helping them to win two championships and an FA Cup. Since his appointment as manager at Chelsea in 1951, he'd guided them to the championship a few years later, but his style of management was now out of date and out of step with modern times. Having had no luck with Eastham, Ted turned to Motherwell's Willie Hunter only to enjoy a similar lack of success, an exercise that must have been repeated five or six times that summer.

I never felt I got close to Ted. We'd sit in his office and talk about the Chelsea players but he never seemed to engage with me. I'd enthusiastically outline my plans for training, or inform him of tactics we were to deploy, and he would listen but never reacted in the way I hoped. I wouldn't say he resented my presence at the club, but I had the feeling that at best, I was tolerated.

I gained a little insight as to Ted's attitude towards me when

I read his article in the *Chelsea Official Handbook* published before the start of the 1961–62 season. Near the end of his piece Ted made mention of the backroom staff at the club. 'We commence the season with Harry Medhurst as trainer. He fills the vacancy created by the retirement of Jack Oxberry . . . We have an excellent backroom staff at the club. The second team trainer will be another of our old players, Derek Saunders, whilst Dicky Spence will continue to assist the admirable work of Dickie Foss with the youth team.' Conspicuous by my absence, wouldn't you say?

In the opening match of the 1961–62 season, a 2–2 draw against Nottingham Forest, Peter Sillett broke his leg. Ted immediately switched his attention from trying to sign an inside-forward to finding a replacement for Peter at full-back. His target was the Huddersfield Town left-back Ray Wilson, who would go on to become a key member of England's 1966 World Cup winning team. Unfortunately Wilson had no desire to sign for Chelsea. Things were becoming darker for Ted, even players from lower divisions didn't fancy a move to the Bridge. Only one victory in our opening six matches did not go down well with directors and supporters alike. Desperate for some consistency that would take Chelsea into the top half of the table, the rumblings from the boardroom were becoming louder by the match.

In early September Ted dropped a bit of bombshell. He said the defence needed an experienced head and told me he wanted me to play left-back that Saturday against Sheffield United. I pointed out that it had been nine months since I had played a competitive match and was nowhere near match fit. It was arranged that I would turn out in midweek in a London FA Challenge Cup tie against Wimbledon. One game was hardly ideal preparation but better than no match at all.

The game against Sheffield United on the Saturday could not have gone better. Though now managed by Johnny Harris, they still played the sweeper system they had used when Joe Mercer was in charge of the team. What's more the defence was almost the same: Hodgkinson in goal, Coldwell and Graham Shaw the full-backs, and Joe Shaw sweeping behind a central defence of Gerry Summers and Brian Richardson, the latter being the only change for Tommy Hoyland. Before the game I went through my strategy with the Chelsea players for playing diagonal balls behind their back four to a point between the full-backs and the goalkeeper. My plan was for Bobby Tambling to be the forward who would get on the end of those passes. I don't think I ever stopped shouting instructions to the youngsters in the team for the entire ninety minutes. The score was 1–1 at half-time but during the interval I told the lads to be patient and play those diagonal balls at every opportunity. It worked a treat. Bobby Tambling notched a hat-trick and we ended winning the game 6–1.

The result was another false dawn. We lost 2–1 at West Ham, Cardiff City completed the double over us by winning 3–2 at Stamford Bridge and then we struggled to draw 1–1 at home to Blackburn Rovers. Then on the Thursday after the Blackburn game, 15 February, Joe Mears asked me to meet him in the boardroom and said, 'Tommy, Ted Drake is leaving Chelsea by mutual consent. We're going to call a press conference this after-noon. If you are willing, the board would like you to take charge of all matters concerning the players on a caretaker basis.'

This at last was a dream come true, even if I was to be manager in all but name. I assured Joe that I would do the job to the very best of my ability, thanked him and his fellow direc-tors for the opportunity they had given me and left that board-room on silver wings. The first thing I did was telephone Agnes to give her the news – she was, of course, delighted. The second call I made was to Ted Drake to express my regrets (although in truth I knew he had to go) and to wish him well and good luck in whatever he chose to do. He never wished me good luck.

I knew I wouldn't be able to improve things overnight. The club was beset with problems that would take some time to sort out. For a start I believed the training was nowhere near adequate and the players were not as fit as they should have been; some of them were coasting, not only in training but in matches. Chelsea also had a number of players I believed were simply not good enough. If I did get the manager's job on a permanent basis, I would have to plan long term if Chelsea were to be a force in English football again. But being only caretaker manager I was still not in a position to make sweeping changes. By mid-December Chelsea had a strong team – we were holding up the rest of Division One – with Manchester United only two places above us.

As I have said we had some terrific young players. The problem with young players, however talented, is they are notoriously inconsistent. On fire one game, virtually anonymous the next. An experienced quality pro will never have a bad game, he may have matches in which he is a shade off the mark, but he will never have a stinker. I was also worried that Chelsea's promising youngsters would pick up bad habits from certain senior pros who I couldn't yet get rid of. I desperately wanted the job full-time and to strengthen my claim for that I needed good results, but the results were not forthcoming. It was Catch-22.

Increasingly I put my faith in youth, and though results did not improve, our performances did. At Stamford Bridge we met a Burnley side that were top of Division One and played them off the park only to lose 2–1. It was after this match that I went to see the board and advised that it was high time we had a clear-out. I said I was confident of selling some players for half-decent money which could be used to sign better players. The board gave me permission to start looking for new blood.

I arranged for four players who didn't feature in my plans to play for the reserves in a Football Combination match against Southampton and made a few telephone calls to other managers to let them know these players were in the 'shop window'. The players were John Sillett, 25-year-old brother of Peter, who was still out with a broken leg; Sylvan Anderton who I felt would do a good job for a lower division club; centre-half John Mortimore; and David Cliss, a pint-sized forward who had been a sensation with England schoolboys but following a broken leg had failed to fulfil his early potential. On the day of this game I flew up to Scotland in the hope of signing the Motherwell inside-forward Pat Quinn who I had been tracking for some weeks. In the event I couldn't agree a deal with Motherwell, but it wasn't all bad news: the shop window brought in some customers.

I finally sold Sillett, Anderton and Cliss, retaining John Mortimore, who subsequently left to play for Queens Park Rangers before embarking upon a career as a coach; I later made him first-team coach at Chelsea. I was disappointed not to have got Quinn but on 2 January 1962, I did get what I had long hoped for – the offer of the manager's job at Chelsea on a permanent basis.

I attended a board meeting to make my routine report on what I had to admit was still an unsuccessful team. I outlined the problems of the team as I saw them and informed the directors that I felt the problems were so acute, relegation was a distinct possibility. Having given them the bad news, I then said I believed, such was the potential at the club and the depth of young talent that with the right manager at the helm, should relegation happen, the club could win promotion straight off.

As I got up to leave, with the team sitting on a coach waiting to go to Euston for the train to an FA Cup tie against Liverpool, acting chairman Mr Pratt called me back. 'Tommy, the board feel that it is time we asked you to take over fully as manager,' he said. 'Since Ted left we think you have done a fine job in very difficult circumstances. Will you accept?'

'I'm delighted to accept. I have a lot of ideas as to how this club can improve, and I think when we start clicking, we'll go places.'

Mr Pratt asked me about the terms I wanted. 'I'll leave that to you. Money has never bothered me that much. I know you'll be fair. You sort my contract and I'll get on with what I have to do.'

Happy as the birds in spring, I left to join the players on the coach. I stood at the front and said, 'Boys, the board have just appointed me manager on a permanent basis, or at least as permanent as a football manager can ever be.' I gauged their reaction to be, in the main, favourable.

We were out of luck at Liverpool, where we lost 4–3 to again exit the competition in the third round. The following Saturday my first league match as a fully fledged manager proved a mirror image of my first Cup match, when we beat Fulham 4–3 at Craven Cottage. Thereafter things did not get better; on the contrary, they got worse. In the final analysis there was no consolation whatsoever in the fact I had begun my career as a manager by being proved correct in what I had said to the board – at the end of the season Chelsea were relegated.

I had not made a sensational start to my managerial career, far from it. Of my first ten games in charge, we lost six. I had been left such a mixed legacy, even with my self-belief and bubbling optimism I couldn't see us getting out of trouble.

In the doomed run-in I made my first two signings for the club, one a big-money deal that didn't work out, and the other one of the best signings I was ever to make in my time as a manager. The signing that didn't come off was centre-half Graham Moore who cost £50,000 from Cardiff City. Graham had played very well against us and was a nice lad, but he never fitted in at the Bridge and was soon to be on his way.

The other signing I made went on to become a Chelsea legend, and I picked him up for a song. I had flown up to Scotland with the intention of watching two Arbroath players. On the day Arbroath were playing East Stirling and after only five minutes I found I had eyes for only one player on the park, East Stirling's no-nonsense, tough-tackling left-back, Eddie McCreadie. Immediately after the game I eased my way into the East Stirling boardroom which was so small, someone had to step outside to make way for me – and there were only around eight people in the room. I located the chairman and after introducing myself asked, 'How much would you take for that young McCreadie?'

'Hm, well, he's a fine player, very fine player indeed. You have to be talking big money for a player of his quality and potential. Say, five grand?' the chairman said cautiously.

'Done,' I said. 'Can I go and talk to him?'

It didn't take long to persuade Eddie that his future lay with Chelsea. Results were not going our way, relegation was looming, but his signing gave me a tremendous lift. A £5,000 signing from East Stirling understandably failed to inspire the Chelsea supporters, but I knew I'd unearthed a gem, albeit at that time a very rough diamond.

Good as I knew Eddie would become once he had settled in London, I couldn't take the risk of playing such an inexperienced youngster in a side which had lost many more games than it had won and was heading for the drop. I signed no more players that season. Those I had in mind to sign I would do so when the season was over, that way they would not come into a team that was struggling. I knew relegation was inevitable and felt it better to take that medicine whilst at the same time making preparations and plans for the fightback the following season. I informed the board of my plans for a big clear-out of the playing staff and that we had enough young players of sufficient quality to win promotion back to the First Division. As it turned out, my words proved to be no idle boast.

9

BLUES REVIVAL

The summer of 1962 saw Chile host the finals of the World Cup. Brazil retained the trophy beating England in the quarter-finals along the way. The consensus was England stood a very good chance of doing well, but manager Walter Winterbottom was handicapped by the loss of three key players: Peter Swan, Bobby Smith and Bobby Robson. For England's first match against Hungary Winterbottom replaced Robson with the young West Ham wing-half Bobby Moore who only a week previously had made his international debut in England's final warm-up game against Peru. Maurice Norman (Spurs) was also awarded his second cap when taking over at centre-half from Peter Swan, while Middlesbrough's Alan Peacock earned his first cap in England's second match against Argentina.

Like Walter Winterbottom, I had little option but to place my faith in youth as I prepared Chelsea for the new season. During the summer I pondered over the players I had at Stamford Bridge. I took stock, and decided that I would not splash money in the transfer market, at least not at first. My plan was to create a team of talented young players with a sprinkling of experienced pros from whom they would learn good habits. That year I trimmed the playing staff by eighteen. Amongst those to leave were Dennis Butler (who went to Hull City), Terry Bradbury (Southend United), Colin Huxford (Swindon Town), Ray

Corney (Gravesend) and Terry More (Guildford City); more departures were soon to be in the offing.

Winger Peter Brabrook was the first of the next batch to go just a few weeks into the new season. Peter told me he was unhappy and unsettled at the Bridge. This he did the day after I had ordered him back for special training along with a group of others whose efforts had not impressed me. Peter was a flying winger, skilful and with an eye for goal. I acceded to his request for a number of reasons. In Bert Murray I had a ready replacement; Peter was a good player who would command a decent fee, which I could then put towards buying a player to fill a priority position in the team; and when a player doesn't want to stay at a club, you might as well let him go rather than have a disgruntled member of the squad who could cause you problems. So I sold Peter to West Ham United for £35,000, not a fortune but an amount that would give me some bargaining power in the transfer market. More than four decades on, Peter is still with West Ham where he continues to do a fine job with the youth players.

I didn't necessarily want Peter to go but he, Andy Malcolm, centre-half Mel Scott and winger Mike Harrison refused the terms I had offered, saying that the basic wage on offer was not enough. Mike was to play only one more game for me in the new season in the Second Division, whilst the other two never played for Chelsea again.

As stated I sold Brabrook to West Ham and not in the mood to mess about, I threw the other three out. Mel Scott ended up joining Brentford, Andy Malcolm went to Queens Park Rangers and Harrison to Blackburn Rovers. When all four had left I told the remaining players. 'You've seen how it is. If you're not 100 per cent behind what we're doing – then you're out of here. This club will be back in the First Division next season, if you want to be like some of them others and play your football in Division Three – you know how to go about it.'

Having assessed the players, I looked at my backroom staff and have to say I was happy with what I saw. Head trainer Harry Medhurst was a former Chelsea goalkeeper who had left the club in 1952 to join Brighton only to return the following year as assistant trainer. Harry obviously had his own thoughts about training but I was happy to have him on board because he also showed enthusiasm for new ideas, i.e. mine. Harry was quite expressive, often imaginatively so. Once at training Barry Bridges complained he couldn't run because the new boots he was wearing were chafing. Harry dug out an old pair of baseball boots which many players wore for training and said, 'Here, son, wear these. It'll be like running over the breasts of maidens wearing carpet slippers.'

My assistant trainer was Dave Sexton who I'd appointed in February. Dave began his career with Luton Town and subsequently played for West Ham, Leyton Orient, Brighton and Crystal Palace before his career was prematurely terminated by a serious knee injury. Dave was a fully qualified FA coach who I had met at Lilleshall. I had warmed to him and liked his ideas, so when I heard he was looking for a job I contacted him and 'sold' him Chelsea. Dave was more than just an assistant trainer, I greatly valued his expertise as a coach, our ideas were complementary and he became an invaluable member of my staff.

The youth team manager Dickie Foss had a reputation for developing young players that was second to none (in addition to his role as manager he also seemed to be chief cook and bottle washer – he did everything for the youth team). He began his playing career in 1936 with amateur club Southall before being signed by Chelsea. Dickie was one of the founders of the Chelsea youth system back in 1947, though he didn't actually end his playing career until 1952. The Chelsea youth team played on the Welsh Harp ground which was situated near Staples Corner in Hendon. Whenever I went along to watch them, before the game I would find Dickie sitting outside the Welsh Harp pub having a pint. 'My front office,' he used to call it. His style wouldn't go down well with Arsène Wenger, but I didn't mind one bit. Under Dickie the Chelsea youth side had won every competition going, including the FA Youth Cup in two successive seasons. The youngsters learned a great deal about football from Dickie and respected him. When you have a member of staff on board like that, a manager is willing to turn a blind eye to the fact he may have a pint before and after a match. As Dickie once told me. 'A pint helps me relax and assess them boys in me 'ead. Then when ya ask about so and so, I can tell ya if he's gonna be quick burn, slow burn or never burn.' Rarely, if ever, was Dickie wrong on that score.

Richard 'Dickie' Spence was the youth team trainer who had given sterling service to Chelsea as a winger from 1934 to 1950. He won two caps for England and was a product of football in the 1930s but, unlike Ted Drake, he readily embraced new ideas and methods. Listening to Dickie's accounts of the events of a match was an entertainment in itself – 'He gets in the penalty area, and goes down like an 80-year-old butler who's just heard tragic news'; 'The boy was like dog dirt, Tommy, he got everywhere'; 'The boy needs building up, he looks unhealthy, like a mummy with its wrappings off'.

Like Dave Sexton, my chief scout Les Bedford was a relatively new addition to the staff. He joined us the previous season after spending over seven years as a scout with Sheffield Wednesday. Les was a very good all-round sportsman. He played professional cricket for Sheffield in the Yorkshire League, was an excellent tennis and badminton player and had a golf handicap of 10.

I was happy with my backroom staff and, after the clear-out, happy with the players under my charge. We were a very young team but not without a little experience. Frank Blunstone, a former England international, was the only remaining player from the Chelsea team that had won the League championship under Ted Drake in 1955. Frank was a super pro, I could have asked no more of him in the way of attitude and application.

He set a fine example to the younger players. I was only sorry I didn't have three or four experienced pros just like him.

To emphasise we were not just about to embark upon a new season, but also a fresh era for the club, I went to the board and asked them to give every pro on the books a pay rise of £5 a week. The pay rise was also a little 'thank you' for the effort and loyalty the players had shown to me and, I also believed, served as an incentive to them to do well.

The team I picked for our opening game of the season at Rotherham United was as balanced as it could possibly be given most of the first-team squad was under 22 years of age. I needed experience in the side and so reinstated John Mortimore, the one player from the reserves 'shop window' I hadn't sold the previous season, who took his place in the following side: Peter Bonetti; Ken Shellito, Eddie McCreadie; Terry Venables, John Mortimore, Frank Upton; Bert Murray, Bobby Tambling, Barry Bridges, Graham Moore, Frank Blunstone. Seven of the team were only 19, and only three were over 20. I caused a bit of a stir when I made Bobby Tambling captain. He had just turned 21 and became the youngest captain in the entire Football League. It turned out to be a great season for Bobby as he was also chosen by Walter Winterbottom for England against Wales and played in Alf Ramsey's first ever game in charge, against France in Paris. I couldn't have asked for a better start to the season. Bobby Tambling scored the only goal of the game against Rotherham and we followed that with two convincing victories at the Bridge, 3–0 against Scunthorpe United and 5–0 against Charlton Athletic.

The defensive frailties of before were no longer in evidence; we conceded only 9 goals in our first 11 matches, which pleased me no end. Peter Bonetti was emerging as a goalkeeper of real class, whilst the full-back pairing of Ken Shellito and Eddie McCreadie was first rate. The only thing that concerned me was we weren't scoring enough goals away from home. Four goals in six matches on our travels was not championship form.

On 8 September we entertained Sunderland who I believed would be one of our closest challengers in the promotion race. They had only just missed out on promotion on the last day of the previous season. In Brian Clough the Black Cats possessed one of the most prolific goalscorers in the country. Clough had scored 197 goals in 213 appearances for Middlesbrough and had continued to find the net for Sunderland. Prior to playing against us Clough had scored six goals in as many matches and was to have 28 to his name come Boxing Day when he suffered a serious injury against Bury that effectively ended his playing career. Sunderland were lying in second place on goal difference behind leaders Huddersfield Town. We were in ninth position but only two points behind Sunderland. A win would take us above them on goal average; what's more, it would give me a very good indication as to our credentials as genuine promotion candidates. Midway through the first half Graham Moore played in Frank Upton who rounded the Sunderland skipper Stan Anderson before slotting the ball home. The second half was touch and go for a time as Sunderland pressed forward to get something from the game, but John Mortimore stuck to Cloughie like a limpet and never gave him a hint of a chance. The victory moved Chelsea up to third. Another pleasing aspect was the attendance for that game, 32,901. The supporters were coming back.

By December we were flying. Preston were beaten 3–1 at Deepdale. I didn't recognise the Preston team when they ran out, with only Tommy Thompson remaining from my days at the club. The roll continued with victories against Rotherham, Charlton and at Luton. By this time I had introduced more youngsters. A very timid lad with a deft, genteel tackle by the name of Ron Harris had come in at left-half whilst at left-back Allan Harris had again established himself following a broken leg. I was delighted with how things were going. As we made the short trip from Luton back to SW6 on Boxing Day we enjoyed a seven-point lead at the top and I couldn't see what on earth would stop our momentum. Then the snow came.

Some parts of the country had snow in mid-December, it fell across the rest of the country on Boxing Day, and on the following day, the day after, the day after that and it kept on falling. Temperatures plummeted. Within a week or so the weathermen were telling us it was the worst winter since 1947. The severe weather lasted for weeks. The newspapers dubbed it the 'Big Freeze' and not without good reason. On 29 December 14 inches of snow fell in parts of London and on 23 January the temperature in Hereford was −20.6°C, the lowest ever recorded in England. Television showed pictures of the sea frozen up to 100 feet offshore at Eastbourne, and pack ice on the Mersey, Humber and Solent. The River Thames froze with ice measured at three inches deep at Windsor, which was nothing compared to the nine inches recorded on parts of the River Tyne. The snow lay deep for 67 days and yet I can never recall a school closing. Certainly my children attended classes every day. The trains ran, many were late, but they ran thanks to the work of snowploughs. People went to work every day. Irrespective of how much snow had fallen overnight, or how freezing the temperature, the Chelsea players never missed a training session, albeit mostly indoors.

The Big Freeze played havoc with the football fixtures. Only three third round FA Cup ties out of 32 went ahead on the day they were scheduled. Fourteen of these ties were postponed ten or more times. Having drawn their third round tie on 3 January, Blackburn Rovers and Middlesbrough had to wait until 11 March before replaying. On one Saturday in January only four games took place in England, and only five on 2 February. The following Saturday there were seven games in England but the entire Scottish League programme was wiped out. Having beaten Spurs 1–0 on 8 December, Bolton Wanderers did not play another game until 16 February. The severe weather also put paid to the run we were enjoying at Chelsea. Having beaten Luton Town on Boxing Day we only managed to play four matches between then and March, two of which ended in defeats to Swansea and Cardiff.

I had the Chelsea players clearing snow from the Stamford Bridge pitch on several occasions only to find the playing surface frozen underneath. We hired a tar burner in an attempt to defrost it, but it was futile. Clubs came up with all manner of ideas in an attempt to beat the freeze. Flame-throwers were used on Blackpool's Bloomfield Road pitch. Leicester City hired a hot-air tent. Birmingham City rented a snow-clearing tractor from Scandinavia, while Wrexham shovelled eight tons of sand on to the Racecourse Ground. QPR moved to the appropriately named White City Stadium in the hope the pitch there would be more accommodating. The ice was so thick and permanent at The Shay, home of Halifax Town, that in a desperate attempt to generate income the club opened it as an ice rink on Saturdays and hundreds of people came to skate on it.

The weather eventually loosened its grip and Britain more or less returned to normal in mid-March. So many games had been postponed that the Football League decided to extend the season, the last game taking place at Workington on 1 June!

The pools companies lost thousands of pounds as week after week the coupons were declared void. To stem the losses the companies united to create the Pools Panel to predict the results of postponed matches, as it does today. When the Pools Panel first sat and passed judgement, their 'results' were the subject of much interest in the press. One newspaper in Scotland, the *Forfar Dispatch*, actually ran a 'report' of a Forfar Athletic game based on the 'result' given by the Pools Panel. The influence of the panel even found its way to Stamford Bridge when, one Friday lunchtime, Frank Upton came into my office brandishing his pay packet.

'You've paid me short in my wages, boss,' said Frank.

'Short? How come?'

'The Pools Panel put us down for a win last Saturday, I haven't received my win bonus.'

'You don't qualify for the win bonus,' I responded, 'you weren't in the team.'

When we started playing football again regularly, Chelsea couldn't win a match. In March we lost five out of seven games, our seven-point lead over Sunderland was cut to two, and eventually vanished altogether. In the space of four weeks in April we had eight matches. Following a 2–1 defeat to Manchester United in the Cup, our third match in a week, I knew I had to bring an experienced head into the forward line as Frank Blunstone was struggling with an injury. I tried in vain to get Jimmy Bloomfield from Birmingham City then switched my attention to trying to sign a robust traditional style centre-forward. I rang Joe Mears, who was on holiday in the south of France, and said, 'Mr Chairman, I'm seeking your permission to buy Derek Kevan from West Bromwich Albion. We must get some goals or we're not going to go up.'

'How much are they asking for him?' asked Joe.

'Forty-five thousand,' I replied. 'Hello? . . . Hello? . . . Mr Chairman, are you still there? Hello?'

That was a lot of money in Chelsea's books. I had previously paid a large fee on Graham Moore who was not setting the world alight, and that fee had eaten a large hole in the club's finances.

'Forty-five grand,' repeated Joe eventually, 'Or we'll not go up.'

'No,' I reiterated.

'Do it,' said Joe. I thanked him.

'A funny thing's just happened to me, Tommy,' Joe said, laconically. 'The temperature is around eighty-five degrees out here,' he told me. 'I've been sitting out in the sun for over two hours, but I've just turned white.'

It was a mistake. Derek Kevan arrived at the club overweight. He didn't take too kindly to my training routines and balked at whatever I asked him to do. He was forever saying I was able to get the other players to do exactly what I wanted, because they were largely kids and would do anything they were told. It cut no ice with me. I insisted he did the training I asked of him. He did, but I knew he resented it. He mistook discipline for dictatorship and we were forever at odds. I couldn't have this as it was undermining my position as manager. I knew I had to get rid of him. I cut my losses, which, to the eternal relief of Joe Mears, wasn't too hefty, and sold Derek to Manchester City for £38,000. But not before he made one last vital contribution for me, one that proved a key factor in our promotion.

One signing that did work out cost me peanuts. That was Tommy Harmer, the former Spurs player, whom I signed from Watford. I brought Tommy to the Bridge primarily to play in the reserves and bring on the youngsters. He had bags of experience, was a super player and though I had him down as a fringe first-team player because of his age, he ended the season with a remarkable first-team record, five appearances, every game won. Tommy was the antithesis of Derek Kevan when it came to training. He put everything into it and seemed to enjoy every moment. At 5ft 5in and 9 stone he didn't possess the physique of your archetypal footballer, but he was wiry and strong.

With three matches remaining we were locked in a battle for promotion with Stoke City and Sunderland; Middlesbrough had an outside chance too. Two of our remaining three games were against Stoke and Sunderland, the latter away from home. We met Stoke at the Bridge on 11 May. Stoke's manager Tony Waddington had done the opposite to me, created a team of very experienced pros with one or two youngsters to do the running. The Stoke team included the mercurial Jimmy McIlroy, Eddie Stuart and Eddie Clamp, two formidable defenders who had won championships with Wolves, the former Blackpool and Scotland inside-forward Jackie Mudie, Dennis Viollet, a former Busby Babe who was a wonderful player, and a certain Stanley Matthews. On the day Stoke had just too much experience for us. Jimmy McIlroy showed his class and composure in scoring the only goal of the game We ran ourselves into the ground but spent much of the time merely chasing the ball. The attendance that day was 66,199 with an estimated 10,000 locked out. Some consolation for the board in this defeat came in the form of receipts of £10,155, which was a record for a League match at Stamford Bridge. I hadn't expected us to lose to Stoke, but our destiny was still in our own hands. I was determined nothing would distract us from achieving our aim.

So we embarked upon the last desperate stanza, with three clubs in contention for two promotion places. We were due to play Sunderland at Roker Park in a match postponed from mid-January. They needed just a point before their own supporters to go up. We had not only to beat them, but also win against Portsmouth the following Tuesday. From the Saturday night immediately after our defeat against Stoke I deliberated on the team I should play against Sunderland. I had no problem fielding the same defence, my dilemma was in choosing a midfield and forward line that would shut them out but also snatch a precious goal.

We travelled up to the north-east early on the Friday morning and stayed at the Seaburn Hotel which is right on the promenade. Adjacent to the hotel is a recreation ground. That afternoon I took the players across the road for a loosener on the rec and pondered my options. Watching them finish the session with a game of one-touch football I mentally named the forwards and promised myself I would stick to my decision.

The following morning I called a meeting in the hotel and announced the team. I dropped Moore, Bridges and Murray, and brought back the two toughest players I had at my disposal, Frank Upton and Derek Kevan. I switched Frank Blunstone over to the right wing in place of Murray and brought back little Tommy Harmer. I told Tommy that as a player of his experience I didn't have to tell him what to do. But I told him anyway: 'Sit in there, hold on, and keep the line together.'

I instructed Upton and Kevan to hustle and harass Sunderland centre-half Charlie Hurley unmercifully, and manfully they carried out the task. Hurley was what we called a 'footballing centre-half', he liked to bring the ball out of defence in much the same style as Bobby Moore. Hurley cut a majestic figure on the pitch, but not on this day. From the kick-off Frank Upton raced across to Hurley and aimed a wild, hard tackle at the Sunderland pivot. Hurley managed to steer clear of this challenge but turned straight towards Derek Kevan who executed a similar tackle. Hurley went white. He wasn't used to this type of game.

From that moment on, wherever the ball was, one or more Chelsea players ruthlessly hunted it. We never allowed Sunderland to settle, and just before half-time we scored the goal we so desperately needed. We were attacking the Fulwell End when we won a corner on the right. I'd talked about corners before the game and decided to vary them as I believed Hurley would have the beating of Kevan in the air. From watching Sunderland I had also noticed their full-backs, Cec Irwin and Len Ashurst, manned the posts at corners but tended to stay there, with goalkeeper Jim Montgomery taking up a position on his line towards his far post. Bobby Tambling took the corner and drove it hard at around waist height towards the near post. Little Tommy Harmer sprinted towards the ball, but it was at such an awkward height he could do no more than meet it with the lower part of his stomach. That was good enough. Tommy bundled the ball over the line and we went in at the interval one goal to the good. As I expected, Sunderland upped the ante in the second half, but we stuck so diligently to our task they never looked like scoring, until a heart-stopping moment in injury-time.

The Sunderland left-winger George Mulhall for once got the better of the peerless Ken Shellito. Mulhall had a terrific turn of speed and an explosive shot, once timed by a newspaper at nigh on 80 mph. Mulhall ran into our penalty area and hit a thunderbolt of a shot just inside the near post. A goal at that moment and Sunderland would have won promotion by a matter of seconds. But the green hurtling figure of Peter Bonetti was quickly down at his near post and somehow managed to palm the ball away. Almost immediately the up-flung arms of the Chelsea team told the despondent Roker Park faithful the result.

Back in the dressing rooms we were ecstatic even though we still had to beat Portsmouth at home to secure promotion on goal average. Tommy Harmer went around showing the spot on his lower stomach from which the ball had rebounded for the all-important goal. From that moment on he was to be known in the dressing room as Tummy Harmer, the man who scored one of the most important (albeit bizarre) goals in the club's history.

The Sunderland manager Alan Brown, his players and directors were gracious in defeat even though it was apparent to me they were shattered. Promotion wasn't completely impossible for them as we still had to beat Portsmouth, but I detected they knew we would not foul that one up. The Sunderland players were riddled with angst, as I should imagine were their supporters. Having been denied promotion on the final day of the previous season by a single point, it now appeared they had blown it again on the final day, this time on goal difference.

I don't know who was the more anxious, Sunderland awaiting news of their fate, or the 55,000 Chelsea supporters who packed Stamford Bridge in the hope of seeing us beat Portsmouth and clinch promotion. The terraces were tense and so too was our dressing room. John Mortimore was so wound up before the game he suffered a nose bleed. When the match got under way I detected plenty of nerves in our side as Portsmouth, who had nothing at stake, knocked the ball about comfortably. We were soon on the offensive, however, and after only three minutes Bobby Tambling broke down the left, centred and there was the head of Derek Kevan to power the ball home. The relief around the Bridge was palpable. Before the game I had told the team to be patient, that I knew we would score and once in the lead there would be more goals. So it proved. Having made the first,

Bobby Tambling scored a second and then a third before half-time. Three goals up at the interval, the remainder of the match was a victory parade. Tambling ended the game with four goals to his name. The final score was 7–0 and the scenes at the end remain with me to this day.

Immediately after the final whistle supporters ran on to the pitch and carried Bobby Tambling, Tommy Harmer and Frank Blunstone shoulder high towards the tunnel. I took the players up into the grandstand to celebrate our promotion and accept the cheers and applause from the 50,000-plus crowd, many of whom had by now congregated on the pitch in front of the stand. A microphone appeared from somewhere and I took it. I thanked the players, the directors and the fans from the bottom of my heart for all the support they had given during what had been a tremendous and historic season for the club. 'I promise that we will give you a team to be proud of,' I said, and I always try to keep my promises.

My luck had certainly changed. First the gamble of playing Tommy Harmer had paid off; then the man I had once told would never play for Chelsea again, Derek Kevan, headed the goal that sent us on our way to the First Division. It was the first and only goal he scored for Chelsea in seven matches before I moved him on to Manchester City. I remember Joe Mears saying to me some time afterwards, 'Kevan's one goal cost me forty-five grand.'

'Not really, Mr Chairman,' I told him, 'I bought him for forty-five but sold him for thirty-eight. But his goal wasn't the sum total of his contribution to our promotion. It was the job he did with Upton for us on Hurley at Sunderland. Now what price could you put on that?'

'Seven grand,' said Joe. He had a mind like an accounting ledger.

Joe Mears was a super guy and a great football club chairman. In a wonderful gesture of his appreciation of our promotion he and the other directors paid for all the squad, backroom staff, our wives or partners to fly off to Cannes for a holiday. Later that summer the team went on a short tour-cum-break to Israel. We visited Jerusalem and I took the players to see the Wailing Wall, but we couldn't get near it for Sunderland supporters.

In finishing as runners-up to Stoke City both teams set a record. Stoke had the oldest average age of any team to have won an English championship (a record that stands to this day), whereas Chelsea had the youngest average age of any team to have won promotion. Over the years I often thought about those facts; I know they tell me something about football, but I've never been able to work out quite what.

Agnes managed to get me away from football in that summer of 1963. We enjoyed two weeks holiday in Las Palmas, the first real holiday we'd had together in fourteen years. The break did us both the world of good. I even managed not to think about football – I think it was between two and three in the afternoon of the third day we were there.

Having enjoyed the 'honeymoon' period following our promotion I set to work planning for how Chelsea would not only stay in Division One, but challenge for honours. The first player I locked into my radar was Marvin Hinton of Charlton Athletic, a fearless but extremely honest player with super vision and an uncanny knack of reading a game. I also liked Marvin because he was a good, versatile pro. He could play in either full-back position or in the centre of defence. What's more, such was his love of the game and positive attitude, he never grumbled about where he was asked to play. Another thing about him was that his challenges were as clean as a whistle, he rarely gave away a foul, an important asset for a defender. The 1963–64 season was only a few weeks old when I netted my man for what turned out to be a bargain fee of £35,000.

I was confident of us doing well in our return to Division One but also conscious that money was now playing a greater and more significant role in the game. In the previous season the championship had been won by Everton, known by the press as the 'Chequebook Champions'. Having spent £50,000 on players in the close season, Everton manager Harry Catterick spent a further £175,000 on five players, then during the Big Freeze he laid out £60,000 on Tony Kay from Sheffield Wednesday and £40,000 on Rangers winger Alex Scott. In the early 1960s this was a phenomenal level of spending. In retrospect Everton's title success now seems a watershed for English football. The age old adage of club chairmen – 'Money doesn't guarantee success' – still held true, but in a rapidly changing game Everton had shown you never achieve success without money, a statement more true and relevant today than it has ever been.

I knew Chelsea couldn't compete in the money stakes with Everton, or anywhere near them. If I was to create a team that was to challenge for honours, I knew I'd have to rely on home-grown products and my eye for an emerging gem, such as Marvin Hinton.

We began the season with three successive draws and gained our first victory when beating Burnley 2–0 at the Bridge. I was soon to be given notice of how much work had to be done if we were to be amongst the top teams in Division One when Liverpool arrived at Stamford Bridge and beat us 3–1. We won only once in our next five matches, which included a 3–0 home defeat to Spurs followed by an ignominious defeat at Swindon in the League Cup by the same score.

I made six changes from the team that had lost to Spurs for that League Cup game at Swindon, with Marvin Hinton and John Hollins making their debuts. It wasn't that I didn't take the League Cup seriously, I did. I made the changes to give some of the youngsters who had been knocking on the door their opportunity in the first team and also to emphasise to one or two who felt they had regular places in the team that they could not take this for granted.

I was very pleased with the progress of the youngsters at

Chelsea, and I wasn't the only one. On the opening day of the season we drew 0–0 with West Ham, a game watched by England manager Alf Ramsey. After the game Alf called into my office for a cup of tea. He told me he had come along with the intention of watching four West Ham players – Martin Peters, Bobby Moore, Johnny Byrne and Geoff Hurst as well as our own Bobby Tambling, but in doing so had also made a note of Peter Bonetti, Ken Shellito and Terry Venables. I told Alf that in addition to those players for his senior England team, he should also keep an eye on John Hollins – a few weeks later John was in the England youth team. Interestingly his brother Dave played in goal for Newcastle United and Wales, because they were born in different countries.

John was a baby-faced midfield player with a crash-tackle, a terrific shot, amazing work-rate and the resilience of a rubber ball. John was also one of the most intelligent players I had on the books. He picked up things very quickly and even at a relatively young age was able to work out what was going wrong during a game and do something about it. John made his mark from the first moment I saw him. He came up from Redhill for a trial at the Welsh Harp Ground. It was the practice of Harry Medhurst to watch trialists loosening up, and then to test their reactions, and see how they shaped as they moved to the ball. Harry would kick a ball to a youngster and say, 'Come on son, have a crack at me.' Harry still retained his goalkeeping skills and could cope with anything a youngster sent his way. Not on this occasion though; John Hollins connected with the sweet spot on the ball time and again and Harry didn't have time to move a muscle. In the practice match John Hollins, metaphorically speaking, was head and shoulders above every youngster on the pitch. When the game was over Dickie Foss nodded in the direction of John and said, 'Quick burn. Emphasis on quick.'

I had 31 full-time pros at the club, 14 apprentices and five junior amateur players. Of the 31 pros, 19 had come up through the ranks of the Chelsea juniors. It was a remarkable achievement on the part of the club, as normally a youth policy was considered a success if two players from the same 'A' side graduated to the first team. As fate was to have it, none of the new batch of apprentices in 1963–64 went on to establish themselves in the Chelsea first team. There were some unusual names amongst them. I had a Vowles, a Mallard, and best of all, a goalkeeper called Herbert Haggis. To my dying day I will regret that that lad never made the grade. I did, however, have two junior amateurs who would go on to play a significant part in the future success of the club: John Boyle and Peter Osgood; the latter becoming a Chelsea legend. Peter Osgood developed into a great footballer. I always got on well with Peter and on hearing of his untimely death in 2006, mourned his passing deeply.

On Chelsea's return to the First Division I gave six young players an opportunity in the first team, all of whom I subsequently moved on. It was never pleasant telling a youngster he was not quite good enough and it would be better for him to try his luck elsewhere. The task was a little easier when the players were older and professional. Those players who didn't make it were Dennis Brown, Jim Mulholland, Errol McNally, Dennis Sorrell, Ian Watson and Tommy Knox.

As with Derek Kevan, I had to admit to myself that I had made a mistake in signing Graham Moore. Graham was a likeable lad, but quiet. I knew he was unhappy and felt he had never settled at the club or in London. He lost his form and adopted a negative attitude which I didn't want influencing any of the youngsters – hence my decision to sell him, Manchester United picking him up for £35,000. Neither player, good as they were, fitted into my style of play or way of thinking. I was on a learning curve as a manager. I knew I would make mistakes, what I wanted to ensure was that I didn't keep repeating them. McCreadie, Harmer and Hinton were great signings, those other two were not. My experience thus far had taught me when signing a player I had to ensure that not only

was he a good player, better than I already had on the books
in that position, but also that his attitude, character and lifestyle
were in keeping with the culture I had created at the club. I
knew I had the ability to spot potential in a youngster, and had
an eye for a bargain. As my experience grew I also felt I was
developing a knack for the big-money signing who would not
only justify his fee, but would repay it many times over.

After a period which I would describe as Chelsea finding our
First Division feet, we began to post good results. Following the
home defeat against Birmingham we picked up a well-deserved
point at West Bromwich Albion, beat Arsenal 3–1 at home then
won 4–2 at Leicester City and ended November with a 4–0
home win over Bolton. On Boxing Day we met Blackpool at
Bloomfield Road and played them off the park, winning 5–1.
Not only had we established ourselves in the top flight, but we
had become a force to be reckoned with. In the dressing room
immediately after the match I listened to the radio expecting
our 5–1 away win to have made the football headlines, but it
passed almost without comment due to the most extraordinary
set of results ever to have been produced in the First Division.
Ten games produced an amazing 66 goals. I couldn't believe my
ears as the announcer read out the results. The goal glut of 6.6
goals per game was a First Division record. I remember talking
to Blackburn manager Jack Marshall a few days later, Jack
couldn't believe his Rovers team had scored eight but were still
not the highest scoring First Division team on the day.

We went into the New Year in fabulous style. Spurs enjoyed
a two-point lead at the top of the table over Blackburn Rovers
who were followed by Liverpool, Sheffield Wednesday, Arsenal
and Manchester United with Chelsea in seventh place.

I couldn't have asked for a more exciting tie in the third
round of the FA Cup: away to Tottenham Hotspur. Terry Dyson
gave Spurs the lead but just before half-time Bert Murray
levelled the scores and that's how it stayed. The replay at
Stamford Bridge drew the largest attendance on any ground that

season – 70,123. As lifelong Chelsea supporter Sir Richard
Attenborough remarked, 'The good old days have well and truly
returned to this club.'

The replay turned out to be a terrific game of football. Bobby
Tambling gave us the lead in the first half and Bert Murray put
the issue beyond doubt in the second. We had done remarkably
well in the league and now victory over high-flying Spurs in the
FA Cup. What's more we achieved the cup result in spite of
injuries to key players. Reserve keeper John Dunn did well in
both games against Spurs, as did Marvin Hinton who was filling
in at right-back for the injured Ken Shellito.

Victory over Spurs was enough for some of us to set our
sights on Wembley, but pride came well and truly before a fall,
because in the next round we failed at what seemed to be a
comparatively simple task, that of beating Huddersfield Town.
The Yorkshiremen's win was a mixture of guts and of professional know-how defeating enthusiasm on the part of my youngsters. Although we never threatened to land the championship
trophy, I was delighted with our final placing of fifth. Liverpool
were champions, finishing four points ahead of Manchester
United, with Everton and Spurs above Chelsea. We completed
the season only seven points adrift of Liverpool which filled me
with confidence for the future.

Veterans Frank Blunstone and John Mortimore only missed
one match each as did young Ron Harris who had developed
into a superb left-sided defender. My other seasoned pro, Frank
Upton, played in 24 matches. The other mainstays of the team
were youngsters Bobby Tambling, Barry Bridges, Peter Bonetti,
Terry Venables, Eddie McCreadie, Bert Murray and Ken
Shellito. I was never afraid to pitch a young player into the team
to see if they would sink or swim. Several youngsters, as I have
previously mentioned, didn't show me enough to make me feel
they could be part of the future of the club. Two young players,
however, John Hollins and Peter Houseman, had produced
performances that suggested to me they were ones for the future.

I was delighted to see my old club Preston, still in Division Two, reach the FA Cup final. I was particularly pleased for Jimmy Milne, who had been trainer in my days at the club, and who had taken over as manager from Cliff Britton in 1961. 'And about time too,' I said in my telegram of congratulations at the time. In one of the most exciting finals for years Preston lost 3–2 to West Ham United, Ronnie Boyce scoring the winner for West Ham in the second minute of stoppage time. It was cruel on Preston who had been equal to West Ham in every department. Whilst West Ham United were to build on their FA Cup success, winning the European Cup-Winners' Cup the following season, sadly Preston rather than progressing, slipped into further decline.

The success of West Ham United in the 1964 FA Cup final poses an interesting question. When a club previously devoid of trophies wins a cup and then goes on to enjoy further success, is their cup success simply the first evidence of a successful team in the making? Or does success in the cup inspire the team and their manager to greater self-belief and act as a springboard to greater success? This question was in my thoughts as Chelsea prepared for the 1964–65 season. I was confident the team's development would continue apace, we would mount a serious challenge for the league title and win one of the domestic cups. I told the press so, too. Some football writers saw this as no more than me being bullish and indulging in what today we would call 'spin'. Others thought me arrogant and big-headed. How could they all be right? In the event it proved to be a momentous season for Chelsea. Spurs had won the double in 1961, but in 1964–65 Chelsea were going for the Treble.

10

BRIDESMAID REVISITED

Every decade assumes an identity of its own: the 'Roaring Twenties', the 'Hungry Thirties', the 'Frugal Fifties'. The 'Swinging Sixties'? Perhaps, though not for everyone. Each decade takes a few years to establish its identity and the sixties was no exception. The first few years were little more than a hangover of the fifties, but by 1964–65 the sixties had exploded into a decade of vibrant, new, radical ideas that encompassed just about every stratum of society.

I felt we were living in a new, modern age and wanted Chelsea to reflect this. I changed the old familiar strip and even the club badge. I introduced a new streamlined Chelsea strip of blue shirts and shorts and white stockings with the novelty of numbering appearing on the shorts as well as on the back of the players' shirts. I also changed the kit of the goalkeepers. Traditionally keepers wore a green jersey and the same shorts and socks as the outfield players. I decked my keepers out in all green. The old club badge, that of a dragon rearing on its hind legs and clutching a staff, I replaced with the letters 'C.F.C.' which were embroidered on the shirts at a sloping angle. I was always looking at ways of generating publicity for the club. Not only as means of raising our profile, but also to convey the message that Chelsea were a successful, modern, go-ahead club that any talented young player would want to join. As part of this policy I came up with what I called an 'identikit' for training.

I dressed the first-team squad in sky blue shirts and sweat tops, black and white striped shorts and white stockings with blue tops. I then devised a strip for the reserves which consisted of red shirts and tops, red shorts and white stockings with red tops. This was to enable the players to readily identify one another in practice matches. To coin the phrase of the time, Chelsea were said to be very 'with-it'. I was aware that some might see the introduction of separate training kits for first team and reserves as possibly creating a 'them and us' culture, but I was happy about this innovation as the spirit and camaraderie amongst the players was first class and they felt they were one big happy family.

At the pre-season press call I asked the players to don their new training kit. They loved it. The pre-season photographs were usually of two types: a team group of the entire playing staff formally organised into rows and wearing the club strip, and individual shots of the players. The latter consisted in the main of two poses. A simple head and shoulder shot of a player, or one of him swinging a leg in the air like some London Palladium dancer as if he had just struck a sweet forty-yard cross-field pass. I had nothing against these stock poses, but once they were in the can I invited the photographers to stay on and take more shots of the players and myself, in training, talking tactics and informally sitting having a picnic lunch on the grass. It was this type of shot that appeared in the newspapers, football magazines and annuals. One in particular I remember. It showed me on my hands and knees over a 'Subbuteo' board with a bare-chested Dave Sexton at my side, the pair of us explaining a tactical move to the players who were either seated around us on deckchairs or lying on the grass. Curiously, this shot appeared in countless newspapers and football books, usually under the headline, 'Chelsea on the Chessboard'.

As a boy I remembered once seeing Celtic's Jimmy Delaney walking down a Glasgow street. I had, of course, seen Delaney playing at Parkhead, but to see him at such close quarters left me slack-jawed and excited beyond belief. To me as a boy it seemed inconceivable that the world of a footballer, particularly my hero, should ever cross mine.

I had never forgotten the Delaney experience and thought it would be a good idea to set aside an hour or so one morning, and invite Chelsea supporters to come along to the training ground and meet me, the players and the backroom staff. So I became the first manager to hold a club open day. I knew the national press wouldn't be interested in my idea, but after a news conference I collared a reporter from the local weekly paper, I think it was the *West London Observer*, and asked if he'd do me a favour. I told him about the open day and asked if he'd give it a plug in his paper, saying the supporters were welcome to bring autograph books and cameras.

I revealed my idea to the players who were all for it. There was no local radio in 1964, so the only publicity was the five or six lines the local reporter gave it at the foot of his column. It was the school summer holidays and I was expecting around a hundred or so young people to turn up. On the day in question I was flabbergasted to see what we estimated to be some three thousand people attending! I originally thought the exercise would take about an hour, two hours tops. We began at ten in the morning and supporters of all ages just kept rolling up. It was a great day, but in the end tiring for the players, so I had no choice but to draw it to a close at around four in the afternoon.

When it was all over, Ron Harris told me he might have to report to the physio for treatment as he had signed so many autographs he thought he'd strained his wrist. Ron then started to get worried because Terry Venables started to wind him up. Terry saying, 'In the end Chopper, you weren't taking any notice of what you were signing. I definitely saw two cheques slipped under your nose that you signed. For big amounts too!'

During the summer I'd had meetings with Joe Mears and the board to sort out a new pay and bonus structure for the players and staff. I was confident I had a team good enough to challenge for the championship, if not win it, whilst at the same time winning one of the domestic cups. I wanted to leave nothing to chance, so asked the board to agree to a set of financial incentives that would spur the players to even greater effort.

Every player was given a three-year contract for which he would be paid a weekly wage of £40. At the time Chelsea had 30 professionals on the books (it had been 47 when I'd first arrived at the club as player-coach), of whom 27 were under the age of 23. The incentive lay in the bonus scheme we had agreed upon. In the main this concerned the team's position in the First Division on a weekly basis. Following a match, if we reached half-way in the table, the playing eleven plus the reserve on the day, would receive an extra £5 each. This amount increased in line with how far up the table we were. If we were tenth each player received an extra £10 and so on. Top position at any stage of the season would realise an extra £55 in the weekly wage packet. The players were also to receive match bonuses of £2 for a draw and £4 for a win. In addition to which the players were to be paid a crowd bonus based on £1 for every thousand supporters above 25,000 that came through the gate.

The scheme kicked in after our fifth game of 1964–65 by which time Chelsea were unbeaten and top of the league. We drew at Leicester City 1–1 which meant the eleven players who played in that game plus the travelling reserve earned £97 each that week. Our terrific start to the season brought the supporters flocking to Stamford Bridge. In a home match against Fulham, Terry Venables didn't seem to get into the game from the start. He seemed to be gazing about the ground, disengaged from the play that was taking place around him. I was screaming at him to wake up and get involved when Harry Meadows turned to me and said, 'You know what he's doing don't ya? He's counting the bloody crowd, working out how much bonus he's gonna get.' Harry said it tongue in cheek, but knowing Terry, I sometimes wonder.

The team I chose for our opening fixture at Wolves read as follows: Peter Bonetti; Ken Shellito, Eddie McCreadie; John Hollins, Marvin Hinton, Ron Harris; Bert Murray, Bobby Tambling, Barry Bridges, Terry Venables, Tommy Knox. Of that team Ron Harris was to play in every league match, in all FA Cup ties, six League Cup ties and two prestigious friendlies against Benfica and West Germany 'B' respectively. Ron also played in five representative England teams. That is sixty games in total and Harris was just eighteen years of age. Goalkeeper Peter Bonetti was even busier, with 62 appearances.

Bobby Tambling started us off on the right foot at Wolverhampton. He scored twice and Terry Venables added another to get us off to a flying start. I was very happy with the squad but one thing bothered me. Tambling was a goal machine and Barry Bridges knew where the back of the net was, but I didn't have a forward who was good in the air to give us other options in attack. I watched games in all standards of football at any given opportunity, and had seen one young player who I believed would fit the bill. I had seen this 19-year-old playing for Aston Villa reserves. I contacted the Villa manager Dick Taylor to ask how much he wanted for the lad. I tried to play down the fact I was very keen on this player, as I didn't want Dick Taylor to bump up his asking price. Dick obviously didn't rate the lad as highly as I did, so we agreed on a fee of £5,000. I couldn't believe my luck at having paid such a nominal fee for George Graham.

We remained unbeaten for the first ten matches of the season. We suffered our first reverse at home to Manchester United on the last day of September. United had too much experience for us, but it was one of their younger players who made me sit up and take notice. I had never seen a winger give Eddie McCreadie the run-around, but this lad turned Eddie inside out that afternoon. The United player in question was George Best.

It was just before the United game that I received an offer to manage Sunderland. Alan Brown, who had guided the club to promotion, had sensationally left in July to take over at Sheffield Wednesday. I was flattered by Sunderland's offer but there was never any likelihood of accepting it. I had started a job at Chelsea and I wanted to see it through. I was very happy at the Bridge, had a wonderful squad of young players, a super chairman and had a good relationship with the supporters. My family were settled in London, there was just no way I would have moved.

Following our first defeat of the season we embarked upon a run that saw us lose just three from 21 league matches, reach the semi-final of the FA Cup and the final of the League Cup. George Graham settled in straight away and had solved our problem in the air. I could see no one stopping us in our quest for glory.

Chelsea's path to the final of the League Cup began with a 3–0 win at Birmingham City. There followed victories over Notts County, Swansea, Workington (after a replay), and a 4–3 aggregate win over Aston Villa in the two-legged semi-final. All of which led to us meeting Leicester City in the final.

Leicester were the holders and had a very good team that included Gordon Banks, Richie Norman, Colin Appleton, Graham Cross, Davie Gibson and Len Chalmers. Both legs turned out to be close and tough encounters. Goals from McCreadie, Tambling and Venables gave us a 3–2 lead to take to Filbert Street, the Leicester goals coming from Colin Appleton and Jimmy Goodfellow. McCreadie's opening goal was talked about for years and, I am sure, will still be remembered by those present on the night. Picking up the ball in our own half of the field, Eddie set off on a run that took him past two Leicester players before he unleashed a shot from 40 yards that flew past Banksy (no mean feat – especially from that range) and into the roof of the net. The goal was as uncharacteristic as the position McCreadie found himself playing that night. With Barry Bridges injured I played McCreadie upfront alongside George Graham and Bobby Tambling, with Ron Harris taking over at left-back. Harris's place on the left went to John Boyle but that wasn't the only change to the regular team. John Mortimore was also out, his place being taken by Alan Young who was playing his only game of the season.

Playing Eddie McCreadie at centre-forward in a Cup final made headlines. For weeks McCreadie had been begging me to try him upfront saying, 'I don't know why you keep playing me in defence, boss. I have too much ability to be playing left-back.' McCreadie did have a lot of ability. I had seen him playing centre-forward in practice games, and had it in mind to try him as a striker one day. I made the decision to play him upfront against Leicester not as a publicity stunt as some of the press believed, but because he had pace and was very direct. It was a calculated decision on my part.

The return leg at Filbert Street took place on a wet and windy night at the beginning of April. The home side exerted considerable pressure but could find no way through our defence, in which Peter Bonetti was outstanding. When referee Jim Finney signalled 'finish' I raced on to the pitch to embrace my boys. We celebrated in style that night. The League Cup was the first domestic cup the club had ever won and the first trophy since winning the Division One league championship ten years previously. We paraded the cup around Filbert Street showing it off to the Chelsea fans who were grouped all around the unsegregated ground. The Leicester fans were gracious in defeat, every side of the ground breaking out into applause as we passed with the trophy held aloft.

Though we had been presented with the cup, oddly the players did not receive their winner's tankards at the same time. I don't know why this happened, and I don't think anybody was too concerned about it. Back in the dressing room whilst the players were in the plunge bath handing around bottles of champagne, a Football League official turned up with a box containing the tankards. As soon as the official left the room, our secretary John Battersby took two tankards from the box.

'Say nothing, here's yours,' said John handing me one and putting the other in his briefcase.

The tankards were meant for players only, but John was obviously keen to keep one as a souvenir of the night. I was happy to receive a memento too, but concerned two players would be going without. Seeing the concerned look on my face John said, 'Don't worry. Nobody will miss out. I'll get in touch with the League and tell them I need another two tankards for squad players.'

In winning the League Cup I was especially pleased for the board, particularly Joe Mears, who had given me the opportunity to manage and backed me all the way in everything I had done. 'Europe here we come,' said Joe. He was right.

We were flying. The League Cup had been won, and we were sitting on top of the First Division three points ahead of Leeds United and five clear of Manchester United with ten games to go. In the FA Cup we had fought our way though to the semi-final where Liverpool awaited. But for some reason, around mid-March we started to wobble. It was then that we visited Old Trafford for a game the press believed would have great bearing on the destination of the title. I had a few forebodings as I looked around the dressing room before kick-off. For the first time during the season I noticed the players were showing signs of nerves. It was too quiet in there.

If we had started well and got an early goal against United, I am sure we would have settled down to control and eventually win the game, but we were jittery and the goal never came. Roared on by a 56,000-plus crowd, United tore into us from the very first whistle. When we did have the ball no one wanted to put their foot on it and slow down the tempo of the game. United dictated from the start and after six minutes took the lead. The normally confident and composed Eddie McCreadie lost the ball to George Best who went on to score that all-important first goal. I normally watched games from up in the directors' box, simply to gain a better all-round view of play, but after the United goal I came down to the dugout. The players were bowed by the United pressure and the volatile home crowd. Harry Medhurst and I were shouting and, very soon, screaming at them to get their act together. It was so desperate even Dave Sexton, normally the soul of restraint, raised his voice. Shout as I did, it was all in vain. We conceded a second to David Herd on 25 minutes and had a mountain to climb. During the interval I tried to be composed and reason quietly with the players, but to no avail. David Herd made it 3–0 within four minutes of the restart and we were clinging on for dear life. When Denis Law scored a fourth some ten minutes from the end calm descended. At last United eased up, but by then the game was well and truly beyond us.

Two weeks later my young team were given another football lesson by Liverpool in the semi-final of the FA Cup at a packed Villa Park. Bill Shankly's team displayed no signs of weariness from their hectic fixture schedule as they outplayed my boys. Once again the players were a bag of nerves, but we had no excuse. Liverpool beat us 2–0 and we were lucky to get nil. I've always believed that the worst type of match to lose is a semi-final. Being so close to Wembley only to lose out in the semis flattens emotions and dulls spirits, much more so than going out of the Cup in, say, round three. So near yet so far – that's a hard feeling to shake off, and following our defeat I detected morale was low in training. More disturbingly confidence seemed to have evaporated from the team. It was as if they had suddenly come to think, 'We've done well this season but now we've been found out.'

In an attempt at injecting some confidence into the team I told the players that I had belief in them, and that they were great as individuals and as a team. I picked the same eleven against Everton the following Wednesday night. But when we drew 1–1, it felt more like a point lost than one gained. This momentous season was building to a dramatic climax that put the club, and me, on the front page of the newspapers rather than the back.

With a handful of games left we dropped a point at home to West Bromwich Albion, and on the Sunday we took the train north for the return league match with Liverpool. We'd beaten them 4–0 at the Bridge but up at Anfield we lost by a brace to nil. After the game I'd planned for us to take a break in Blackpool, which we would make our base for our last two games, against Burnley and Blackpool. A break by the sea at Blackpool was something I had introduced whenever we played in the North West. The players enjoyed the break from our regular routine of daily training. At night I allowed them to go out for a drink (two pints maximum) as long as they were back in our hotel before midnight. Previously there had never been a problem: no one had ever abused the midnight curfew. This time, as it was essential that we won our remaining games, I told the players they had to be back in the hotel for 10.30 p.m.

I spent the evening in the hotel talking football over a pot of tea or two with Harry Medhurst, our club doctor, Dr Bowen, and the Blackpool manager Ron Suart, with whom I was very good friends. At around 10.30 the players arrived back in the hotel, some of them were a few minutes late but I was happy to give them leeway. At around midnight Harry, Dr Bowen, Ron and myself were just winding up the night when the hotel porter came up and said quietly: 'Mr Docherty, your players are causing a terrible rumpus upstairs and disturbing the other guests. Could I ask you to sort the matter out?'

My reaction was one of disbelief. A rugby team was also staying in the hotel and I have to say my first thought was it was the rugby players who were up to high jinks. I was convinced the rumpus had nothing to do with my players and told the porter so. He went away only to return within minutes. The porter informed me the trouble had, if anything, got worse, and the source of the commotion was not the rugby players, but my Chelsea lads. What's more the door of the fire escape had been opened which was in breach of fire regulations.

We went upstairs with the porter's pass key to check the

players' rooms and found all but two to be empty. By now all was quiet. Whoever had been causing the rumpus had seemingly left the scene by the fire escape.

I returned to the hotel lounge and simply sat and waited. At around 3.30 a.m., the porter came up to me and said, 'I heard them come in, they're all back now.' Up I went again with the pass key, this time to find eyes blinking at me as I turned on the lights in every room. I was not surprised to find that one of the rooms that had previously been empty was now occupied by John Hollins and Barry Bridges, both great lads and consummate professionals.

I asked them if they were sleeping OK and both told me they were.

'Did you go out tonight after the curfew?' I asked them.

'No, boss,' they replied in unison.

'Don't lie to me!' I snapped back.

I strode across the room and whipped the covers off their beds. It was like something out of a Whitehall farce – both players were lying in bed dressed in their suits, shirts and ties. I could have laughed if I hadn't been so fuming mad. I knew I had a serious matter on my hands and that if I faltered, my position as manager would be seriously undermined. I told both players to get undressed, get back into bed, get to sleep and report to me first thing in the morning.

I told the other miscreants the same, eight in all, including Eddie McCreadie and Terry Venables. I suspected Tel had been the ringleader in all this. Tel was a superb player who to this day holds a unique record, that of having represented England at every level of football, England schoolboy, amateur, youth, under-23 and full international level. He had also played for the Football League that very season. He was the dominant character in our dressing room not by bullying players or playing childish pranks on unsuspecting team-mates as some dressing-room characters are apt to do. He was the 'leader' of the dressing room, who the other young players followed and looked up to.

Terry told me he had not left his room all night. I said I

respected every player and had always treated them as responsible adults, allowing them out in the evenings (this was the third night in succession). But we were in Blackpool to prepare for important matches, not cause trouble or skylark about in the early hours of the morning. I went on to say everyone else had admitted going out to a club, except him.

'This is your last opportunity to come clean, Terry.'

He didn't change his story and remained adamant he had not gone out after curfew.

The following morning after breakfast I gave the eight players rail tickets back to London with the simple word, 'Home!' The four who had gone to bed as requested and had not broken the curfew, Peter Bonetti, Ken Shellito, Ron Harris and Marvin Hinton, remained at the hotel with me.

I got on the phone to the club, spoke to Harry Medhurst, and told him I would need to dip into the reserves for our game against Burnley.

'How many are you taking out of the reserves?' asked Harry. 'Eight,' I told him.

'Eight?' gasped Harry incredulously. 'What's happened up there, an outbreak of bleedin' typhoid?'

My next call was to Joe Mears who was on holiday in France. I told him exactly what had happened and what my action had been. Joe said he had every confidence in me, and backed me totally in whatever further action I felt necessary. He later sent me a telegram reiterating his support.

The following day I came down to breakfast to find a familiar face on the front of the newspapers. Mine. The headlines were lurid. Seemingly the hotel porter had tipped off the Blackpool *Evening Gazette* from which the national papers had picked up the story. It didn't make for pleasant reading. Within half an hour the TV cameras arrived at the hotel. I gave an interview which amounted to little more than me saying there had been a breach of club discipline, nothing serious, and that I had dealt with the matter, which was true.

I had too much experience of dealing with the press to think
the 'Blackpool Incident', as it had been dubbed, would run in
the newspapers for just one day. Every last drop of interest was
squeezed from the story. Football writers, many of whom were
personal friends, took the high moral ground. The copy read
along the lines of: 'Chelsea players reflecting a society in which
the young had no respect for their elders or authority', and
'Loutish behaviour now rife amongst footballers'. The story was
further fuelled when reporters rolled up at Bontau Road,
Dagenham, the home of Terry Venables. Terry was asked for his
side of the story and didn't help matters one bit by giving it.
Terry told reporters that the players had not done what had
been suggested. This only served to make the reporters more
inquisitive, because no one had suggested what the players had
been doing. Terry proceeded to dig a hole for himself, climb in
it and scrape the earth over his head. Not realising he was
inflaming the situation Terry told the reporters, 'We went out
for a few drinks and picked up a couple of girls.'

I subsequently had to deal with an irate father of one of the
girls who, understandably, took great exception to Terry's use of
the phrase 'picked up' and all that it appeared to imply. The
father was so incensed he threatened to take legal action.
Fortunately I managed to calm him down and get him to see
reason. I told him that as a parent I understood exactly how he
felt, but that Terry had not been implying anything untoward
when referring to his daughter. I went on to tell the gentleman
the phrase Terry used was thoughtless, but no matter how
distasteful he found it, it was a terminology widely used by young
men at the time. I concluded by saying that I firmly believed
his daughter had been treated with nothing but respect. To my
great relief the girl's father said he would let the matter rest with
me, hoping I would take 'necessary action'. I did. I imposed
severe fines on all eight players and warned them as to their
future conduct at the club.

I wasn't angry with the press for running with the story and in the way they did. I had used the press to my advantage in the past, and would do so many times in the future. Every football writer and reporter was made welcome at Stamford Bridge thereafter. It was foolhardy to make an enemy of the press, so I prepared to ride out the storm. As Joe Mears said on his return from France, 'You've told me what went on up there and I've read what the papers are saying. Don't worry, everyone will have forgotten about it in – ten years.'

After all that kerfuffle, needless to say we lost 6–2 at Burnley and 3–2 in our final game at Blackpool and ended up finishing in third place behind Manchester United and Leeds. Many believed I had blown Chelsea's chance to clinch the title by fielding so many reserves in our crucial final two games. I suppose one could say that I forsook what chance we had of winning the championship on a matter of principle. However I felt I had to make a stand, discipline the players who had overstepped the mark and did not regret my action in the least.

We had won the League Cup and qualified for Europe, but I wasn't satisfied. At one stage I really believed we could win the Treble but we had come off the rails, in the end, in dramatic and sensational fashion. Things were never the same after Blackpool. I still trusted the four players who had done as I had asked and, of course, those players who had not been on the trip. As for the eight I had reason to send home, I told them they had to learn from the experience, that we had to put the matter behind us and move on. The trust I felt they had abused was slowly rebuilt, but it was never quite complete again. I remember once reading a quote from the Roman writer Cicero – 'Trust, like the soul, shall never return once it has departed.' That's how it was with those eight players. I did place trust in them all again, but it was never to be the wholehearted, implicit trust we had once enjoyed.

It was during 1965 that Dave Sexton left Chelsea to take over as manager of Leyton Orient. When the Orient job became available Dave approached me and told me he was thinking of applying. I told Dave I would be sorry to see him go, but would not stand in his way. Orient chairman Harry Zussman called me to ask my opinion of Dave. In short I recommended him for the job. I had been impressed with his coaching and work on the training field. He had some very good ideas and the players liked him. He had proved himself a responsible member of my staff, and I was always happy to leave him in charge of the players in my absence. Dave is a smashing guy but there were two aspects of his character I felt might prove a handicap to a possible career as a manager. He is very quiet and unassertive when dealing with a problem. That can be an advantage but there are often occasions when a manager has to be more forceful when handling players. The other characteristic I felt handicapped Dave was that he was never comfortable with the press, even though as a coach he had never found himself in the firing line. One of the best jobs in football is as a number two, as you have the involvement and input but not the flak. I did wonder how Dave would cope if results at Leyton Orient didn't go his way and he came in for criticism from the media and supporters. I never voiced my concerns to Harry Zussman. I felt Dave's qualities outweighed the negatives. In the event he was appointed manager at Leyton Orient but remained in the job for little over a year.

We faced up to 1965–66 with much the same squad of players as we had finished the previous season. One new face was coach Jimmy Andrews who replaced Dave Sexton. Jimmy, who had been on the same FA coaching class at Lilleshall with Dave and me, had managed QPR where he had proved himself one of the best coaches in the game. Jimmy and I got on famously and everybody at Chelsea loved his happy-go-lucky attitude to life and cheerful disposition. The only addition of note to the playing staff was goalkeeper Jim Barron, signed for the princely sum of £5,000 from Wolves, ostensibly to compete with John Dunn as cover for Peter Bonetti. I did, however, have another player in reserve for whom I had very high hopes. This was Peter Osgood, and what a 'reserve' he turned out to be.

This season substitutes were allowed in English domestic football for the first time. Each club was allowed to name one substitute, who supposedly would be called into action only in the event of an injury to a team-mate. In no time at all, however, managers were making tactical substitutions. The first substitute ever to be called into action was Keith Peacock who came on for Charlton Athletic against Bolton Wanderers at Burnden Park. Charlton's goalkeeper Mike Rose sustained an injury to his ankle, Rose was replaced in goal by my old Scotland team-mate John Hewie, and Peacock came on to ensure his place in English football history and countless pub quizzes. I used my first substitute in our third match of the season, at Fulham. Bobby Tambling was injured and John Boyle replaced him in what turned out to be a good afternoon's work for all twelve players – we won the derby 3–0.

Everyone was looking forward to another great season. We were competing on four fronts, as we had qualified for the Fairs Cup, my first venture into European club competition. I relished the prospect. Players mature more quickly playing in Europe, they learn new techniques, greater discipline is instilled and generally they will become better players. And for me, it would prove a fresh insight into match planning and different tactics.

We began our Fairs Cup campaign with a plum tie against Roma. The very nature of a two-leg competition encourages the visiting team to place emphasis on defence. Once I knew our draw, I flew to Rome with Jimmy Andrews and Terry Venables on a scouting mission to see our opponents in action. Such was the Italian style of play at the time, favouring the *catenaccio* system, Roma even played defensive football when in front of their own fans. As the visitors, Spal, also played an ultra-cautious game, the match did not make for spellbinding viewing. I wasn't there to be entertained, however, and I had spotted one or two weaknesses which I felt we could exploit.

The first leg against Roma at home was a niggly, bad-tempered affair. This often occurred when two nations with contrasting football cultures met. The general feeling at the time was Italian players were skilful, possessed wonderful technique but were given to gamesmanship, petty fouls and antagonistic gestures such as spitting or pinching the skin on one's back. The robust, tough-tackling style of British football was anathema to the Italians who saw us as little more than thugs on the pitch.

The first flashpoint of the game concerned the dismissal of Eddie McCreadie. After half an hour of what the *Daily Mail* described as 'punching, butting and wild senseless kicking on the part of the Roma players', Leonardi kicked McCreadie on the shin causing a gash that later required six stitches. Eddie carried on playing and won the ball from Francesco Carpenetti with a shoulder charge on the Roma full-back. The shoulder charge was considered a perfectly legitimate way to win the ball in British football but frowned upon on the Continent. As soon as he had won the ball McCreadie was grabbed by the throat by Leonardi. He hit out – and the referee gave McCreadie his marching orders.

Considering we were down to ten men what followed was nothing less than a superb performance from the Chelsea players. Terry Venables scored a hat-tick and George Graham added another in a 4–1 success. I was keen to emphasise that we were by no means home and dry. The second leg in Rome would be difficult, but deep down there was just no way I could see the Italians scoring four goals without reply. I had looked through their results in this and previous seasons. In three years the best they had done when scoring four goals was in two separate matches.

I guessed there might be a little repercussion from the rough-house of the first leg, and was aware that the Italian press had built up something of a hate campaign against us, but never in my wildest dreams did I envisage anything quite so torrid as what took place that night in Rome.

I had an inkling of what might lie ahead when we arrived at the airport a fortnight later to find no one from the club to greet us. When Roma had arrived in London, the club sent a welcoming party to Heathrow, a policy I continued in every European game I was involved in. We sorted ourselves out at the airport, only to find no one from Roma at our hotel. No messages, nothing.

We had been under the impression that the game was to be held in the national stadium. It was only when Brian James of the *Daily Mail* informed us otherwise that we learnt that the match had been switched to a much smaller ground belonging to Tibitsi Roma who played in the Italian equivalent of the Third Division. The atmosphere in that little stadium was hostile. Joe Mears, his son David and some of the directors walked out to inspect the pitch and were treated to a chorus of verbal abuse and a cascade of missiles. When David popped his head around the dressing-room door to wish the players good luck he was visibly shaken and the jacket of his suit was stained with tomato. I thought then, if that is the sort of reception they are giving to our directors, heaven knows what will be in store for the players.

They took to the pitch dodging a hail of missiles. I looked about to see what the reaction of the police would be to this, only I didn't see a single policeman in the ground. By the time the kick-in had ended Peter Bonetti's goalmouth was littered with fruit, bottles and cans. No one made any attempt to clear the area but Peter himself. I had been very pointed about the need for self-discipline and restraint in my pre-match talk to the players. I told them irrespective of what the Roma players got up to, under no circumstances should they retaliate. To respond to provocation would simply play into their hands. Throughout the game the lads rose to the challenge magnificently. In all my time as a manager I don't think I ever saw players face such provocation and hostility. Not that we on the bench were immune: for the whole game we were subjected to verbal abuse and a barrage of missiles, at least four of which were cups filled with urine. To his credit the Roma coach took to his feet on more than one occasion and tried to appeal to the crowd, but to no avail.

At one point in the game Marvin Hinton was cynically chopped down by Benaglia. The referee seemed on the point of dismissing the Roma player but, wisely to my mind, thought better of it. As for Benaglia having scythed down Hinton, he then staggered away feigning injury, a trait I was to come across often in Italian players in the 1960s.

During the half-time break with the game goalless, I told the players to stick close to a Roma player when they returned to the pitch in the hope it would prevent another barrage of missiles. Some hope. I can still picture the scene now, the Roma players trying to run away from Chelsea players who, at the same time, tried to follow them as closely as they could.

The worst incident of an incendiary second half occurred when John Boyle was laid out by a bottle that hit him on the head as he was about to take a throw-in. As John received medical attention the game was held up for some five minutes, during which two humorous incidents occurred. As Harry Medhurst administered the 'magic' sponge and smelling salts a Roma player leaned over the pair. At that very moment a tomato meant for John or Harry hit the Roma player square in the face. Boy, was he mad. He immediately ran over to the crowd and with a shaking fist launched a torrent of abuse at his own team's supporters. The other moment of levity occurred when Harry got John Boyle on to his feet. John was complaining bitterly about the bottle that had hit him on the head, only for Harry to reply, 'Oh, come on, John, get on with it. That bottle was only on your head for a second.'

Later in the game another bottle hit Eddie McCreadie on the shoulder, and a length of iron stanchion landed on the pitch, but by then we were becoming blasé to it all. The game ended goalless which was a good result for us, but I was more delighted with the way the players had conducted themselves in that very violent atmosphere, on and off the pitch.

As our coach left to take us back to our hotel it was pelted with fruit and stones. One window was smashed by a lump of iron and pieces of glass cascaded all over us. Later it took a while to remove all the shards of glass that had become embedded in David Mears' wife, June. As the coach paused before turning out of the car park a pock-marked, snarling face pressed against my window. A mouth that seemed to contain all the bad teeth in Italy yapped muffled abuse at me, then a fist the size of a ham shank hammered angrily on the glass. Unnerving, yes, but believe me, the men were much worse.

The post-match banquet was a gloomy affair. The two teams ate in an uncomfortable atmosphere of silence, as if there was a coffin in the room. The Roma President apologised for the crowd's behaviour; Joe Mears' reply was dignified and straight to the point: that Chelsea, having undergone the greatest provocation any team had ever been asked to face, had conducted themselves with grace and dignity.

Before our party flew home I gave an interview to the Italian media. At one point a journalist commented that my players had shown great restraint in not retaliating to such provocation. 'But we did retaliate,' I told him. 'We retaliated in the best possible manner, by keeping our cool and going through to the next round with our three-goal advantage intact.'

Back home, we received official recognition of our exemplary conduct in the form of a letter from the Minister of Sport, Denis Howell, himself a former Football League referee, who wrote, 'Please convey to everyone connected with Chelsea Football Club my congratulations on their conduct and composure which reflects great credit on British sport and themselves.' I received a similar letter of praise from UEFA, who went on to impose a record fine on Roma and banned them from all European competition for three years.

Happily our next venture in the Fairs Cup passed off without any incident whatsoever. We were drawn against Wiener SK and though we lost the first leg 1–0 in Austria, goals from Peter

Osgood and Bert Murray took us through to the next stage against AC Milan. As ever, Milan had a team full of stars: 'Golden Boy' of Italian football, Gianni Rivera, Cesare Maldini (father of Paolo), Sormani, West Germany's right-back Karl-Heinz Schnellinger and Brazil's Amarildo. We lost 2–1 at the San Siro only to beat them by the same score at the Bridge thanks to a super all-round performance and goals from George Graham and Peter Osgood. With the aggregate score 3–3 we tossed a coin to decide the venue for the play-off. Ron Harris called incorrectly so it was back to the San Siro.

Chelsea and AC Milan were two well-matched teams, at the end of normal time the score was 1–1 and even another thirty minutes of football failed to prise us apart, which resulted in what I think was the most ludicrous way of settling any football match – we tossed a coin. This time Ron Harris called correctly. In our first season in Europe we were through to the semi-finals of the Fairs Cup, only it hadn't been fair on Milan. I went straight to the Milan coach Nils Liedholm to express my condolences to him. Nils shrugged his shoulders and said philosophically, 'Tommy, they have to decide the outcome someway, we couldn't go on playing for ever.'

'No,' I said, 'but a better way would be to play on until one side scores, at which point the game would end. It's not perfect, but at least football and not a coin would decide the outcome.' Years later FIFA and UEFA introduced the 'Golden Goal' or sudden-death extra-time goal to decide ties in major tournaments, before reverting to the cruel drama of the penalty shoot-out.

TSV Munich 1860 played open, entertaining football and were renowned for their sportsmanship. Our three games against AC Milan produced some fine play but I knew our matches against TSV would result in more fluent football. A week prior to our meeting in the first leg in Munich, TSV, along with West Ham United, had been presented with a special award from UEFA and Unesco in appreciation for the superb football and sportsmanship both sides had demonstrated in the previous season's Cup-Winners' Cup final. West Ham had beaten TSV at Wembley in a classic game of football. The referee that night was Istvan Zsolt from Hungary, who later officiated at England's opening World Cup match of 1966 against Uruguay. Mr Zsolt was designated to officiate in our games against TSV. I knew all supporters were in for a football treat.

I had changed our away kit from yellow shirts and blue shorts to an all-white strip as worn by Real Madrid, though we would later revert to the yellow and blue. The choice of the all-white strip nearly backfired on me the night we met TSV in Munich. It was mid-March but the Grunwalder Strasse pitch was carpeted in snow which fell intermittently throughout the game, making it difficult for our players to pick one another out at distance. But even on such a tricky surface, both teams produced terrific football. Kohlars gave TSV the lead with Bobby Tambling equalising just before the interval. In the second half Konletzka scored for the home side but again Tambling was on the mark to help us secure a very creditable 2–2 draw.

The second leg drew a crowd of 42,224 to the Bridge with gate receipts of £20,382, and the vast majority went away highly satisfied, having seen a pulsating game of football and Peter Osgood score the only goal of the game. This was my first season as a manager in Europe and we had reached a semi-final. Characteristically I felt we would go on to win the Fairs Cup – and the league, and the FA Cup to boot! Though not the League Cup; even though Chelsea were the holders I had decided that due to our European commitments, it would be asking too much of the players to compete in four major competitions, particularly with my small squad. So I opted out of the competition. The size of the squad was a matter of concern to me, so whilst our European adventure continued apace, I was also getting out and about looking for players who could bolster the squad. My scouting trips were not fruitless. I bought a wonderfully gifted winger from Dundee who was blessed with football genius –

Charlie Cooke. I paid a bargain £35,000 to bring Joe Kirkup from West Ham and £20,000 for Tommy Robson from Northampton Town. I did, however, sell one player, Jim McCalliog, more of which later.

We needed to adapt our style of play slightly for European matches. In domestic football Chelsea were known for taking a game to opponents. We liked to attack because we had the sort of players who didn't give the ball away easily and we had pace. There was nothing complicated about it. Football is a simple game; coaches, if they are not careful, can over-complicate. To ensure I never did that I set myself a little benchmark. Whenever I had an idea for a game plan or tactic, I used to think, would my milkman understand this? If he didn't, I'd dump the idea and come up with something simpler.

In Europe I warned the players that Continental teams, particularly the Italians, were happy to fall back and defend the territory in and around their penalty area. Then they would suddenly break and should they score, they would shut up shop, content to defend their slender lead, irrespective of how early in the game they had scored. It wasn't pretty football but it had proved highly effective. So we couldn't just attack regardless.

With only one representative from each country, plus the holders, competing in the European Cup the quality of teams competing in the Fairs Cup was very high. The other three semi-finalists were Leeds United, Real Zaragoza and Barcelona. I didn't mind who Chelsea were drawn against; whoever we got I knew we would have a really tough game on our hands. As it was we drew Barcelona. The first leg at the Nou Camp left us with a mighty task on our hands. Goals from Fuste and Zaldua gave Barça a healthy two-goal advantage to bring to the Bridge and it would have been worse but for a fantastic one-handed save by Peter Bonetti from Muller two minutes from time. Before the second leg I told the players that should we get one goal, it would rattle Barcelona and I fancied us for another one – at least.

We scored the all-important first goal when a shot from Charlie Cooke was deflected into his own net by Gallego. In the second half we had Barcelona rocking on their heels. I thought we had equalised when Bobby Tambling went for a 50–50 ball with goalkeeper Reina. There was no doubt Tambling touched the ball but in so doing the pair collided. The ball broke free and Ron Harris, following up, swept it into the net. To my dismay the referee disallowed the goal for a foul on the goalkeeper. It was another example of how the rules were interpreted differently in Britain and on the Continent. Had Tambling's challenge taken place in a league match, the goal would have been allowed. Shots rained in at their goalkeeper Reina and I felt it would be only a matter of time – it was.

I had noticed the Barcelona keeper Reina was not comfortable taking crosses and often left them to his centre-backs, Montesinos and Torres. Under pressure Reina tended to flap at the ball. One of our ploys for corners was to have the ball hit with the inside of the foot so that it curled just under the bar. I had assigned George Graham to challenge the keeper when this happened, hoping Reina would do his flapping bit. It worked: ten minutes from time a corner was driven into the box, George Graham went up at the near post, Reina panicked and palmed the ball into his own net. Stamford Bridge erupted. It was a terrific performance from my boys to have come back from a two-goal deficit against such quality opposition, but try as we did, we couldn't get a third goal. So it was back to tossing a coin to decide the venue for the play-off.

We met Barcelona at the Nou Camp and after such an exhilarating performance at the Bridge, I was desperately disappointed in the way we played in the decider. We made uncharacteristic and silly mistakes at the back and were two goals down inside twenty minutes. When Rife added a third before half-time I knew we were on our way out of Europe. We gave it a go in the second half, but Barcelona were such a good team they soaked up our pressure only to launch lightning-quick counterattacks. Barcelona had too much European experience for my boys, and ended up beating us 5–0. It was gut-wrenching stuff to have been beaten in a semi-final for the second year running.

We had a particularly tough sequence of league fixtures in the New Year when we were also pursuing the FA Cup. In little over six weeks we played four of the top six sides in the table. In addition to this difficult sequence of league matches we also drew tough ties in the FA Cup. By the time the draw for the third round was made, our opponents Liverpool had a seven-point lead over us. I just couldn't see Bill Shankly's consistent team hitting a slump to let us catch them. Liverpool against Chelsea in the third round: even at this early stage of the competition, the press were saying this would have made a great final.

Only the foolhardy would underestimate the Reds, but I was certain we wouldn't lose. Like Chelsea, Liverpool had an arduous fixture list. I knew Shankly had set his sights on winning the league title, and at the time they were also still in the European Cup-Winners' Cup. Liverpool were contesting three major competitions, which I reckoned would prove too much even for a team of their quality. In the previous year we had secured a fine win against them at Stamford Bridge, but before that had flopped horribly against them in the FA Cup semi-final. That, if nothing else, was going to be the spur Chelsea needed to pull off the win of the season.

I had nothing but the highest regard for Bill Shankly, as a manager, a man and as a plotter of the downfall of rival clubs. Apart from playing what was arguably the best team in Britain at the time, we once again had to do it before the noisiest set of fans in the country. When in full voice the singing could sometimes be not only awesome, but moving as well. The Kop was becoming a legend in football, the name deriving from the battle of Spion Kop fought during the Boer War. When soldiers from Merseyside regiments returned home from South Africa, those who supported Liverpool and had fought at Spion Kop congregated on the terrace behind one of the goals.

Anfield in those days was a great place for humour. I had become very good friends with Jimmy Tarbuck, who was arguably Britain's top comedian then. Jimmy's rise in the comedy business became synonymous with the Mersey Beat. He sported a similar haircut to the Beatles, wore similar suits and shared that Scouse humour. Jimmy was, and still is, Liverpool through and through, but when he moved to London to host *Sunday Night at the London Palladium* he became a regular visitor to Stamford Bridge and often sat next to me in the stand.

It seemed everyone in Liverpool thought themselves to be a footballer, a musician or a comedian – they are what put the city on the map in the mid-sixties. Even Bill Shankly, Liverpool's most famous adopted son, was noted for his ready wit. Every time I went to Anfield I would hear witticisms and the latest jokes, some from Bill himself: 'Last home game, Tommy, I was walking to Anfield when I stopped at the kerb. Next to me was one of our more senior supporters who was wearing a Liverpool scarf, woollen bob hat, and carrying a red rattle. At that point a funeral cortège passed by and the old boy doffed his hat and bowed his head. I thought to myself, "Aye, we have the best, most respectful supporters in the world." So I turned to the chap and said, "That was a very decent thing you did there, taking off your hat and bowing your head as that coffin passed by." And he turns to me and says, "Mr Shankly, it was the very least I could do. I was married to her for forty years."'

After a game at Anfield, in keeping with most managers, I would be invited into the 'Boot Room'. There Bill Shankly and his backroom staff of Bob Paisley, Joe Fagan, Ronnie Moran, and later, Roy Evans, would talk football with me over a pot of tea or a dram of whisky. If Liverpool hadn't performed well, Bill would keep away from the players after the game. He didn't want to say, or hear the players say, anything that would later be regretted. Following that rarest of events, a Liverpool defeat, Bill always reserved his comments for Monday morning at the club's Melwood training ground, after a weekend of considered thought.

Bill Shankly and I were very good friends. He spanned the
two ages of football. His playing days were those of boots with
bulging toe-caps, shorts like the sails of a tea clipper and short-
back-and-sides hair. When he was in his pomp as a manager, it
was in the age of relatively long hair, tight-legged Gola track-
suits and strips of a single uniform colour of which Liverpool
were pioneers in British football.

One good team may make a manager's reputation for years.
But it is the continuity of achievement that proves beyond doubt
the prowess of his power as a football manager. It is because
Bill Shankly spanned successive eras in football that I believe
our recollections of him are so strong. He built success upon
success. For these two reasons Bill Shankly has, for a long time,
been revered for being more than simply a great football
manager. Along with Jock Stein and Matt Busby who, like him
came from good Scottish stock, Shankly became one of football's justified and ancients, a football sage who to this day is
still the daddy of the elders of that great functional family we
call Liverpool Football Club.

English football has had more successful managers – his
successor at Anfield, for example, Bob Paisley, guided Liverpool
to a haul of nineteen major trophies. But never has the game
produced such a complex character who, at the same time, could
come across as being uncomplicated and straight talking. It was
that that made Bill Shankly so appealing to me. Bill was, at
various times, outrageous, obsessed, totally focused, ironic,
passionate, funny, honest, compassionate and totally uncompromising and ruthless. Above all, he was human, and I think that
is the reason why everyone felt they knew and understood him.

When Alan Ball left Blackpool and signed for Everton, Bill
rang to offer his congratulations. 'Well done, Alan, son,' said Bill.
'You'll be playing your football next to the greatest club in the
world.'

Liverpool had a player called Bobby Graham who became
fed up with constantly being named as substitute and voiced his

feelings on the matter to Bill. 'Jesus Christ, son, you've no cause to complain,' Bill told him. 'When you started out in this game, you would have settled for being the twelfth best player in the world!'

The Chelsea performance against Liverpool was to my mind the most satisfying since I had taken over as manager – better even than the way we had come back against Barcelona, or when we had secured the draw in Rome. Before the game I told Peter Osgood that I wanted him to play even deeper than usual, but that he would have to make goal-breaking runs whenever the opportunity presented itself. When we lost possession when in attack, it was Peter's job to get back as fast as possible, if not faster! I knew I was asking a lot of a 19-year-old, but such was Peter Osgood's talent and football brain, I knew he could do it.

I asked John Boyle to man-mark Liverpool's top goalscorer, Roger Hunt. John Hollins was to harass Ian St John and play alongside Osgood in midfield. I had Terry Venables in a central role, with Marvin Hinton sweeping behind the defence. This left Bobby Tambling and George Graham as the twin spearhead in attack. Again it was nothing complicated, but I was confident it would stem the red tide.

My confidence took a dent as early as the second minute. The Liverpool right-back Chris Lawler, often the originator of so many of their moves, hit a raking ball up to St John. A flick carried it on to Peter Thompson and the Liverpool winger took off like a rat out of a viaduct, hitting a cross to the far post. St John headed the ball down on the six-yard line and Hunt blasted it past Peter Bonetti. As Jack Harkness wrote in the *Sunday Post*: 'The net behind Bonetti suddenly developed a brute of a gumboil.'

We had been caught cold from the off. Jimmy Andrews and I issued some less than genteel reminders to Boyle and Hollins of their responsibilities regarding Hunt and St John, after which we settled down to play some of the fine football we were so eminently capable of producing. Five minutes later we won a corner. Tambling took it, Boyle rose at the near post to flick the ball on his with his head which wrong-footed the home defence and Osgood soared to nod the ball into the net. It was a simple play we had practised on our Hendon training ground. It flummoxed Liverpool, and as the game featured on BBC TV's *Match of the Day* that night, soon every team in the country at every level of football was trying it.

Marvellously balanced, the game eventually swung our way. Bonetti threw the ball to Venables, who found Ron Harris, and on the ball went to Tambling. As Liverpool defenders converged on him, he slipped the ball to Graham and stayed on his own course down the middle to meet the inevitable cross from George and place a downward header past the flailing arms of keeper Tommy Lawrence.

It was a tremendous performance and a great victory. Discussing the game in the Boot Room later, Bill Shankly told me, 'That was one of the greatest games you'll ever see. Fantastic entertainment. Your boys did grand.' Meanwhile up in the board-room the Liverpool chairman said to Joe Mears, 'We have to send the Cup back to the FA in London. Could you do us a favour and take it back with you?' We did. On the train back to Euston the FA Cup had pride of place on the table. I was convinced that for the next three months the FA would be simply looking after it until the Queen gave it back to us in May. But there's many a slip . . .

After our titanic battle with Liverpool I could have wished for an easier fourth-round draw than Leeds United. Nobody wanted to draw Leeds – nobody ever wanted to play Leeds. Don Revie's team were a superb side capable of brilliant football, if very physical. It wasn't the physical aspect to their play that made them unpopular opponents, but their tendency to indulge in cynical play that was often snide and sly. Leeds had no qualms about intimidating opponents and since their promotion in 1964 had made few friends in the First Division. Leeds were often loathed, at best admired, but never loved.

Chelsea, more than most teams, had some epic battles with Leeds. A feud developed between the players. The Leeds lads seemingly thought of Chelsea as a bunch of southern, fashion-conscious softies who needed taking down a peg or three, whereas the Chelsea players saw Leeds as crude antagonists and thus spoilers of the beautiful game.

We met Leeds at Stamford Bridge, the tie being sandwiched between our meetings with AC Milan. It was a very tight and physical game and there was nothing between the two sides except a single goal from Bobby Tambling. How many times did that lad get the winner in an important match?

After disposing of both Liverpool and Leeds one would think ties against Shrewsbury Town and Hull City would have been relatively easy, but not a bit of it. Shrewsbury came to the Bridge in round five and put up a very spirited performance. Their line-up included the former Wolves and England inside-forward Peter Broadbent, one of football's true gentlemen, who proved he was also still one of the game's better players. We beat them 3–2 but it had been a battle from start to finish. Likewise our tie against Hull City in round six. Hull came to the Bridge and went away with a well-earned 2–2 draw. I wasn't concerned about the replay – I felt they had missed their chance at the Bridge. We had been a little out of sorts that day, but I knew there would be no repeat performance at Boothferry Park, and so it proved. We ran out comfortable 3–1 winners and Wembley was just one game away.

It was a filthy day at Villa Park for the semi-final against Sheffield Wednesday. About an hour before kick-off a rainstorm of biblical proportions turned the pitch into molasses. The heavy surface didn't suit my players who were also up against a very quick and tough-tackling Wednesday outfit. We ended up losing 2–0, the architect of our downfall being the player I had sold to Wednesday some months earlier, Jim McCalliog. I had consid-ered Jim to be a fine prospect for Chelsea but as he was unhappy at not having a regular place in the first team, I sold him to Wednesday for £35,000. Unfortunately he went on to prove one of my unwritten laws of football – a player will always return to score against you.

We were devastated to lose another Cup semi-final. Bill Holden writing in the *Daily Mirror* was given to parodying Oscar Wilde: 'To lose one semi-final can be considered unfortunate, but to lose two in the same season following a similar defeat the previous year, makes one wonder if Chelsea are destined to be bridesmaids and never the bride.' When I read that I thought, 'We'll show them. Next season we'll be back in another semi and this time there will be no slip-ups.'

11

A BRIDGE TOO FAR

On 1 July 1966 Joe Mears collapsed and died aged just 61 whilst on a trip to Oslo accompanying the England squad on their warm-up tour for the World Cup. Joe had been chairman of Chelsea since 1940 and a key figure in the Football Association since 1963. His death affected me deeply; he was Chelsea through and through and had been a wonderful chairman to work for. In fact, I will go as far as to say Joe Mears was the best chairman I ever had. I loved him not because he gave me my chance at Chelsea. I loved him for being the man he was. He was wise, caring, understanding of the needs of others, often to the detriment of his own; he was objective, receptive to new ideas and innovations, witty and, win, lose or draw, always affable and in control of his emotions. Only after his untimely death did I realise just how great and positive his influence at the club was. Nothing would ever be the same for me at Chelsea following his death, and I think most would agree the club was never the same.

I was devastated, but I had a job to do and I got on with it to the best of my ability. Though we had only won one trophy in my time as manager, Chelsea had embarked upon a colourful and exciting odyssey. As I prepared the squad for a new season in the wake of England's World Cup victory, I was very optimistic of our chances of winning a major trophy – or two.

Yet there was a disturbing undercurrent at the club. Whether

the winning of some silverware would have erased this is hard
to say. Perhaps the fact we had been bridesmaids on more than
one occasion fuelled a certain discontent. All I know was that
1966–67, for all it promised, saw this disturbing undercurrent
rise to the surface in no uncertain fashion.

For some months during the previous season I had been
turning over in my head the possibility of selling Terry Venables.
I knew that to sell Tel would be a very unpopular decision with
the players, supporters and the board, but the more I dwelt on
the matter the more I knew it had to be done. Tel was 21, a
wonderful player and a very popular figure around the club. As
I have said, younger players looked up to him and followed his
lead. He had a great interest in the tactical and technical side
of the game even then. I was happy to encourage this interest,
which is the reason I had asked him to accompany me when I
flew to Italy to watch Roma and later AC Milan.

I must emphasise my decision to sell Terry had nothing at
all to do with the Blackpool Incident. My decision to move
him on was simply because he had become a bit of a luxury
at the club, particularly out on the training field. Also, his presence in the side was, I felt, no longer benefiting the team. His
great interest in managing, coaching and tactics meant that he
tried to run the playing side of the club, which made it increasingly difficult for me to do so. I would often ask the players
to do such and such during training, only for Tel to pipe up
with an alternative suggestion. There were even occasions when
I felt he was trying to belittle me in front of the players.
Sometimes I would rap back at him, other times I would ignore
his interference and when the training session was over, ask
him to step into my office for a chat. There was, after all, only
room for one manager. Tel was always apologetic when I
pointed out that his behaviour had undermined my position,
but interestingly he only ever offered an apology when in
private, never in front of the other players.

There was another problem: I felt he was having a detrimental effect on how we played as a team. Tel's sway in the dressing room was matched by his influence on the pitch. He was a wonderful player and I could never fault his commitment, effort, or skill. He was the hub around which almost every Chelsea move revolved – and that was the problem. Such was his influence on the other players it reached a stage where we couldn't mount an attack without the ball being played to Tel. We had become predictable in that sense. If you closed Terry down, you stopped Chelsea playing.

When I told Joe Mears my thoughts, he backed me to the hilt, as always, yet I did detect some disappointment in his voice. I think, though, he accepted it had to be done.

I called Tel into my office and broke the news that I had placed him on the transfer list and that he would not be in the team for the trip to Milan. He was visibly shocked, and said, 'Why? What have I done?'

'It's not so much what you have done, as what you haven't done lately. You haven't been doing the business for the team, you've been playing for yourself. I can't have that Terry, I've put you on the list.'

I wasn't happy, but, for the good of the team it was the right thing. Tel left my office that morning a very perturbed young man. He was popular with the press and had a lot of friends in Fleet Street, seemingly more than I did because the media came down firmly on his side. They said he was one of the best ball players in the game; loves football and possesses a great knowledge of football for one so young; a good pro absolutely first class in his punctuality for training, and so on. That was all true. As I said in an interview for the *Daily Sketch*, 'One day Terry will become a great coach or a manager. Of that I have no doubt. And one day when he comes up against a situation similar to that which he created for me, knowing him, he will take the same action as I have done. Because, as a manager, he will know that is the right action to take.'

To this day I have remained a great admirer of Terry Venables.

Whenever we meet it is always warm and friendly, and we can even laugh about the old days. But it wasn't a laughing matter when I put him on the transfer list. I was the only person on the playing or administrative staff not to be invited to his wedding. As for my attitude to Tel, a framed photograph of the two of us holding the League Cup remained on my office wall during my time at Chelsea.

I received an offer of £70,000 from Bill Nicholson at Spurs for Tel. I told Bill the true value was £10,000 more. Bill said, 'I think you're probably right', offered £80,000 and the deal was done in May 1966.

Two players surprised me by saying they wanted to leave. I considered Peter Bonetti and Bobby Tambling as two of my most loyal players. Both had refused new contracts and a pay rise offered by the board to all the first-team squad as a thank you for the efforts of the previous season in reaching two semi-finals and finishing fifth in Division One. All of which had realised a sharp upturn in revenue at the turnstiles.

I still have Bobby Tambling's letter asking for a transfer which suggests Bobby's gripe at the time had much to do with his quest to buy a house. It reads:

> Dear Sir,
>   As I can see no possible settlement as far as the house is concerned, whereas we could buy it through the club at the promised price plus the decorating estimate from A.C. Whyte Ltd, I feel that there is no alternative but to ask for a transfer to another club.
>   Yours sincerely,
>   Bob Tambling

It was following the transfer requests of Bonetti and Tambling that Joe Mears did something that surprised me. Without consulting me he decided to pay each of them an extra £10,000. I have to say that on learning of this I felt let down by Joe for the first, and subsequently only time, since I had joined the club. There were other players who had accepted the new terms without anything extra, players who were just as important and equally loyal to Chelsea as Bonetti and Tambling. I didn't mind one bit if all the first team received an extra £10,000, but not just two of them. I feared that if news of this got out in the dressing room, it would lead to wholesale unrest.

I told Joe of my concern and displeasure at the payments made to Bonetti and Tambling. Joe pointed out that the two players had also complained of being away from their families too often. I was taken aback to hear this.

'I don't keep them away from home deliberately,' I informed Joe. 'If we are successful we have to travel, often abroad. It's part and parcel of the job. If they don't like it they should get a nine-to-five job in an office, or find a club that isn't in contention for trophies. If you're going to give in to every demand from players, I might as well leave here.'

Joe Mears, as I have said, was a very objective and fair-minded man. He told me that I was right, and apologised for interfering. What a man. For a chairman to admit he was wrong was very rare. Joe was rarely wrong on any matter, but he obviously realised the error of his ways on this occasion. The offers were retracted, which I believed to be the right course of action for Joe to take. I dare say both players were unhappy about it, but they were a long way from the bread queue on their wages, I can assure you.

Peter Bonetti and Bobby Tambling both remained at Chelsea. Peter stayed at the club until 1979 before ending his playing career with a spell in the NASL for St Louis Stars. In twenty years at Chelsea Peter amassed 729 appearances and I guess you could count the number of poor games he had on the fingers of one hand. Bobby Tambling was also a great servant of the club. He went on to make 370 appearances for Chelsea before ending his career at Crystal Palace. His 202 goals for Chelsea remains a club record.

★

Our opening fixture of 1966–67 was a peach – away to West Ham United. Not only was this a London derby, it was the first opportunity to see England's triumphant World Cup trio of Bobby Moore, Geoff Hurst and Martin Peters in action since that glorious July day when Alf Ramsey's team had beaten West Germany. Moore, whose middle name, somewhat unbelievably, was Chelsea, had captained England in the World Cup, Hurst was the hat-trick hero of the final whilst Peters scored the other goal. Upton Park was full to capacity with 35,918 supporters bathed in glorious sunshine as England's World Cup heroes took the field to wild applause. The game also marked the league debut of Charlie Cooke.

It was not long before the Hammers fans were silent. John Hollins scored direct from a free-kick and we dominated the play for the remainder of the half without adding to our tally. The second half produced more fine flowing football. Ronnie Boyce put West Ham back on level terms but we were not going to be denied. At last the goal I expected came, in sensational fashion. Having beaten one West Ham player Charlie Cooke was then confronted with Bobby Moore. Cooke dropped a shoulder as if about to run wide but instead cut inside. While Moore struggled to adjust his weight from one leg to the other, Cooke cut inside and raced clear before driving the ball low and hard past keeper Jim Standen. The goal capped what had been a mesmerising league debut for Charlie. In no time at all he had become a favourite of the Chelsea fans.

We remained unbeaten in our opening ten league matches and beat Charlton 5–2 in the League Cup. In mid-September we travelled to Aston Villa where Bobby Tambling scored five in a 6–2 victory to in some way exorcise the demons that had beset us on that ground in two losing FA Cup semi-finals. We followed up by beating Arsenal 3–1, another two goals from Tambling, who was on the mark again in our next match, a 4–1 success at Manchester City. We had equalled the club record for the longest unbeaten sequence at the start of a season, were sitting pretty at the top of the league and had drawn Blackpool in the League Cup. In addition to this we were playing fluid, attacking football that opposing teams had real difficulty coping with. What could possibly go wrong?

The victory at Villa was George Graham's last game for Chelsea. George had been unsettled for some time and wanted away. As to why he wanted to leave a club that was flying high, I never did find out. Perhaps he didn't like my style of management. Whatever, I sold him to Arsenal for £50,000 and they threw in a young striker I had been watching for some months, Tommy Baldwin. I put Tommy straight into the team and he scored on his debut in our win at Manchester City.

During our League Cup tie against Blackpool at Bloomfield Road there was a crunching challenge from Emlyn Hughes on Peter Osgood who fell awkwardly and lay still on the ground. I knew straight away that he had broken his leg. It turned out to be a bad break that was to take quite some time in the healing.

The loss of Osgood, one of the most talented players in Britain, was a big blow. Peter had been invited for a trial at Arsenal but at that time didn't have enough confidence in his own ability to attend the trial. He had been associated with Chelsea as a boy but on leaving school went into the building trade with his father. He began playing amateur football with Spital Old Boys on a Saturday and Windsor Corinthians on a Sunday. His uncle, Bob Snashell, wrote me a letter reminding me of Peter's talent and asking if there was any chance of our having another look at him. After a practice match at Hendon we signed him as an amateur, and I subsequently offered him pro terms in 1964. He developed into a player with an abundance of skill, a good football brain, terrific vision and an eye for goal. He could drop a shoulder, jink, and be past opponents before they saw the trouble coming. His control of the ball, even on mudheap pitches, was immaculate, and he was naturally two-footed. It was almost impossible to mark Peter because he timed his runs from deep to perfection, and when he had the ball at his feet, had the capacity to screen it from opponents.

Peter, despite his fine career at Chelsea and Southampton, was perhaps never quite as good following his horrendous injury. That said, he would always be in my 'dream team'. We remained the best of friends. To the end of his life he always called me 'boss'.

With our exit from the Cup (Blackpool won the replay 3–1 at the Bridge) following the ending of our unbeaten run in the league, we needed new impetus. Having sold George Graham to Arsenal and with Peter Osgood sidelined, I set about signing a forward. The player I had in mind was Aston Villa's Tony Hateley (father of Mark), but I knew we would have to move quickly because Bill Shankly was also interested in him.

Our last game of the previous season had been at home to Aston Villa. It was mid-May and the pitch was so bone-hard that some of the players had taken to wearing lightweight boots with moulded rubber studs like training shoes. In this footwear Hateley had no problem controlling the ball. He did for us that night – it was mainly down to him that we lost 2–0. He was also nigh on unbeatable in the air and headed the ball with such power, you'd think he had a boot between his ears.

Another interested spectator at the match was Bill Shankly. At the end of the game Bill said to me, 'What about that Hateley, boy? He's the fellow for me, Tommy. Only problem is, persuading my board to come up with the money.' Villa valued him at around £100,000, a very large fee at that time and one that the Liverpool board would not agree to. Tony Hateley was still with Aston Villa the night Peter Osgood broke his leg at Blackpool, so I wasted no time in contacting the club.

Villa manager Dick Taylor confirmed Shankly had sounded him out about the availability of Hateley and that Matt Busby at Manchester United and Alan Brown from Sheffield Wednesday had also made enquiries. 'If you're really up for him, you'd better put a concrete offer in and soon,' advised Dick.

'Villa won't accept anything less than a hundred grand.' I knew I had to act quickly so I asked my board for permission to sign Tony Hateley for this huge fee. The board agreed.

I was well aware that many Chelsea fans of a certain age, and indeed Brian Mears, son of Joe, believed the signing of Tony Hateley was a waste of money. I wouldn't go that far, though I do admit he didn't turn out to be anywhere near as successful as I had hoped. I once said of Tony's passes they should have been labelled 'To whom it may concern'. As the saying goes, many a true word spoken in jest. Tony didn't score many goals for Chelsea, but some of them were important, goals that would help take us to the FA Cup final. The main problem was that Tony didn't really fit into the Chelsea style of playing. Our game relied a lot on running off the ball whereas Tony expected the rest of the team to, as he put it, 'lob the ball across to me in the middle'. We tried to compromise our approach to fit in with his style but it didn't work, although I had nothing but admiration for the way Tony applied himself to the task of making things happen for himself and the club on the pitch. When the time came to move him on the club didn't lose a penny. Tony was sold for the same fee for which he had been purchased – £100,000 – and the buyer? Bill Shankly at Liverpool.

Following our first defeat in the league against Burnley in mid-October we lost only once in ten matches before losing at home to Liverpool on Christmas Eve. Prior to that defeat there was a run of five consecutive draws, the most amazing of which took place at the Bridge before Christmas when a thrilling game against West Ham United ended 5–5. At one stage West Ham were leading 5–3 before we pulled them back. With the score at 5–5 and only a minute remaining, Charlie Cooke broke free of Bobby Moore and hit a ball at waist height across the penalty area. Hateley was on to it like a flash but instead of guiding the ball home with his foot, for reasons only known to him, he stooped and tried to head it into the net. He missed it completely, an absolute howler.

The fans that day had witnessed as open and fluid a game of purist football as you are ever likely to see. They had seen ten goals and fortunes swung throughout the game in dramatic fashion. A bumper crowd had provided healthy receipts. Yet all some Chelsea directors could go on about was the sitter that Hateley missed. If the game had been dull, drab and goalless up to the last minute and had Hateley scored the winner from Cooke's cross, would they have been happier? Hateley was being selected for special criticism. No one said anything about the fact our defence had conceded five goals at home, no one but me that is!

Inconsistency throughout the New Year cost us dear in the league. We finished the season in ninth place (16 points behind champions Manchester United), the lowest in my time as manager. If Peter Osgood had not missed the rest of the season I believe Chelsea would have won the title, as a lot of skill and momentum went out of the team, particularly in the forward line. To finish so far adrift was very disappointing, but whilst our league form in the New Year had been far from scintillating, our form in the FA Cup was the opposite.

We began our Cup campaign with a visit to Huddersfield Town, a tricky test as at the time they were lying fourth in Division Two and had lost only one match at Leeds Road. Their squad included two youngsters who went on to carve fine careers in the game, Trevor Cherry and Joe Harper. It proved to be a very tight but entertaining game. Huddersfield gave it a go and for a time the tie was finely balanced at 1–1, but once again Bobby Tambling produced yet another crucial goal to take us through to the next round.

In the fourth round we travelled the fifty or so miles to Brighton. A Goldstone Ground crowd of 35,446 witnessed yet another tight and pulsating Cup tie. Bobby Tambling scored a wonderful goal sprinting down the middle before unleashing a terrific shot from just outside the box that tore into the net. The goal rocked Brighton for a time, but we were reduced to ten men when John Boyle retaliated to a tackle in an unsavoury way. Having the extra man seemed to spur Brighton on. They threw men forward and after a period of concerted pressure from the home side, David Turner steered the ball into the net during a goalmouth scramble for the equaliser.

On the Thursday before the game I received a telephone call from club secretary John Battersby, informing me of a board meeting to discuss remarks I had made over the allocation of tickets for the Brighton match. Seemingly the board were annoyed I had spoken to the press about what they considered to be an internal club matter. Less than a week before the players had grumbled about the allocation of tickets for the Brighton match: they could have two tickets each and could also pay for up to ten ground tickets and ten tickets for the grandstand seats, evidently not enough for players like Marvin Hinton, John Hollins and Peter Bonetti who lived in and around the Brighton area.

Wanting to support my players I asked if the chairman or secretary could come and explain the circumstances in more detail and smooth the matter over. Mr Pratt told me that neither he nor the club secretary should have to come down and defend themselves to the players, and that the allocation had been agreed upon to prevent a flood of tickets 'ending up where they shouldn't'. I was livid. The inference was that the fact the players were having to pay for tickets had more to do with him and the board than it did Brighton Football club or the FA. That he used the word 'defend' suggested that he did, indeed, have something to defend.

'You think yourself clever don't you, Tommy?' said Mr Pratt.

'It's not a miserly allocation by any means,' I informed him, 'but asking the players to pay for all but two of their tickets is. By the way, will you and the board be paying for all the tickets you receive?'

Mr Pratt looked at me as if he'd trodden in something rather unpleasant in the street. I bade him 'good day' and that was that. Only it wasn't.

The players resented the implication that they wanted more tickets to sell to touts, and told me to tell the club that they refused the allocation, except for the two complimentary tickets per player. The press had got wind of this story, which in my mind amounted to little more than a storm in a teacup, and I was asked for my opinion. I gave it. I said I was totally behind my players and would hand back my own ticket allocation. I repeated my stance during a TV interview and in a newspaper article I penned. The board accepted the tickets back.

By then, it was a matter of principle. It was the first time in five years as manager of Chelsea that I had not been consulted on a matter involving my players. All I had asked was for Mr Pratt or John Battersby to see the players and explain their decision over the allocation. They refused. I felt a wall had gone up between myself and the board, a wall of their making. I was sure that had Joe Mears still been alive, none of this would have happened. Joe would have listened to what the players had to say. He would have come up with some solution, one that appeased both parties. I knew at the time that in the wider scheme of things it was a trivial matter. But trifling matters can decide the future of a manager.

The board were far from happy with me and my stance. On the day of the Brighton replay I attended the board meeting. Mr Pratt did most of the talking. Len Withey had his say, and then Viscount Chelsea spoke rather gravely about the rights and wrongs on both sides. John Battersby and Brian Mears said nothing.

I was issued with a reprimand and warned as to my future conduct. I was also reminded that it was not in keeping with my position to air personal views about internal club matters in the newspapers. But to my bewilderment, following the meeting, John Battersby held a press conference outlining details of my 'misdemeanour'. I felt humiliated by this and not a little miffed. Seemingly it was all right for the board to air their views about internal club matters to the media, but not me! That this all took place a few hours before the match was hardly helpful preparation for an important Cup tie.

But the lads put it all to one side as they played Brighton off the park, Bobby Tambling scoring twice and Hateley and reserve defender Alan Young also netting to give us a comfortable 4–0 victory. Even so, and despite my recent signing of a new five-year contract, as I drove home after the game I felt like handing in my resignation. Then I thought: 'Why should I? I've spent over five years building a team, why throw all that hard work away now because of a few tickets and a bust-up with the board?' I decided to soldier on.

That night I did something that was out of character. I told the whole story to Agnes whilst the children – who now numbered four, Peter having been born in 1964 – were tucked up in bed. Agnes was a good listener but I rarely talked football with her because I was a devoted family man and tried never to bring my problems home. That night, however, I talked matters over with her, and the more I did, the less I felt like walking out on Chelsea. When I had taken over as manager the club were still a bit of a music-hall joke; now we were one of the most respected names in football. Having done all the spade-work, I didn't fancy handing my team over to someone else.

My tetchy relationship with Mr Pratt continued unabated. On one occasion he called me into the boardroom to ask why I had not told him the team that was due to play in a five-a-side tournament at Wembley Arena. I was flabbergasted. Joe Mears had never asked to see the team sheet before a game, nor had the other directors, even though I knew Brian Mears had his own views on how I ran the team. Brian felt I discarded players too easily, those who I felt didn't fit into my system of play, and also that I enjoyed playing 'psychological war games' with people. He was entitled to his views but he kept them to within the confines of the boardroom, which was fine. He never interfered in team matters. Unlike Mr Pratt.

Sheffield United had the unenviable task of visiting the Bridge in the fifth round. United were pretty handy up front but we never gave them the opportunity to provide the ammunition for their forwards. Tony Hateley scored with a bullet header, and Bobby Tambling was also on the mark to ensure our safe passage. In the quarter-final we had the chance to avenge that painful semi-final defeat by Sheffield Wednesday of the previous season, though it was a close-run thing. We had most of the possession and pressure but the Wednesday keeper Ron Springett continually denied all our efforts to open the scoring. During the second half Bobby Tambling sustained an injury to his calf and I replaced him with Joe Kirkup. I asked Joe to play left-back and put Eddie McCreadie up front. With the game goalless at 90 minutes the referee allowed three minutes for the hold-up caused by the injury to Tambling. In this time added on, the ball was played to McCreadie on the left who made ground before driving the ball into the Wednesday penalty area. Up went Tony Hateley to nod the ball down into the path of Tommy Baldwin. Tommy's momentum didn't allow him to connect sweetly with the ball, but he stuck out a leg and the ball hit his shin. Springett had raced to his far post and spread his body in readiness to block a thunderbolt of a shot. As if in slow motion the ball dribbled off Baldwin's shin which deceived Springett completely. He was already committed and although he threw out a hand as he hit the ground, Tommy's 'shot' evaded him. Once past Springett the ball had only a yard to cross the line, but in that short distance it must have bounced three times as it bobbled apologetically into the net. The Bridge erupted. Springett, now on his knees, glanced back, then placing his hands on his hips looked up to the heavens in disbelief and dismay. Another semi-final beckoned.

Once again the venue was Villa Park, but this time our opponents were Leeds United. We had had some ding-dong battles with Leeds and there were to be more acrimonious meetings to come culminating in the most physically contested FA Cup final of all, in 1970. I knew Leeds would provide our stiffest challenge to date in the Cup, and that it would be a very tight game with few clear-cut chances. In such a situation a manager needs a player who can produce that little bit of magic, that something different to break the deadlock. His name was Charlie Cooke.

Ten minutes before half-time Cooke latched on to the ball just inside the Leeds half and set off with the terrier-like Billy Bremner snapping at his heels. Bremner had two or three lunges, but on each occasion Charlie evaded him and carried on with the ball bouncing on the toe of his boot. Bremner made one last effort to win the ball only for Charlie to dance away from him and float the ball into the Leeds penalty area. Tony Hateley soared into the air above Paul Madeley, and at first it looked as if Hateley had mistimed his jump. But it was as if some invisible hand had come down from heaven, grabbed the back of his shirt and held him suspended in mid-air. Hateley met the ball with the meat of his forehead and it lanced past Gary Sprake and into the net. The Holt End burst deafeningly into life with undulating humanity bedecked in blue and white.

In the second half we tried to keep possession of the ball as much as we could. Leeds could play wonderful football, if you allowed them. The second period was not for the football purist but from our point of view we had a job to do and did it. There was one heart-stopping moment a minute from time when Norman Hunter was bundled off the ball just outside our penalty area by John Hollins. Referee Ken Burns was in the process of ensuring our wall was ten yards back when Johnny Giles slipped the ball to Peter Lorimer too early. Lorimer let fly in characteristic style and the ball flew into the roof of the net. I slumped back into my seat in despair. Until, that is, I saw the referee was ordering the kick to be retaken. Lorimer couldn't possibly do it a second time. He didn't.

When the final whistle blew it was almost as if all the angst and frustration of the disappointment of previous semi-finals had suddenly been lifted from our fans. I could not contain myself and ran on the pitch to embrace the players as did Peter

Osgood who had been sitting with me on the bench. And so we were through to meet Tottenham Hotspur in the first ever all-London FA Cup final, which the press wasted no time in calling 'the Cockney Cup Final'.

In his autobiography, Jimmy Greaves said of the build-up to the final, 'Stories were getting back to me that all was not well in the Chelsea camp. There was disagreement over a bonus payment. Regarding the allocation of tickets, the Chelsea players believed they had received a miserly allocation from the club and once again voiced their dissatisfaction. When you hear stories like that coming out of your opponent's camp, there is only one thing a player can do. Believe them.'

He wasn't wrong.

The trials and tribulations that accompanied our build-up to the final began with the composition of the party for our close-season tour of the United States and Bermuda. Peter Osgood had not played since breaking his leg but his rehabilitation had been such that he was on course to start training in the summer with a view to being match fit for our opening game of the new season – which he was. I wanted Peter to accompany us on the tour, even if he didn't play. I felt he deserved some reward for the way he had applied himself during his rehab. The club doctor, Dr Paul Boyne, however, recommended that Peter stay at home and continue his treatment, which possibly he could not get while we were travelling overseas. The board agreed and refused to allow Peter to go. Unhappily the matter was made public, not by me I might add, and Peter didn't exactly help matters by airing his views to the press, comments for which he later apologised to the board.

Having put that little matter to bed, more problems arose. Ten days before the final the players asked for a meeting with me about a rumour that all they were likely to receive as a bonus for reaching the final was £50 per man, and twelve tickets each for the match – two complimentary and ten which they had to buy. I told the players there was little the club could do about the ticket allocation which had been imposed by the FA. Each club had been allocated a totally inadequate 25,000 tickets, and I reminded the players that many regular supporters would be unable to get a ticket. The FA needed the remaining 50,000 tickets to distribute to various bodies; it was generally believed that many of them ended up in the pockets of leading touts such as Stan Flashman and Johnny Goldstein.

I could have done without these niggling problems whilst preparing the team for the final, particularly as my emotions and thoughts were elsewhere. Agnes had a serious illness which culminated in her having to go into hospital for a major operation which, she told me calmly, would decide whether she would ever be able to walk again.

I could do nothing about the tickets but sought to clarify the £50 bonus payment. At a board meeting on the Thursday before the final, the directors announced that the players were to share a £12,000 bonus between the squad of nineteen should we win. Otherwise they would get £50 appearance money. As a financial incentive it went down like a parachute with a hole in it. I was cross that this had dragged on throughout our preparations, and had only been resolved two days prior to the final. Discontent was further fuelled with the news that Spurs players would receive a handsome bonus for having reached the final even if they lost, and, an even better bonus should they win.

It was such a shame. At last we had won our way through to Wembley, and it should have been the source of a great deal of joy and pleasure. Instead, we had mean-mindedness and bickering. I appealed to the players to set aside their gripes, to think of the supporters, the club, themselves and give it their all.

The press portrayed the finalists in very different terms. One newspaper compared the two teams to a film of the time, *The Cincinnati Kid*, in which Steve McQueen, a young, swaggering poker hustler battles for supremacy with an old, experienced hand, played by Edward G. Robinson.

We stayed at the Hendon Hall Hotel. I had no selection problems, and picked Joe Kirkup an substitute. Chelsea lined up as follows: Peter Bonetti; Allan Harris, Eddie McCreadie; John Hollins, Marvin Hinton, Ron Harris; Charlie Cooke, Tommy Baldwin, Tony Hateley, Bobby Tambling, John Boyle; substitute Joe Kirkup. The Spurs team presented to the Duke of Kent was: Pat Jennings; Joe Kinnear, Cyril Knowles; Alan Mullery, Mike England, Dave Mackay; Jimmy Robertson, Jimmy Greaves, Alan Gilzean, Terry Venables, Frank Saul; substitute: Cliff Jones. The referee, and a very good one too, was Ken Dagnall of Bolton, a very popular figure amongst players and managers alike, who had impressed everyone with his handling of two World Cup matches.

Dave Mackay and substitute Cliff Jones had been members of the great Double-winning Spurs team of 1960–61, and they, along with Jimmy Greaves, had also played in the team that had beaten Burnley in the 1962 final. Of the chosen twelve, only Joe Kinnear and Frank Saul had graduated from the youth squad. The remainder of the team had cost considerable fees for their day. True I had spent £100,000 on Tony Hateley and £70,000 on Charlie Cooke, but the rest of my team had come up through the ranks or had been purchased for nominal fees.

There was quite a family atmosphere about Chelsea. On the pitch, for only the third time in the history of the FA Cup, were brothers – Allan and Ron Harris. On the bench were trainers Harry Medhurst and his son Norman, and next to me was my ten-year-old son Tommy. And I knew that, watching from her bed in St Mary's Hospital in Paddington, Agnes would be very proud to see young Tommy take his place next to me.

This final was the last to be broadcast in black and white. This required both teams to use a variation of their normal kit, for purposes of identification for viewers at home. We wore an all-blue strip, while Spurs opted for all-white.

I assigned Ron Harris to mark Jimmy Greaves and he did a very good job of it. The aerial threat of Mike England at corners and dead-ball situations was countered by Tony Hateley coming back to pick him up. In the event they were to cancel each other out at both ends of the field. John Hollins managed to close down Terry Venables for long periods of the game. Assigned to mark Alan Gilzean, Marvin Hinton stuck to his task manfully, but it was the wily Spurs striker who won that contest.

I had anticipated Charlie Cooke causing Spurs all manner of problems. That he didn't had much to do with Alan Mullery and Dave Mackay, who ran their legs off to snuff out the service to Cooke. It was a good tactic on the part of Bill Nicholson. Presumably Bill knew Charlie had the beating of any defender. Rather than have his players converge on Charlie and create gaps behind them, Bill opted for preventing our players playing the ball to him. Starved of the ball for long periods of the game Charlie's sublime talent withered on the vine.

Spurs edged things in the first half and took the lead before the break. Mullery fired in a shot which rebounded off the legs of Ron Harris. The ball fell kindly at the feet of Jimmy Robertson and he made no mistake from a point just beyond the six-yard box. During the interval I was still confident we could go on and win, but we were never allowed to play to our potential in the second period. To my acute disappointment Spurs' second goal came at the end of a good spell of pressure from us. Having broken down one of our attacks the ball went out for a Spurs throw-in. Dave Mackay's long throw floated deep into our penalty area, Robertson flicked it on and Frank Saul turned to lash the ball past Bonetti. My heart sank.

I got up from the bench and urged the boys to greater effort and to push forward. To their credit they did, though Spurs repelled our every attack. Four minutes from time we were handed a lifeline. Pat Jennings was always struggling to collect a swerving cross from John Boyle and when he only managed to fingertip the ball away, there was Bobby Tambling lurking with intent at the far post to head home.

We poured forward and Spurs were now struggling to contain

us. Their older legs were tiring, not so ours. It was all to no avail though as once more experience triumphed over youth. The Cup belonged to Spurs.

The post-match banquet was a great night for Spurs but very low-key for the Chelsea party. Often finalists staged their own post-match banquets but on this occasion both parties dined together at the same venue where I offered my congratulations to Bill Nicholson and his team. The speeches droned on. I was not on the official list of speakers but grabbed the microphone following Mr Pratt's speech in which he went on and on about Chelsea players of the past without ever referring to, let alone thanking, the current team who had taken us to Wembley. At one point during my brief words I said, 'I was beginning to think that the people responsible for this club getting to Wembley – the players – were not going to get any mention at all. So a big thank you lads, you've been terrific.'

And they had been. I knew my words would not have pleased Mr Pratt, but by this stage I couldn't care less what the board thought of me. If it hadn't been for me the players wouldn't even have been present at the banquet. They were so incensed with the attitude of the board over the matter of the bonus, they had voted to boycott the night. However, I managed to make them see reason and the folly of such a decision.

Two weeks later, we embarked upon our tour of the USA and Bermuda and it was whilst abroad that I was to fall foul of not only the board yet again, but also the Football Association. We were playing a Bermudian side and winning 7–0 with about three minutes to go. There was a local referee in charge of the match who wasn't doing a particularly good job of it. Suddenly he took exception to something Tony Hateley and Barry Lloyd had done or said and sent off the pair of them. Neither player was hotheaded, and they obviously thought they had done nothing untoward because they refused to leave the pitch. I walked towards the touchline and was just about to persuade both of them to go when, seeing this, the referee rounded on me and said tersely: 'Get off the pitch, white man.'

I said, 'What's that?' Which prompted him to reiterate what he'd said to me in the first place.

I should have kept my calm, I know that. Instead I said the first thing that came into my head which was derogatory and politically incorrect. The comment I made referred to him and trees, but contrary to what some reports said, there was no swearing on my part, nor had I referred in any way to the colour of the man's skin. The referee said, 'I'll report you for what you just said.' 'As you wish,' I replied. I spoke to an official of our host club and apologised for what I had said. I told him I regretted the remark and it had been purely an impulsive re-action to being referred to as 'white man'. The official told me not to worry, that neither he, nor anybody else at the club had taken offence and hoped I felt the same about the remark the referee had made to me.

The referee filed his report to the Bermudian FA who, in turn, passed it on to the Football Association. The FA conducted a meeting, I can't refer to it as a hearing because I wasn't invited to attend and give my side of the story. This was early October 1967, and the announcement came like a bombshell to me and Chelsea. I was suspended for a month for having made 'ungentlemanly remarks to an official'. Apparently the FA had taken into consideration other complaining remarks I had made about match officials during the tour and also the fact I had received a £100 fine for making, again, according to them, 'ungentlemanly remarks to officials' following a youth team match at QPR nine months previously. I had complained about match officials on the tour simply because the standard of much of the refereeing was poor. What do you do, just accept sub-standard refereeing?

I didn't mind having a reputation for being outspoken or opinionated, but I had gained what I thought was an undeserved reputation as a troublemaker. And though my number two, the former Blackpool boss, Ron Suart, could look after things for the month of my ban, my relationship with the board, in particular Mr Pratt, had deteriorated to such an extent that we had some serious talking to do.

Early results in 1967–68 were fair, and happily Peter Osgood was back in the team. But before long we crashed 5–1 at Newcastle and 6–2 at home to Southampton and after a run of draws and defeats slipped into the bottom half of the table. It was clear the board wanted me out, and I too wanted out. When they convened an emergency board meeting, the writing was on the wall.

When I walked into the boardroom Mr Pratt asked me to sit down. 'We just can't go on like this, Tom,' he said in a serious tone.

'Mr Chairman, gentlemen, will you excuse me one moment,' I said. I got up and left the room, collected some bottles of champagne I had left in the corridor and returned with them to the boardroom.

'I knew what was going to happen. Say no more Mr Pratt, have a drink!' and I poured him and his fellow directors glasses of champagne. Chelsea finis!

The board didn't sack me, I quit.

12

PICKFORD'S FAVOURITE CUSTOMER

I had no idea what lay around the corner, all I knew was that I wanted to continue my career as a manager. Only a few days after the news of my departure from Chelsea, I received a telephone call from Greece. The voice on the other end of the line told me his name was John Pateras and that he was the president of Panathinaikos. John informed me he would like me to become the manager of his club and, as he had business interests in London, perhaps we could meet to discuss the situation. I had never considered going abroad to manage but agreed to meet John in a London hotel.

The meeting went very well, I warmed to John and his ideas for the club. I pointed out that I was still serving a suspension imposed by the FA, but that didn't seem to matter to him.

'That's OK, if you want to come, join us as soon as your suspension is over,' he said. He offered me £10,000 a year, plus a villa and car. I said I wanted to discuss the matter with Agnes and he invited us both over to Athens so that he could show us around. Happily Agnes had made a good recovery from her operation. I thought the trip to Greece would do her good and, after everything that had gone on, I felt in need of a holiday too.

'Just one thing,' said John. 'The chairman, Mr Karavitis, a small, rotund man with a beard, wonderful man, but very proud, fiercely Greek. He needs reassuring that whoever we appoint is not coming just for the money. Tell him you are delighted to be in Greece, that it has always been an ambition of yours to manage Panathinaikos.'

In the days that preceded the trip to Greece, I received three more enquiries for my services. The first was Karl Rodyn, the president of the Sydney club Hakoah. I had visited Australia on tour with Chelsea, and seemingly I had made an impression. The thought of managing in Australia with its different culture and lifestyle was not unappealing, but the more I thought about the offer from Hakoah the more I knew I would have to turn it down. Uprooting the family just wasn't an option at that stage.

The second enquiry came from Peterborough United who had just parted company with their manager Gordon Clark. Soon there was much press speculation as to whether I would leave London for London Road. I never got as far as a meeting with the Peterborough board. I had heard that some directors wanted to appoint from within, and sure enough, a few days after receiving the initial call, Peterborough announced their new manager was to be Norman Rigby, their former centre-half.

One call I received that I was definitely interested in taking further came from Jimmy Hill. He had managed Coventry City for six years and in that time had taken the club from the Third Division to the First. Jimmy had transformed the club from top to bottom, introducing all manner of innovations that left the majority of clubs looking as if they were still trapped in the 1950s. Coventry had been promoted to the top flight the previous season but Jimmy was about to leave the club to pursue a career in television. The thought of managing such an innovative club that was riding high appealed to me. I told Jimmy I was very interested in taking the matter further so he arranged a meeting with the Coventry chairman Derrick Robins.

On the Tuesday night prior to the meeting I was watching the news on television when it was announced that Coventry City had appointed the former Manchester United skipper Noel Cantwell as their new manager. Needless to say I was a little taken aback. A minute later Agnes came into the room.

'So, what do you think your chances are of becoming manager at Coventry then?' she asked.

'Not very good,' I informed her.

A few days later Agnes and I flew out to Athens as arranged, and I found myself saying to a small, rotund man with a beard that I was delighted to be in Greece, and it had always been an ambition of mine to manage Panathinaikos.

Agnes and I were both very impressed, me with the club, Agnes with Athens. I learned Panathinaikos had won the Greek league in five of the previous six seasons. In 1966 they were runners-up and were currently third in the table. John Pateras was very keen that the club should once again rise above their closest rivals Olympiakos and AEK Athens and promised I would have a good budget to spend on players to make sure that happened. I was shown around their stadium which was tidy but not the largest with a capacity of around 30,000.

Having seen the set-up, Agnes and I went sightseeing. We were staying in a stunning villa owned by the club which would be one of our options for a home should I accept the job. 'It's beautiful isn't it?' said Agnes.

'It is,' I agreed. 'But I want to work in England.'

'It might not be so bad. Living and working here, I mean,' she suggested.

'No, things could be worse,' I said. 'I could be manager of Rotherham United . . .'

Two days later we were back home when I answered the telephone to hear Jimmy Hill on the other end of the line. 'Don't tell me they've sacked Cantwell already,' I said.

'No, no, nothing like that,' said Jimmy. He told me he felt bad about the fact Derrick Robins had not kept the meeting with me. Seemingly Matt Busby, not knowing I was being considered for the vacancy at Coventry, had contacted Derrick to recommend Noel Cantwell. 'If Matt had known you were up for the job . . . well, he didn't,' he added.

Jimmy went on to say that Rotherham United had parted

company with Jack Mansell and were keen to appoint me as their new manager. He went on to explain he was sounding me out because the Rotherham chairman Eric Purshouse was a little shy about making the initial approach.

'A chairman who is shy? I'm interested,' I told him, and I was. The following day I drove up to Rotherham to meet Mr Purshouse and his son Lewis. I liked them straight away. They came across as friendly, warm and genial people who had the best interests of their club at heart.

'I don't know much about football,' Eric Purshouse told me. 'In fact I'm not fanatical about football at all. But I do know how important this football club is to the town. I became chairman not for me you understand, but for Rotherham folk.'

It was November, Rotherham were struggling at the foot of Division Two and looked to have a long hard season ahead of them.

'We're ambitious,' Mr Purshouse told me.

'Good,' I said. 'I'll take Rotherham out of Division Two.'

I did. I took them into Division Three.

Mr Purshouse and his son gave me a tour of Millmoor. Mr Purshouse told me that if I agreed to be their manager I would have complete control of the playing side of things and could make any changes around the ground I thought fit. At that point we turned a corner at the back of the main stand and I spotted an old dilapidated wooden hut.

'Well, that eyesore will have to go for a start,' I said.

'That's your office,' he informed me.

Chelsea to Rotherham United seemed a curious move to many people, and I suppose it was. It has often been said to me, 'Why didn't you bide your time? With your record at Chelsea a First Division club would have come in for you.' That may well have been the case, in time. But I am notoriously impulsive. I will often make a snap decision and hope for the best. Also I hated being out of work. At the time Rotherham was the only job that was available, they wanted me – snap decision. Not that I have ever regretted it, mind you.

To show my commitment to the club, the job and the area, we moved from London and bought a house in Whiston, not far from Rotherham, and only an hour or so by car from Burnley, where my son Michael had recently signed professional forms. Agnes and our three-year-old son Peter went along to see Michael sign the forms and the moment was captured by both local and national press. Burnley had an excellent youth policy and a reputation for giving youngsters their chance in the first team. I knew Michael would be in good hands and I was delighted. I admired the work of the manager Harry Potts, who was a good friend, as was the Burnley skipper and coach Jimmy Adamson.

It was still the first half of the season and was perhaps a little premature for Rotherham to be involved in a relegation struggle, but after assessing the playing staff, I knew that was what lay ahead. The Rotherham players saw their big games as being against the likes of Aston Villa, Ipswich Town, QPR, Birmingham City and Blackpool, teams at the top of the division who drew healthy attendances. The truth was very different, however. The chances of gaining points at the expense of Ipswich or QPR were not good. But if Rotherham were to survive, it was essential we gained points at the expense of the other teams like Plymouth, Bristol City, Derby or Preston who I expected to be near the bottom – teams I felt we were capable of beating.

On 25 November 1967 I took my seat in the dugout at Millwall for my first game as manager of Rotherham United. I was escorted to the dugout by about 25 cameramen, and received a warm-hearted standing ovation from the Millwall supporters which for me was very moving. We earned a point the hard way by defending for most of the game. There was one close call when a corner from Millwall's Eamonn Dunphy (the future author and broadcaster) was headed past Alan Hill our goalkeeper by our own defender Harold Wilcockson, but team-mate Andy Burgin flung himself full-length to head off the line. I was happy with a point in my first game in charge and away from home too.

True to form I pitched a youngster into the lion's den. Neil Hague was only 18 and was making his debut for Rotherham but he did a fine job in shackling Dunphy. The post-match press conference lasted over half an hour as so many reporters were present. Rotherham United hadn't buzzed like this for months.

The players were a good bunch who didn't see themselves as big-timers, and everyone at the club, from the chairman down, was friendly, honest and easy to deal with. I quickly decided that a lot of pruning had to be done. Poor players get managers the sack, and Rotherham had a few.

Some decisions, I knew, would be hard to take and unpopular with some, but I pressed ahead as I had to act in the best interests of the club. Just as I had done at Chelsea I had a clear-out and brought in some young players. On my arrival the first-team squad consisted of 29 full-time pros but within a few weeks I had cut this to 20. I made both the club physiotherapist Bernard Grimmer and the groundsman Eric Scott redundant. Both had been with Rotherham for a number of years and I was sorry but it had to be done – their output and workload could not justify full-time salaries. In addition to coaching the players I was also taking them for the majority of the training sessions, so I made the head trainer, Albert Wilson, an assistant trainer but also gave him the responsibility of being groundsman and physio.

The squad were a great group of lads. Alan Hill was a capable goalkeeper but I released his deputy and promoted the club's junior goalkeeper Roy Tunks into the reserves as cover for Hill. I was happy with the captain Brian Tiler, but I cleared out many senior pros and replaced them with juniors and a few signings. Come the end of the season, of the 22 full-time pros on the books, 17 were products of the youth team. I dismantled the team and rebuilt it in such a short space of time the Sheffield 'Green Un' described me as 'the friendly hurricane'.

As always, I got myself out and about watching games at all levels in the hope of unearthing a gem – and I did. I had gone to watch a Football Combination Division Two game at Meadow Lane. After only 15 minutes I knew I had to sign the Notts County centre-half Dave Watson. After the game I spoke to the County manager Billy Gray who told me the lad could also play at centre-forward. I couldn't understand why the boy was playing in Notts County reserves and offered him guaranteed first-team football at Rotherham. I paid £5,000 for Dave Watson, who went on to win 65 caps for England. Rotherham later sold him on to Sunderland where he was a key member of the team that won the FA Cup in 1973. By that stage his value had increased to £275,000 when he was bought by Manchester City.

As an extra incentive to avoid relegation I met with the board who agreed to my idea of paying the players an extra £25 for every point we gained, which I thought was good money at the time without being outrageous. The board was a small one, but they supported me in everything I did. One of the older members, Mr Ferguson, a lovely gentleman who would do anything for Rotherham United, was once asked by a reporter from the *Sheffield Star* for his opinion of me which he duly gave.

'But he's not very tactful is he?' said the reporter referring to the way I had dispensed with so many players and staff.

'Some people are tactful,' said Mr Ferguson. 'Others, like Tommy, just tell the truth.'

The £25 bonus per point obviously worried Eric Purshouse at times. During one game at Millmoor, Neil Hague played a great through-ball that split the opposition defence. Jim Storrie was on to it like a flash and raced clear on goal, only for Mr Purshouse to jump to his feet and shout, 'Offside! C'mon ref – he's got to be offside!'

It has often been said that I spent a lot of money at Rotherham, but that isn't true. My total outlay on transfer fees was £43,000, but I netted the club £54,000 from the sales of players, the best fee received being £25,000 from the sale of centre-forward John Galley to Bristol City. The club also made a healthy £29,000 profit from a run in the FA Cup that saw us beat Wolves 1–0 at Millmoor, Aston Villa by the same score at Villa Park before losing 2–0 at Leicester City in a replay. There was a healthy increase in gate receipts with the average home attendance up 3,000 compared to the period before I joined the club. Added to which has to be the £95,000 profit the club made when they later sold Dave Watson.

Following the changes I had implemented the team became harder to beat, but not unbeatable. With eleven matches remaining we were still embroiled in a fight to avoid the drop. A glimmer of light appeared when we beat Huddersfield Town 1–0 at home and followed this with a fine 2–0 win at Bolton and a 1–0 win at Bristol City. But we won only two of the remaining eight matches. Rotherham finished the season second bottom on 31 points, four adrift of safety, and with Plymouth Argyle we were relegated.

I was very disappointed not to have guided Rotherham to safety but Mr Purshouse and his board were very philosophical about it. 'You had an uphill task from the start,' he told me. 'The club was in a bad way but at least we are on a better footing, finance wise.' In recognition of this, the board paid for the team to go on a holiday to Spain to thank them for their efforts since my arrival at the club. I believed they were in a good enough financial state to achieve promotion at the first time of asking – only I wasn't going to be there long enough to see my plans come to fruition.

The 1968–69 season created a little bit of football history before a ball had been kicked. It began on 10 August, the earliest ever start to a new season. The only additions I had made to the squad during the summer were my former Scotland team-mate, Graham Leggat and former Arsenal and Liverpool goalkeeper Jim Furnell. Jim had come into professional football a very odd way. In 1954 young Jim Furnell was unemployed. He went along to his local Labour Exchange in Burnley and when asked what line of work he was pursuing told the clerk, 'Football, I'm a goalkeeper.' Jim never expected anything to come of that throw-away comment, but the dole office subsequently fixed him up with a trial for Burnley who were so impressed they offered him professional terms.

Rotherham began life in Division Three as if we had no intention of staying there any longer than necessary. After an opening 3–3 draw at Orient we went on to lose only one of our next ten matches. By early November, Rotherham were handily placed in sixth position.

I had no intentions of leaving Rotherham United, though I did miss the big match atmosphere. In the Third Division the biggest crowd we played in front of was 10,164 in September when we drew 2–2 at Brighton. Even accepting the lack of high-profile matches, I was thoroughly enjoying the experience at the club. I had a great bunch of players who gave it their all and gave me no trouble. The board were supportive in everything I did and were lovely people, and I had a great relationship with the supporters and the local media. I remember being at a supporters' club fund-raiser, chatting to the fans about our last game against Gillingham and our forthcoming match against Bristol Rovers. Suddenly I realised how much I was missing the First Division, and pitting my wits against the best managers and players in the game. I felt that if I was to become a better manager and derive greater job satisfaction, I had to be challenging my managerial skills against the very best. Curiously, I was also missing the daily cut and thrust with the national press. That night as I drove home something was gnawing away inside me, I just knew I had to get back into the First Division, little knowing that in just over a week such an opportunity would be coming my way.

My final match in charge of Rotherham United saw us involved in a goalless draw at Walsall. As we travelled back from Fellows Park, if anyone had told me the following Saturday I would be preparing Queens Park Rangers for a First Division match against Burnley I'd have thought they had taken leave of their senses. It was about this time that the press came up with the phrase 'managerial merry-go-round' and not without good reason. Hold on tight. The following occurred within the space of a few months in the autumn of 1968, all of which was to have a bearing, at some time or another, on me.

Alec Stock, who had guided Queens Park Rangers from the Third Division to the First and won the League Cup in 1968, puts in a bid for Fulham's Johnny Haynes. Haynes decides to stay at Fulham (that's relevant, don't worry). Bobby Robson is sacked as manager of Fulham. Ronnie Allen resigns as manager of Wolverhampton Wanderers. One national newspaper reports I am in line for the vacant Wolves job, I tell the press I've had no contact with the club, which is true. A few days later Bill McGarry is appointed manager of Wolves. Bill Ridding leaves Bolton Wanderers after eighteen years as their manager. The *Daily Express* reports Bolton are on the verge of offering me the vacant manager's job, I tell the newspapers I've had no contact with the club whatsoever. Again, true.

Bobby Charlton signs an eight-year contract with Manchester United, the longest contract ever to be agreed with a player. Manchester United also pay £100,000 to Burnley for Willie Morgan. Aston Villa bid for their former centre-forward Tony Hateley, but Hateley chooses to leave Liverpool for Coventry City; the fee is £80,000 and Hateley becomes the first British footballer to command combined transfer fees in excess of £300,000. The Aston Villa directors come in for increasing criticism from Villa fans who feel they do not have the financial wherewithal to take the club forward.

On 4 November Alec Stock is sacked as manager of QPR after a poor start to the season in Division One. Johnny Haynes is appointed 'probationary' manager of Fulham. On 5 November, having read I was linked to the jobs at Wolves and Bolton, QPR chairman Jim Gregory approaches the Rotherham board asking for permission to speak to me. It is granted. On 6 November I become manager of QPR; Stock's former number two, Bill Dodgin, is confirmed as my number two. My former Scotland team-mate Allan Brown resigns as manager of Luton Town, replaced by Alec Stock. On 10 November Bill Dodgin leaves to become assistant to Johnny Haynes at Fulham. On 5 December I resign as manager of QPR after only 28 days in charge. On 12 December, the Aston Villa board, who tried to sign Hateley, resign en bloc and agree to sell their shares to a company called Birmingham Industrial Trust. On 15 December members of Birmingham Industrial Trust approach me about becoming the new manager of Aston Villa. On 18 December I am the new manager of Aston Villa . . .

All these years on just recording the events of those few weeks is tiring. Believe me, at the time it was as if a hurricane was propelling the merry-go-round. At this juncture in my story you might be wondering about the significance of Bobby Charlton's contract and United's signing of Willie Morgan. Patience – this will become apparent later.

It wasn't the lure of London or the salary increase that induced me to return to the capital after only thirteen months in Yorkshire. When Mr Purshouse informed me of QPR's enquiry I found I couldn't resist the challenge of a move back to a struggling First Division club to try and resurrect it – something I seemed to do all my working life. The offer was made and I accepted in the course of the same phone call.

Looking back I should have given considered thought to the QPR job. Alec Stock had taken what had been a mediocre Third Division club to the First Division and won the League Cup at Wembley. When, after four months, QPR had not set the First Division on fire it was Alec who had come in for fire from Jim Gregory. How could I have not read the signs?

Alec Stock was a good manager though, to me, he never looked like a football man. When managers as prim as Quakers gave way in the late 1950s to the Walter Winterbottom-inspired tracksuit manager. Alec Stock remained untouched. Beneath tweed jacket or light sports coat he'd wear a crisp white shirt, with open collar and cravat. In light cavalry twill trousers and brown brogues polished like glass, Alec resembled the director of the local amateur dramatic society more than a worldly-wise football manager. It was fitting, because somehow the words he spoke, the ideas he nurtured about football were often theatrical. He once told me, 'Most managers would enjoy relative success, if they were not troubled by the great ambitions of their directors.' On the subject of football in general he once said, 'In football, like life, from the sublime to the ridiculous is often just one step.'

With the odd exception – at QPR it was Rodney Marsh – Alec's teams did not boast big-name players, yet he always created teams which played attractive, entertaining football. It was his ability to mould and shape a squad of players who were not individually outstanding into an attractive, capable team that made Alec the manager he was. A team is a reflection of its boss and Alec's were honest, stylish, entertaining and, in the football sense, cosmopolitan. That Jim Gregory had so quickly dispensed with the services of a manager who had picked QPR up by the bootlaces should have served as a warning to me. But so keen was I to return to the First Division, it never did.

Initially everything seemed to be good about my move to QPR. Jim Gregory came across as being amiable, enthusiastic and very ambitious for the club. A very ambitious chairman – perhaps that should have been a warning. Jim Gregory was the very antithesis of Eric Purshouse as a club chairman. Jim was the sort of person who when he said, 'I'll think it over and let you know' – you knew. He had various business interests in London in, I believe, transport and cars and was successful in his dealings. In very little time, however, he struck me as the sort of person I wouldn't like to have business dealings with. I found Jim arrogant to the point that he appeared to have no interest in any ideas about the team and club but his own. I couldn't help but wonder how, during the good times at the club, he and Alec Stock had got on. They seemed a very unlikely pairing.

Bill Dodgin had worked with Alec Stock but left the club two days after my appointment to join Fulham. Remember the 'managerial merry-go-round'? Alec had put in a bid for Johnny Haynes, only for Haynes to turn down the move to QPR. The word was Haynes had chosen to stay at Fulham as he'd been tipped off that Bobby Robson was about to be sacked and he would be offered the job as his first managerial appointment. Johnny seemingly felt he needed a more experienced hand to guide him, hence the recruitment of Bill Dodgin.

When I took over at QPR they were rooted to the bottom of Division One and were destined to stay there, not only for the duration of my 28 days at the club, but also until the end of the season when, under the charge of Les Allen, Rangers were relegated with a meagre total of 18 points. I was reunited with Ian Watson and Barry Bridges, the latter who had joined Rangers from Birmingham City, to whom I had sold him in my days at Chelsea. The Rangers squad also included Rodney Marsh, Les Allen, Bobby Keetch, Tony Hazell, Dave Clement, the Morgan twins Ian and Roger, Frank Sibley and the ex-Sheffield Wednesday and England goalkeeper Ron Springett, who was vying for the number one jersey with Mike Kelly.

It took me no time at all to see that that squad was overloaded with too many older players. Over half of them were thirty plus, so the metaphorical pruning shears were about to be taken down and oiled once again and young legs called for. In the event my stint there was to last just three matches: Burnley at home, lost 2–0; Everton away, lost 4–0; Nottingham Forest at home, won 2–1. The victory over Nottingham Forest was, in fact, a very spirited performance.

In addition to being keen to give promising youngsters an opportunity to show what they could do, youngsters such as fullback Ian Gillard who would later go on to play for England, I had also made a list of players I wanted to sign, top of which was Brian Tiler, my-skipper at Rotherham. As the days passed

I became increasingly frustrated in my attempts to see Jim Gregory to discuss bringing new players to the club. I don't know how many times I rang requesting a meeting, but he never returned my calls. I simply imagined he was so busy with his various business interests that he couldn't find the time to meet. I kept on ringing him, hoping to discuss over the telephone the matter of new players as Jim had, after all, secured my services over the phone. All to no avail. After almost four weeks of this I happened to speak to Dennis Signy who, at the time, was involved with the League Managers Association. He intimated that Jim Gregory wielded absolute power at the club and was the type of chairman who, if you wanted a player and he agreed, you would get him. But if he didn't agree, there was no way on earth the player would come to QPR. I told Dennis I could never get hold of him. Dennis told me he believed Jim Gregory was at a health farm in Tring, and suggested I find the number and try him there. I gave it a go and succeeded.

'Mr Chairman, Tommy Docherty, remember me? Your manager at Queens Park Rangers,' was my opening gambit.

'Tommy, what is it?'

'Mr Chairman, I would like to buy Brian Tiler from Rotherham United. Super young player, will do us a great job,' I informed him.

''ow much?'

'A hundred thousand.'

'I don't agree. Now I'm busy, get back to the players you've got.'

'Mr Chairman, it isn't going to work between us. I'm leaving.'

And I did. It turned out to be the shortest managerial reign of my much-travelled career. When the club announced my departure the press had a field day. Not privy to my frustrated attempts to sign new players, the newspapers understandably portrayed my departure from QPR after only 28 days as another chapter in what was increasingly being seen as my 'tempestuous' career as a manager. I returned to our home in Whiston, livid with how I was being portrayed in some quarters of the press, and pondered on what I should do next.

I did not have long to contemplate the future. Within two days of having resigned I received a telephone call from a pal of mine, George Sturrock. He and his son Richard had contacts in Spain. George told me that Atletico Bilbao were looking for a new coach and their president was keen on speaking to me. I duly did so and the following day he flew over to London to meet me. Things were looking up.

The meeting took place in the Royal Lancaster Hotel and it went well. Atletico were mid-table at the time, but in the eyes of their president this was not good enough (they later went on to win the Spanish Cup that season). He told me he believed I was the man who could put his club back at the forefront of Spanish football. The idea of managing a leading Spanish club appealed to me. When I had been offered the opportunity of managing Panathinaikos, I turned it down because I wanted to manage in England. Now, with the sour taste of my brief stint at Queens Park Rangers still with me, I thought a spell managing in Spain might prove the making of me. We verbally agreed a deal and our meeting ended with him saying he would have contracts drawn up. Only a day later I received a telephone call relaying tragic news. The Bilbao president had been killed in a car crash. I never heard from the club again.

While I was debating my next move I received another telephone call from another old friend. The caller in question was Charles Tagwright, an avid Chelsea supporter. Charles, his wife, Helen and their sons David and John were great friends of Joe Mears, my old Chelsea chairman. Charles asked if I had ever heard of a business consortium called Birmingham Industrial Trust, which at the time I hadn't. Charles went on to say that BIT were on the point of a successful take-over at Aston Villa and that a guy called Pat Matthews, 'a high-flyer at the First National Bank', wanted to meet me. Although they were struggling near the foot of Division Two, Villa were

a club with a rich history and tradition, not to mention potential, and they interested me greatly, so I agreed to meet Mr
Matthews.

Pat Matthews looked every inch the successful financial man
he was, immaculately dressed in dapper pinstripe suit, white shirt
as crisp as a new banknote, dark hair grey at the temples.
Matthews surprised me with the nature of his opening question,
asking me what I knew about Aston Villa's playing staff. I listed
the players, beginning with goalkeepers John Dunn and Colin
Withers and proceeded to run through the squad which included
Charlie Aitken, Mick Wright, Len Chatterley, Alan Deakin, Willie
Anderson, Peter Broadbent, Mike Ferguson, Brian Godfrey,
Brian Greenhalgh, Tommy Mitchinson and Barrie Hole. In so
doing I offered a personal appraisal of the ability and character
of each player in turn. When I had finished I could see he was
impressed.

'For a chap who hasn't even been there, you seem to know
a hell of a lot about them,' he said.

'It's a manager's business to know players,' I told him.

'Do you think the team can avoid relegation this season?' he
asked.

'With one or two new faces, yes,' I told him.

'Should you become manager, would the current squad be
good enough to win promotion?'

'No.'

'How do you find your relationship with players differs when
you're not in a manager's job?'

'I don't win so many games of golf.'

'Do you know anything about high finance and company
take-overs, Tommy?'

'No.'

'Do you know when the best time is to buy anything?'

'In my experience, usually last year.'

'What would you be looking for in the way of a contract?'

'A three-year deal.'

'And salary?'

'The terms of the job are more important to me than the money,' I told him in all honesty.

'How does eleven thousand a year, plus bonuses and a car sound?'

'Good to me.'

'Have you heard of a chap called Doug Ellis?'

'Yes, he's a director of Birmingham City.'

'I think the pair of you should meet,' he suggested.

There was obviously a close link-up between Pat Matthews and Doug Ellis because Doug and I met the very next day. Even at this early stage of proceedings, there was a little tension to our conversation.

'Pat has told me you want to manage Aston Villa,' ventured Doug.

'Yes, but I didn't ask. He asked me, Doug,' I pointed out.

'"Mr Chairman", if you don't mind,' said Doug.

'You're not the chairman yet,' I reminded him.

'Well, true,' agreed Doug. 'Now Pat tells me you want eleven thousand a year. There is no way the club can afford that.'

'How do you know? As I said, you're not the chairman yet,' I reiterated. Doug smiled and there was warmth in his smile, about half a firefly's worth. That initial salvo over, we agreed on the deal.

'I think we will get on very well together, Tommy,' he said.

'I hope so, Doug,' I told him.

The take-over went through. Doug Ellis became chairman and he was joined by Harry Kartz, a super guy who could see the importance of developing long-term plans, such as a youth policy. They in turn were joined by Harry Parkes, a former Villa full-back, with whom I was to enjoy a working relationship as companionable as that of a cat and canary.

Before I relate events at Villa as I saw them, let me tell you I have remained good friends with Doug Ellis to this day. Like him or dislike him, Doug has always had the best interests of

Aston Villa at heart. To me he is and always has been a good guy. We often don't see eye to eye – who does with Doug? He's also such a contrary guy. During my time at Villa Park Doug and I had numerous run-ins, much verbal sparring, often to comic effect, but nothing has affected our friendship.

I was appointed manager of Aston Villa on 18 December 1968 and got down to work straight away. The following day Johnny Haynes resigned as 'probationary manager' of Fulham after having been in charge of the club for only four matches. The headlines that greeted Johnny's resignation, however, were nowhere near as sensational as the ones that followed my resignation from QPR. To this day Johnny has never officially appeared in the records as being manager at the club.

There had been no sort of youth policy at Aston Villa. The apprentices were wandering about like lost souls, as were many of the other players, and little wonder as the previous owners had sold the training ground. The first thing I set about doing was to strike a deal with a local company for the use of their sports ground for daily training. It wasn't an ideal situation, but at least the players now had a regular base. With the assistance of Arthur Cox and Peter Doherty, the former Irish international who, as manager of Northern Ireland, had guided them to the 1958 World Cup, we set about organising a structured youth policy. Peter Doherty was not only a brilliant inside-forward in his day, he knew how to spot emerging talent in young footballers. Peter was also a great character and wonderful wit. He once told me, 'I've never lost a football match in my life, I've just run out of time.' One of the first youngsters Peter brought to the club was Brian Little, who went on to become something of a Villa legend before entering management himself. He also brought down from Scotland two wonderful young talents in Jimmy Brown and Billy Kellock.

The team was in a state. With half the fixtures completed Villa were near the foot of the table and the spectre of relegation was beginning to loom. They had been conceding too many goals, so Arthur Cox and I set about working to tighten the defence. My first game in charge was at home to Norwich City and though we did concede a goal, we scored twice to make it a winning start. We went on to lose just one of the first thirteen league matches under my charge, and come Good Friday when we beat Millwall 1–0 at the Den, we had pulled well clear of the drop zone. A week after Easter the Villa fans were ecstatic when we beat local rivals Birmingham City at Villa Park before a crowd of nearly 53,000. Our final position of eighteenth in Division Two was nothing to shout about, but nonetheless satisfactory given the wretched state of affairs I had walked into.

As fate would have it, that season Aston Villa drew QPR in the FA Cup. I didn't think I had a point to prove to anyone, nor did I bear any grudges – I'm not the type. The team did the talking. Every player performed extremely well on the day and we ran out 2–1 winners. In the fourth round we earned a hard-fought 2–2 draw at Southampton before overcoming the Saints 2–1 at Villa Park. I was hoping for a plum tie in the fifth round and we got it when we were drawn out of the bag to meet Spurs at White Hart Lane. It was something of an anti-climax when every fifth round game and almost the entire Football League programme, was wiped out due to heavy snow across the country. We travelled to White Hart Lane in midweek for what turned out to be a classic Cup tie. It was end-to-end stuff from start to finish and though we lost 3–2, I was proud of the boys for the way they applied themselves and for the football they played against a quality Spurs side. We appeared to have come a long way in only a matter of weeks.

We'd had to work extremely hard at Villa to achieve the results that took us to safety. In its end-of-season assessment of the club the *Birmingham Mail* said, 'Tommy Docherty has revitalised Aston Villa, so much so the club and its players will be looking forward to next season with great optimism.' I was optimistic, but I knew changes had to be made and new blood injected into the team. The only signing of note I'd made in my first four months in charge had been Brian Tiler from my old club Rotherham United. We were so high on enthusiasm and team spirit, several members of the team had played above themselves. I knew it would be too much to expect them to replicate that type of performance, never mind improve upon it, the following season. If Villa were going to live up to their motto and be 'prepared', I realised we had to bring in some players of superior quality. The problem was there wasn't the money available for to me to do that.

I had to wheel and deal. Over the first few months of 1969–70 there were quite a few players coming and going. I brought in Bruce and Neil Rioch (Luton Town), Ian 'Chico' Hamilton (Southend, who was with me as a youngster at Chelsea), Pat McMahon (Celtic), goalkeeper John Phillips (Shrewsbury Town) and George Curtis (Coventry City). No big names, though Bruce Rioch would go on to make a considerable impact in the game. They were all budget buys with the exception of the Rioch brothers who arrived together at a cost of £100,000, the lion's share of that being for Bruce. This was a large fee at the time and so to offset part of that outlay I sold Barrie Hole to Swansea, Dick Edwards (Torquay United), Alan Deakin (Walsall), John Griffiths (Stockport County), Mick Ferguson (QPR), whilst Peter Broadbent retired.

In the close season we had spent six weeks in the USA representing the city of Atlanta Georgia, in a tournament which included Wolves, Sunderland and Dundee United. In keeping with the other clubs involved, Villa had no connection with the city they were representing. As there was a dearth of football talent in the US, cities 'adopted' a British team which represented them in the tournament, the purpose of which was to generate interest in soccer in the USA amongst ex-pats and young people.

It was during our stay there that I came across Emment Kapengwe and Freddie Mwila who had arrived from Zambia that summer to play for the Atlanta Chiefs in the NASL. I invited both to train with us and was impressed by their skill and application. They were both smashing lads and from our conversations I learned both had been playing for the Zambian club Rokana United, but it was their ambition to play in England. Of the two, Emment was the better player. I had my doubts about Freddie being good enough to play in the Second Division but decided to sign them both. I did so because I was aware that life in Birmingham would represent a total change of culture and lifestyle for Kapengwe and felt if he had his pal with him it might help him settle. Besides which Mwila was only nineteen and keen to learn. I felt if I worked at his game he might have a good chance of making the grade in England. It was not unusual for a manager to sign two players to get the one he really wanted, I had done it previously when signing the Rioch brothers from Luton. But it was unusual for a manager to sign African players at the time. African football interested me, I was aware that many countries, within that contintent, were beginning to produce very talented and skilful players and for some time had wondered if they could adapt to the speed and robust nature of the English game.

The UK had yet to join the European Community and as Zambia is a member of the Commonwealth, there were to be no problems regarding work permits for the pair. When Villa left Atlanta I promised Kapengwe and Mwila I would be in touch and kept that promise. I brought them over to the UK, signed both, arranged their accommodation and wrote to their respective parents to let them know their boys would be well looked after. Emment Kapengwe and Freddie Mwila both made it into the Villa first team though, as I had suspected, Freddie found life hard in Division Two and only played a handful of matches, albeit both remained at the club following my departure.

We started the season with some optimism but, Bruce Rioch apart, because I had not been given the financial wherewithal to bring in players of real quality, I never felt we were good enough to win promotion. Far from it, I thought it was going to be another tough season, only I didn't realise just how tough. We made a disappointing start by losing at home to Norwich City, and it went from bad to worse, with no victories in our opening nine league matches.

In mid-September we played Bolton Wanderers at Burnden Park and it was there I gave a debut to Jimmy Brown who at 15 years and 349 days old was (and remains) the youngest player for Aston Villa. Within a few days Jimmy celebrated his sixteenth birthday and within a week I had made him captain. The story of Jimmy's appointment made for sensational headlines. Many football writers questioned the wisdom of making a 16-year-old captain of a team that included seasoned professionals such as Brian Godfrey, Mick Wright and Charlie Aitken. I have to admit there was an element of spin to it. The appointment made national headlines at a time when the club rarely featured in the morning papers. I also made Jimmy captain because, young as he was, he was a terrific player who had a presence on the pitch. We'd had a bad run of results and I felt some of the senior pros had become a little complacent. I thought having a youngster shouting the issue on the pitch would shame them into greater effort.

Jimmy was one of the most gifted youngsters I ever came across during my time as a manager. Peter Doherty had spotted him playing for Edinburgh and District Schools and brought him down to Villa Park. Jimmy seemed to have it all but never came anywhere near to fulfilling his true potential. He only played some 70 or so first-team games, though he did win an FA Youth Cup winners' medal with Villa in 1972 before being sold to Preston North End. In my opinion Jimmy's family had a detrimental effect on his development. They were forever interfering and complaining to him and me that this or that wasn't right. No doubt they believed they were acting in his best interests, but I thought their frequent intrusions affected Jimmy's attitude and state of mind. He was a fine young lad, it was such a shame he never developed into the great player I knew he was capable of being.

Our poor form at the start of the season was not helped when we were knocked out of the League Cup at the first time of asking, beaten 2–1 by local rivals West Bromwich Albion in front of a Villa Park crowd of 40,303. Following our September defeat at Bolton in which Jimmy Brown had made his debut, I told the players he was to be the new captain. This certainly fired up the more experienced players. In our very next match we beat Hull City 3–2, our goals coming from Brian Godfrey, Lew Chatterley and David Rudge. The crowd that day at Villa Park was a disappointing 23,590. I knew the directors would think the fans were voting with their feet, but I was confident we were on the right track.

Arthur Cox and I had been working at organising the defence to make it less porous. We hadn't been scoring a lot of goals and elementary mistakes in defence had cost us dear. Our following two games against Portsmouth and Preston both ended goalless. The defence was looking a lot tighter; now we needed to work at the sharpness in front of goal.

All this time I felt I had the support of the board with the exception of Harry Parkes. Harry had played for Villa in the 1930s. He was forever going on about the old days and how modern football and footballers were not a scratch on the game and players he had known. Whenever Parkes went on like that, for some reason he always reminded me of Albert Steptoe.

Though I felt I had the support of Doug Ellis, I was wary of him, rightly so as it was to turn out. When we were having our sticky spell at the start of the season Doug had said to me, 'Don't worry, Tommy, I'm behind you.' 'I don't want you behind me, I want you in front of me where I can keep an eye on you,' I told him. On another occasion Doug said to me, 'To every problem in football, if you just think about it, Tommy, there will be a simple and easy solution.' 'Yes, but to your mind it will be wrong,' I replied.

It wasn't all verbal sparring. Doug has a great sense of humour and we had many a laugh together, and with the players.

At the time hotels did not provide TV sets in individual guest rooms. During one away trip we had all gathered in the hotel TV lounge as Doug took command of the set's controls. It was around Christmas and he located a programme about the Christmas Day football match played between British and German troops at the Somme. Thinking, probably correctly, that many of the players would not know of this poignant and historic occasion, Doug began an explanation. 'This is about a football match that took place over fifty years ago, between the British and the Germans on the Western Front during the First World War,' said Doug, only for me to interrupt his flow by saying, 'Anyone who doesn't want to know the score, should look away now!'

The hard work on the training ground began to pay off. When we met Huddersfield Town they were top of the league (and were to finish as champions). Goals from Brian Godfrey, Barrie Hole, Brian Tiler and Lionel Martin gave us a fine 4–1 victory. I told the players, 'If we can convincingly beat the team that's top of the table, we need fear no team in this league.' In our very next game at Cardiff we came unstuck, losing 4–0, in the main due to the aerial prowess of the home side's young centre-forward John Toshack. It was back to the training ground and more work with the defence in preparation for the big derby game against Birmingham City which resulted in a 0–0 draw. By Christmas I thought we were turning the corner: from mid-September we had played sixteen league matches and had suffered only five defeats. To use a term Pat Matthews would have understood, the trend was good.

The country suffered another severe spell of winter weather between Boxing Day and mid-January. The only games we managed to play were in the FA Cup against Charlton Athletic. After having drawn 1–1 at Villa Park we lost the replay at the Valley by the only goal of the game. When we returned to league action in mid-January after a break of three weeks, we were beaten 5–3 in a thriller at Portsmouth. The former Burnley centre-forward Ray Pointer and Jim Storrie, whom I had signed for Rotherham, did for us that day. If ever one needed reminding of the fine line between success and failure in football, you only had to look at the Portsmouth substitute that day, Mike Trebilcock. Less than three years before Trebilcock had been the hero of the 1966 FA Cup final when he scored twice for Everton, as they came back from being 2–0 down to beat Sheffield Wednesday. Little over two years after we visited Fratton Park, Trebilcock was playing for Torquay United reserves. Following the Portsmouth game I was disappointed that we had scored three goals away from home without getting a point for our efforts, but I wasn't panicking. Unfortunately the Villa board did. Two days after our visit to Portsmouth I was sacked.

I remain convinced that given time I would have turned things round at Villa Park. But the Cup defeat against Charlton and the 5–3 reverse at Portsmouth had the local papers ringing the alarm bells. My off-the-pitch critics, such as Harry Parkes, were having a field day. No doubt there was an element of the Villa support who were not enamoured with me either, but by and large I think the supporters could see we were making progress. Indeed thousands of Villa supporters signed a petition and wrote accompanying letters demanding my reinstatement and sent them to the Birmingham *Evening Mail*. The *Mail* forwarded the petition and letters to a local councillor, Mr Tilsley, who, in turn, passed them on to the club who, for some reason sent them to me. The efforts of the Villa fans meant so much to me that I still have their petition and letters of support. There were over 8,000 signatures on that petition but it cut no ice.

I told Doug Ellis I hadn't been given long enough to steer the club in the right direction, but I think he and other directors had been egged on by some people who were happy to put the knife in. Doug said he was sorry things had not worked. We shook hands, wished each other good luck and I said 'Goodbye, Mr Chairman'. He looked genuinely sad. I bore no hard feelings when I cleared my desk, bade my farewells to the players and made my exit. I was sad for everyone connected with the club when Villa were relegated to Division Three at the end of the season.

The first offer of work came from Bob Findlay at the *Daily Mail* who asked if I fancied writing about football for his newspaper. The thought of being on the other side of the fence was not unappealing. So I wrote for the *Mail* for a time, but was always keen to return to managing. Such an opportunity was not to be long in the offing.

I then received a phone call from the president of FC Porto who informed me his club was looking for a coach on an eighteen-month contract that would last until June of the following year. This was more like it. The thought of resurrecting my career as a manager with a top continental club would be a new experience and, at the time, I felt I needed a new and different challenge.

I flew out to Oporto, met the president and we agreed a deal there and then. I began work in earnest the following week. Agnes joined me in Oporto as our children, with the exception of Michael at Burnley, attended boarding school in Staffordshire. On my first day the president told me, 'They are your players. You train them, coach them, pick them for the team. That's it. Any financial problems, we handle them. Just the team Tommy, that's all you are responsible for. Oh, and getting results of course.' I didn't have much time, so I didn't waste any. There was no time for sightseeing. When not working with the players, I went to see other Portuguese teams in action. I didn't speak the language so I hired a teacher who gave me lessons every evening, though I did have an interpreter alongside me in training for the first two months. It was very much a crash-course, but I did my homework and ended up being able to converse quite well. As language courses go it must have appeared strange to my teacher. Not only did I want to learn enough of the language to converse, I also needed him to teach me Portuguese for football terms such as 'Push up from the middle', 'Indirect free-kick' and 'Come off your marker'.

Porto's stadium, Estadio do Dragao had a capacity of 80,000 but results had been so poor they had been lucky to attract 20,000 to matches. The stadium is situated in a sleepy district of the city though I quickly discovered Porto, known locally as the Dragons, was the best supported of the city's three clubs. The others being Boavista, and Salgueiros, which both looked to me to be on a par with an English Fourth Division club.

Having assessed the squad and done a little scouting I went to see the president and told him I needed to sign two players, one from Academica Coimbra, the other a squad player from Vitoria Setubal. I outlined to him my reasons and asked if he could convene a meeting of the board to discuss the matter.

'There is no need,' he informed me. 'We will get them for you.' And they did.

Today such a situation is common to British football, but in 1970 managers handled the financial side of things with players, from negotiating transfer fees to agreeing wages and bonuses. It was easier then because players didn't have personal agents, image agents and lawyers and a deal could be agreed in a matter of minutes. Now when a top player moves clubs, the negotiations may take up to a month, or even longer. I found it refreshing not to have to handle the financial side of things at Porto, it allowed me to concentrate on team matters. In fact I found the whole experience of managing in Portugal to be refreshing. It is a very accommodating and friendly country whose footballing reputation was built on the riches of its former colonies. African players have long played a key role in Portuguese football, none more so than the great Eusebio.

The Porto players treated me with great respect and always called me 'Mr Docherty'. The one mistake I made with them was training them too hard at the beginning. The pace of the game in Portugal was much slower than in England and, of course, the climate much warmer. Having realised my error, I adapted. We trained early in the morning, occasionally late in the afternoon and just about everything we did involved the use of the ball.

Results began to improve. When I arrived at the club, they were fourteenth in a league of eighteen teams. When the season ended we were sixth, though some way behind champions Sporting Lisbon and runners-up Benfica. During the close season I took myself off to Mexico to watch the World Cup. In addition to seeing a good many matches and a Brazilian team that was arguably the greatest international side of all time lift the World Cup, I also bumped into a lot of English managers out there. Like me they had come to see what they could learn. I once went along to watch Brazil train and saw some familiar figures lolling in the sun on a grassy bank at the side of the pitch: Don Howe, the Arsenal coach, Bobby Robson, then manager of Ipswich Town, and Tony Waddington, the Stoke City manager. I joined them for a time and as we marvelled at the Brazilians in training we put the football world to rights. They talked of this player or that player and mentioned games played in mud and slush in February. All of which made me think about how convivial the climate and conditions were for football in Portugal.

'We [Stoke] played at Sheffield United one night. The pitch was so icy the teams had difficulty turning round at half-time,' quipped Tony.

'Yes, you won't have that with Porto,' said Bobby. 'Bet you don't miss us one little bit.'

But I did.

I spent the 1970–71 season fulfilling my contract as manager of Porto. I enjoyed my time with the club who I guided to third in the league, four points behind champions Benfica and just one point away from Sporting Lisbon who took the runners-up spot. It meant the team qualified for the next season's UEFA Cup. We also had a good run in the Portuguese Cup only to suffer a narrow defeat to Sporting, the eventual winners, in the semi-finals.

Though I never guided Porto to trophy success, the president and his fellow directors were delighted with the progress I had made. I had enjoyed my time immensely, but I was hankering after a return to the English game in some capacity. Part of me hoped the president might ask me to stay on but I knew he wouldn't. Knowing my contract was coming to an end and that my ambition was to work in the UK again, the club had lined up my replacement.

In June 1971 I flew back to England to be reunited with my family and was hopeful of work. After being sacked by Aston Villa, my standing as a manager had taken a knock, only for it to have been restored following my spell in Portugal. Word had reached England about the good job I had done and within a day of my return Terry Neill, the manager of Hull City, rang to ask if I would like to become his assistant at Boothferry Park. 'I think the pair of us would work well together,' said Terry, 'and who knows, it might open a door for you at another club.' But within three months, rather than it being another club, it was Scotland who opened the welcoming door.

13

TILL A' THE SEAS GANG DRY

I think Terry Neill knew when he offered me the job as his assistant at Hull City that I wanted to be my own man and manage. I accepted his offer because I wanted to be involved in British football again. Also I liked Terry and felt I could help him in his quest to bring success to Hull, a club with oodles of potential.

I had known Terry since our days together at Arsenal. He reminded me of Danny Blanchflower. Both hailed from Belfast, both went on to captain and manage Northern Ireland, and both made their name by playing in North London. The similarities, however, do not end there. As was the case with Danny, Terry is a highly articulate and intelligent guy though, and I know he won't mind me saying this, Danny was more poignant and profound in what he said about football and the superior wit. Then again, there have been few in the history of British football to match Danny Blanchflower on that score.

Terry began his career playing for Bangor youth team, was spotted by an Arsenal scout and signed for them in 1959. In 1969–70 Terry contracted jaundice which put him out of the game for some time. When he regained health and fitness he was offered the job of player-manager at Hull City. He was only 28 and became one of the youngest managers in the game. There are those given to believing you can't be a player-manager, that it is impossible to do both jobs. Terry proved that notion wrong.

Whilst at Hull he also became player-manager of Northern Ireland!

Terry later had two years managing Spurs before being asked to take over from Bertie Mee at Arsenal. He steered Arsenal to three FA Cup finals, though they only won one, but in his time at Highbury made some super signings such as Pat Jennings and Malcolm Macdonald. He left Arsenal in 1983, worked in the media and later opened a chain of sports bars in London which, to the best of my knowledge, he still owns.

I was appointed as Terry's assistant on 2 July 1971. I was looking forward to working with him as I felt the two of us together could build on his excellent work at the club. The previous season Hull City had finished fifth in Division Two, their highest post-war placing, and had also reached the sixth round of the FA Cup. The club had great potential and still has. I once took my Chelsea team to Boothferry Park for an FA Cup replay in 1966 which was watched by a crowd of 45,328. Though I felt it unlikely we would ever attract attendances such as that, I knew Hull had the sort of support worthy of the First Division.

There was one little caveat to my being at Hull and Terry mentioned this during our initial telephone conversation. Hull's general manager was Cliff Britton. Yup, the same fellow who had been my manager when I had left Preston. I told Terry, Cliff Britton's presence at the club did not bother me one iota and that I was looking forward to seeing him again. Well, at least the first part was true.

Having been there a few weeks I couldn't work out what Cliff did, so I asked Terry. 'Not a lot,' he said. Cliff was Terry's predecessor. To be fair to Cliff he had overseen heady days at the club. He had become manager in 1961 and in 1966 steered them to promotion from the Third Division by playing some excellent football. Hull chairman Harold Needler rewarded him with a ten-year contract. When Terry took over the reins, it wasn't in Harold Needler's nature to be so cold as to pay Cliff's contract up, because he'd been a good manager. So Cliff was moved 'upstairs' and given the title of 'General Manager'.

The only moment of friction between Cliff and me took place during pre-season training only a fortnight or so after my arrival. He was standing on the touchline watching me work with the players, following a training routine that I had devised during my spell with FC Porto.

'Didn't I used to do that with you when we were at Preston?' asked Cliff as I walked off the training ground.

'You could have fooled me,' I told him.

I carried on walking so didn't hear what Cliff then said. But it must have been a remark at my expense because Terry Neill walked up to my side and said, 'Whatever you do, Tom, don't hit him.'

I never thought I would work for as good a chairman as Joe Mears, but even in what was to be a short stay at Hull City, Harold Needler came very close. Harry was a wonderful man who had saved Hull City from going under in the 1940s by investing £10,000 in the club. After the Second World War he and his brothers assumed control of the club and revitalised it. Harold was never shy about bringing big-name managers to Hull. He appointed Major Frank Buckley who had enjoyed success with Wolves, and after Buckley, Raich Carter as player-manager in 1948. Carter was indisputably one of the greatest players of his generation, and to have him managing the club raised the profile enormously. During Carter's three-year reign Hull City was forever being written about in the national press which, I suppose, was part of the idea. In 1963 Harold Needler floated his company Hoveringham Gravels and gave £200,000 worth of shares to the club. The shares leapt in value and Hull City enjoyed a halcyon period in the mid-sixties under the management of Cliff Britton. They had their own railway station, Boothferry Park, alongside the ground and attendances in excess of 37,000 were common.

Hull City had some quality players. The pedigree of Chris

Chilton, Ken Wagstaff, Ian Butler, Ken Houghton, Ken Knighton and goalkeeper Ian McKechnie was not in doubt, but for me they were all the wrong side of thirty. When Terry Neill asked me what I thought would improve the squad I replied, 'Young legs'.

Hull lost the opening game of the season at Charlton, then squeezed a 1–0 victory against Oxford United. I had been impressed by a local youngster who was playing centre-forward for the reserves and suggested to Terry we should give him a chance in the first team. His name was Stuart Pearson and he scored in our very next match, a 1–1 draw at Cardiff. The next two matches both resulted in one-goal victories, over Birmingham City and Blackpool respectively, and it was Pearson who scored on both occasions. It wasn't the last I'd see of Stuart.

It was great to be involved in English football again and Terry Neill and I worked well together. I was, however, only with Hull for those five matches as the first of what I consider were the two greatest opportunities of my managerial career was about to come my way.

Kenny Gallagher, a freelance football writer in Manchester who later went on to work for the *Daily Record*, phoned me to ask if it was OK to pass on my home telephone number.

'Who's the guy?' I asked.

'Hugh Nelson,' said Kenny. 'You know him?'

'Yes, lovely fella, Chairman of Arbroath and the Scottish FA,' I said.

'That's right,' said Kenny.

'The big time! I've got the Arbroath job!' I exclaimed in good humour.

'Oh, no,' said Kenny earnestly. 'I think he might want to speak about something a wee bit bigger than that.'

My mind was doing cartwheels. Bobby Brown had resigned as manager of Scotland in July after four years in charge of the national team. Two months had passed and there had been a lot of speculation as to who his successor might be, but my name had never been mentioned. 'Surely not . . .' I thought.

On 11 September Hull City played at Bristol City. Bristol appears an unlikely venue for a meeting between Scottish Football Association officials and a prospective national team manager, but it was in a hotel in that city that I met Hugh Nelson and other representatives of the SFA. Hugh told me Scotland were due to play two important European Championship qualifying matches against Portugal and Belgium, also coming up was a prestigious international against Holland in Amsterdam. Scotland needed an experienced manager at the helm for those games, and that he and his colleagues would like me to take temporary charge of the national team. A heady cocktail of emotions and feelings coursed through my body – astonishment, excitement, joy, elation, pride and unbounded enthusiasm. I had never felt like this before about any job in football – ever.

'How are you fixed with Hull City?' Hugh Nelson asked.

I told him I would have to speak with Harold Needler and Terry Neill, though I imagined there would be no problem in me taking up my duties with Scotland. This proved to be the case. I couldn't have asked more of Harold Needler. He was delighted for me, and insisted he continued to pay my Hull City wages in case 'things don't work out' with Scotland.

Hugh Nelson concluded the meeting by saying other senior members of the SFA would like to 'interview' me before a final decision was made. The second meeting, at a hotel near Glasgow, lasted little more than fifteen minutes. In the chair was Wullie Allen, the secretary of the SFA who came across as being tetchy and terse and who I didn't warm to.

'Has Hugh spoken to you?' Allen asked.

I confirmed he had.

'The post hasn't been advertised, you know that?'

There was further confirmation from me.

'For the time being we want to keep the lid on this. You haven't spoken to any pressmen regarding this matter have you?' Allen asked.

'Only Kenny Gallagher,' I replied.

'You had no right speaking to him,' said Allen, very vexed. 'No right at all. That's a breach of confidence and as far as . . .'

I jumped into his conversation. 'Just hold on a minute, Mr Allen,' I intoned. 'It was Kenny Gallagher who Mr Nelson first contacted, asking if he could, in turn, make contact with me.'

There was a pause in the conversation.

'Well, I find that situation most unsatisfactory, most unsatisfactory indeed,' said Allen.

'I know Kenny Gallagher,' I said. 'He won't go public with anything until he is told it is OK.'

'I'd prefer if the press never found out about your appointment at all,' Allen said much to my bewilderment.

'They'd find out eventually,' I told him. 'They'd see me sitting on the bench at Scotland matches and work it out. They're very good like that.'

I noticed one or two other SFA panel members suppressing smiles, but Mr Allen didn't see the joke.

'Yes. Yes. You know what I mean,' said Allen.

I did glean meaning from what he had said. He had used the phrase 'your appointment'. I took that to mean the decision had been made. That this meeting had been convened for reasons of protocol, so that the lofty members of the SFA who were not present in Bristol could be said to have had an input in the selection of the new national manager. I was to be put in temporary charge of Scotland with a view to earning a four-year contract should all go well. I was to be paid £7,000 a year, have a Rover car and be allowed to claim 'legitimate out-of-pocket expenses'.

I did see my role as assistant manager at Hull City as a stepping stone, but to what and where I was never sure. But I was happy there and gave my all to the club. I was aware that some people had seen the move as indicative of my career having shifted into a backwater of English football. I sensed that in some quarters there was an element of distrust of my record at club level,

while others looked at my career to date and reckoned I did a
great job at Chelsea, a sound one for Rotherham and a lot of
valuable spadework at Porto. Some people simply harped on
about the turmoil that accompanied my final year at Chelsea,
the fact I had walked out on QPR, and saw my sojourn at Villa
Park as a failure. Rejuvenating a Portuguese club and guiding
them to European qualification didn't seem to cut much ice in
the English game. I have to say this division of opinion concerning
my managerial ability affected me, though I didn't think so at
the time. Looking back to my time with Hull, I now recognise
that my trademark ebullience had been somewhat muted.

The offer to manage Scotland rejuvenated me. The confidence the SFA had placed in my ability was an enormous boost
to my morale. I thanked them for having faith in me when others
were closing doors. I was also grateful to those members of the
media whose support had been unwavering. A few days after the
news of my appointment was made public I attended an England
game at Wembley. Afterwards I headed for the press box and
was courteous to the well-wishers I knew had been writing negative things about me. When reports had been filed I grouped
together a bunch of football writers I felt had been supportive.
'I want you to know that I realise who helped me get the
Scotland job,' I told them. 'It was you lads. I want to say a big
thank you for your support, and for you to know I shall never
forget it.' It isn't often you see football writers lost for words,
but to a man they were at that moment.

To have captained my country and now be the manager of
Scotland filled me with great pride. I also felt very humble that
it was me the SFA had chosen. I was mindful of the fact, and
later emphasised the same to the players, that we were the representatives of every person in Scotland, football fan or not. I went
on to tell the players at our first squad meeting I did not expect
them to be paragons or live like monks but, like me, they had
to be mindful that any indiscretion would reflect not only on
Scottish football but the nation.

'We've been given the honour of representing our country and with honour comes responsibility,' I told the players. 'Everyone stamps his own value on himself. Whether we are to be remembered as having been good for Scotland, will really be decided by our own individual will.'

Then I set out targets and objectives, the first being to beat both Portugal and Belgium. At this stage of the campaign damage had been done; even if we won both games the chances of qualification for the European Championship Finals were remote. I considered it vital to win those two games, however, for in little over a year we would be involved in qualification for the World Cup. I wanted to embark upon that tournament with confidence high. I sought to create a positive and vibrant culture within the squad, whereby all players would want to be selected and be enthused by what we were doing. I took notes concerning the team ethic, clarity of communication in every area with the players, identifying problems early and demonstrating to all that I solved them. I planned the training and coaching, tailoring it to individual needs and, collectively, focusing on our next game and opponents. In truth an international manager has little, if any, time to coach players. The majority of the job is taken up with explaining the system of play you have devised.

I travelled extensively in both Scotland and England watching Scottish players. I checked the lineage of English players who had not played for England but were of international standard to see if they qualified to play for Scotland. This was not wasted effort. I discovered the Arsenal goalkeeper Bob Wilson, though seemingly as English as roast beef, had Scottish grandparents which qualified him for Scotland. Bob became one of my goalkeepers. No home international manager had done this type of research before, though Jack Charlton would later make it a fine art when manager of the Republic of Ireland. I was diligent in everything I did and paid meticulous attention to detail. I couldn't wait for our opening game.

Not for the first time, nor indeed the last, Scotland were

having a bad run of results. Earlier they had played three European Championship qualifiers against Belgium, Portugal and Russia and lost each game without scoring a goal in the process. Something was very wrong, because when I looked at the players available there were several top quality internationals on that list. The SFA had told me I, and I alone, would have complete control of team affairs, so I set about drawing up my squad in preparation for my first game in charge, against Portugal.

I recalled Celtic's Jimmy Johnstone which, as I have said, surprised a lot of people. Jimmy still was a great player in my eyes and if he had caused previous Scotland managers one or two problems, I felt I could handle him and, more importantly, get the best out of him as a player. He needed coaxing; emotionally he was often up and down, and when he was down he was liable to do things with no thought of the impact his actions would have on others, or himself. Jimmy once jumped off a train when travelling to a match at Wembley and, for reasons known only to himself, made his way back home to Glasgow. He was taken to task for that and went into his shell. Jimmy needed understanding. Even when you didn't get what he was up to, you had to pretend as if you did. As Jock Stein once said, 'Keep telling him you know what's going on in his heid. By the way, if you ever find out what that is, be sure to tell me.'

The players seemed to welcome my appointment and our sessions together went very well. While my appointment was, at this stage temporary, I was able to convince them we were embarking together upon a new and exciting era for Scottish football. As if to emphasise this, for our game against Portugal I made ten changes to the team that had lost the previous qualifier against Russia. I didn't rule out any player for the future, but the only player who survived was Hibernian's Pat Stanton.

The team I selected for my first game as manager of Scotland on 13 October 1971 was: Bob Wilson (Arsenal); Sandy Jardine (Rangers), David Hay (Celtic); Billy Bremner (Leeds United),

Eddie Colquhoun (Sheffield United), Pat Stanton (Hibernian); Jimmy Johnstone (Celtic), Alex Cropley (Hibernian), John O'Hare (Derby County), George Graham (Arsenal), Archie Gemmill (Derby County). Substitutes: Martin Buchan and Scott Murray (both Aberdeen).

The squad also included: Bobby Clark, Asa Hartford, Lou Macari, Eddie Gray, Peter Lorimer, Willie Donachie; Jim Bone, John Hansen, Alex Forsyth (all three Partick Thistle), Denis Law, Colin Stein, and a young teenager from Celtic – Kenny Dalglish.

You can have a super squad of players and plan meticulously for games, but if you are going to be successful you need a little luck. The luck I had was in knowing the strengths, weaknesses and idiosyncratic ways of the Portugal players from my days at Porto. Three of the Portugal team were Porto players, one of whom was the majestic winger Simoes. Portugal also included the great Eusebio, Nene, Graca and Baptista. They were not the best team in Europe but they were right up there. I couldn't have been happier with the way the players responded to my claim that we were the new Scotland. We set about Portugal with vigour from the start and though far from having it all our own way, as the game unfolded I was confident of victory. John O'Hare gave us the lead. Receiving a raking pass from Bremner, he leaned beautifully into his stride before striking a crisp shot wide of Damas. We seemed comfortable until, suddenly, Eusebio, with the deftest of touches, played in Rodrigues who accelerated through a tiny gap to glide in the equaliser.

As the second half progressed we asserted our authority. Billy Bremner was doing a fine job of marking Eusebio and 'Jinky' Johnstone was back to his former self, twisting and turning Adolto and often the supportive Calo into the bargain. After 20 minutes of the second period, Archie Gemmill, coming up from deep, was fed the ball by Jinky, and fired past Damas to make it 2–1. A sound that had not been heard for some time rent the heavens – it was the return of the Hampden Roar.

After the game I was overjoyed and buoyant. It had not only been a good result for Scotland it had also been a very good performance. I felt all the players were with me in my aim to put Scotland and Scottish football back on the map. For a time my career had slumped, but I felt I was now back in the big time. I was loving every minute, my old enthusiasm had returned. During my post-match press conference I told the media, 'We have a long way to go. This is just a start, but it's just the start we needed.'

The progress continued for a month when we beat Belgium 1–0 before a full-house at Pittodrie. For this game I played home players Bobby Clark in goal in place of Bob Wilson, Martin Buchan for Colquhoun and Scott Murray for Gemmill, whilst Eddie Gray came in for George Graham. Never one to hold back when it came to giving talented young players the oppor-tunity to show what they could do, I named Kenny Dalglish as one of my two substitutes. He had been at Celtic for little over a year and had only played a handful of first-team matches, but had impressed me greatly. At the time Belgium were a better team than Portugal. They had won their six previous inter-nationals, which included 3–0 victories over both Scotland and Portugal. Belgium did prove sterner opposition but a wonder goal from John O'Hare settled the issue. I felt we were really up and running.

Little under three weeks later we encountered our sternest task to date when we took on Holland in Amsterdam. Today it would be billed as a friendly international, but there was no such thing in 1971. This was a major game for Scotland and I knew Holland would test the progress we had made. That, however, didn't stop me giving Kenny Dalglish his first full international appearance.

Holland were in the throes of developing their 'total football'. The key players in their team now reads like a who's who of the cream of football talent in the seventies: Cruyff, Neeskens, Krol, Hanegem, Schrivers and Israel. The mark of the strength of the

Dutch side being Arnold Muhren named as one of the substitutes, whilst Johnny Rep and Franz Thijssen, though in the squad, didn't get a shirt.

Holland were formidable and, of course, the star of their team was Johann Cruyff. At the time he was on the cusp of being hailed the greatest player in the world. For me he combined just about everything. As he demonstrated against Scotland that night, he was a marvellous team man. Every move seemed to start, and often end, with Cruyff. His brain was lightning quick and he was no more dangerous than when in our penalty area.

For a player whose artistry was never in question, Cruyff was never afraid to dive in where it hurts. For me that is what gave him the edge as an all-round player. Against Scotland he demonstrated that he was more of a leader than Pelé. With Pelé everything seemed to start from his physique, with Cruff it started from his brain and I think that was the difference between these two football greats. There was more than a touch of arrogance to Cruyff's play, but I admired the man all the more for that. At one point in the game he paused with the ball on our right-hand side, Pat Stanton came to close him down and having been given a tantalising glimpse of the ball Pat went for it. With the swiftness of a striking rattlesnake Cruyff's left foot dragged the ball away from Pat's outstretched boot and he was off on his travels again. His tremendous acceleration took him down the wing before he cut inside only to find Eddie Colquhoun blocking his path. Cruyff flicked the ball to Eddie's right and rounded him on his left before meeting the ball on the other side. It all seemed so effortless. Cruyff's ability to make the most accurate passes over long distances meant that he could open up any defence, which is what he did to ours playing the ball forward to Keizer who held it long enough for the great man to make up ground. When Cruyff took the return he danced around Colquhoun and Jardine before stroking the ball wide of Bob Wilson.

The Scotland team of a few months earlier would have caved

in; this Scotland side were made of sterner stuff. Far from caving in we took the game to Holland. In the second period I introduced John O'Hare for Jinky and replaced Eddie Gray with Peter Cormack. O'Hare's presence up front caused Holland problems. He was very good at holding the ball up which allowed our midfield to push on and exert greater pressure. During one attack Archie Gemmill beat goalkeeper Schrivers only to see his effort came back off the foot of the post. But we would not be denied. Minutes later George Graham put us on level terms. This stung Holland into action again, but we soaked up the tremendous pressure created by Cruyff and Neeskens. At one point we broke from defence only to be denied the lead when a header from John O'Hare hit the bar.

As the game entered its closing stages a little bit of magic from Cruyff swung the game in Holland's favour. He turned Davie Hay and hit a slide-rule pass across the face of our goal and Hulshoff, arriving at the far post, side-footed the ball into the net. I took to my feet and asked an official how long there was to go. He checked his watch before saying, 'One minute.' I instinctively threw my head back and gritted my teeth. The agony and frustration was almost too much to bear.

The press were full of praise for our performance. For my part I was very proud of the way we had played against what was one of the best teams in the world. After the game I gave an interview to Arthur Montford, one of the best TV match commentators there has ever been. After answering characteristically searching questions from Arthur, he asked if I had been disappointed with any aspect of the game. 'Yes,' I told him, 'I'm disappointed we didn't get at least the draw our play deserved.' Arthur picked up on my comment in his summary: 'Holland away from home is a formidable task for any side. The fact Tommy Docherty and the Scotland team are disappointed not to have won tonight, may be taken as indicative of the progress that has been made these past weeks.'

Arthur Montford was not the only person of the mind that

progress was being made. Before the Scotland party left Amsterdam, Hugh Nelson and Wullie Allen took me to one side. They told me the SFA were delighted with my work so far and offered me a four-year contract. The caretaker tag had been removed. I was now a fully fledged international manager.

When news of my permanent appointment was made public I gave an interview to Ian Archer, then of the *Glasgow Herald*, during which I said, 'Scotland must succeed. No country in the world possesses as much natural talent as we do. Possibly Brazil, but that's all. We've made a good start, there is a lot of work to do but we will do it. Scotland will have a football team to be proud of.' My claim that Scotland possessed natural talent second only to Brazil raised a few eyebrows, but after five years of approaching games with appropriate modesty, I knew it was just the bullish statement the fans wanted to hear.

It was then that I discovered a downside to being manager of Scotland. It was to be almost five months before we played our next game, against Peru. Having been in charge of the team for three matches in six weeks, to be without a game for such a period of time was detrimental to the spirit and momentum I had instilled in the squad. If there was to be any semblance of continuity I knew I had to see the squad in the meantime for regular 'get-togethers', so I contacted every manager of Scotland's top clubs to a meeting-cum-lunch, where I could outline my plans for the national team and ascertain their take on things. This I duly did, but the response I received disappointed me. Not all the managers turned up, one didn't even bother to reply. Four months later I repeated the exercise, and the response was to be equally disappointing.

In the months that led to the Peru game I constantly negotiated with club managers for the release of players for get-togethers. I never had my preferred squad together at any time. Having been informed of players who were unable to be released, I would call up others, only to have some of them pull out at the last minute due to injuries sustained in the preceding club match. It seemed to me that whatever the nature of the injury it would only last for the duration of the national call-up; the player was invariably and miraculously fit again for the next league match! Now that's good medicine.

The real downside to the job was that I spent much of my time on my own, particularly during the intervening months between the Holland and Peru games. I saw as many matches as possible on both sides of the border. I talked to players and managers, but I sorely missed the day-to-day involvement with players. I spent more time with the press than the players and knew that wasn't right. The time spent in giving interviews and press conferences raised the profile of the Scotland team and helped generate greater optimism among supporters, but I didn't want to be seen as just 'talking a good game'.

When the time came to announce the squad for the Peru game in April I found I had lost a number of players. I was keen on making Bob Wilson my number one goalkeeper, but Bob had sustained a serious knee injury which was to keep him out of the game for some time. With Bob out of the picture I selected Ally Hunter and Bobby Clark and also called up the young Leeds keeper David Harvey. Two other youngsters I called into the squad were Leeds' Joe Jordan and Kenny Burns of Birmingham City. I also added Bobby Moncur (Newcastle), Asa Hartford (West Bromwich Albion), Willie Carr (Coventry City) and Willie Morgan (Manchester United) and gave a recall to Denis Law. I played all five in the match against Peru, who were on a four-match tour of Europe. I had done some homework on them and realised they had three excellent players in Chumpitaz, Cubillas and Murante. Six years on it was to be this trio who were to destroy the hopes of Ally MacLeod and Scotland in the 1978 World Cup in Argentina.

Peru were young and skilful but always second best at Hampden. Goals from John O'Hare and Denis Law gave us a comfortable 2–0 victory and a good confidence booster for the Home International Championship that began the following month. The tournament had changed much since my days as a Scotland player. Then games were played over the course of the season, in 1972 they took place over seven days in May at the end the season. Whilst one might question the wisdom of players playing three internationals in the course of a week after a gruelling domestic season, this format did have its advantages. I found I was able to work with the same squad of players for the duration; what's more, there were no problems in obtaining their release from clubs.

The Home Internationals were not the draw they had once been, evidenced by the 40,000 who attended Hampden for our opening game against Northern Ireland. It was a decent crowd but nothing compared to the attendances that once gathered for this competition. The game had been designated to be played at Windsor Park but due to security problems the venue had been switched to Glasgow. The Irish included Pat Jennings (Spurs), Pat Rice (Arsenal), Sammy McIlroy (Manchester United), Derek Dougan (Wolves) and my good friend, the 'multi-tasker' Terry Neill. Noticeable by his absence, was George Best who at the age of 26 was taking a self-appointed sabbatical from football in Spain at the time.

I picked Manchester City's Willie Donachie at left-back, recalled Celtic's Billy McNeill in the heart of defence and also Jimmy Johnstone on the wing. This was a bit of a gamble as, according to Jock Stein, Jinky had been out of sorts. Jimmy did OK in the game, but just OK, and I did replace him with Peter Lorimer in the second half. There was a lot more cohesion and balance to the Scotland side now, particularly where defence was concerned. For a second successive match we kept a clean sheet whilst goals from O'Hare and Law saw us to victory. The win looked even better when Northern Ireland then beat England 1–0 at Wembley, their goal coming from Terry Neill.

Wales provided stiffer opposition for us at Hampden. Bob Moncur and Billy McNeill did an admirable job of coping with the twin aerial threat of Ron and Wyn Davies, a threat compounded when Mike England joined the attack at set pieces. A goal from Peter Lorimer settled what, was in truth, an unmemorable game, but I was delighted with our third consecutive clean sheet, something Scotland had failed to achieve under my predecessor.

My one big disappointment came when we lost by the only goal of the game to England at Hampden. Twelve months previously 30,000 Scots at Wembley had booed Bobby Brown's side off the pitch following England's 3–1 success. With the occasional exception – Scotland's victory at Wembley in 1967 comes to mind – the Home International Championship had been a canter for England for years. The game was a volatile affair. Alf Ramsey had struck a note of animosity as soon as the England party arrived at Glasgow airport. A journalist called out, 'Welcome to Scotland, Sir Alf,' to which Alf replied, 'You must be 'king joking.' It was an ungracious remark to say the least and, I must say, out of character with the Alf I knew, but his curt response set the scene.

From the earliest stages sparks of anger and animosity flickered across the pitch before fully igniting. It was not a match for faint hearts or weaklings. The only goal was scored by Alan Ball, to send the vast majority of 120,000 spectators away to drown their sorrows and boost the profits of the breweries and distilleries. I was not in the least happy with the result, but I was philosophical. England were one of the top three teams in the world. We'd had them under pressure for long periods without ever making that pressure tell, but their superior quality came through and they squeezed victory out of the game. I took comfort in the fact that on this performance, there didn't appear to be too much between the sides.

After the game I had a few words with Alf, who was gracious in victory, though when it came to beating Scotland that wasn't always the case. He said he had been surprised at how well Scotland had played. I took that as a compliment. He told me he was aware of the improvements I'd made with the team, though until this game didn't realise how marked that improvement had been.

I got on well with Alf, though I found him a curious character. In public he appeared cold and somewhat terse, but once
you got to know him you discovered his warmth and wit. He
respected his players and the England team returned that
respect. The years that followed England's 1966 World Cup
success witnessed a radical change in how football was played.
Alf's uncompromising functionalism won the World Cup and
set a trend that was copied throughout the country, though not
by me. In the late 1960s and early 1970s the emphasis was on
not conceding goals rather than scoring them. Fear crept into
the game and as coaches increasingly exerted their influence the
price to pay for better organisation was fewer goals and less
open, fluid football. With the old system of only three defenders,
the full-back on the far side was always covering behind the
centre-half so the winger always had space when the ball was
played out to him. Having four defenders enabled the full-backs
to get tight on the winger and deny him his acceleration space.
Without that first few yards the effectiveness of the winger was
lessened. A good example of how Alf implemented his system
is Alan Ball. He originally played wide in the England midfield,
always looking for an opening. Alf saw it better to opt for work-
rate, for a player who will go again and again, display his courage
and not be confined to hugging the touchline. It wasn't Alf's
fault that many managers and coaches slavishly aped his style
of play.

Here's a good pub quiz question: when did Scotland represent
England in an international tournament? The answer to that is
1972, the tournament in question the Independence Cup held
in Brazil. The original idea behind the tournament was to involve
all past winners of the World Cup but when it became apparent
this was not feasible, the tournament went ahead by invitation.
England had declined to attend. The Scottish FA was very sceptical about a request to stand in for England, but I managed to
persuade them that with the likes of Brazil, Uruguay, Portugal

and West Germany competing, the tournament would provide excellent preparation for our forthcoming World Cup qualifying campaign.

Having received the blessing of the SFA I then had to persuade club managers to release players. The tournament was taking place at the beginning of July and many managers were not keen to have players reporting back for pre-season training after a long-haul trip to South America, also fearing the possibility of injury. I once again invited the managers of all the leading Scottish clubs to attend another meeting-cum-lunch at SFA headquarters. The response I received was mixed, to say the least. Most did turn up including Jock Stein, but one or two didn't, including Dundee United manager Jim McLean. In the main Jock was fine about releasing his Celtic players, though on occasions I felt his compliance had more to do with the situation suiting his needs rather than those of the national team. Jock and I were great friends and he did what he could to help my situation. Though the same cannot be said of the Rangers manager Willie Waddell, who I found to be belligerent, obstinate and most unwilling to help the national team.

The squad I took to Brazil was: Jimmy Bone, Martin Buchan, George Graham, Denis McQuade, Bobby Clark, Ally Hunter, Eddie Colquhoun, John Hansen, George Anderson, Willie Donachie, Alex Forsyth, Donald Ford, Asa Hartford, Willie Morgan, Colin Stein, Denis Law, Lou Macari and Billy Bremner. There were others I would have liked to have taken such as Lorimer, Gray and Dalglish but they were unavailable to me, but all things considered I was happy with the strength of the 18-man squad.

My backroom staff consisted of only two, trainer Ronnie McKenzie and Jimmy Steele who was our masseur-cum-physio, kitman and first-aid man. The squad did not have a retinue of superfluous coaches and personal fitness trainers. They were already at the top of their game and supremely fit, so what would have been the point?

Our first match was against Yugoslavia in Belo Horizonte on 29 June and we flew out some five days earlier and arrived in Rio de Janeiro. It had always been an ambition of mine to see the Maracana Stadium, that whale amongst a shoal of football grounds peppered throughout the city. It truly was a wonderful sight as our plane descended over Rio Bay itself, seeing the city below nestling amongst the peaks that slide down to the shore, the sand of which gleamed as yellow as the Brazilian shirt itself. At the heart of it all there was the Maracana, from the air looking like a giant flying saucer that had just landed on earth. When we came through customs we were amazed to find a familiar welcome in the form of a pipe band which, we soon discovered, was formed of expatriates living in the Rio area. The players were in peak fitness and keyed up for the tournament but I knew they had to relax. I introduced a routine of swimming sessions in the morning, a light lunch, rest then training in the after-noon. In the evenings we relaxed with a drink in the hotel, or else went for a walk and did a little sightseeing. The Rio St Andrews Society held a party in our honour and later acted as our guide on a shopping trip along the Copacabana. Invaluable as this relaxation time was, I couldn't wait to get down to the serious business.

Yugoslavia were a more than useful team who'd enjoyed a month's acclimatisation by playing four matches against South American teams, remaining unbeaten on their tour, with victor-ies including a 2–1 success against Peru and a 10–0 thrashing of Venezuela. I was expecting a closely fought game, which is exactly what it turned out to be. Lou Macari scored both our goals in 2–2 draw, but we fluffed a great opportunity of winning the game when we were awarded a penalty towards the end. Willie Morgan elected to take it and if there had been a town hall clock nearby, he would have knocked the hands of it.

We then travelled to Porto Alegre where we were involved in a second draw, this time 0–0 against Czechoslovakia which proved good enough to take us through to a semi-final against the hosts, Brazil. This would be a real test of our international credentials, our character and resolve, playing as we were in front of 133,000 volatile and fanatical supporters. This was the game I had been longing for. In the dressing room I talked to the team, telling them they had nothing to fear, that we too had marvellous players and an abundance of skill. I was confident, I knew the boys were at optimum both physically and mentally, but minutes before we were due to take to the field, a problem arose.

We were all ready and up for it but an official called into our dressing room to tell us the kick-off was to be delayed for 'thirty minutes, perhaps more' – the Brazilian team bus had been held up in traffic. We were inundated with apologies and I had no alternative but to tell the players to relax, but the delay had an immediate effect. Irritation and frustration crept into the team.

I was later told that rather than there having been a genuine delay, this late kick-off was a ploy used by Brazil on several other opponents, including England. A couple of Scottish journalists told me they had seen some members of the Brazilian team entering a rest room in the Maracana, prior to the official informing us of the supposed problem. I was left with a team champing at the bit and becoming increasingly fidgety and nervous which, I was given to think, may well have been the whole point of it all.

The team I chose against Brazil was: Bobby Clark (Aberdeen), Alex Forsyth (Partick Thistle), Eddie Colquhoun (Sheffield United), Martin Buchan (Manchester United), Willie Donachie (Manchester City), Billy Bremner (captain – Leeds United), Asa Hartford (West Bromwich Albion), George Graham (Arsenal), Willie Morgan, Denis Law (both Manchester United), Lou Macari (Celtic). Subs: Colin Stein (Rangers), Jimmy Bone (Partick Thistle). It was a team geared to attack but also one I felt provided us with the cover in defence we would need when facing Brazil on home turf. The one disappointment for us all was that there was to be no Pelé. The boys had been relishing the thought of playing against the great man, and when news arrived that Pelé was injured and his place was to be taken by Leivinha, there was an audible sigh in the dressing room.

The Brazil team still contained plenty of world class players; Tostao who, in the absence of Pelé, wore the number 10 shirt, Brito, Clodoaldo, Gerson, Rivelino and Jairzinho, the core of that wonderful team that had won the 1970 World Cup by playing such superlative football. But I have to be honest and say I was very disappointed with the way Brazil applied themselves to this game. The match was littered with petty fouls, not so petty fouls, off-the-ball antagonism and much gamesmanship. It was a performance I felt unworthy of them, and we were to see it repeated less than two years later in the 1974 World Cup. While there were occasional flashes of stylish samba football from the Brazilians, for a lengthy spell in the first half it was Scotland who had the upper hand, without us ever converting our pressure into an all-important goal.

As the game ran down I grew more confident of us achieving a sensational result. A prolonged bout of pressure on the Brazilian goal in the second half saw Brito hook an effort from Morgan off the line, and Graham fizz a shot just the wrong side of the post. A minute later Leago displayed tremendous reflexes when finger-tipping to safety a goal-bound header from Macari. I knew we were doing very well because the Maracana was eerily silent.

Rather than seeing the efforts of Morgan, Graham and Macari as a foretaste of a goal to come, I began to fear we may have missed our best opportunity of taking the lead and would be punished for it. My concern was proved well placed. Ten minutes from time the Brazilian midfield suddenly and characteristically burst into action. There seemed no danger as Brazil hugged and stroked the ball to one another across the middle of the pitch, then the deadly moment arrived. Rivelino, who we had subdued for long periods, hit an exacting ball from the middle to the left. Tostao helped the ball on its way and Jairzinho cut inside to fire low past Bobby Clark. Just like that, from indolent play to deadly strike all in a matter of a few seconds. Suddenly the Maracana was alive, fireworks and rockets shot into the sky and, at the end of it all, the whole stadium was aflame with the bonfires of victory. It was fiesta time and we felt like unwanted guests.

As the newspapers and television reported, there was no disgrace in our defeat, far from it. We had come to South America, played three matches and narrowly lost one. As Jack Harkness wrote, 'Scotland has found a new hope under Tommy Docherty. When once we looked set to approach the World Cup qualifying matches with due caution there now reigns a buoyant mood of optimism throughout Scottish football.'

Scotland were drawn in a World Cup qualifying group of three, as were England. England awaited their fate at the hands of the Poles and the Welsh, whereas Scotland took on Denmark and Czechoslovakia. Characteristically, I was supremely confident of our qualification. Czechoslovakia had a good team, but I had seen nothing in our game against them in Brazil to cause concern. Denmark were the dark horses, their football having come on in leaps and bounds in recent years. They had beaten Scotland in a European Championship qualifier little over a year previously, during the managerial reign of Bobby Brown, and since then their results had included wins against Iceland, Mexico and Poland.

The performance against Denmark in Copenhagen on 18 October 1972 was to my mind the best during my spell as manager of the Scotland team. At half-time we held a 2–1 lead courtesy of goals from Lou Macari and Jim Bone, and in the second half we tore Denmark apart. Further goals from Joe Harper (Aberdeen) and Willie Morgan gave us what was to prove an unassailable 4–1 lead and it would have been six if the Danish crossbar hadn't played a blinder. Confident of victory, 15

minutes from time I brought on young Kenny Dalglish for Lou
Macari and saw enough to convince me that Kenny, for all his
tender years, was a prodigious talent.

I included Dalglish from the start in the return match with
Denmark at Hampden in November. For shielding the ball,
scoring from seemingly impossible angles and creating chances
for others, Kenny Dalglish had no equal. Even at this stage of
what was to be a much-garlanded career, he was superb at
making space in the penalty area and then laying the ball off.
His finishing was clinical and he always appeared to have so
much time to do things on and off the ball. For me Kenny was
a master of the footballing arts and I had no compunction about
giving him his chance in the Scotland team. Typically he marked
the occasion with a wonderful goal against Denmark, a second
from Peter Lorimer gave us a 2–0 victory and put Scotland top
of our group. Happily that is where we were to stay.

It had been my great ambition to lead Scotland into the World
Cup finals in Germany in 1974, but fate was to intervene and
I would never have that honour. Fate came in the form of
the most fabulous offer of management there could ever be,
one that presented me with the biggest decision and greatest
dilemma of my career.

I have never been a great drinker, I enjoy the occasional glass
of wine or a dram, but that's about it. But I was never one to
deny players their pint when the time was right. Scotland's win
over Denmark was such a time. When the work was done and
the interviews over I joined some of the players and a few
members of the press in our hotel for a nightcap. Some of the
team had gone to their rooms, one or two who lived in Glasgow
I had allowed to return to their families, but there were several
still present.

Victory was ours, the road to the finals beckoned and, just
as important, pride had been restored in the national team. I
had an extremely talented squad of players who were a great
bunch of lads. I was in my element that night. There was much

talk of football, of the optimistic variety too. There were jokes, japes and a really super atmosphere prevailed. Suddenly, from across the room, someone sang the opening line of 'Scotland the Brave'. Almost immediately others joined him. The song finished, there was a moment's silence, then one of the press boys began to sing Robbie Burns' 'A Red, Red Rose'. That did it. The patriotic atmosphere swelled to bursting point.

Burns is not a tradition in Scotland; to this day he remains a living force. Scotland lives in every word he wrote and uttered, and his influence has never waned. If there is ever anything to fire the patriotism of us Scots, it is Burns. Centuries of repression spoke in him, his works proof to any Englishman that Scotland is indeed another country. Burns fuels the passion of Scots as no other can ever do. The pressman ploughed deliberately on through the song, sometimes closing his eyes, the better to remember it, only to reach the third verse, 'Till a' the seas gang dry, my dear', and have everyone in the room join him. We sang with gusto, with pride of our undying love of Scotland:

> Till a' the seas gang dry, my dear
> And the rocks melt wi' the sun,
> And I will love thee still, my dear
> While the sands o' life shall run.

The pressman looked around the room triumphantly, delighted to have the majority of the Scotland squad and a good many of his colleagues fall into his vein, and so we continued to sing, reaching an emotional finale:

> And fare thee weel, my only love
> And fare thee weel, a while . . .

14

FOLLOW YOUR BLISS

I received a telephone call from Crystal Palace manager Bert Head. He was keen for me to see Tony Taylor, a young defender who Bert told me had been playing exceptionally well for Palace, and who he was recommending for the Scotland squad, so I agreed to travel down to Selhurst Park to look at the boy play against Manchester United on 16 December 1972. At the time I thought it would be an intriguing one, as both Palace and United were struggling near the foot of the First Division and in desperate need of points. The game would also provide me with an opportunity of meeting my old Preston team-mate Frank O'Farrell who was the United manager. I suspected he might be in need of a friendly face. With United not doing well he was coming in for increasing criticism from the media and United fans alike.

Taylor played at left-back but the game didn't really offer him an opportunity to show his worth. Palace dominated and won 5–0. United were dreadful that day. They were without Bobby Charlton, while George Best had gone missing again, but to my mind still had enough talent on the field to have given Palace more than a run for their money. Willie Morgan and Martin Buchan only showed flashes of their talent. Ted McDougall, Ian Storey-Moore and Wyn Davies were virtually anonymous, whilst David Sadler, Brian Kidd and Eric Young were not even that good. Denis Law was substitute on the day. When Denis came on for Tony Dunne in the second half, he appeared to have lost his former spark. I was taken aback. Of Law's many assets, one was certainly his enthusiasm. He never gave up a lost cause. After the game he wouldn't come out of the dressing room and join his team-mates for a drink and a bite to eat before the journey back to Manchester. Something was definitely wrong at United.

I was sitting in the Selhurst Park tearoom when a pal of mine, Basil Graham, who organised the travel for United, came and sat next to me with his cup of tea. 'Sir Matt's looking for you, Tom,' Basil informed me. 'It'll be about your Scottish lads.' It never occurred to me there might be any significance in this. I finished my tea and went in search of Sir Matt Busby. When I found him he was deep in conversation with the United chairman, Louis Edwards.

'Bad news, Tom,' said Matt. 'There's a lot of trouble in the camp.'

'Gathered that from what I saw today,' I told him.

'Fancy the job?' asked Matt.

I was stunned. The sudden and matter-of-fact proposition really did shock me. I immediately lost control of my senses and found myself suppressing laughter. It was laughter of the nervous type. Matt and Louis Edwards had obviously noticed the shocked expression on my face as both smiled.

'Think about it,' said Matt, acknowledging I needed time to take this all in. 'Willie, Denis and Martin rave about you. You know I've always rated you, Tom. As I say, have a think and let us know the result.'

I caught a taxi to the airport and sat trying to take it all in. It seemed a perfectly normal winter's night in London, but I knew it was going to be far from a normal night for me. I kept telling myself I'd just been offered the job of manager at Manchester United. It seemed surreal. The conversation with Matt had lasted less than a minute and I had been offered the manager's job at arguably the biggest club in the world. I was still struggling to come to terms with it when I eventually arrived at our home in Largs.

There was no mention in the morning press of United being about to dispense with the services of Frank O'Farrell. I felt I was privy to some great secret. The only person I told about this was Agnes who, of course, was delighted for me.

My mind was in a whirl. I was the Scotland team manager with a very good chance of leading my country to the World Cup finals. I had been offered the opportunity to manage Manchester United because of the success I had made of the Scotland job. Simple as that, only it didn't make my decision any easier. I turned the matter over and over in my head. What if I accepted the United job, but things got worse at the club and they got rid of me after a year? How would I feel about having given up the Scotland job then? I had done a lot of spade-work with Scotland and turned things round. I was now sitting comfortable as the manager, everyone thought I was doing a grand job – why should I take on a giant of a club that, in Matt's own words, had a 'lot of trouble'? For a moment, only a brief moment mind, I did wonder whether I'd be better off staying where I was. A case of better the devil you know than the red devils you don't.

All these thoughts were taking place on the Sunday morning, the day after Matt had made the offer. That afternoon I settled down at my desk at home with the intention of catching up on Scotland work, only there wasn't much catching-up to do – Scotland's next game was the SFA Centenary match against England in February, the three Home Internationals were in May, and we were due to play against Switzerland and Brazil at the end of June. There was then a gap of three months before the World Cup qualifiers against Czechoslovakia in late September with the return scheduled for November. Eight games in nigh on a year, with the next one not for nine weeks. I loved being manager of Scotland, but there simply wasn't enough work to keep me occupied and energised. That after-noon as I sat at my desk, I made my decision to say yes to Matt. Once I had made that decision, I knew it was the right one and was left wondering why I had deliberated most of the day. Love and respect of my country I suppose.

That Sunday evening after dinner, Matt rang. 'Are you interested, Tom?' he asked.

'Yes. Scotland, great job, but not enough work for me,' I told him.

'Good. Let's keep the wraps on it, we have to sort things our end,' he said. 'You know it won't be easy? It'll be like turning an oil tanker round, only bigger.'

'I can do it,' I told him.

'I know you can, that's why we're offering it to you. But there are all sorts of problems. You might find yourself having to take a step back in order to take a leap forward,' said Matt.

At the time I never thought Matt might be alluding to United being relegated – I can't think what else he could have meant.

'How're you fixed with Scotland?' Matt asked finally.

I told him the first thing I would have to do was ring the SFA for permission to speak to him and his co-directors. Strictly speaking Matt had made an approach for my services contrary to football rules, so I was keen to go through the official channels as soon as possible. 'There's nothing in my contract that says I shouldn't be given permission to speak to an interested club,' I informed him.

'Good, I'll leave you to get it sorted,' said Matt.

I was keen to move things forward, and quickly, but I couldn't just then, not whilst Frank O'Farrell was still manager at Old Trafford. On Monday I received a call from SFA secretary Wullie Allen. Wullie informed me Louis Edwards was seeking permission to speak to me about the possibility of becoming the new manager at Manchester United. Wullie asked if I wanted to speak to United, I told him I did, though I reminded him that to date they still had a manager in Frank O'Farrell. 'Seemingly not for much longer,' said Wullie.

The following afternoon I was driving home to Largs when I heard on the radio the news that Frank O'Farrell had been sacked. It was time to make my move. I spoke to both Wullie Allen and Hugh Nelson to confirm I had permission to speak to the United directors. Permission was confirmed though both informed me they hoped I would reconsider my position and remain with Scotland. Hugh was a club chairman himself and I sensed he knew Manchester United had already spoken to me. Hugh never said anything to that effect, probably knowing that's the way it is in football, binding contract or not, things are rarely, if ever, done strictly by the book. It was common for a club chairman, or a friend or associate of his, to sound out a possible manager before making an official approach for his services. Such an approach was referred to as 'tapping' and, though in violation of a contract, it was so common people turned a blind eye to it. It happened because a chairman wanted to avoid making an official approach to a would-be manager only to be turned down and suffer the stigma of such a refusal. Tapping, it would appear, is as common today as it was thirty years ago.

The sacking of Frank O'Farrell made headline news but the photographs on the front pages were not of Frank, but of George Best who, on the same day, had also been sacked by United. For a number of years, before his sad death in 2005, it was generally said that George saw Matt as a father figure and that Matt had nothing but warmth for, as newspapers often put it, 'his wayward genius'. I have no doubt whatsoever that George did see Matt as a father figure as he did, after all, ignore Matt's advice often enough. George may have felt love in his heart for Matt but that feeling was, for a number of years at any rate, not reciprocated. In December 1972 at the time of Best's sacking by United, Matt was fed up to the back teeth with George. I still have the front pages from several newspapers of that day. They paint a very different picture to the one that has often been portrayed of mutual fondness between mentor and prodigy. On the subject of George, Matt is quoted as saying, 'We've finally had enough of him. Thankfully, we've finally got him out of our hair. All of us had enough of George and his [night]clubs and his way of life.'

United had made a clean sweep. In addition to sacking Frank and George, chief coach John Aston and assistant manager Malcolm Musgrove were also relieved of their duties. The newspapers reported Pat Crerand and Bill Foulkes had been put in charge of team affairs as 'United begin their search for a new manager'. Tucked away at the bottom of the *Daily Record*'s report was a sub-headline that immediately grabbed my attention, it read – 'Now They Are Going After The Doc'. The piece ran to only half a dozen three-line paragraphs. It said bookmakers in Manchester had me the clear favourite to succeed Frank O'Farrell and that others in the running were Jock Stein, Brian Clough, Preston boss Alan Ball senior and Burnley's Jimmy Adamson. The article concluded by saying United was to advertise the post. I wondered whether or not to apply.

I flew down to Norwich to watch their League Cup semi-final against Chelsea. I was on Scotland business but as soon as I arrived at Carrow Road I was button-holed by a bevy of pressmen, all of whom wanted to know if I was about to become the new manager of Manchester United. I did my best imitation of a politician by never providing a direct answer to any question. I adopted the strategy of having the beginning and end of my reply very close together. Then I got out as early as I could.

On my return to Scotland, Hugh Nelson and SFA vice-president Jimmy Aitken both tried to persuade me to stay on with the national team, but my mind was made up. They were publicly full of praise for my work and my results as Scotland's team manager.

Early in 2001 Craig Brown sent me a table he'd compiled of the record of every Scotland manager to have been in charge for three games or more. I had met Craig at a dinner during which he told me that I had the best record of any Scotland manager. As proof, he sent me the table:

SCOTLAND INTERNATIONAL TEAM MANAGERS
Record in all Matches

		P	W	D	L	F	A	%
Andy Beattie (first term)	1954	6	2	1	3	6	14	42
Matt Busby – two games only	1958	2	1	1	0	5	2	–
Andy Beattie (second term)	1959–60	12	3	3	6	19	23	33
Ian McColl	1960–65	28	17	3	8	77	52	65
Jock Stein (first term)	1965	7	3	1	3	11	11	50
John Prentice	1966	4	0	1	3	4	9	13
Malcolm McDonald	1966	2	1	1	0	3	2	–
Bobby Brown	1967–71	28	9	8	11	37	35	46
Tommy Docherty	1971–72	12	7	2	3	17	8	66
Willie Ormond	1973–77	38	18	8	12	55	38	58
Ally MacLeod	1977–78	17	7	5	5	26	21	56
Jock Stein (second term)	1978–85	61	26	12	23	80	70	52
Alex Ferguson	1985–86	10	3	4	3	8	5	50
Andy Roxburgh	1986–93	61	23	19	19	67	60	53
Craig Brown	1993 to date	47	22	11	14	58	39	59

In 2006 Craig told me, if one took into consideration his complete record as manager, also that of Bertie Vogts and Walter Smith to date, I still topped the table.

I wouldn't have left my role as manager of Scotland for any other job. For me it was the chance of a lifetime, I couldn't wait until my appointment was made official and I could get down to work.

On Friday 22 December Manchester United called a press

conference at Old Trafford and, to no one's surprise I am sure, unveiled me as their new manager. I had no backroom staff, I had yet to meet the players, United were bottom of the league and at home to Leeds the following day. After the press conference I was taken by car to meet the players at The Cliff, the United training ground. Introductions over, I returned to Old Trafford to sign the contract. Up to this point no one had mentioned a salary. It was Matt who first talked money prior to the signing of the contract. He told me my salary was to be £15,000 a year, plus a car. When asked if I was happy with that, I told them I was more than happy.

Against Leeds United I only made two changes from the team I had seen demolished at Crystal Place the previous Saturday. Denis Law replaced Eric Young, and Bobby Charlton was back in place of Brian Kidd, who I made substitute. Ted MacDougall put us ahead in the first half against Leeds, one of the best teams in Europe at the time. It looked as if I was going to enjoy a dream start but, two minutes from time, Allan 'Sniffer' Clarke lived up to his nickname. Seizing on an error in defence, Clarke advanced before slotting the ball past Alex Stepney.

Though I was very disappointed not to have made a winning start, the performance had been pretty good, but I wasn't deluding myself. The team had big problems. If I only thought it then, I definitely knew it three days later when we were second best in just about everything and lost 3–1 at Derby County, sending us to the bottom of the First Division again. I wasted no time in making changes. The very next day I paid £120,000 to bring George Graham from Arsenal, the day after that I travelled to Glasgow to sign Partick Thistle full-back Alex Forsyth for £100,000. There were no mobile phones in those days so when travelling the length of the UK to sign Graham and Forsyth, I rang the people I wanted for my backroom staff from hotels and even public phone boxes. In addition to the 'names' who had been sacked along with Frank O'Farrell, a retinue of trainers and scouts had also been dismissed so I had a lot of calls to make.

I made Tommy Cavanagh my right-hand man to supervise training and help me with the coaching. Tommy had been in Preston reserves when I was a player at Deepdale but had never really made it into the first team. When his playing days were over he became a trainer and when I was assistant manager at Hull City, Terry Neill asked if I knew a good trainer for the club. I recommended Tommy and he was duly appointed. I knew he would do a great job for United, and for me, so he was my first port of call. I also engaged Jimmy Curran to work with the youngsters; and appointed the former United keeper, Gordon Clayton, alongside Norman Scholes, and former United skipper and ex-Blackburn Rovers and Nottingham Forest manager, Johnny Carey as scouts. I also re-engaged two of Matt Busby's old staff, Jimmy Murphy and Jack Crompton, two very seasoned men in football who did not have a specific task, other than being around to help with the training and give youngsters the benefit of their considerable experience in the game.

Ted MacDougall made it known that he wasn't happy at the club and wanted a move back down south. This made me happy as he didn't really feature in my plans. In a matter of weeks I sold him to West Ham for £150,000. I travelled back to Glasgow to talk to Jock Stein about the player I wanted as Ted's replacement, Celtic's Lou Macari who had asked for a transfer. But I found I had competition for his signature from Liverpool. I was confident, however, that due to the relationship we had formed during my time with Scotland I was going to get my man. On 6 January we lost 3–1 at Arsenal and were still firmly rooted at the bottom of the table, not the best position to be in when trying to compete with Liverpool for the signature of one of the hottest properties in British football.

Liverpool were due to play Burnley in an FA Cup replay at Anfield. I went along that night to see my son Michael in action for Burnley. When I saw Lou Macari sitting in the stand I wobbled a bit but went over for a chat. The temptation was to try there and then to persuade Lou to come and join me at Old

Trafford, but I had yet to receive permission from Celtic to talk to him so didn't raise the subject. I knew, however, he would be talking to Bill Shankly later and, in a curious way, I felt Bill talking to Lou would make him lean towards joining me at United. I knew that when Bill talked to prospective signings he sung the praises of Liverpool, but also tended to exert pressure on the player to sign. Knowing Macari as I did, I felt he would not want such pressure, and that he would have misgivings about a manager who attempted to do that.

What was said between Bill and Lou I have no idea. All I know is the following day, with Celtic's consent, I spoke to Lou and suggested he had to weigh up his prospects, as well as those of Manchester United. Lou thrived on a challenge and I told him, should he join United, no other club could offer a greater challenge than the one that would await him at Old Trafford. The following day the way was clear. After Lou's meeting with Bill Shankly had not resulted in him agreeing so sign, Liverpool withdrew their offer. What came first I don't know, but also on that day Lou Macari told me he had made his decision – he was coming to United.

I paid £200,000 for Lou Macari, it was a massive fee for the time, but he proved to be worth every penny. On the same day I also signed midfielder Mick Martin from League of Ireland club Bohemians for £20,000. A couple of weeks later I bought a granite-like but raw young centre-half from Shrewsbury Town by the name of Jim Holton. The bricks were being put in place but I knew that 'Rome wasn't built . . .'

We went out of the FA Cup in the third round, beaten 1–0 at Wolves. Lou Macari made his debut in our next game against West Ham and United fans took to him straight away. Trailing 2–1, Lou popped up towards the end with a great equaliser to top what had been a sparkling display from him. The Stretford End immediately burst into song in praise of their new hero, singing 'Who put the ball in the West Ham net, who put the ball in the West Ham net, who put the ball in the West Ham net, skip to me Lou Macari!'

Towards the end of February I had a long chat with Bobby Charlton. Bobby's status as a truly world class player was never in doubt, but he was now coming up to 37 years old. He had been with United from the age of 15 and had given the club sterling service, but he told me he was to make this season his last. Bobby was a true football great, a thoroughbred player of real class. He was still a great player and felt he could do a job for me, but not the job he once did for United, and that was the crux. I respected him for the decision he had made, moreover for recognising that, at his age, he could no longer play for his beloved United in the way he wanted.

The Manchester United team that had won the European Cup in 1968 was without a doubt a great team, but many members of that side had been allowed to grow old together. Matt Busby's successors Wilf McGuinness and Frank O'Farrell had made the mistake of keeping faith with the old guard, a mistake Liverpool never made or indeed Celtic manager Jock Stein. Jock said to me that the trick is to get rid of the ageing star *before* he isn't doing the business for you any more.

Bobby Charlton had taken the decision to retire and I had made some decisions of my own. I knew what I had decided would prove very unpopular with many people but it had to be done. I set out my stall to end the United careers of amongst others Denis Law, Tony Dunne, Pat Crerand and David Sadler. Of these I knew far and away the most controversial decision would be that of Denis Law. Denis was hero-worshipped at Old Trafford, he too was a world-class player, but I could see Denis wasn't playing anywhere like he used to. At 33 he should have had another season in him at Old Trafford, but he was now going through the motions in games. There was no room for sentiment. I had to be realistic and practical. I knew I would receive a mountain of criticism, but Denis had to go.

At the end of March I had been in charge of United for thirteen games of which we had won four, drawn five and lost four. Prior to me joining the club, United had won five from twenty-two. Progress was being made but to my mind nothing like I wanted. Due to contracts which still had a year, or, in some cases two years, to run, I was stuck with a number of players I didn't want. Unless another club came in for them they would have to stay – for the time being.

It was around this time that George Best re-emerged from his Spanish sabbatical. George announced that he was ready to play again, but only for Northern Ireland. I was asked by the press for my opinion on this and gave it – George was currently serving a FIFA ban, so he couldn't play for Northern Ireland. I believed George was hoping United would make contact and ask him to return to the fold at Old Trafford. I wasn't ruling out a return for him, but given his previous shenanigans it would have to be on my terms not his. I wasn't going to jump to George's call.

I also appointed United's former centre-half Bill Foulkes and Pat Crerand to be in charge of the United youth team. Bill worked out fine, but when I later promoted Pat to assistant manager I was to have monumental problems with him.

We enjoyed an unbeaten run of eight matches from mid-March to mid-April which elevated us to safety. The final game of that run was a 0–0 draw in the Manchester derby watched by the Football League's highest attendance of the season, 61,676. We ended the season by losing both at home to Sheffield United and away to Chelsea to finish fifth from bottom, seven points clear of the relegation places. I had inherited a mess, and although we had preserved our First Division status, I knew I was far from having finished the necessary clean-up.

Sadly that Sheffield United defeat marked the last appearance at Old Trafford by Bobby Charlton. A crowd of nearly 58,000 bade an emotional farewell to Bobby who, before the game, was presented with an inscribed silver salver by Matt Busby as a token of the club's gratitude for the 22 wonderful years of service he had given the club. There was another presentation for Bobby from both Chelsea and the Football League prior to the game at Stamford Bridge.

When I took United to Stamford Bridge for what was our final game of the season, I was heartened by the reception I was given by the Chelsea supporters as I took my seat on the bench. The stands hummed with warm applause and the Shed chanted my name. I was very touched by this and reciprocated by holding my arms aloft and applauding all corners of the ground. The Chelsea directors and their guests were also welcoming – no hard feelings then.

For Bobby Charlton's last game the Stamford Bridge turnstiles were closed half an hour before the start, and every available inch of the fractured ground in the process of reconstruction was taken by the 44,000 crowd. Both teams provided a guard of honour for the man himself as he took to the stage alone, amidst rapturous applause. The game itself was nothing to write home about. The best touches came from Osgood, who scored the only goal, and Hollins who was superb in midfield. When it was all over Bobby shook hands with the opposition as normal, quickly waved farewell to the crowd and was gone. I should imagine that was the way he wanted it to be, given he was never a man for nostalgic junketings.

Ageing footballers, unlike old soldiers, do not simply fade away, as football has little affection for dwindling skills. Even eminently successful careers invariably end with an almost callous abruptness, as decline is a fact of football life and has to be accepted without question. The season ended with some illustrious names moving from the spotlight to the shadows. Bobby was unquestionably the most revered name, and his last game for United was on the same afternoon his brother Jack pulled on a Leeds United shirt for the final time. I had given a free transfer to Denis Law to Manchester City, whilst tragic circumstances – in the form of a car crash – had contrived to remove Gordon Banks from top-flight football. The finale to the 1972–73 season seemed to mark a change in the old guard, fittingly, for that was what I was trying to at Old Trafford.

I came in for a tremendous amount of criticism from some

quarters of United supporters and the media for dispensing with
the services of Denis Law. Some also accused me of having
ended the career of Bobby Charlton, though of course this
wasn't true – that was a case of guilty by association. Denis Law
had done a great job for me when coming on as substitute for
Scotland, he had a bubbly presence in the dressing room which
was good for team spirit, but he was no longer producing the
goods over 90 minutes. When I called Denis in to my office and
I told him I was giving him a free transfer he was, understandably, far from happy. Denis had a year of his contract to run
but I told him he was now drifting in and out of games, at best,
and I couldn't have that. When I had played him in matches,
his performances had simply not been good enough. He didn't
agree with that, but as far as I was concerned it was fact. The
atmosphere between us was, not surprisingly, strained; Denis
was very unhappy, but there was no animosity. The fact that he
had a year of his contract remaining meant he didn't have to
go. He could have stayed if he had wished, but I believe he saw
little point. In the event the directors gave Denis £5,000 tax-
free for the remainder of his contract, and also granted him a
testimonial match, a fitting reward for the excellent service he
had given United.

Initially Matt Busby told me he felt Denis had another season
in him at the club, but I convinced him the decision to free Denis
was the right one. I pointed out that he was spending more and
more time in the treatment room, often only being declared fit
to play on Thursday afternoon or Friday morning. I reminded
Matt that under my predecessor, United had played 22 league
games and Denis had started only five, two of which had resulted
in him being substituted. He had hardly been a first choice of
Frank O'Farrell. Under my management Denis had made only
four starts, in two of which I'd had to substitute him just after
the hour mark. The corners of Matt's mouth made a downturn
and he nodded his head solemnly.

★

At the end of 1972–73 I released thirteen players. As far as I was concerned I had only made a start in changing the personnel at the club. In July I persuaded Frank Blunstone to leave his post as manager of Brentford and join me at United. Frank had, of course, played for me during my days at Chelsea. He was great with young players, and had that most wonderful gift, the ability to spot ability. He was to bring much fine young talent to the club. Whenever a youngster had self-doubt, Frank had the knack of pin-pointing strengths the boy never realised he had and developing those, as well as being able to improve the weaker aspects of his game. I knew Frank would do a great job for me and the club and he did. He proved to be one of my best signings.

The season began with a 3–0 defeat at Arsenal in front of a Highbury crowd of 51,501. In our first home match of the season we entertained Stoke City, a goal from defender Steve James gave us a 1–0 victory but what I remember most from this match was Stoke's George Eastham being booked for the first time in his career. George was cautioned for mildly contesting a decision and when his name went into the book I could see what was going through his mind. 'Twenty-two years in the game, never so much as a booking then this twerp spoils it all. It's time to pack it up.' Four weeks later he did.

Goals from Jim Holton and Sammy McIlroy gave us a 2–1 victory over QPR in our third game but I knew we were flattering to deceive. What followed was a disastrous run of results that saw us win three from nineteen League matches, the third victory coming at the end of December and mercifully ending a run of nine matches without a win, four of which were drawn. Inevitably after such a poor run of results we were struggling at the foot of the table.

One player to arrive before Christmas was Stewart Houston who, having been strongly recommended to me by Frank Blunstone, I had seen playing for Brentford at Stockport County. On the strength of Frank's recommendation and Houston's

performance at Stockport I paid Brentford £50,000 for his services. Again, it was to prove money well spent. The arrival of
Stewart Houston provided a little chink of light during the power
crisis that had beset the country and saw the nation working to
a three-day week to conserve energy supplies.

The New Year brought little, if any, respite from angst at
United. We were beaten 3–0 at QPR on New Year's Day and
that set the tone until the end of March. Two wins in twelve
meant that by March we were contemplating the unthinkable:
Manchester United were on course for relegation. In an attempt
to boost our goals tally which was still at this time woeful, I paid
Wolves £60,000 for Jim McCalliog. Jim made his debut in the
middle of March in a 1–0 defeat at Birmingham City, not the
best of starts. Jim had a keen eye for goal, worked hard, had
some nice touches, could hold the ball up when required and
was a good team player. He soon made his presence felt in the
team and played a key role in a sequence of results I felt was
going to lift us to safety.

That sequence began with our 3–1 win at Chelsea and thereafter we enjoyed victories over Norwich (2–0), Newcastle United
(1–0) and Everton (3–0) and draws against Burnley and
Southampton. McCalliog scored four goals in three matches and
with three games remaining our fate lay in our own hands. That
advantage did not last for long. In our very next match we lost
1–0 at Everton on a day when our rivals at the bottom collected
points. The prospect of relegation loomed if we did not win our
next and penultimate home game – the derby against
Manchester City.

The situation at the foot of Division One at 3 p.m. on
Saturday 27 April 1974 was very tight. Birmingham City were
at home to Norwich City, Southampton were away to Everton,
whilst West Ham United faced Liverpool at home. It was a time
when two points were awarded for a win and was the first season
of three-up and three-down promotion and relegation between
the First and Second Divisions. Should we win our final two

matches we would finish with 36 points; a win against Manchester City, and a win or a draw for Norwich at Birmingham would give us a chance of safety, with Stoke City our final game.

A scriptwriter couldn't have come up with a more dramatic story than the one that was about to unfold before 57,000 spectators at Old Trafford. The atmosphere was a heady cocktail of nervous tension and excitement as the game began with the City supporters making no secret of their ambition to see their team apply the fatal blow on United. There was also a heavy irony in the situation, as in the ranks of the City team was Denis Law – you couldn't have made it up.

Within minutes of the start news filtered through from St Andrews that Norwich had taken the lead against Birmingham City. Hope sprang eternal. Shortly before half-time our ardour was dampened with the news of Birmingham scoring twice in a matter of minutes to lead 2–1, which was how that game would remain. We gave it our all against City and though both teams went at it hammer and tongs the score remained goalless – until eight minutes from time. Under pressure from City we failed to clear our lines, a City shot was blocked, Francis Lee knocked the ball to the feet of Denis Law who, with his back to goal, lazily back-heeled it. When the ball entered the net my heart sank. It was a fortuitous goal but, of course, they all count and they look the same in the record books come May. Denis didn't celebrate, not in the least. Knowing there were seven minutes of the game remaining he seemed to realise what the consequences of his laconic back-heel would be to the club he loved and had served so admirably for 12 years. His team-mates rushed to congratulate him, but Denis just held his arms by his sides.

Thereafter it all turned ugly. This was a period when some clubs were blighted with a small fraternity of criminals who followed them about – at the time Manchester United were one such club. I refrain from referring to these people as football fans; they were hooligans who had nothing to do with genuine football supporters. The hooligans were very much in the minority, but group dynamics being what they are, they found it none too difficult to encourage the weak and gullible to fall into line with their antics. No sooner had Denis scored than hundreds of hooligans took to the pitch, not from the Stretford End where the core loyal United fans gathered, but from the Scoreboard End (East Stand). The game was halted, the pitch cleared, the game restarted for a couple of minutes during which time Denis Law was substituted, then finally abandoned as more hooligans spilled onto the pitch. Matt Busby made an emotional appeal to these people via the Tannoy system but I knew he was wasting his time, those on the pitch were not lovers of the club or the game.

The result stood. What had been the unthinkable had become reality. Manchester United, once the kings of Europe and for many years one of the clubs at the very top of the English game, had been relegated to Division Two. What's more I had the stigma of being manager when it happened. It has often been written that Denis Law's goal relegated Manchester United. It didn't. If we had beaten Manchester City 10–0 that day it wouldn't have changed a thing. Our relegation was sealed by results elsewhere, primarily Birmingham's defeat of Norwich City. It has also been written that the City match was our final game of the season. It wasn't; on the Monday we travelled to Stoke City. In the event the game at the Victoria Ground was a meaningless match for both teams which we lost 1–0, but had we beaten Manchester City and had Birmingham even drawn with Norwich, a win at Stoke would have made United safe. Likewise we would have been safe had Birmingham lost and we had collected three points from our games against City and Stoke. Hark – is that the sound of water under a bridge I hear?

How can I explain how I felt the night of the Manchester City game? For the first and only time in my life I was to know what depression was. That night as I sat at home I had no enthusiasm for anything. I felt like an empty shell. To be honest I was expecting the sack and thought what the future might hold for a manager whose last job was tainted with the stigma of having taken Manchester United down to Division Two. Low as I was that night I wanted to remain in the job and see it through. I was still confident that given the time, I could revive the fortunes at United and bring them success. Fortunately I was to be given that time.

Matt and Louis Edwards made it very clear they did not like the situation the club were now in, but that I still had the unanimous support of the board. Matt reminded me that when he first spoke to me about the United job he said it would be like turning an oil tanker around, only bigger. 'I knew it would take time, so we are going to give you the time,' he told me. With that he gave me a case of champagne and said, 'I know you're not a drinker Tom, but at least have a few glasses of this, then get on with getting the club back to the First Division.' It was a marvellous gesture on his part, but grateful though I was for the champagne my real gratitude was for the time Matt and his fellow directors had given me.

The lot of a manager is a strange one. I had endured an awful first full season with United but was still in a job. I consoled myself with the thought that in time I would ride out the storm. Frank O'Farrell rang that weekend to offer his condolences and best wishes for my future success at the club. Frank had spent the season as manager of Cardiff City but told me he'd resigned to take up a new job. 'I'd had enough of the troubles at Cardiff,' he told me. 'I've taken a job where I can get on with things in peace, where there'll be no turmoil or animosity flying about. It's a job as a national coach.' I asked him where. 'Iran.'

When we started our 1973–74 campaign at Arsenal I was already toying with the idea of bringing George Best back to the club. George was 27 and, if he had been handled right and looked after himself, such was his talent he could have gone on playing at the top into his thirties. During the summer of 1973, on more than one occasion George had hinted at a return to football, initially only for Northern Ireland as I have said. However, invariably when interviewed he waxed lyrical about Manchester United, the inference being that if he were to come back, United would be the club. George was a great lad and, of course, a genius of a player. What I needed was very good players, never mind a football genius. Though I had never managed George, I was familiar with his character and lifestyle and thought if I talked to him we could sort things out. He was a very intelligent and objective guy. I thought George coming back to United and playing football again would be good for both him and the club, and that his presence on the pitch and in the dressing room would have a very positive influence on the team – as long as he returned with his professional head on.

Some time in late August I spoke to George and we arranged to meet on 6 September. He was articulate and easy to talk to and after some social niceties it was George who first brought up the subject of returning to United. This pleased me; perhaps he was even keener to play again than I had first thought. A highly motivated George Best – there was no way I was going to do anything but pave the way for his return and help him all I could. We concluded our meeting with me saying. 'George, I'm delighted to have you back and I am delighted for you, but you do know this is your one and only chance with me?' He showed a little irritation at this but nodded and said, 'Yeah, right, no problem.' Of course, such was George and his life, it was only to be a matter of time before there was a problem.

Four days later George reported for training and, for a time, everything went well. When I saw him in training I told him he was a good month's work from being able to play again, and to his credit he buckled down. In mid-October we travelled over to Ireland to play a friendly against Shamrock Rovers. George had been training hard for over a month and the Shamrock Rovers game presented a good opportunity for him to get some match practice. The news George had been included in the team for this friendly made headlines. Shamrock Rovers' ground could hold around 25,000 and it was full to capacity with thousands locked outside. George did not disappoint me, the club, or his legions of fans. He was scintillating. With ten minutes to go and us leading 2–1 a few young fans ran on to the pitch to embrace George; in no time at all they were followed by hundreds of others. He disappeared into a swarm of his young admirers. Somehow we managed to get George and the other players off the pitch. Once safely inside the dressing rooms the referee announced that in the interests of the safety of the players and officials he was abandoning the game.

Five days later I included George in our 1–0 victory over Birmingham City. He did well but he was still lacking match fitness and as he tired in the second half I replaced him with Mick Martin. Our main problem was our inability to score goals. The goal against Birmingham was only our tenth in twelve matches, and was scored by goalkeeper Alex Stepney from the penalty spot. As a mark of how ineffective we were upfront, having scored from the spot earlier in the season against Leicester, Stepney was our joint top goalscorer!

George had a run of eleven matches until the end of December, he did well enough but it was obvious he was not the George of old. He scored our goal in a 2–1 defeat at Tottenham and one in a 3–2 home defeat to Coventry City, but generally speaking his contribution was lacking. It was sad to see. When he first came back into the team you could sense the expectation of the crowd whenever the ball came near him, but this was quelled after he produced a number of journeyman performances.

On New Year's Day 1974 we suffered a 3–0 defeat at QPR. It was a shocking performance and George seemed uninterested from start to finish. I gave the players the following day off and when they reported back on 3 January George wasn't there. He turned up for training the following day saying he'd had a

24-hour bug. I asked why he hadn't rung the club to let us know and he mumbled something about being so poorly he'd slept all day. He did his training so I included him in the squad for the following day, a third round FA Cup tie against Plymouth Argyle. I made up my mind to play him against Plymouth but whilst in the process of making that decision, George was reaching for the self-destruct button.

The players assembled at noon for a light lunch – minus George. Come 2.15 p.m. George still hadn't shown. I had the team sheet to hand in, so named Mick Martin in place of George. At around 2.35 p.m. I was in the dressing room with the players when George turned up and told me he was expecting to play. I said there was no chance of this, that I had already picked the side and handed in the team sheet.

'George, rather than thinking about playing football, you should be thinking about being breathalysed,' I told him as the smell of alcohol hit me. George wasn't happy with the situation and neither was I.

We beat Plymouth, though it was another unconvincing performance. George didn't turn up for training on the Monday, the next day or the day after that. On 12 January, seven days after the Plymouth game and having had no contact from him, I suspended George for two weeks and placed him on the transfer list. What was the point of suspending George when he wasn't turning up? First of all, I felt his behaviour was intolerable and merited disciplinary action. Second, I didn't want George turning up at the ground or The Cliff as the mood took him, and his presence possibly having an adverse effect on the other players. George never did show up again. The day before his suspension was up he announced his retirement from football, although he would later play for a variety of clubs on a short-term basis.

George Best's genius as a footballer has never been in doubt. At 23 he was the finished article. As a young man he was a smashing lad: intelligent, witty, honest, warm and, for all his fame, modest. But in my opinion for the majority of his time at Old Trafford he was badly handled. George was the first footballer to achieve fame and stardom – and they are two different things – outside of the game. Before him football stars enjoyed a fame that never transmitted beyond the game itself. To an extent George's fame was a product of the times, the heady and, for many in the spotlight of popular culture, hedonistic sixties. George's face was to be seen adorning not only football magazines but a wide range of publications from colour supplements to the *Daily Mirror*. He also appeared in TV commercials, one of the most memorable being for the Egg Marketing Board which featured George having a boiled egg for breakfast and extolling the virtues of eggs to a young fan, the strapline for the commercial being 'E for B and B your Best'. Because of his fame George met and mixed with the wrong people – sycophants, hangers-on and those out to make a killing off the back of his fame. Having ingratiated themselves with him they would invariably say, 'I have a little business project you might be interested in.'

At Manchester United George was never really subjected to discipline in the way players at other clubs were, a commonsense discipline whereby his life outside football would have been monitored and advice and a regular routine provided. That he fell prey to all manner of bad influences is true, but is only part of the story. Many of the things that happened to George, good and bad, were engineered by himself. Those close to him knew they had football's first superstar on their hands, but he drove them mad.

Matt Busby was of the old school. Matt was two generations removed from George. It wasn't so much he couldn't handle George, moreover that he didn't know how. I don't think Matt ever understood what was happening to George – he was only vaguely aware of the Beatles, let alone the impact they were having on popular culture. George had an agent, Ken Stanley, who was a good old boy. Ken was decent, honest and of mild temperament, but often George's antics drove him to distraction. Ken would make appointments for him with potential sponsors and commercial people but quite often he simply wouldn't turn up. Ken was a good agent, but maybe George should have also had a personal manager to help him deal with the press and all the demands that were being placed upon his time. Though for years after finally hanging-up his boots, George had a personal manager in his close friend Phil, but even he struggled to keep him on an even keel.

About four weeks after his comeback game George called into my office and asked if we could have a chat. He wanted someone to have word with a young woman who was following him around which, I suppose, we describe today as stalking. The fact that George had sought my advice on the matter heartened me. I felt I was getting somewhere with him. I suggested that surely plenty of young women were obsessed by him. 'But this one is different, boss,' he told me. The young woman would be on the pavement outside his house when he left home for training, she would follow him to The Cliff, be there when he left, only to turn up again outside his house in the evening. He said he recognised her from a photograph she had enclosed with a letter she had sent him. He hadn't replied to the letter, but the woman had enclosed her phone number and he'd rung her for a chat.

'What possessed you to do that?' I enquired.

'Well, in her letter she said she'd seen me interviewed on television and had seen in my eyes that I understood her loneliness and pain,' he said. George was an intelligent guy. I couldn't work out whether he was just being naive in this particular matter, or whether he genuinely felt a connection with this woman.

'George, didn't you hear, even far off in the distance, the sound of an alarm bell ringing?' I asked.

'No, not really,' he said and gave a little chortle, which I took to mean it was me who had misread the situation and was getting it all wrong.

George never found a way to change his lifestyle or reinvent himself. He was forever elevated, and his elevation set him apart. He wasn't alone in the world, so much as unmoored and, at times, unhinged.

I last saw George in 2001 when we appeared at a dinner together in Salisbury. He was accompanied on the night by Alex, who came across to me as being a loving and devoted wife. That night, not for the first time, I feared for George. He had about him an aura of undiminished and inappropriate genial detachment, the sort common to every alcoholic I had ever come across. I wish I could say on that night he delivered a sparkling, witty speech that enraptured his audience, but it was far from the case. Often swaying on his feet, occasionally placing his hands before him on the table for support, he gave a disjointed, slurred speech that was uncomfortable to listen to. When George eventually sat down to sympathetic, rather than appreciative, applause the MC turned to me and said, 'He started off brilliant, lost his way, but stumbled through to the end.' He could have been summing up George's life.

The bigger the club, the bigger the politics. Manchester United is arguably the biggest club in the world and I found it riddled with political subterfuge. I had my own taste of it whilst I was there, and the source of much of it was a group Tommy Cavanagh dubbed the 'junior board'.

Irrespective of its size, every club will have its equivalent: successful local businessmen, often in their thirties or forties, who are not quite successful enough, and consequently not rich enough, to acquire sufficient shares to enable them to become directors of a club. They have sufficient disposable income, however, to purchase season tickets that afford them 'Vice-President' status. The Vice-President season ticket was a step-up from a normal stand season ticket. They cost considerably more but those afforded Vice-President status had their own room where they took tea and sandwiches before a game and at half-time. Also, after a game, players would often visit the Vice-Presidents' Room for a drink, or, alternatively Vice-Presidents were allowed to enter the Players' Lounge after a match. Nowadays you are more likely to find such people in executive boxes or a club's banqueting suite. Because they come into contact with directors, players and occasionally the manager and his backroom staff, the junior board believe they have the ear of the hierarchy and the players which, in certain instances, may well be the case. At Old Trafford some members of the junior board had an unhelpful and unhealthy influence.

Paddy McGrath was a United supporter who was a bookmaker who also had business interests in the Playboy and Cromford clubs in Manchester. The Playboy Club was situated off Canal Street and on a Saturday night Matt Busby was a frequent visitor along with Pat Crerand and occasionally players such as Willie Morgan and Denis Law. The group would join Paddy and his friends for dinner and while away the wee small hours talking football, in the main Manchester United. Matt invited me to join this group at the Playboy. I think I went twice before deciding the scene was not for me. It doesn't pay to socialise with your players: it leads to accusations of favouritism, a reluctance to give a rollicking when deserved, and can be seen as a potential sign of weakness.

After a game on a Saturday the routine was for Matt and his friends to go to a well-known Manchester establishment called Dougie's Bar, then gravitate to the Playboy or, occasionally, the Cromford Club. Apparently my management was often questioned during these nights and plenty of criticism heaped my way. The kindest description I can give of the junior board is that of hangers-on. They were like bloodsuckers, feeding off the success of the club, and providing the poison when things weren't going well. They were supposedly ardent supporters but in truth they did more harm than good. Constructive criticism is fair enough, but some of the stories that came back to me seemed geared to getting me out of the club simply

because I was disliked. Why was that? Because I had dismantled the old guard. On a visit to Old Trafford, former United
full-back Shay Brennan, a member of the 1968 European Cup-
winning team, called into my office. Having talked about football in general and, United in particular, our conversation
turned to the junior board. Shay told me to be wary of what
he termed 'the United clique', at one point telling me someone
had said, 'He gets rid of great players such as George and
Denis and brings in Macari and Martin, what sort of United
team is he creating?' The truth was that the glory days had
gone and I had been called in to be the unpopular guy whose
job it was to clear the decks for the future. All I can say is, I
would have been a darned sight more unpopular had it not
been for the common sense and wonderful gesture of Bobby
Charlton.

The sniping against Lou Macari was down to the fact that
he had not made the impact in the team I had hoped. Not just
the junior board but others began to ask why so much money
had been spent on Macari. Lou was playing nowhere near his
potential and for this, I hold my hand up. Initially I had asked
Lou to lead the line, though he felt the role suited neither his
style of play nor temperament. I persevered because, at the time,
I felt he was the best player we had to do it. Perhaps unfairly,
I suspected he was not even trying to make a go of the role I
had asked him to play in the team. In light of this I dropped
him for our game against Derby County at Old Trafford in
October 1973. Lou, naturally, wasn't happy and we had words.
In midweek a United XI containing reserves and a few youth
team players was due to play a friendly at non-league Mossley.
In view of this I asked Lou to train with the reserves on the
Monday. Needless to say, he was furious, particularly when I
rang him on the afternoon of the game and told him he was in
the side for the Mossley game.

When Lou refused to play, I said that if he persisted in being
obstructive he would be fined and put on the transfer list. He

slammed the phone down. I later found out, from Lou himself, that following our conversation he then telephoned Cliff Lloyd at the PFA. Cliff told him that he was out of order refusing a request from his manager to play in a friendly. Not at the time knowing of Lou's call to Cliff Lloyd, I drove to Mossley's ground to watch the game and found Lou sitting there changed and ready for action. We bandied words yet again, so I told him he was to be fined and placed on the transfer list. Lou didn't travel back on the team coach, he hitched a lift home with a pressman. Inevitably the story of Lou's transfer listing and our spat made headlines in the newspapers of the following day.

The fact Lou had turned up and played against Mossley as requested broke the ice. Having established my authority as manager and made my point, I was more inclined to discuss his role in the team. I told him that he had to buckle down and accept that his name and reputation were not sufficient to gain him popularity at Old Trafford. As far as United fans were concerned, the 'jury was out'. I believed him to be a brilliant player and consummate pro and I was going to give him an opportunity to make his name at Manchester United in his preferred position. Instead of being target man, I would play Lou much deeper, and it soon began to reap benefits for all. I admit to having initially made a mistake with Lou. He wasn't the same player I had known and admired in Scotland because leading the line was not his game. He became a different player making runs into the penalty box. Our differences were buried and forgotten and once more he became the darling of the Stretford End – and all other parts of the ground too. As things were to turn out Lou was not the only one to regain popularity amongst the United faithful . . .

15

THE THRILLING FIELDS

Having been given the support of the United board a day or so after our relegation was confirmed, I began preparing for 1974–75. The only break I took from United work was to travel to Germany for the World Cup, but even then I was on United-related business.

Willie Ormond had succeeded me as Scotland manager and encountered numerous problems with players during the warm-up games, particularly in Norway when Jinky Johnstone and Billy Bremner went AWOL one evening. There was talk of the pair being sent home, but with the World Cup only a fortnight away both were given a reprieve. I wondered how Willie was fairing in his attempts to understand Jinky's heid – he had never struck me as the understanding type when it came to problematic players.

The Scotland squad as a whole were not happy that 10 per cent of the players' 'perks' pool, that is money earned from World Cup-related commercial work, was to be paid to the SFA. At one point several players threatened to fly home unless the SFA agreed to allow the squad to keep all the money. Prior to leaving for the warm-up tour there had also been discontent in the camp over what constituted 'legitimate expenses', which reminded me of my own days as a Scotland player, when the issue was equally contentious.

Thankfully Scotland's 1974 World Cup squad managed to put their internal squabbles behind them. Though they failed to qualify on goal difference for the second stage they remained undefeated in the tournament, having beaten Zaire 2–0 and secured draws against both Brazil (0–0) and Yugoslavia (1–1). Being a club manager at the World Cup in those days was like being a child looking into the window of a sweet shop, but knowing the shop was shut. Apart from the obvious stars of the tournament such as Beckenbauer, Muller, Cruyff and Neeskens, there were several players I would have loved to have signed for United, but couldn't. It was all but impossible to obtain work permits for players from nations such as Argentina, Yugoslavia and Brazil. And in practice, it was not much easier where players from, what was then called, the Common Market, were concerned. The United Kingdom had only been a member for just over two years, and membership had yet to afford freedom of movement for labour. So apart from support of Scotland, the 1974 World Cup for me was a chance to catch up with the latest in tactics and coaching. As for the players who caught my eye, Mario Kempes, Carlos Babington and Ruben Ayala of Argentina and Lato and Gadocha of Poland, they would have to continue playing their football in their native countries.

The one player I did sign in the summer was Stuart Pearson, the young striker I had spotted in Hull City reserves. Stuart had continued to develop apace and I knew he would not only score goals, but his style of play would also present United with more options in attack. To offset some of the £200,000 fee I had paid for Pearson, I sold Brian Kidd to Arsenal for £110,000. At this time I was still searching for a young winger who could provide us with width and penetration. I would eventually land my man, but as I prepared United for the new season I was content with Willie Morgan, who was a fine player.

Though United were now in the Second Division, I knew the fame we enjoyed and the wages the club paid would enable me to attract the quality players I was looking to add to the squad. One of my responsibilities as manager was to discuss contracts and wages with players, particularly during the close season, the time when many contracts were up for renewal. I still have the salary structures for 1974 which I always kept to hand when negotiating with players. Looking back at them now, they make for interesting reading, not least when you compare the wages of then to those of Manchester United players today.

Player	Gross Weekly Wage £	Appearance Bonus £
Arthur Albiston	35.00	20.00
George Best (cancelled)	175.00	–
David Bradley	30.00	20.00
Martin Buchan	160.00	–
Gerry Daly	80.00	–
Ron Davies	130.00	–
Alex Forsyth	90.00	–
Tony Grimshaw	30.00	20.00
Brian Greenhoff	80.00	–
Jim Holton	140.00	–
Stewart Houston	90.00	–
Steve James	85.00	–
Lou Macari	160.00	–
Mick Martin	80.00	–
Willie Morgan	160.00	–
David Morris	35.00	20.00
Jim McCalliog	125.00	–
Sammy McIlroy	80.00	–
Jimmy Nicholl	45.00	20.00
Stuart Pearson	100.00	–
Paddy Roche	65.00	20.00
Arnold Sidebottom	50.00	20.00
Alex Stepney	135.00	–
Peter Sutcliffe	30.00	20.00
Tony Young	80.00	–

To which added in the season were:

David McCreery	35.00	20.00
Steve Coppell	60.00	–

Staff Wages

	at **June 1974**	**Increase 1975**
Frank Blunstone (Coach)	75.00	8.25
Laurie Brown (Physio)	58.00	12.00
Tommy Cavanagh (Asst to Mgr)	96.25	11.00
Gordon Clayton (Scout)	47.80	5.20
Pat Crerand (Coach)	120.00	11.00
Tommy Docherty (Manager)	288.00	–
Jimmy Murphy (Asst Youth)	15.00	1.50
Les Olive (Secretary)	95.00	9.40
Norman Scholes (Scout)	60.00	63.40

Regarding the staff wages you will have noticed the disparity between Pat Crerand's pay and that of Frank Blunstone and Tommy Cavanagh who, at the time, held more senior coaching positions. To the best of my knowledge agreement had been reached concerning Pat's salary before my arrival. Also a few eyebrows may be raised at the wage of Jimmy Murphy though no one, least of all Jimmy himself, considered the money he received a wage. Jimmy had retired but returned to the club at my request, and was happy to be involved in return for 'expenses' as he called them. There were all manner of other occupations at the club such as groundsmen, office staff, cleaners and laundry ladies. Their wages were referred to me, though they were nego-tiated and set by others, usually secretary Les Olive.

The fact many first-team players were on a basic wage with no appearance bonus money was down to the fact their basic wage was considered a good one. The fringe players, whose basic wage was much less, received an appearance bonus when playing in the first team both as a reward and an incentive. (This is in sharp contrast to the contracts of players nowadays.) In addition to a salary the club did pay each player a sum of money every six months or so as a contribution to his pension fund. There was also a system of bonuses for a win and a draw but these never amounted to much, perhaps £20 and £10 respectively.

The season began with two great managerial names bowing out of the game, Bill Shankly (Liverpool) and Bill Nicholson (Spurs) both announcing their retirement from football. The old guard was certainly changing and the United team I fielded at Orient in the first match of our Second Division campaign was far different in composition to the one I had inherited. The team that beat Orient lined up as follows: Alex Stepney; Alex Forsyth, Stewart Houston; Brian Greenhoff, Jim Holton, Martin Buchan; Willie Morgan, Gerry Daly, Stuart Pearson, Lou Macari, Jim McCalliog; sub: Sammy McIlroy. Of the twelve only Stepney, Buchan and Morgan remained from the squad I had inherited. There was a vibrancy about the team that I liked. Many teams were still playing defensive-minded football. That had never been my style. I placed the emphasis on attack and we played to a simple philosophy: when we had the ball we were all attackers, when the opposition had the ball, we were all defenders.

We started our Second Division campaign like a whirlwind. We won our opening four matches and enjoyed an unbeaten run of nine games that ended in late September when we lost 2–0 at Norwich City. Pearson, Macari and Daly were firing on all cylinders and producing plenty of goals. At the back the cerebral and stylish Buchan and the no-nonsense, rugged Holton had formed a great pairing.

In October Frank Blunstone demonstrated his loyalty to United when Chelsea, having parted company with Dave Sexton (this time permanently), offered Frank the job of manager. It was a tremendous opportunity, but Frank turned it down. 'I'm staying here at United out of job satisfaction and loyalty,' he told me. 'We're going to see the job through.'

At the end of November when United met Sunderland at Old

Trafford we were sitting five points clear at the top of the League having played 19 games, of which just three had been lost. Sunderland, along with Norwich City, Aston Villa and Bristol City presented the biggest obstacle to our quest for automatic promotion. Sunderland had sensationally beaten Leeds in the 1973 FA Cup final and though a number of that team had since moved on, they had players of First Division quality in Jim Montgomery, Dave Watson, Bob Moncur, Bobby Kerr, Billy Hughes, 'Pop' Robson, Vic Halom and Tony Towers. Those who saw our 3–2 win over Sunderland still talk about the game today, and it was featured on *Match of the Day*. At a time when the moronic hooligans were dragging our national game through the gutter, our match against Sunderland was seen as a fine advert for football. It had everything: excitement, drama, open, fluid attacking football from both teams and, as *MOTD*'s Jimmy Hill said, 'The problem we had in showing the highlights of this game was what to leave out.'

Jimmy was not exaggerating. Pearson gave us the lead only for Hughes to equalise. Just before half-time McIlroy dashed down the touchline, sent across a swift low centre to Morgan whose shot was a model of timing. If anything the tempo was upped in the second half as both teams went at it full pelt. Sunderland's equaliser might have come earlier than it did but for some fine saves from Stepney. But the Wearsiders were not to be denied. Just after the hour Kerr played the ball through to Halom who helped it into the path of Hughes who unerringly swept the ball wide of Stepney. The remaining quarter was witness to furious exchanges from both sides. Minutes from the end, the close dovetailing between Macari and Daly produced an opportunity for McIlroy. He didn't disappoint the United fans and Old Trafford erupted. At the final whistle the whole ground gave both sides a standing ovation. It was a good day for United, but also a good day for football in general – there was not one reported arrest by the police.

I was so concerned about the problem of hooligans following

United that I arranged a meeting between myself, the players and United supporters' groups. I knew in the big scheme of things we would solve little, if anything, but I hoped we could evolve some ideas for dealing with the issue. The supporters in attendance were genuine United fans, never ones to cause trouble and who were just as alarmed about the problem as the players and the club. Encouragingly they were willing to identify those who were causing trouble, but the problem was how to relay this information to the authorities on the day of a game. Regular United fans simply didn't know who many of these trouble-makers were. Many were travelling from other cities, such as London and Birmingham, and masquerading as Manchester United supporters. Willie Morgan spoke well at the meeting and I summed up. I went along with Bob Paisley's line that rather than being a part of football, hooligans were parasitical, able to do their worst, then individually blend into the crowd. Significantly I can't recall anyone suggesting all-seater stadiums as part of a possible solution. But much of the trouble took place away from grounds. The key to preventing hooliganism was information, liaison with the police and early identification of troublemakers. In the days before CCTV, however, no one really had an idea as to how this could be achieved.

Looking back now I am grateful that football is not beset with such problems today. The game is different now, some changes have been for the better, some not so. The fact football is now a family game again heartens me. I thoroughly enjoyed football in the seventies, but I shudder every time I think of the hooligan problem and how, at that time, not one of us could come up with a solution. It would take fifteen years and a tragedy that resulted in the loss of many lives before football finally got its act together.

The Sunderland game was not the only big match of November. In the second round of the League Cup we enjoyed a 5–1 victory over Charlton Athletic, and when the draw for the third round was announced we couldn't believe our luck when paired with Manchester City. This had all the hallmarks of a classic derby encounter, and would provide a pointer to our pedigree as a prospective First Division team. At the time City were riding high with Derby County and Liverpool at the top of the First Division. Another bumper crowd of 55,159 saw a ding-dong game that was settled from the penalty spot by Gerry Daly. United were deserved winners on the night.

The character of the players was further emphasised in December when we found ourselves 3–1 down at half-time against Sheffield Wednesday at Hillsborough. Tragedy then struck when Jim Holton, executing a typically brave challenge for the ball, twisted and broke his leg. We pulled a goal back through Lou Macari only for Wednesday to make it 4–2. That day the team showed it had plenty of mettle and a never-say-die attitude. Roared on by a sizeable following of United fans we took the game to Wednesday, and in a thrilling finale scored twice through Macari and Pearson to earn a 4–4 draw.

After many very good performances and some superlative ones, the New Year produced a blip. From losing to Oldham on 28 December until the end of February we produced only two victories from seven league matches. We were also beaten by Walsall in the third round of the FA Cup and lost over two legs to Norwich City in the semi-finals of the League Cup.

With Jim Holton sidelined, I played Steve James alongside Martin Buchan in the heart of defence. James took a while to settle into the role but when he did, it coincided with an upturn in our fortunes. I hadn't been happy with the form of Jim McCalliog and during the lean spell replaced him for three matches with Eric Young. Eric was a grafting player, but he too failed to provide the penetration I was looking for. I had previously mentioned to our scout Norman Scholes that I wanted a young player who could play on the wing or, as an attacking right-sided midfield player. Towards the end of February whilst we were enduring our blip I received a scouting report from

Norman to say he had found such a player at Tranmere Rovers, so I drove to Prenton Park to see the lad in action for myself. I took Jimmy Murphy with me and after only ten minutes Jimmy turned to me and said, 'Sign him'; I had already come to the same conclusion. I paid £40,000 for Steve Coppell and recouped the money immediately by selling Jim McCalliog to Southampton for the same amount. In effect I acquired Steve Coppell for nothing; though such was to be his impact and contribution at United he would have been a bargain at £150,000.

Steve's only request when signing was for him to continue studying for a degree in economics. I assured him that with the free time players enjoy, there would be no problem. Steve was not the only United player to have embarked upon a university degree course as Martin Buchan was studying languages. The days when teams travelled to away games by train were now over. In keeping with every club, we travelled by coach. Being Manchester United we had our own team coach which boasted two tables similar to those one finds in railway carriages. Some players whiled away the time on journeys by reading newspapers or books, others gathered around one table for Lou Macari's card school (stakes were matchsticks). More often than not the other table would be occupied by Coppell and Buchan, on which they would spread out their college books. Steve Coppell made his debut as a substitute in a 4–0 win over Cardiff City, a result which ended our slump and signalled the beginning of an unbeaten run of eleven matches that took us to the end of the season. I had seen enough in Coppell's appearance as a substitute against Cardiff to know we had signed a rare talent, and he was soon to become a regular fixture in the team.

With five matches remaining we entertained Oldham Athletic. In front of an Old Trafford crowd of 56,618, goals from Macari, McIlroy and Coppell, his first for the club, gave us a 3–2 victory that all but clinched promotion. It was still mathematically possible for Norwich, Aston Villa and Sunderland to overhaul us, but they would have to win their remaining matches and we lose ours. Unlikely, but until we were absolutely certain of promotion I kept the champagne on ice, the champagne in question being the case Matt Busby had given me when we were relegated. A 1–0 win at the Dell against Southampton sealed our promotion and we clinched the title two games later when sharing the points at Notts County. Our final game of the season turned out to be a victory parade as we put four goals past Blackpool without reply. At the end of this game 59,000 spectators roared their approval as the players did a lap of honour around Old Trafford. I went on to the pitch to thank the fans for the magnificent support they had given us throughout what had been, a very memorable season. No sooner had I set foot on the pitch when the crowd began to chant my name. I acknowledged the fans by raising my arms above my head and clasping my hands together. Besieged by well-wishers, I made as dignified an exit as I could as I wanted the players and supporters to enjoy the moment together.

Promotion at the first attempt came as a great relief to me. My responsibility as manager had been to effect changes at the club, but also to maintain United's First Division status. I shouldered the blame myself for our relegation and though I eventually brought success to Manchester United, to this day it still rankles that relegation should have happened under my management.

At the time there was a body of opinion that felt a season in a lower division had been a good thing for the club, though it was a view I never subscribed to. I would have much preferred to have rebuilt the side whilst in the First Division. A successful team in a lower division will invariably attract bigger attendances to home matches than when consolidating in a higher division, and I suppose this is why some believed United's relegation had been no bad thing. That season over a million people watched our games at Old Trafford, more than any club in the First Division. United's relegation was good for the Second Division because of our huge following. But I could have done without the club having had that experience.

I knew much work still lay ahead. The oil tanker had turned but 180 degrees, but it was turning all the same. For me the pleasing thing about the side that won the Second Division championship was, not only were they a very good team, they were a great bunch of lads. Lou Macari and I had resolved our differences and, in his preferred role as an attacking midfield player, he had developed into an even better player than he had been at Celtic. Macari scored a total of 18 goals that season, the same number as Stuart Pearson. It was evident even at this stage in his career that Lou had a very good football brain and I was not surprised when later he went into management. Gerry Daly, who I signed from Bohemians, was an unsung hero in the United team. It was often the likes of Pearson, Macari, McIlroy, Coppell and Buchan who stole the headlines, but Gerry was a consistent performer whose contribution to the side was exceptional. He took over the role of penalty taker from Alex Stepney and I can't recall him ever missing from the spot. Along with Macari and Stewart Houston, Daly was one of the most vocal players on the field. Despite all the running they did, the trio never stopped talking and shouting to team-mates. In the main it was all positive stuff and there is little doubt their on-the-field advice helped youngsters such as Steve Coppell, Arthur Albiston and Jimmy Nicholl. Gerry Daly and Lou Macari were like chalk and cheese. Lou is teetotal and has never smoked, whereas Gerry liked to do both. It was pointless me nagging Gerry to stop smoking, as he once said to me when I did raise the subject, 'You've seen me on the pitch, boss, I'm not a quitter.' Gerry was never much for going out to clubs, though he did stay up a little later than I would have liked, but only because he was a movie buff and loved to watch late night films on television. Smoking and the odd drink apart, the other aspect of Gerry's lifestyle that left a lot to be desired was his diet. If I didn't keep a close eye on him prior to a game he would eat a bag of chips washed down by a can of Coke.

Alex Forsyth had a very strong Glasgow accent, so pronounced even Lou Macari and I had trouble understanding

him at times. Alex was consistently good at full-back and, as
full-backs tend to be, the regularity of his good performances
were often taken for granted, though not by me. I had never
come across a player who was so particular in his pre-match
preparation. Everything had to be just so for Alex, the lie of the
tie-ups around the top of his socks, the way his boots were laced
and tied, how his shirt was tucked into his shorts, nothing
haphazard. He would also apply to various parts of his upper
body and legs just about every embrocation, ointment and cream
there was in the physio's bag. Alex would rub Vaseline on his
heels to stop chafing, and apply Vick vapour rub to his nostrils
with a dab on his shirt so that he could inhale it at a point
during the game. He would smother his legs in Buxton Rub or
Sloan's Liniment, place sticky plasters around his shinguards
and so on. On Fridays before a home game I told the players
what time I wanted them to report to the ground the following
day. Often I would say. 'Twelve-thirty, except you Alex, you'd
better get here for around eight-thirty in the morning.'

Martin Buchan was extremely intelligent, studious, quiet and
unassuming, added to which, of course, he was a top-class
defender. He always liked to do his own thing, which was fine.
I remember once during a tour of Australia he asked me for
permission to visit an uncle of his, which I duly granted. Martin
left our team hotel in a hire car before most of us had risen
from our beds and did not return until late at night. If it had
been anyone but him I might have been concerned but, as I say,
Martin is a very bright person and full of common sense. When
he eventually returned I asked why he had been so long.

'Oh, yes, sorry about that, boss,' he said. 'It took a little longer
to get to my uncle's than I thought and, of course, I then had
the drive back.'

'How far does your uncle live from here then?' I asked.

'I clocked it at just under 450 miles,' he told me.

The fact that Martin had driven almost 1,000 miles that day
didn't surprise me. He would often embark upon things no one

else in the squad would dream of doing. He liked being a part of the team set-up, but at the same time, also appeared to enjoy doing things that would set him apart from the other players. In asserting his independence, he found a greater sense of identity. Which, to a man of Martin's intellect and objectivity, I am sure he was only too aware of.

As I made my preparations for 1975–76 my priority was to find a left-winger to complement the work of 'the student prince' Steve Coppell on the right. I believed if United had direct wingers on either flank who could take full-backs on and beat them, we would stretch defences and provide more opportunities for goals from Pearson and Macari.

My desire for another winger was made more urgent by the departure in June of Willie Morgan. Willie was a good player and a good professional. Unfortunately he had sustained a bad eye injury during the close season whilst playing tennis and, for me, was never the same player again, although Willie might disagree. I was looking to build for the future and as a consequence sold him to Burnley. Seemingly Willie was aggrieved at this; he would later make a very derogatory remark about my ability as a manager in a TV programme which, as events unfolded, led to a nightmare scenario for me, one in which my very liberty would be at stake.

One man I did fall out with, irreparably as it turned out, was Pat Crerand. Pat is Manchester United through and through and had given the club sterling service as a player. Matt Busby thought a lot of Pat and was often on at me to promote him as my number two. Pat had a good knowledge of the game and I initially liked Matt's idea. But after only a few months of the 1975–76 season I went to see the board to tell them I had made a mistake in appointing Pat Crerand as my assistant. Managers make mistakes, and I always said you should admit it and cut your losses. That is what I decided to do regarding Pat Crerand. Of course, I realised it was a delicate situation and could cause a few ructions. Following Pat's appointment as my assistant, Matt and I had been the catalysts in obtaining Pat a testimonial at Old Trafford after seven years' service, when usually the requirement was ten. As a result Pat received some £46,000, which I felt appropriate and deserved. But I felt there was no alternative but to tell the board I had made a big mistake when appointing him my assistant. We just weren't compatible in terms of our working practices – time keeping, how to present yourself in a managerial capacity, that sort of thing. We had different ideas on it. Pat remained at the club on his salary but had no further involvement with the first team. In the event this situation only lasted a few weeks as Pat left of his own accord and was later appointed manager of Northampton Town.

All these years on, I still feel it necessary to stress that I never sacked Pat Crerand. At the time of his testimonial, he informed me and the board that he had decided to try his luck in coaching, perhaps even management. The board were more than accommodating, paying him a year's wages and letting him keep his club car. I knew it would get back to Pat that I had said I'd made a mistake in appointing him, and he was to harbour animosity towards me for giving the board my opinion of him as my assistant.

I was never the sort of manager to promote someone just to get rid of them. When another club enquired about someone's suitability for a certain post, I always gave an honest opinion whether good or bad. In 1976 I was sitting in my office with Jimmy Murphy when I received a call from Northampton Town chairman Neville Ronson and his general manager Dave Bowen, about Pat Crerand becoming team manager of Northampton. Seemingly Pat had been recommended by Matt Busby and Joe Mercer and Messrs Ronson and Bowen were sounding out my opinion. I spoke to Dave, who I knew well from our days together at Arsenal, and told him in my opinion Pat would not make a suitable manager for their club and offered some reasons. I then put Jimmy Murphy on the line and he endorsed my view that

Pat was not the right man for the Northampton job. Presumably on the strength of the recommendation by Busby and Mercer, Pat subsequently became manager at the County Ground but lasted just a few months.

One thing that appeared to bug Pat was the notion, quite wrongly as it happened, that I had deprived him of a job at Celtic. Jock Stein was manager at the time, but coming back from a holiday, he was injured in a car crash. Celtic were looking for someone to work as an assistant during Jock's absence and I received a call from an old friend, Jim Farrell, a Celtic director. Jim explained they were looking for a number two because Jock was to be away from the club for some time, and asked about Pat Crerand. I told Jim that socially Pat was a great guy but didn't think he would be any good as an assistant manager for his club.

Word got back to Pat that I had not recommended him to Celtic, and he tackled me on the subject saying I had done him out of a job. I told him that was not the case, that I had, when asked, simply offered an honest assessment as to his suitability. 'So you deprived me of the job,' said Pat again.

'No, I didn't, I gave an honest opinion,' I told him. 'I would have been delighted to say that you would have been a great man for the job, Pat, but I don't think that is the case. You may not think of me as the right manager of this club, but that is your opinion and you're entitled to it. Don't you think if Jock had really wanted you as his assistant, he'd have appointed you himself, or at least asked Mr Farrell to see you. He didn't have to ask my opinion of you. Jock's knowledge of the abilities of people in the game is second to none. Jock is his own man. He sorts his own staff out.'

Pat's antagonism towards me was fuelled by the aforementioned events, but regarding his work as my assistant, let's just say it wasn't what I was looking for. The fact that, following Pat's voluntary departure I then guided United to two FA Cup finals, to within four points of winning the championship

and into Europe didn't serve to make him warm to me any
the more.

The 1975–76 season saw United visit Wolves on the opening
day. We stormed to a 2–0 victory at Molineux, our powerful
display giving fair warning to those who thought we wouldn't
last the pace back at the top. The game was a personal triumph
for Lou Macari who, in scoring both our goals, was outstanding
in what was a superb team performance. In our second match,
at Birmingham City, we recorded another two-goal victory.
Goalless just after the break, I had to substitute our keeper Alex
Stepney when he suddenly bent over double in pain – suffering
from lockjaw! Brian Greenhoff had to take over in goal and did
a great job, keeping a clean sheet, while at the other end Sammy
McIlroy scored twice to give us a 100 per cent return from our
two away games.

A crowd of 56,000 was at Old Trafford for our first home
match and the vast majority went away joyously happy as we
beat Sheffield United 5–1. The Manchester *Evening News* had
no compunction about saying, 'The Glory days are back at Old
Trafford again with all the glamour and excitement that the
world associates with Manchester United.' The hyperbole could
not disguise the fact that we had made an excellent start in our
return to Division One which, when the first league tables were
published, saw United sitting proudly at the top one point ahead
of Newcastle United.

In my programme notes for our next game, the visit of
Coventry City to Old Trafford, I exercised caution saying, 'We
have done better than expected. I never really considered the
possibility of us winning our first two away matches . . . though
I am delighted with our start I do not intend to go overboard
about our prospects this season, and I hope you fans won't
either. There is an awful long way to go yet and we shall most
certainly have setbacks.' We experienced a setback that very
night. Leading 1–0, an unfortunate back-pass from Brian

Greenhoff failed to reach Alex Stepney, and Coventry striker Alan Green nipped in to latch on to the ball and clinically dispatch it for a share of the points.

A workmanlike win at Stoke City set us up nicely for our next match at home against Tottenham Hotspur. Prior to the Spurs game I gave an interview for BBC TV's Saturday lunchtime preview programme *Football Focus*. This was a time when broadcasters were not even allowed to announce the identity of the match they were to feature in highlight form later on *Match of the Day* because the Football League felt it would affect the attendance, but the 'live' appearance of a manager on the lunchtime preview offered viewers a pretty good indication. During the interview I played down the notion that United were possible championship contenders saying. 'With only five games played I don't see how anyone can talk in terms of being in contention for the championship. But what I can promise you is that we shall have a darned good try and no matter what, we will stick to our style of playing entertaining, attacking football. It isn't in the make-up of this team to be negative and cautious, we want to entertain.'

I knew our attacking style of play meant we would concede goals, but to be honest, I wasn't bothered if we conceded two goals as long as we scored three. I don't think that is an attitude prevalent with too many managers today. At times our positive attitude also left us vulnerable to counterattacks. So it proved against Spurs when Chris Jones gave them the lead after four minutes before which we had laid siege to Pat Jennings' goal. Undaunted, we played the only way we knew how and a thrilling, open encounter finally ended 3–2 in our favour.

Mid-September was not a happy period. We suffered our first reverse of the season when losing by the only goal of the game at Queens Park Rangers. Alex Forsyth had picked up an injury against Stoke and missed our midweek League Cup defeat of Brentford. The prognosis was not good – I was told Forsyth could be out for three months. I brought in Arthur Albiston for the game against QPR which meant, with Jimmy Nicholl at left-back, we had two teenage full-backs flanking Houston and Greenhoff in the centre of defence. It is an old adage of football that it only takes a second to score a goal and so it proved during this game. Rangers, from the kick-off, won a free-kick wide of our penalty area. It was a taken short by Gerry Francis who tapped the ball to Stan Bowles. There was a centre by Bowles, a header from Ian Gillard that hit the bar, and David Webb, bustling up on the far post, bundled the ball into the net. I turned to Tommy Cavanagh. 'How long?' I asked. 'Forty-five seconds,' said Tommy. 'Good start,' I said. 'Cracking,' he said, 'we haven't touched the ball yet.'

Try as we did we couldn't pull that early goal back. After the game I told the press conference, 'Rangers were the better side, but we'll continue to play the way we do. We'll lose some games, give away goals, but attacking football is the only way to attract supporters in large numbers into grounds.' The disappointment of losing at Loftus Road was compounded when I received the news that Jim Holton had broken his leg again when making a comeback in the reserves. I now had two players who I'd hoped to feature regularly, on the sidelines with long-term injuries.

Bobby Robson's Ipswich Town were defeated 1–0 at Old Trafford which reinstated us at the top of Division One. Ipswich did not play well, possibly suffering a hangover from their midweek victory over Feyenoord in the UEFA Cup. Then in November I signed the winger I had been looking for to complement Steve Coppell. I paid Millwall £70,000 for Gordon Hill which, even at the time, was a modest fee. Gordon was a fast, direct winger who was not only a maker but a taker of goals. He had tremendous ability, and his attitude and character were first class. Little wonder that, in time, I would sign Gordon on three occasions during my management career.

The period from October to Christmas saw United play fourteen league matches in which we suffered only three defeats.

My first day at Chelsea as player-coach. *Left to right*: Frank Blunstone, Bert Murray, Bobby Evans, Ron Tindall and John Brookes.

Left to right: Dave Mackay, Cath, Agnes, Mick, me and Tom. Dave stayed with us when he arrived at Spurs from Hearts.

I loved to embrace new ideas, here specialist colour-coded training kit for the Chelsea first team and reserves. Not that I thought it suited me, you'll note.

I always had a great rapport with supporters. Here with a group of Chelsea fans who arrived at Sheffield Wednesday only to find the game postponed. We went for coffee together before they returned home to London.

A rare shot of me getting a word in with my great pal, Bill Shankly.

SPORTS PRESS

helsea players Peter Bonetti and Tommy Baldwin can't hide their
isappointment after the 1967 FA Cup final against Spurs. The BBC are about
) collar me for an interview – good luck to them with the mood I was in.

ome of the wives of Chelsea players
1ow their reaction to the news I had
ecided to stay at the club.

MIRRORPIX

SHEFFIELD NEWSPAPERS

With a very youthful
Rotherham United squad;
D for Doc and D for demoted.

QPR, with Alan Harris and Barry Bridges. 'Now listen carefully, lads, I don't have much time to tell you this – 28 days in fact.'

In the team hotel the night before an Aston Villa away game at Portsmouth. The sign above the door was to prove prophetic!

...he wasn't always, as I was to discover

)n arrival at Old Trafford it was
lear changes were needed. Bobby
Charlton chose to retire in April
973.

I eventually got to the end of my
tether with George Best's antics.

nd Denis Law moved to City and relegated us a year later with a back heel.

I look longingly at the FA Cup as Southampton skipper Peter Rodrigues holds it aloft after the 1976 final. I told him, 'Look after it, it's only on loan until United have it next year'.

It had to be a special occasion for me to light a cigar. It was. With Tommy Cavanagh after Manchester United's victory over Leeds United in the 1977 FA Cup semi-final.

My remark to Rodrigues comes true.

ith Mary in 1977.
till claim to be the
ly manager sacked
r having fallen in
ve.

rrive at the Old
iley and clear my
roat before being
eared of charges of
rjury in October
81.

Mary and me, still happy after 30 years.

JOHN O'CONNOR

And with all the girls: *from left to right*, Helen, Grace, Lucy, me, Jane and Mary

The day after Boxing Day a fervent festive crowd of 60,000 saw us beat Burnley 2–1, a result which made United joint leaders of the First Division with Liverpool on 33 points.

It was in January that we embarked upon a run in the FA Cup that was to take United to Wembley, and in that month we also moved ahead of Liverpool at the top of the table. There was still a long way to go but it didn't stop the *Guardian* saying, 'They can smell the championship around Old Trafford, and the taste is like a drug to United. It drives them on to a peak of performance that keeps going higher and higher.'

As the New Year shed its days and with it the hopes and resolutions of many, we remained resolute in our twin pursuit of the championship and the FA Cup. An exciting battle was developing at the top of the league between United, Liverpool, Queens Park Rangers and Derby County. In February we drew 0–0 at home to Liverpool before another capacity 60,000 crowd, leaving only two points separating the top four clubs. It was anybody's title, even Leeds United and Manchester City in fifth and sixth places were not out of the running. Our match against Liverpool proved an intriguing and entertaining game between my fiery attacking young team and experienced masters. After the game Liverpool manager Bob Paisley popped into our dressing room and paid the players, and I suppose me, a wonderful compliment. Bob said, 'Your side must be one of the easiest teams in the league to referee, hardly a foul. As well you know, football is basically about winning, but if you can win the right way by playing the type of football you lads play, then it is something special.'

Following the Liverpool game a defeat at Aston Villa in late February put paid to an unbeaten run of eleven League matches stretching back to mid-November. These were heady days for United. Following defeat at Villa we built another unbeaten run, this time of six matches, two of which were drawn. The pace at the top was unrelenting. Our form was matched by that of Liverpool, Queens Park Rangers and Derby, and as we entered

April only one point separated the top four clubs. Leeds still had a chance of the title, but really it was any one from four. We began April with a trip to Portman Road having just reached the final of the FA Cup. It was there that Ipswich pulled the rug from beneath us by winning 3–0. Football writer Mike Langley summed up our performance thus: 'Don't tell me it is impossible to see the towers of Wembley from 70 miles away in Portman Road. Because 35,000 of us will swear that Manchester United played as though they could see nothing else. The team famed for bright, attacking football were too often the jump-out-of-trouble team. The don't-get-hurt-and-miss-the-final-team.' Langley had a point: only three remained wholly steadfast through the battle, Stepney, Buchan and Coppell. It was our heaviest defeat of the season and, as QPR and Liverpool kept up the pace, we slipped to third, a point behind Liverpool but now five points adrift of Rangers.

With Wembley just two weeks away we had five league matches in which to close the gap, beginning with a home game against Everton. In front of the biggest crowd of the Football League season, 61,879, we fell behind to a first-half goal from George Telfer, which seemed to galvanise us, particularly after half-time during which we heard QPR were losing at Norwich and Stoke were a goal up at Liverpool. We tore into Everton after the interval and when the inevitable goal came, it was one of the most fortuitous and ridiculous goals I have ever seen – but they all count. Gordon Hill tried his luck with a free-kick from about 20 yards. The ball deflected off Everton defender Ken McNaught into the face of Mick Lyons, on to the back of Roger Kenyon, from where it bounced off the shoulder of keeper Dai Davies, who had readjusted position with every pinball deflection. Somehow the ball left Dai's shoulder and went into the net. Unbelievably, after the game, Gordon Hill tried to claim it. Everton eventually succumbed to our pressure when, after replacing Steve Coppell, substitute David McCreery scored our second to secure two crucial points. In the dressing room we were listening intently to the radio as the results filtered through from the other matches that had a bearing on the destination of the title. The news was encouraging. Liverpool had beaten Stoke 5–3, but Derby County had drawn at home to Leicester City and, most significantly, Queens Park Rangers had been beaten at Norwich City. The only downside to the afternoon was the injury to Coppell, sustained when challenging for a fifty-fifty ball with Mick Lyons – proof if ever it were needed that minds were not simply on Wembley. Coppell's injury resulted in him missing all but one of our remaining games. It was some blow. All was still going to plan when we secured a one-goal victory at Burnley thanks to a Lou Macari effort. This was another crucial victory, but with both Liverpool and QPR winning that day, we needed to win the two games we had in hand on both clubs to overhaul them.

Have you ever noticed how often a manager receiving a Manager of the Month Award coincides with a crashing defeat for his side? Or, in cricket, when commentators say a batsman looks set for a big score, he is bowled next ball? I was driving to Old Trafford for our midweek game against Stoke City, when I heard on the radio that United and QPR boasted the only unbeaten home records in the First Division. 'United have become impregnable on their own turf,' said one national newspaper writer. I was confident of victory over Stoke but from the back of my mind a little voice warned me about tempting fate.

Stoke's keeper, Peter Shilton, defied everything we sent his way. On those rare occasions when we were not on the attack, the foraging of Terry Conroy and Jimmy Greenhoff was a nuisance. The game seemed to have 0–0 written all over it; the more the clocked ticked, the more we looked leg-weary and frantic in our attempts to batter down Stoke's stubborn massed defence. Deep into injury time, Stoke defender Alan 'Bluto' Bloor abandoned his defensive responsibilities to join a swift counterattack. Conroy played the ball out to Alan Dodd who looped the ball towards our far post, and there was Bloor to apply the killer blow with the meat of his forehead. His goal was greeted with numbed silence from 54,000 spectators. I felt pretty numb myself.

On the same night Derby County lost at home to Everton, which effectively ended their title hopes. With Liverpool having previously won against Manchester City and QPR defeating Arsenal, in the course of 90 minutes we had made a quantum jump from short odds to very long odds for the title and, as well you know, the bookies rarely get it wrong.

Our fate was sealed the following Saturday when we travelled to Leicester City and lost 2–1. I think Wembley and the FA Cup final were in our thoughts that day. Whilst we lost, Queens Park Rangers rounded off their season by beating Leeds United. Liverpool didn't play that day. Their remaining game was away to Wolves who had to beat Liverpool to avoid relegation. We were now out of the title race, but Rangers had to sit and await the outcome of Liverpool's match at Molineux.

Liverpool's record away from home did not bode well for QPR, or Wolves in their fight to avoid the drop. Liverpool had conceded only nine goals on their travels though, curiously, 21 at Anfield, an unusually high number for them. Liverpool fell behind in their final game at Wolves, only to storm back to win the match and the championship. Less than a week later Bob Paisley's side also added the UEFA Cup to their trophy cabinet when beating Bruges 4–3 over a two-legged final. Of course I was disappointed that Manchester United had not won the championship when we had led the First Division so often, but our return to the First Division had, all in all, been a very good season and a magnificent effort from the players.

The disappointment I felt at United's title challenge having petered out at the end was, however, nothing compared to the disappointment I was to feel at Wembley that May. United's quest to win the FA Cup began at home to Oxford United, where two Gerry Daly penalties overhauled Oxford's Derek

Clarke's opener which had stunned Old Trafford. Oxford were doughty fighters as were to be our opponents in the fourth round – Peterborough United.

Man for man I believe we had the most skilful team in the country at the time. While I emphasised teamwork, I was always at pains to encourage individuals to express themselves and never to be afraid to try something out of the ordinary. That philosophy paid dividends against Peterborough. We appeared to have put the game beyond their reach as early as the tenth minute, when we led through goals from Forsyth and McIlroy. Driven on by the former Sheffield Wednesday and West Ham United defender Peter Eustace, Peterborough never gave up and pulled a goal back through their centre-forward John Cozens just after the half-hour mark. This inspired Peterborough to even greater effort, which they continued into the second half. I was feeling a little uncomfortable until, after 70 minutes, a wonderful piece of individual skill from Gordon Hill put paid to Peterborough's spirited incursions. Hill was 25 yards from goal when the ball was played to him from wide on the right. I expected him to control the ball and lay it off. Instead he conducted a half-turn of his body, got his head over the ball and volleyed it with his left foot. Eric Steele in the Peterborough goal stood frozen to the spot, and little wonder, the wind-chill factor from the ball as it torpedoed past him must have made the temperature around him plummet. A matter of a second after leaving Hill's boot the ball jerked the centre of the net into the shape of an elbow. It was a tremendous goal, worthy of winning any Cup match.

Another sparkling display in the next round saw United defeat Leicester City 2–1 at Filbert Street. First-half goals from Macari and Daly put us in the driving seat and even a reply from Bob Lee in the second period failed to disrupt our progress or, indeed, our control of a match in which Leicester played their part in the superb entertainment. Somewhat ominously the newspapers were given to talking of United's success in the FA

Cup as being a foregone conclusion. The *People* was, quite literally, given to flights of poetic fancy: 'What a day it's going to
be! What football we're going to see! When Tommy Docherty's
Red soldier ants swarm into Wemb-ley.'

It was the tenet of such reports from the press, television and
radio that served to imbue the United camp, and I include myself
here, with that enemy of all good sides – over-confidence. Even
the broadsheets talked up our chances of winning the Cup, the
normally objective *Observer* saying, 'This season the name of
Manchester United appears to be written on the trophy, as no
team appears capable of halting their inexorable march to the
FA Cup.' Whilst I was always at pains to keep the players' feet
firmly on terra firma, I too was beginning to be swept along
with the tide of hyperbole.

I should have taken a step back and re-evaluated everything.
Especially as we were given a reality check in the sixth round,
when held to a 1–1 draw by Wolves. It was amazing how goalkeepers produced fantastic performances against us at Old
Trafford. Wolves' goalkeeper Phil Parkes gave full vent to his art
and was only beaten by a deflected shot from Daly which – John
Richards having previously put Wolves ahead – took us to a
replay at Molineux.

I felt it would be a different game there, and so it proved. On
their home turf the emphasis was on Wolves to take the game to
United, and with us knowing no other way but to attack, what
unfolded was an epic Cup tie, more open and fluid than at Old
Trafford. Wolves rocked us with two swift goals from Steve Kindon
and Richards, and we suffered a further setback when Macari
limped out of the game. At 2–0 down we at last began to do all
the probing and pressing, instilling in me a belief we would get
back into it. On 35 minutes Pearson scored with a fine header
after a corner kick had been flicked on by Brian Greenhoff. Once
again when finding ourselves in trouble we rallied magnificently.
With Nicholl in the back four and Greenhoff taking Macari's place
in midfield, we continued to surge forward with tremendous deter-

mination. Wolves' resilience held until the 73rd minute as Coppell's persistence paid off when he burst in from the right and hit a low centre into the penalty area. McIlroy guided the ball to Greenhoff who gleefully rifled it into the net. The game went into extra time with United still in the ascendancy. The additional period was only five minutes old when McIlroy slotted home the winner following a neat interchange of passes between Daly and Pearson. Wolves gave their all in search of the equaliser, but we held our nerve to progress to a semi-final against fellow championship challengers Derby County.

The other semi-final saw Southampton of Division Two pitched against Crystal Palace from Division Three. Prior to our game I said, 'This is the real final of the Cup, we should have been meeting at Wembley, not at Hillsborough in the penultimate stage of the competition.' People saw this as disrespectful of Southampton and Crystal Palace, though this was never my intention. I simply believed as two teams locked in battle for the First Division title, United and Derby would have produced a classic FA Cup final, particularly as both teams loved to attack and were, respectively, the highest and second highest goalscorers in the First Division.

Our game against Derby was, indeed, worthy of the final itself. In the end two goals from Gordon Hill separated the teams, and I doubt Hill ever scored any that could match the majesty and importance of the brace he netted that day. Hill blasted away Derby's hopes of reaching Wembley. The first, from fully 20 yards, was a beauty that ballooned the net. His second, from a free-kick, took a slight deflection from Powell but the shot was goalbound anyway.

In the dressing room before the game I told the players that they should make the most of a great occasion and simply go out and enjoy themselves. This is exactly what they did. They played expansive, entertaining football because that is what they liked doing, and it proved the decisive factor. Southampton, a team which boasted even more experience than Derby, triumphed over Palace at Stamford Bridge. For the third time in four years Wembley would play host to a final that pitched First Division against Second Division. In 1973 Sunderland had sensationally triumphed over Leeds United, while in 1975 Fulham had failed to gain the better of First Division West Ham United. The press had little doubt, however, that United would triumph against Southampton. As the *People* were moved to say after our victory over Derby. 'It makes United the biggest ever certainties to win English soccer's glamour trophy.'

I think we began to believe our own publicity in the build-up to the final. Not for one moment did I think United winning the Cup was a foregone conclusion. I emphasised to the players we had to be at our best to overcome Southampton, but the fact most people had us as certainties suckered us into not being on our mettle as we should have been. As a consequence the merest hint of complacency took a substantial edge off our game on the day. To their credit, Southampton set their stall out well, and didn't allow us to play our normal game.

The Manchester United line-up in the 1976 FA Cup final was as follows: Alex Stepney; Alex Forsyth, Brian Greenhoff, Martin Buchan, Stewart Houston; Steve Coppell, Gerry Daly, Lou Macari, Gordon Hill, Stuart Pearson, Sammy McIlroy; substitute: David McCreery. The Southampton side was Ian Turner; Peter Rodrigues, Mel Blyth, Jim Steele, David Peach; Paul Gilchrist, Jim McCalliog, Nicky Holmes; Mike Channon, Peter Osgood, Bobby Stokes; substitute: Hugh Fisher.

Southampton played to the absolute limit of their ability. We were frustrated by an offside trap operated with robot-like efficiency, catching us offside five times in the first seven minutes. In my mind this set the tone for the game. When we did manage to circumnavigate the trap, we found Saints' goalkeeper Ian Turner, who recovered from a shaky start, to be in inspired form. Semi-final hero Gordon Hill found no headway against Southampton's experienced skipper Peter Rodrigues. As Hill gradually wilted away I was moved to substitute him with McCreery after 67 minutes.

Pearson always found himself battling against two minders in Blyth and Steele, both playing the game of their lives. Coppell kept pegging away on the right but too many of my players were under par, not only Hill but also McIlroy and Macari. For Southampton, Channon was a livewire, whilst two former players of mine, Osgood and McCalliog, found their old swagger. As the game progressed growing menace crept into the play of both players. We went close to breaking the deadlock when a McIlroy header thumped against the post, but what was proving to be a decent final needed a goal and the game seemed destined never to produce one. When it did materialise, it was right out of the blue. There appeared to be little danger when from the right Channon played off a goal-kick to McCalliog, who struck an immediate pass behind our defence that was pushing up. Reaching the ball after it had bounced, Bobby Stokes materialised seven yards clear of our defence running into a penalty area unguarded but for keeper Alex Stepney. Stokes' diagonal left-foot shot beat Stepney all ends up and nestled into the left-hand corner of the net. To be honest I thought Alex was too slow off his line and should have cut down Stokes' angle of vision. We had been caught pushing forward, and I think Alex should have provided some cover by coming off his line until any potential danger had passed, but it's very easy from the touchline.

Try as we might, we couldn't break Southampton down. Such was the experience of Osgood, Channon, McCalliog, Blyth and Rodrigues, as the clock counted down they played the possession game, which only frustrated us even more. All credit on the day to Southampton who were worthy winners. When the final whistle blew I was absolutely crestfallen, but made a beeline for their manager Lawrie McMenemy to offer him my congratulations for a job extremely well done.

There can be fewer sadder sights and gloomier atmospheres

than the losers' dressing room after an FA Cup final. To a man we were gutted, shattered and filled with black despondency. At the time I remember thinking, 'This must be worse than dying. At least when you die you don't have to get up in the morning and read about it in the newspapers.'

It would take time to rid ourselves of the disappointment of defeat in the Cup final, but the fact we had one league match left to play, and this against Manchester City, went some way to helping. It was heartening to see almost 60,000 at Old Trafford only three days after defeat at Wembley. If nothing else local pride was salvaged when we beat City 2–0 to end the season, if not exactly on a high note, then a pleasing one.

As testimony to the way we had played and approached matches throughout the season, United won the *Daily Mail* 'Fair Play League' by some margin from second-placed Liverpool. I was proud of our record of never having a player sent off in 42 League matches and having accumulated only seven bookings throughout the season, which says much for the self-discipline and restraint of the players. The two sides had been in contention for honours all season by playing entertaining, attacking football in a highly sporting manner. I was quoted at the time as saying, 'This augurs well for the future of the game . . . Manchester United and Liverpool, at the risk of upsetting people again, now that would make a terrific FA Cup final.'

Many a true word spoken in jest . . .

16

THE SEASON THEY INVENTED CHAMPAGNE

It was often written that I spent a lot of money on players as a manager, yet I balanced the books at virtually every club I managed. I am certain this was one of the reasons I was offered jobs. Over the years, without any substantiation, the rumour mill has suggested I was one of those managers who took a 'bung'. Sorry to disappoint and all that, but that was never the case. I had an eye for emerging talent, as did the scouts I employed, and the majority of the signings I made as a manager were bargain buys, most of whom went on to be sold for considerably more. You will have noticed how many times I bought a player for a certain fee, only to sell one for a similar amount of money. I felt it part of my remit as a manager to make money for a club in the transfer market or, at least, balance the books. I was involved in countless transfers as the majority of clubs I managed had top-heavy squads containing players who were not up to the standard required. I was involved in a clear-out at most of clubs I managed. Little wonder with so much transfer activity connected to my name there should be rumours of me having accepted the odd bung along the way, but that was never my style. I was an honest player and manager. My policy was always to treat the money of the club and its directors as if it had been my own, and I feel I enhanced the clubs' bottom line by having realised their valuable capital assets. For example, buying Steve Coppell for £40,000 whose market value must have increased tenfold within eighteen months. Lou Macari, Stewart Houston, Alex Forsyth, Gordon Hill and Gerry Daly were five other players whose transfer value to Manchester United far exceeded the original fee paid.

Personally I couldn't wait for the 1976–77 season to get under way. When a team has suffered a deep disappointment as we had done when beaten by Southampton at Wembley, the only way to rid your system of that is by playing games. United's pre-season training went well. Everybody was looking forward to the new campaign, and I knew that once the season got going any remnants of disappointment would quickly evaporate. The season kicked off on 21 August with the temperature in the high 80s. By any standard the summer of 1976 had been extraordinary. On 1 June, Derbyshire's county cricket match at Buxton was postponed because of snow. Only for such unseasonal weather to be followed by, well, more unseasonal weather but at the other end of the scale in what turned out to be one of the driest and hottest summers on record.

The season began with Old Trafford bathed in sunshine and under a clear blue sky for the visit of Birmingham City. It was so hot it was uncomfortable merely to sit in the sun and playing in such heat must have been a test for every player. The first half saw the teams share four goals to keep the 59,000 crowd on its toes, but as the heat began to take its toll, the pace understandably slackened in the second period. As the momentum of the game relaxed no further goals were forthcoming, and come the end I think the teams were relieved to hear the final whistle. I was disappointed not to have got the season off to a winning start, but a draw was a fair result.

On the Monday evening I attended the United reserves match against Coventry City. There was a healthy attendance of 10,879, many of whom, I suspect, had come to see the club's new flood-lights turned on for the first time. I always felt it my duty to watch the reserves matches when I was not involved with the first team, as I felt my presence sent a message to the players that they were very much in my thoughts and encouraged them to greater effort.

There was another reason to my presence at Old Trafford that Monday night. I had come along specifically to see Jim Holton in action. Jim had twice recovered from a broken leg, it was great to see him playing again but after the game I had the onerous task of telling him he was no longer part of my plans. I had built the centre of defence around Brian Greenhoff and Martin Buchan, if anything happened to either of those I had Colin Waldron (signed from Burnley) and Steve Paterson as able deputies, and if required Stewart Houston could also do a job for me in central defence. You can't run a football team on senti-ment. I had to be honest with Jim and inform him he was now down the pecking order and with youngsters soon to be coming through to the reserves, he would be better moving on to find first-team football. Jim was very popular with the supporters and was also well liked in the dressing room, but whilst he had been out injured we had developed a different way of playing at the back, which was more mobile a game than he was suited to. Naturally Jim was very disappointed at the news I gave him, but he was a good pro and understood why I was letting him go.

These days, when chief executives and agents negotiate the transfer of a player, I doubt if you get the good stories that used to occur when two managers were responsible for this element of the game. A good example of this relates to my selling of Jim Holton to Sunderland, then managed by Bob Stokoe, a wily and experienced manager. When a manager wanted to move a player on he would get on the telephone to other managers he thought might be in the market. Sunderland had just sold my former Rotherham centre-half Dave Watson to Manchester City for £275,000. Knowing Bob Stokoe would be looking to replace Watson and that he had money to spend, I rang Bob and began to 'sell' him Jim Holton. Bob didn't appear to be keen at first, so I started to lay it on thick.

'He's a tremendous centre-half,' I told Bob. 'Superb in the air, magnificent tackler, good distributor of the ball, reads a game well, never gives less than a hundred per cent in games and in training. You have to be talking good money for a player of Holton's quality. A hundred thousand wouldn't buy him.'

'I know,' said Bob, 'and I'm one of them.'

For all his initial misgivings I did sell Jim Holton to Bob Stokoe. Sunderland paid £80,000 for him, but it never really happened for him on Wearside and after fifteen matches he joined Coventry City for exactly half that fee.

On the second Saturday of the season the rain came down like stair rods to signal summer was over. Having beaten Coventry City, and their reserves, in midweek we played out a goalless draw at Derby County, leaving us with four points from our opening three matches and lying third. A heavy fixture programme lay ahead in the coming two months which was to total sixteen matches in eight weeks.

Our UEFA Cup campaign got off to a cracking start with a tie against Ajax. Johann Cruyff had moved on to Barcelona but the Ajax side was still full of quality players such as Ruud Krol, Piet Schrijvers, Ruud Geels, Wim Suurbier, Dick Schoenaker, Barry Hulshoff and Frank Arnesen, most of whom had played in three European Cup finals. Though we lost the first leg in Amsterdam 1–0, United's young team just about passed this stern test. The Dutch had never come across opponents who would attack them on their own turf. We had the better of the play and the chances in the first half without making our dominance tell. Four minutes before the interval, it was the experience of the Ajax team that proved telling. Ajax had threatened on the break all night and it was one such break that plunged us into trouble. They broke down one of our attacks and Hulshoff moved the ball quickly out of defence. We raced back to get men behind the ball but to no avail. Hulshoff played a clever ball through to Krol who cut in from the left, played a smart one-two with Arnesen, and then slammed the ball past

Stepney from just inside the penalty box. In the second period we received an unkind rub of the green. Houston tried his luck from the left, Ajax keeper Schrijvers failed to hold the ball and it appeared to have rolled over the line before he finally managed to scoop it away. From where I was sitting I couldn't see if the ball had, in fact, crossed the line but the reaction of my players told me all I needed to know. After the game Macari, Pearson and Coppell were in no doubt it was a goal. It wasn't given so we had it all to do at Old Trafford in the second leg. When asked about the incident during the post-match press conference, I said, 'It was one of those things you get in football. Managers and players make mistakes and officials give what they see. They don't always get it right, but I don't believe they intentionally get it wrong. Whatever, we accept the decisions of officials. I have no gripes, how can I? We are in the UEFA Cup, playing Ajax, which is a great experience for my young team.'

The return leg was another enthralling encounter. With Pearson injured I replaced him with teenager David McCreery, though the absence of our leading goalscorer did not in any way alter our style of play. We set about Ajax from the off and were unfortunate not to score after only five minutes when a Macari effort thumped against the foot of Schrijvers' left-hand post. We continued to apply the pressure and two minutes before the break a capacity 60,000 crowd were in raptures. Schrivjers parried a shot from Hill – in my days as a player we would have said the keeper failed to hold it – and Macari pounced to wipe out Ajax's single-goal advantage.

After an hour, during which we had always lived a little dangerously by taking the game to Ajax, I felt if we were to crack their defence a second time we needed to be doing something different. After 62 minutes I switched Brian Greenhoff from central defence into midfield and it transformed the game. Greenhoff always gave us something extra when playing in the middle of the park, where his qualities as a defender meant he was very good at breaking up attacks from the opposition before

they penetrated deep into our half of the field. He was also a
very good distributor of the ball and his presence in midfield
enabled Macari to push on and McIlroy to have greater freedom.
Of course playing Greenhoff in midfield made us a little more
susceptible at the back, but as ever my philosophy was attack is
the best form of defence. Within five minutes the switch paid
off. Greenhoff dispossessed Van Dord in midfield, made
headway down the right and pulled the ball back for McIlroy
to produce the knock-out blow. Many a team in Europe would
have tried to kill off the game there and then, but that was not
our style. We continued to plug away at Ajax and if it had not
been for Schrijvers would have won the tie by considerably more
than two goals.

On the same night Manchester City's hopes of progress in
the same competition were dashed when they were beaten by
Juventus. On learning of the City result Tommy Cavanagh said
to me, 'Juventus are the team everyone has to beat. I have a
feeling in my water we'll have to do just that in the next round.'
Tommy's 'water' was rarely wrong: United duly drew Juventus
in the second round

We began October with a visit to Leeds United that brought
a 2–0 victory which saw United move to the top of the First
Division for the first time that season. But our lead was a precar-
ious one, based on goal difference from Manchester City,
Liverpool and Middlesbrough. Only a single point separated the
top four clubs from Everton, Arsenal and West Bromwich
Albion, all of whom had ten points. It was early days, but the
First Division was once again shaping up to be very competitive.

Of the sixteen matches United played in September and
October, five were in the League Cup: a 5–0 victory over
Tranmere Rovers at Old Trafford and three epic ties against
Sunderland. The first took place less than a week after our UEFA
Cup match in Amsterdam, in between which we beat
Middlesbrough 2–0 at Old Trafford. With games coming thick

and fast I didn't want to spend any more time than was necessary during our visit to Holland. Usually when travelling abroad I like the players to see something of the city we visited but there was simply no time for sight-seeing in Amsterdam. We had flown in on the Tuesday morning, our game was played on the Wednesday evening, after which we travelled by coach from the Olympic Stadium to the airport and caught a flight home. We landed back in Manchester half an hour after midnight which meant the players were in their own homes at a reasonable time. I gave the players the Thursday off, and everyone reported back to The Cliff for some light training on the Friday morning prior to the league match against Middlesbrough. With the League Cup tie against Sunderland taking place the following Wednesday, I subjected the players to only light training again in the preceding two days. This was to be very much the pattern for us as the season unfolded and our commitment to cup competitions became more involved.

The League Cup tie against Sunderland at Old Trafford ended 2–2. With only four minutes remaining Sunderland seemed on their way to a shock victory only for their centre-half Jeff Clarke to put through his own goal. Up till then Sunderland had survived a merciless second-half pounding, and on the balance of play the draw was no more than we deserved. The replay at Roker Park ended in the same score so it was back to Old Trafford for the second replay. Switching Brian Greenhoff into midfield paid off yet again when he netted the only goal of the game. With the second replay against Sunderland having been hastily arranged the club only had time to issue a four-page programme, simply a sheet of A4 paper folded, priced 5p rather than the normal 12p. I heard many supporters didn't bother to purchase the programme on the night, but those who did and have kept it will have done the right thing as it was very unusual, if not unique, for United to issue such a programme for a first-team fixture and they have since become valuable collectors' items.

It is interesting to note now that in spite of United's heavy fixtures list, the only change I made to the team for the League Cup ties against Sunderland from the one that had beaten Ajax, was forced on me, Greenhoff switching to midfield for the injured Macari, with his place in defence being taken by Colin Waldron. It would never have occurred to me, or any other manager of the time, to field a weakened team, let alone a reserve side, in the League Cup. There was as much, if not more, kudos attached to winning the FA Cup than there was a European competition. Whilst the league title was still the objective of every First Division club, the League Cup had grown in importance since the 1960s and every club took the competition seriously. Whatever the competition, I wanted to field my best eleven, not only because I wanted to win the trophy, but also because I was conscious that we were representing Manchester United, a club with a distinguished history and tradition, deserving supporters and presence in football. I wanted United to be the best in whatever we set out do, be it to win a European match, a League Cup tie or a pre-season friendly.

Of the sixteen matches United played in September and October we lost just four. Having eventually beaten Sunderland in the League Cup we then thrashed their local rivals Newcastle United 7–2 in the fourth round. The Newcastle victory was part of a flurry of four matches in ten days at the end of October which saw United beat Juventus in the second round of the UEFA Cup.

The Juventus team we met at a packed Old Trafford included Causio, Tardelli and Cuccereddu who, the following month, would play a key role in Italy's 2–0 victory over England, a game in which Italy were described as being 'world class' and England merely 'journeymen footballers'. There was nothing journeyman about United that night but Gordon Hill, with a characteristic explosive volley, proved the only player who could breach what was an experienced and superbly organised Juventus defence. For a team that possessed so much quality it was sad to see

Juventus resort to cynical fouls. Three of these were on Pearson who, strangely enough, was the first player to go into the referee's book when he appeared only to be taking evasive action in a skirmish with sweeper Scirea.

Victory over Juventus showed me how far this young team had come in such a short time. I was delighted, but my delight was tempered somewhat when I saw the Juventus players leave the field smiling, delighted to have absorbed all our attacking play at the cost of a single goal. It was as if they knew the return leg would be an entirely different proposition. It was. Two brilliant goals from Roberto Boninsegna and another from Romeo Benetti sent us crashing out of the competition. On a night of incessant rain Juventus had just too much quality, too much skill, above all too much experience.

The glut of fixtures in the autumn saw Pearson, Macari, Buchan, McIlroy, Houston, Daly and Nicholl sustain injuries which resulted in them all missing a number of games at various times. With matches coming thick and fast I found myself having to promote players from the reserves. They did all right, but no more than that. I knew I had to strengthen the squad, find a couple of players who could do more than simply get through a game at this level. I was looking to bring in one or two who could bring an extra dimension to the team, with the ability to produce something out of the ordinary. My quest was only partially successful.

The need to bolster the squad was very apparent during November when we failed to win a single game. We lost to Aston Villa and West Ham, and drew with both Sunderland – our fourth meeting with Jimmy Adamson's side in as many weeks – and Leicester City. By now I was convinced I had to sign a quality goalkeeper. Alex Stepney was number one with Paddy Roche his deputy but I had come to the view that Alex was past his best and I was now looking to replace him. Alex was a vastly experienced goalkeeper with over 600 senior games to his name. When I was manager of Chelsea I signed him from Millwall as cover for Peter Bonetti. Alex wanted regular first-team football, however, and after only one game for Chelsea I sold him to – Manchester United. He had been a terrific servant of the club and was still a fine goalkeeper but for me the consistency he had once deployed had now deserted him.

In the second week of November I received a telephone call from Stoke City manager Tony Waddington. 'I have a player for you, Tommy,' said Tony, 'I've been told I have to sell players, this one is a snip at £120,000.'

'Who are we talking about?' I asked.

'Jimmy Greenhoff,' said Tony.

'I'll buy him,' I said without hesitation, 'and I'll take Peter Shilton off your hands as well.'

The previous week a storm had blown the roof off Stoke City's Butler Street Stand. Tony told me Stoke City were getting no leeway from their bank, and their insurance cover fell far short of the cost of replacing the damaged stand. The Stoke board had told him in order to raise capital he had to sell some of his best players, hence his call.

I jumped at the chance of buying Jimmy Greenhoff, Brian's older brother. Jimmy was a class act as a striker; extremely skilful, he had a very good football brain, a keen eye for goal, was a super team player and a committed professional. Tony Waddington was very loath to part with him, but it was a case of needs must. When the deal for Jimmy Greenhoff was completed I pursued my interest in Peter Shilton.

I saw Shilton as the ideal replacement for Alex Stepney. Shilton, Ray Clemence and Italy's Dino Zoff were, at the time, the best goalkeepers in the world. Such was Shilton's ability I reckoned having him in goal would save us thirty goals a season. Quite simply, I felt his presence would mean the difference between United winning and not winning the championship and, from there, going on to succeed, even dominate, Europe. I was excited beyond belief at the prospect of landing him. So when Peter Shilton indicated he was keen to move to United,

I was thrilled. Stoke were asking £275,000 for him, which was a very large fee but given what he could bring to the club, I knew he would prove to be a bargain. Though the United board had one two reservations about the size of the fee, I persuaded them it would be money well spent. Everything appeared to be going smoothly. At the time Shilton was represented by the agent Jon Holmes. The wages Jon was asking amounted to some £50 more than the highest paid player at United, but to be honest I didn't think this to be unreasonable for a player of his quality and for what he would mean to the team and the club. It was, however, a view not shared by the United board. In keeping with the boards of many top clubs and indeed, some managers of the time, it was considered acceptable to pay huge wages for an outfield player but not a goalkeeper. While this country had, since the 1960s, produced a succession of the finest goalkeepers in the world, many people involved in the game at the highest level seemed not to appreciate the worth of a top quality keeper to a team. The United board had sanctioned £275,000 to buy Shilton and I couldn't believe they were jeopardising the deal for the sake of £50 a week – £2,600 a year.

On hearing of the board's reluctance to make Peter Shilton 'by some way' the highest-paid player at United, there followed a lengthy discussion. I outlined my view of what Shilton's ability would mean in terms of matches won and points gathered; the effect his presence in the side would have on the confidence of the defence; the effect Shilton would have in minimising the opposition's opportunities to shoot. I thought I had presented a strong, rational argument for making Shilton the best-paid player on the books, but my words cut no ice. After a brief discussion I was informed that there was no way the board would accede to Shilton's wage demands or, more to the point, his agent.

I have to say I was pretty devastated. I couldn't believe they could be so myopic, particularly Matt Busby with all his experience as a player and manager. Surely he saw the worth of Shilton to the club. Later in the day I put this to him.

'Of course I do. I couldn't argue with anything you said, Tommy,' Matt told me. 'It's the wages, can't be justified, even here.'

I told Matt that when I arrived at the club George Best was the highest-paid player and his performances rarely justified the amount of money the club was paying him.

'We were tied into a contract,' said Matt. 'Irrespective of how well or indifferent George played, supporters would willingly part with their money to see him. I don't think they would flock to see Shilton.'

'But we are getting capacity crowds as it is.'

'The board are in agreement, Tommy,' said Matt, a serious, definite tone in his voice. 'They feel they can't justify paying the boy what his agent is asking.'

I was left thinking why Matt had referred to the board as 'they'. Was it because he agreed with me but had been over-ruled, or, having seen himself as a lone voice kept his own counsel? Perhaps Matt, too, felt Shilton's wage demands were excessive and was indulging in club spin when speaking to me? If he had been sincere in what he said to me about recognising the worth of having Shilton in goal, I thought it highly unlikely he would not argue the case when the board took umbrage about the salary. Whatever the truth is of Matt's opinion, I never found out. This was the first and only time the United board refused me permission to buy a player, and I was devastated by their decision. I couldn't understand why they had vetoed the deal over a relatively trivial amount of money. Though I didn't think so at the time, I was to come to the conclusion that the machinations of club politics and personal reputations may have been at the root of the matter.

Peter Shilton remained at Stoke City. In September of the following year with Stoke City having been relegated to Division Two, Brian Clough paid £275,000 to take Shilton to

Nottingham Forest, the rest is history, and of the most glorious kind.

Winter came early in 1976. Hard frosts followed by the first snow resulted in United playing only two league matches from our 2–0 defeat at West Ham United on 27 November until 1 January. The first of these was a 3–1 defeat at Arsenal in mid-December, a game that went ahead due to Highbury's under-soil heating. On 27 December we enjoyed a comfortable 4–0 victory over Everton at Old Trafford to exact some revenge for their 3–0 victory in the fifth round of the League Cup at Old Trafford at the beginning of the month. The win against Everton was our first victory in nine league matches stretching back to 2 October. In that time we encountered a series of injuries to key players and whilst no one player, other than Gerry Daly, was out of the team for any length of time, I had not been in a position to field what I believed to be my best eleven.

There was one other game United played in December, this being a friendly I had instigated back in late September. With United playing sixteen matches in two months you may well wonder why, at that time, I offered to play a friendly match. I was often at Old Trafford at seven in the morning; those two hours before the players arrived at The Cliff allowed me to keep abreast of the prodigious amounts of paperwork and letters I received. On arriving at the ground I would make myself a cup of tea and read the sports pages of the morning newspapers before tackling the administrative work. One morning in September I read that Newport County were in dire financial trouble, and that should the club not raise £12,000 by the end of the year they would be declared bankrupt. Irrespective of which club you support, play for or manage, I have always believed, collectively we are all a part of the great family of football. As I read the article it occurred to me that if Manchester United offered to play them in a friendly and waived our normal fee for such a game, the gate receipts may well wipe out the club's debt and ensure its survival. It seemed such a simple solution to their problem, I telephoned the Newport manager Jimmy Scoular and put my proposition to him. I knew Jimmy well from his days as skipper of Newcastle United and he was delighted to take me up on the offer.

As things turned out it was decided it might be better to play the friendly at Cardiff City's Ninian Park rather than Newport's Somerton Park and for Jimmy to field a Combined South Wales XI against United as this might attract a larger attendance on the night and subsequently greater revenue. A crowd of some 15,000 produced receipts of £8,000 for the Newport coffers, a little short of what was required but sufficient to satisfy their bank, most of their creditors and ensure the club's survival. Sadly Newport County eventually lost their Football League status in 1987–88, but as Jimmy Scoular said, my offer to bring United to play a friendly, at the time, 'saved the club from extinction'. Over the years I had made similar gestures when manager of Chelsea and Aston Villa. By offering or, agreeing, to play a friendly against a cash-strapped club, I believed I was not only aiding the club in question but helping the game in general. Whilst I understand top Premiership clubs such as Chelsea, United, Arsenal and Liverpool see their players as capital assets on the balance sheet and do not want to risk them being injured in friendly matches, these clubs do play friendly games in the close season, such as it is now. Such friendly matches are, however, all geared to moneymaking for the clubs concerned, to further promote commercial sales and 'brand awareness' in the Far East, the USA or wherever. At the same time, our top clubs appear to have little or no thought for the smaller clubs of our game, those who live hand-to-mouth but are as much a part of the family of football as the rich and powerful elite of the Premiership.

United's poor sequence of results in October and November of 1976 saw us slip to mid-table in Division One, a position which prompted some newspapers to talk in terms of the club being in 'crisis'. In response to such claims I gave an interview to the Manchester 'Pink' in which I said,

> What the people who are yelling 'crisis' should remember is that basically we are the same team that finished third in the league last season and reached the final of the FA Cup. We are still a very good side . . . It is difficult for me to put my finger on the trouble. We have had more than our share of injuries and I don't think the transfer market can provide a ready answer. Given I am always looking to sign individuals who can improve the team, I wouldn't swap my squad for any other in the First Division, because potentially I think they are the best, particularly if you are looking ahead and note their ages . . . There is no crisis. We shall work our way through this dip in form and move back up the table. I'm very optimistic about the future of the team, and this club.

Our form did pick up in the New Year and the revival of our fortunes coincided with our involvement in the FA Cup. Our victory over Everton on 27 December marked the start of a run of thirteen league matches – which took us into April – of which only two were lost, against Norwich City and title contenders Ipswich Town. The return to form also saw us amongst the goals again – we enjoyed three-goal victories at Birmingham City and Spurs, and at home to Derby County, Newcastle United and near neighbours City. There was also the little matter of a goalless draw against Liverpool who at the time were battling it out with Ipswich for pole position. Our 3–1 victory over Manchester City mirrored our victory at Maine Road back in September. A derby match is an entertainment in itself but such games do not always produce spectacular football as the tension that grips the fans also tends to affect the players. That said I thought our encounters against Manchester City produced more in the way of pure football entertainment than in previous years because both sides had committed themselves to all-out attack. Before the match against City I was presented with the Bell's Manager of the Month Award, usually a bad sign, but not on this occasion as goals from Pearson, Hill and Coppell gave us what in the end was a comfortable victory over a City team that was third and included players of the quality of Joe Corrigan, Dave Watson, Asa Hartford, Brian Kidd, Joe Royle, Dennis Tueart and Peter Barnes.

Having emerged from the so-called 'crisis' our good run elevated United to fourth in Division One with 33 points, seven behind leaders Liverpool who enjoyed a two-point advantage over Ipswich with Bobby Robson's team having two games in hand as we did. Even during our lean spell I had never ruled out another tilt at the championship and I was now determined to give it our best shot.

We followed our victory over City with a 1–0 victory over Leeds United, and a 2–2 draw against a West Bromwich Albion that contained future United players in Laurie Cunningham and Bryan Robson, and one Busby Babe of the past in player-manager Johnny Giles.

We entered April having thirteen games to play in little over six weeks – in April alone we played eight league games and an FA Cup semi-final. On 5 April we visited fellow semi-finalists Everton and it proved to be a lively encounter packed with incidents that kept the Goodison Park crowd thoroughly entertained. They did not have to wait long to see a goal, 40 seconds in fact. Straight from the kick-off we went on the attack and Jimmy Greenhoff smashed the ball twice into the Everton goalmouth. The second time it came off keeper David Lawson's chest and there was Gordon Hill to stab the ball home. Just before half-time a mistake by Everton defender Mick Lyons presented Hill with the ball some 35 yards from goal. Hill looked up to see Lawson standing towards the edge of his penalty area and executed a delightful chip. The ball sailed over the back-pedalling keeper, underneath the bar and stroked the length of the back of the net before coming to rest. Everton proved a different proposition after the break and Martin Dobson reduced the arrears – but it wasn't enough to salvage the game for them – with a goal reminiscent of Hill's second, both strikes prompting a cringe-worthy but nonetheless clever pun headline in the *People* – 'They've Had Their Chips'.

When we then beat Stoke City 3–0 at Old Trafford there was still an outside chance of the title but a 2–1 defeat at Sunderland on a day when Ipswich and Manchester City both won and Liverpool drew at Stoke saw United nine points adrift of Ipswich, still with three games in hand; but it wasn't long before our title dream went up in smoke. Games in hand are worthless if you don't win them. A disappointing 1–1 draw with Leicester City was followed by resounding defeats against both QPR and Middlesbrough which effectively ended our title hopes. We were not the only side to suffer, Ipswich too stumbled and, ominously, with six games remaining Liverpool moved to the top of the table ahead of Manchester City and Ipswich.

United ran down the league programme with victories over Arsenal and QPR, a thrilling 3–3 draw at Stoke City, a sometimes brutal 1–1 draw at Bristol City, and defeats at both Liverpool and West Ham United. With United by this stage in the FA Cup final, the Bristol City game proved tragic for Stewart Houston, who broke his ankle in what was an accident when challenging for the ball with City striker Chris Garland. I felt sorry for him as he was a super lad and a great pro. He was a sad loss and I just hoped we wouldn't miss his presence at Wembley too much.

I had no complaints about the incident involving Garland and Houston but I did have something to say after the game to the media and referee Ray Toseland about Bristol City's Norman Hunter. Hunter's reputation as a hard man is, of course, well known. It says much for how tolerant referees were of overly robust play that in 645 senior appearances for Leeds United where he was an ever-present for five seasons, and in over 100 games for Bristol City, Hunter was sent off only once and booked a mere three times. As a player he was a remarkably consistent performer, a member of Alf Ramsey's 1966 World Cup squad and was the first recipient of the PFA's Player of the Year Award in 1973, always the mark of how highly a player is regarded by his fellow professionals. Against United, however, Hunter had showed his darker side with a reckless challenge on Brian Greenhoff for which he only received a booking. In my opinion had Greenhoff not taken quick and evasive action he and Houston would have been in hospital together. I never had any complaints about hard tackling as long as it was fair but, in my opinion, Hunter continued to overstep the boundary of what was acceptable. Matters began to escalate because when players feel they are not being afforded protection by the referee from unfair challenges they will take matters into their own hands, as my players did on this day.

In the second half another player with a reputation for hardness, Gerry Gow, clattered Sammy McIlroy who had been on the receiving end of a number of rash challenges. McIlroy had had enough of it and on this occasion retaliated. He and Gow exchanged snarls, then blows, before both finally exchanged the pitch for their respective dressing rooms.

After the game when asked about Hunter's behaviour I was quoted as saying, 'I have followed this player for fifteen years and he's always the same. He started the trouble with his tackle on Brian (Greenhoff).'

I chose my words carefully for fear of inciting the wrath of the game's governing bodies and being subjected to that woolly charge of 'bringing the game into disrepute'. I needn't have bothered exercising such verbal caution. The following day the *People* ran with the story that after the game, 'Docherty launched a savage attack on Norman Hunter', whilst on Monday the *Daily Mail* said, 'Manchester United manager Tommy Docherty launched a blistering attack on former Leeds and England defender Norman Hunter after the battle of Ashton Gate', and went on to quote me word for word which, by no stretch of the imagination, amounted to a 'savage' or 'blistering' attack on Norman Hunter.

Having read the newspapers I awaited the letter from the Football League. It's a funny old game, as they say. I had one player with a broken ankle albeit because of an accident, one player sent off and three others requiring treatment. We were lucky the injuries, the result of rash tackles, did not affect the livelihoods of the players concerned. There had been a referee who, in my opinion, had been weak and therefore contributed to the escalation of rough-house play. Yet all the Football League was concerned about was what in my opinion had been my mild and restrained response to these events which had been subsequently blown-up out of all proportion by certain newspapers. Little wonder that even in 2006 I read descriptions of myself, such as one that appeared in the *Mail On Sunday* by Tom Bower, as 'the hard-drinking, foul-mouthed manager of Manchester United'. When I read such a description of myself I don't get angry. But it does instil in me a belief that the article, in this particular instance about 'bungs', is sadly lacking in credibility. The truth is I rarely swear and, as all my former players could testify, was a fitness fanatic and would describe my drinking as always having been far less than even moderate. This type of journalism, if indeed it can be termed 'journalism', perpetuates myth and, I suppose, there are some who prefer to read and hear the scurrilous rather than the substantiated. As TV host Larry Grayson once quipped prior to a charity dinner when introduced to a notorious gossip columnist from a tabloid newspaper, 'If you haven't anything honest or good to say about people, you *must* come and sit next to me.'

United finished the season in sixth position in Division One, Liverpool clinching the championship a point ahead of Manchester City with Ipswich Town having led the table for much of the season slipping to third. The end of the season saw two consummate professionals take their final bows. Bobby Moore played his 1,000th and last first-class match for Fulham

at Blackburn Rovers in May and announced his retirement.
Former Southampton and England winger Terry Paine, with a
then-record 824 League games to his name, played his last game
for Hereford United, appropriately at Southampton for whom
he had made 713 of those appearances. As two famous old
names bowed out as players, two famous old clubs prepared to
meet one another in the FA Cup final. The bookies made league
champions Liverpool 1–2 on favourites to beat us, with United
4–1 against. Strangely enough, those odds rather pleased me.

United's journey to Wembley began with us playing hosts to
Walsall. Tommy Cavanagh and I had been to see our opponents
in action and had been impressed by their total commitment.
Walsall had beaten us in the FA Cup during United's season in
the Second Division. Then we could do no more than a goalless draw at Old Trafford and Walsall deservedly won a thrilling
tie 3–2 at a packed Fellows Park. In the foyer of Fellows Park
there used to be a pertinent reminder of how the FA Cup can
often produce a shock result. A football made of leather in the
old-fashioned way, broad-panelled and the colour of Christmas
pudding sat in a glass case. The ball represented the high-water
mark in Walsall's history, the one used when Walsall produced
their greatest ever FA Cup result when beating mighty Arsenal
2–0 in 1933. I thought about that ball when we were drawn at
home to Walsall. It served as a reminder to me that, though the
club were not doing well at the time in Division Three, the Cup
is about dreams, hope, which may even become conviction, and
upsetting the natural order of things. At the time of United's
defeat at Walsall I didn't shed too many tears, as my priority
was to get United out of the Second Division at the first time
of asking. This time, it was different.

Though still in the hunt for the championship, deep down I
believed the FA Cup represented our best chance of honours. I
was leaving nothing to chance. Frank Blunstone had also been
to watch Walsall and I was happy that we were to meet them

with confidence restored having put an end to our bad run in the league.

What our trips to see Walsall in action told us was, for a Third Division team, they had some decent players. They were a team of variety and balance, muscle and guile, promise and experience, a patchwork quilt of a side enduring a rough time in the league, for whom an FA Cup tie against Manchester United presented a rare opportunity to garland their season in glory. One football writer was foolish enough to suggest that with high wages, increased professionalism and a growing gap between the big and small the age of the giant killer in the FA Cup was over. Mindful that Walsall had upset us two years before, I was taking the tie very seriously.

Walsall had only won four of their 22 matches in Division Three but their limitless courage and desire to shine on the relatively big stage of Old Trafford made them doughty opponents. We camped in the Walsall half of the field but it was not until three minutes before half-time that we took the lead. Nicholl found McIlroy who squared the ball to Hill who drifted past Brian Taylor before placing his shot wide of Kearns. I slumped back in my chair and I don't think I was the only person in the ground to sigh with relief. Far from content to fight a rearguard action, Walsall pushed forward at every given opportunity at the beginning of the second half. Ironically it was their leading goalscorer, Alan Buckley, who fluffed his lines when taking centre stage. Twice in three minutes during the third quarter he failed to convert with the goal at his mercy. When a team plays supposed superiors, when the few goalscoring chances come along, they must take them. On this occasion Walsall failed, which proved their undoing. There was no disgrace in their defeat, far from it. Walsall played very well and could easily have earned a replay to go with their financial windfall from the attendance of almost 50,000.

When the draw for the fourth round was made there were still a number of small clubs ready to contribute an indelible line to the history book of the FA Cup. I sat in my office at Old Trafford listening to the draw on the radio. Just down the road from Manchester, non-league Northwich Victoria had sharp-elbowed their way through and, according to the newspapers, were hoping to draw United. I wondered what their reaction was to a home draw with Oldham Athletic. Eventually there were just two balls left in the velvet bag: Manchester United and Queens Park Rangers.

QPR were in the bottom half of Division One but had reached the semi-finals of the League Cup and the quarter-finals of the UEFA Cup. Our form in the league continued to be good, we were playing more like our old selves and whilst not for one moment underestimating Rangers, I was confident of success on the day. The Rangers team was rich in character. Phil Parkes, who began his career at Walsall, had emerged as one of the best goalkeepers in the country, one who would have surely added to the single cap he had been awarded in 1974 but for the sublime Shilton and Clemence. John Hollins had been under my charge at Chelsea, whilst few opposing players relished an afternoon in the company of the experienced Frank McLintock. David Webb, the central pillar of the side was also a former Chelsea player and had famously scored the winning goal against Leeds United in the replayed FA Cup final of 1970. Don Masson had been a member of my Scotland squad, he was an intelligent midfield player who displayed tremendous ability on the ball that was matched by his pin-point passing. Stan Bowles was an enigma. Slight, small in stature but big in heart, he was blessed with an inordinate amount of skill – and cheek. Leading the line was the unorthodox, unpredictable and perplexing Peter Eastoe, who had been the Football League's leading scorer the previous season when with Swindon Town.

It is an old cliché of football that a game can be of two halves. Our tie against Queens Park Rangers was a game of two pitches. There had been a heavy overnight frost and a watery sun had failed to penetrate the part of the pitch shadowed by Old Trafford's main stand. The referee passed the pitch at around noon but come three o'clock the shaded side was as hard as iron and treacherous underfoot, while the north side of the pitch was soft. The type of stud to wear was a matter of opinion. Not knowing which way we'd be kicking, it was impossible to decide: i.e. short studs or moulded rubber? A toss of a coin was as good a way to decide as any other. An early indication of how tricky conditions were occurred in the first minute when the normally surefooted Bowles slithered on his back after losing his footing in pursuit of Macari. Minutes later Stepney fell over when taking a goal-kick. Whatever Hill was wearing on his feet should have been patented because his faultless darting runs began to cause Rangers all manner of problems. He glided and floated around the pitch seemingly inhabiting a different playing surface and twice tested Parkes' mettle as a goalkeeper. After 18 minutes of largely pantomime frolicking the frostbound pitch appeared to hinder Parkes as he took to his toes to field a shot from Coppell. For a second or so the Rangers keeper lost his footing so that he got down to the ball a fraction later than he would have liked. Always stretching to make contact, Parkes could only push the ball up into the air where it momentarily hung invitingly for Macari who was gingerly making his way towards it. Macari's execution was what we used to call a 'good morning' goal, the ball dispatched with a slight nod of the head.

It proved to be decisive. As the weak winter sun set behind the Stretford End the pitch became even more treacherous. The referee maintained that the surface was not a potential danger to players and the city centre was spared the influx of 58,000 supporters prematurely at a loose end.

The fifth round of the FA Cup is where the really serious business end of the competition kicks in. Every team enters the FA Cup in the hope of glory be it in the first round or thereafter. Those who reach the fifth round begin to sense Wembley in the offing. This time we were to face our Wembley conquerors, Southampton.

The Dell was never an accommodating place for the away team. The fact that the visitors never relished playing there had much to do with the ground itself, which was tight and compact, the crowd only a matter of feet from the action. When Southampton had their tails up, it was as if you had opposing fans standing alongside and bellowing in your ear, an unnerving experience for even the most seasoned professional.

The team we faced at The Dell bore little resemblance to the one that had beaten us at Wembley only ten months previously. Only five members remained: Blyth, Peach, Holmes, Channon and Osgood. Of the new recruits two were very familiar faces, Ted MacDougall who had been the first player I had sold on arriving at United, and World Cup winner Alan Ball. Only Forsyth and Daly were missing from the team I had fielded at Wembley, and even our substitute was the same – McCreery.

The first half produced a thrilling and enthralling forty-five minutes of football – and four goals, two for each team. Southampton's central pairing of Blyth and Waldron struggled to cope with Pearson and Jimmy Greenhoff, particularly in the air, but it was Macari, all five feet and a bit of him who out-jumped everyone after little over ten minutes to head the opening goal. A quarter of an hour later Southampton were on level terms when Peach dispatched a penalty awarded for a foul on Channon by Houston. The defence wasn't created that could have prevented our second goal. Some 25 yards out, Macari casually rolled the ball into the path of Hill who thumped a screamer. The ball fizzed past the angle and upright and the despairing dive of Wells and lodged behind the stanchion.

Our lead was short lived, less than a minute before the break we were caught square across the back by a through ball from Channon, and Holmes, with refrigerated coolness, rolled it past Stepney. Straight from the restart we went down the other end and Macari rattled the Southampton crossbar, the ball was hooked upfield by Blyth, latched on to by Osgood who thumped his shot against Stepney's right-hand post. As the two teams departed the pitch at the interval the stands and terraces of The Dell seemed reluctant at first to believe the evidence of their own eyes but as the players disappeared down the tunnel to the right of the main stand the ground rung with wild applause.

Such an exciting and eventful first half gave way to a cat-and-mouse second period that eventually petered out as a contest as both teams settled for a draw. During the post-match press conference I was asked about Southampton's penalty. Peter Slingsby reported me as saying, 'Houston clearly fouled Channon and I can only apologise to Mick and Southampton fans for that. Though I should think the fact Holmes converted will provide them with ample consolation.' I was genuinely sorry that one of my players had fouled an opponent when he was in a good goalscoring position, as sportsmanship was always very high on my agenda.

The replay developed into a bruising encounter. Jimmy Greenhoff put us ahead with a flying header, only for Buchan to present me with an opportunity to do some more apologising when he upended Steve Williams. Peach struck home a sweet penalty. Referee Clive Thomas was in danger of wearing out his whistle, so often was he penalising Southampton for fouls. Eventually Thomas stamped his authority on the game and the names of four Southampton players into his notebook. Southampton hung on grimly. It was one-way traffic from United and just when I thought it would lead us up a cul-de-sac Jimmy Greenhoff struck once more in the 70th minute to restore our lead. Two minutes later Jim Steele lived up to his name when nearly slicing Jimmy Greenhoff in half. Clive Thomas was quickly on the scene and only said one word, 'Off!'

Our reward for defeating Southampton was a home tie against Aston Villa in the sixth round. Villa had played two gruelling League Cup finals in four days (the first a goalless draw, the replay also a draw – Villa eventually won the second replay – to lift the Cup) which, for the tie at Old Trafford, deprived them of striker Andy Gray, midfield terror Alex Cropley and centre-back Chris Nicholl. At the time we were in fourth position in Division One, Villa two places behind but with two games in hand.

There was some silly talk of Villa not being motivated for the tie in light of their continuing presence in the League Cup final. Nothing could have been further from the truth. Villa were buzzing from the start and within two minutes had scored. Gordon 'Sid' Cowans played the ball to Brian Little who, with the inside of his boot, hit a wonderful curling shot from all of 30 yards that beat Stepney all ends up. We were nothing if not spirited and from this early setback took the game to Villa. McIlroy's headed effort spoilt the pristine whiteness of the Villa crossbar before we restored parity on twenty minutes when Houston netted with a low, venomous free-kick from 20 yards.

I had to reshuffle the defence to accommodate McCreery when Brian Greenhoff limped off with a groin strain, but the change never hindered our momentum. After Macari and McIlroy went close, the enterprising John Gidman combined with Denis Mortimer before whacking a rising drive that must have stung the fingers of Stepney's right hand as he tipped the ball over the bar. As the second half progressed Buchan went close with a 30-yard effort and the crossbar again came to the aid of Villa keeper Burridge when it denied Jimmy Greenhoff. Ten minutes from time, what had been a pulsating tie was finally settled. Coppell attacked on the right, Pearson battled on the by-line but managed to cross to Macari who on the half-volley rifled the ball into the roof of the net with his right boot. Afterwards Villa boss Ron Saunders looked into a TV camera and said, 'It was a wonderful advert for football.' When my turn came to do the same I offered a somewhat sprightlier response.

'After two minutes I thought it was a terrible game,' I quipped. 'At 1–1 it got better, at 2–1 it was very good, and when the final whistle sounded I shook hands with Ron and said, "What a wonderful advert for football, and if you're stumped for something to say to the TV people, Ron, you can tell them that."' Ron Saunders did something people didn't often see him do – he laughed.

The draw for the semi-final paired us with Leeds United at neutral Hillsborough, normally a tie to whet the appetite of the sporting press but on this occasion somewhat overshadowed by the fact that the other semi-final was a Merseyside derby between Everton and Liverpool.

Prior to meeting Leeds, Derby County approached the United board for permission to talk to me about succeeding Dave Mackay as their manager. They offered me a salary of £28,000 a year, £10,000 more than I was receiving at United. As I've already said, money was not a crucial issue for me; I was more concerned with security – that is, the length of the contract. I always wanted time to finish the job I set out to do at a club. I was far from having done that yet at United and so I told Matt Busby and his fellow directors I had no interest in joining Derby at that time. The United board were delighted. Though I had 15 months of my contract to run, they suggested we might enter into discussions ourselves about renewing my current deal. I'd had a difficult ride restoring United to prominence. We had yet to win a major trophy but the board informed me the club were now £400,000 in the black and estimated profits for the current season would be in excess of £750,000. Attendances at Old Trafford had again topped one million and we still had three home matches remaining. Everything was going exceptionally well I was told. I agreed, but said I had only just completed the groundwork. I desperately wanted to bring a major trophy to the club. In little over a week we were to take yet another step to achieving that aim.

Leeds United were managed by Jimmy Armfield, known now as a common-sense radio summariser, and for his work with the PFA and FA. Jimmy had been a redoubtable and stylish right-back for both Blackpool and England and had taken over as manager of Leeds in 1974 after the ill-fated 44-day reign of Brian Clough. Whilst it is true to say Leeds United were not the power in English football they had been under Don Revie they were still a formidable outfit. Under Armfield they had been runners-up in the 1975 European Cup and had beaten Norwich, Birmingham, Manchester City and Wolves to reach the semi-finals. With four First Division scalps under their belt I was determined not to make United their fifth.

The names of most of the Leeds players were synonymous with the club and its previous successes – Paul Reaney, Trevor Cherry, Paul Madeley, Eddie and Frankie Gray, Allan Clarke, Peter Lorimer and Joe Jordan. There was Gordon McQueen, an imperious centre-half and, in midfield, Tony Currie, one of the most talented and skilful playmakers of his generation. Since March, Leeds had been without their first-choice keeper David Harvey, his replacement was another Scottish international, Dave Stewart.

At this stage of proceedings the United team ran off the tongue like a well-known nursery rhyme. Irrespective of how many games we played I was reluctant to change the team, and only did so when forced to through injuries. The players had built up a tremendous spirit, the camaraderie was first-class as was their application in both training and games. We also possessed a ravenous appetite for battle and against teams such as Leeds United, the call was often for sleeves to be rolled up and to give not as good but better than you got.

For me the issue was never in doubt. I told the players before the game to go for a quick kill. A goal, preferably two, in the first half would see Leeds off I was sure. From the first whistle the game was our property. Our pressure created two chances in little over ten minutes and we capitalised on both. First the persistence of the indefatigable Coppell forced a corner that was taken by Hill, flicked on by Houston and volleyed into the net by Jimmy Greenhoff. Three minutes later Coppell himself made it 2–0, hooking home a Hill shot that had cannoned off Madeley. Leeds may well have had McQueen in their side but there was to be no great escape for them. They did get back into the game when Clarke scored from the spot after Jimmy Nicholl tangled with Jordan. Stepney got a hand to the ball but could not keep it out of the net, though he stopped everything else Leeds fired at him. It was an unforgettable semi-final: the second half was a fierce and taut battle which involved every player, every fan, every blade of grass inside Hillsborough. Again we were a force of nature but Leeds showed resolve and commitment to match their skill. Buchan, hampered by a groin injury, struggled manfully to contain Joe Jordan, always a muscular troublemaker up front. As the game neared its finale every minute for me seemed to contain 180 seconds. I kept glancing at my watch and the hands hardly seemed to have moved. Eventually a long shrill blast from the referee put an end to the hostilities. We were back at Wembley but at this point unsure as to whom our opponents would be.

In the all-Merseyside semi-final Everton and Liverpool had played out a 2–2 draw in highly controversial circumstances. Everton had twice come from behind with equalising goals and appeared to have scored a third and won the game when substitute Bryan Hamilton steered the ball into the net, only for the referee to disallow his effort. Everton were furious as they believed they had scored a late and legitimate goal – talk to Evertonians of a certain age even now and they still smart at the very mention of Hamilton's 'goal'. Liverpool rarely if ever gave anyone a second chance; they won the replay 3–0 to set up what was one of the most eagerly anticipated FA Cup finals in years.

The build-up to the final was tainted just a little when the FA announced that in the event of a draw the replay would take place on 27 June – a ridiculous decision given the final was scheduled for 21 May. Asked for his opinion on the matter Liverpool manager Bob Paisley said, 'I am not intellectual enough to find words to express my disgust at this stupidity.' I was a little more lightweight when giving my response: 'We will have to take our holidays on the Costa del Stretford,' I said, adding, 'When I hear of decisions like this, sometimes I wonder if the first item on the agenda of FA meetings is, "How can we upset and antagonise clubs and their supporters."'

The prophets as well as the bookies favoured Liverpool. Having already won the championship and with a European Cup final to follow in only four days, Bob Paisley's side were in contention for a unique Treble. I had the highest regard for Liverpool, their manager and players. I had done my homework on Paisley's team but you could indulge in sufficient study to qualify for a PhD without ever devising a sure-fire plan to overcome Liverpool. I had spotted what I believed to be one or two weaknesses, but really I placed my faith in my players. I felt the team was good enough to beat Liverpool as long as we enjoyed that element required of all winners of Cup competitions be it the World Cup or the Sunday morning League Cup – luck.

Liverpool were a highly skilled and sophisticated team, yet they could also roll up their sleeves and do battle when required. One of their greatest assest was their ability to conduct games at their own tempo, 'bossing it' as Bob Paisley used to say. Liverpool had played in excess of 60 competitive matches, so to have won the league title and reached the finals of two major cup competitions was testimony to their stamina, fortitude and patience. The subtle changes Bob Paisley had made to the team had established a consistency of style and a hard core of first-team players who more or less picked themselves, a situation mirrored at United.

The day of the Cup final dawned fine and sunny. I met the players for breakfast, after which we took a short walk, read, or rather glanced at the newspapers. I felt relaxed but having read the first paragraph of the preview of the final in one newspaper, I suddenly realised I hadn't a clue what I had just read. I tried the paragraph again only for the words to fail to register in my

brain for a second time. I threw the newspaper to one side and
went up to my room to check the suit, shirt and shoes I was to
wear at Wembley were all in order. Nothing had happened to
them since I had last checked them before breakfast. I ordered
coffee and whilst waiting for it to be delivered Tommy Cavanagh
came into my room.

'Grand day for it,' said Tommy.

'Yes, lovely day,' I agreed.

'Take a stud though, I think,' ventured Tommy. 'Always soft
that pitch.'

'Always, even after days without rain.'

Tommy sat down in the only chair in the room, picked up
the hotel's brochure and began to read it. 'It's going to be our
day today,' he said casually.

'Too right it is. We'll do them, no problem,' I said.

'If I was allowed to bet, I'd stick a ton on us.'

'Too right.'

A few moments of silence followed before Tommy cast aside
the brochure. 'I have to say it, you seem very relaxed and confident,' he said.

'So do you.'

'Too right I am, because I know we're gonna win.'

'No doubt about it.'

More silence. 'How are you really?' he asked.

'Bricking it.'

'Me too.'

I was feeling nerves and tension but only because I had nothing
to occupy my mind. I was to hold a team meeting shortly and
knew once my mind was occupied and I was doing my job I would
be fine. In truth I was confident and I wanted my confidence to
transfer to the players. A manager on Cup final day experiences
strangely contradictory feelings. You feel very involved, which you
are, yet also feel detachment because you know there is little you
can do once the game gets under way. Every manager feels this,
whatever the game, but never more so than at an FA Cup final.

I didn't say too much to the players at the team meeting, preferring to keep it simple. We wouldn't be playing anything other than our normal, attacking game. I didn't talk too much about Liverpool, the players knew them well enough. But I was at pains to point out all our individual and collective strengths. Above all I told them to absorb every second of the day, enjoy themselves and commit all to memory. 'It passes in a flash, remember everything,' I said. 'These are the good old days, just you wait and see.'

Liverpool lined up as follows: Ray Clemence; Phil Neal, Tommy Smith, Emlyn Hughes, Joey Jones; Jimmy Case, Terry McDermott, Ray Kennedy, Kevin Keegan, David Johnson, Steve Heighway; sub: Ian Callaghan. Manchester United's team was Alex Stepney; Jimmy Nicholl, Brian Greenhoff, Martin Buchan, Arthur Albiston; Steve Coppell, Lou Macari, Sammy McIlroy, Jimmy Greenhoff, Stuart Pearson, Gordon Hill; sub: David McCreery.

Normally when there was a colour clash in an FA Cup final both teams were requested to play in their second kit. For some reason such a request was not invoked on this occasion; we wore our normal strip of red shirts and white shorts, Liverpool their change strip of white shirts and black shorts.

I was hoping we would take the game to Liverpool from the very start, but it was obvious that the Merseysiders were in no mind to let us have the ball and come at them. I had told the players to close down quickly, especially in midfield so as not to allow them possession and thus dictate proceedings. But almost all the first-half attacking was done by Liverpool. A shot from Case was deflected over the top, Johnson scraped the bar from 20 yards but we replied on the break with a sumptuous drive from Hill that a lesser keeper than Clemence might have struggled to take as easily as he did. As half-time approached Stepney produced the save of the afternoon when denying Ray Kennedy. Stepney had started to go the wrong way when Kennedy headed down a cross from Case at the far post, but somehow managed to readjust and keep the ball out with his knees. A goal for Liverpool then, seconds before the break, would have been a crushing blow to us. As it was, we walked down the tunnel very much in the game but still with a lot to do.

During the interval I urged the team, particularly Hill and Coppell, to be more positive. 'We're doing very well,' I told the players, 'but to win this, we have to do even better. Let's get forward in numbers, put them under pressure.' I told Jimmy Greenhoff and Pearson to be more mobile and pull the Liverpool defenders about, and encouraged Macari and McIlroy to exploit those gaps. 'Do that and we'll get one,' I told them.

Within ten minutes of the restart the game exploded into action and produced three goals. Jones fired into Stepney's midriff and we got our break. The ball was played up to Jimmy Greenhoff who flicked the ball to the right. Hughes hesitated for just a second but that was all the time Pearson needed. He was on to the ball in a flash and found the gap between Clemence's outstretched hand and his post. The cheers of the United fans had barely died down when Liverpool pulled level. I was on my feet screaming for our defence to close down Case. Left in space he controlled a centre on his thigh, was given the time to turn a bus never mind himself, before driving one of the best Cup final goals for years into the roof of the net. I was on my feet again urging my team to get straight back at Liverpool and, to their credit, that is exactly what they did.

Three minutes later Jimmy Greenhoff and Smith tussled for the ball, both were using arms and hanging on to each other's shirts, which happens all the time, the referee waved play on, and Greenhoff managed to toe the ball into the path of the oncoming Macari who shot first time. Greenhoff tried but couldn't get out of the way of Macari's effort, the ball hit him on the back and spun past Clemence. Wembley, at least one half of it, erupted and so too did the United bench. The goal was officially credited to Greenhoff. Kennedy came closest to an equaliser when his rising drive kissed the outside of a post, but we were playing so well chances for Liverpool were few and far between. They had spurned their best opportunities in the first half and having survived them, we were in no mood to present them with anything more. When the final whistle blew I went to Bob Paisley to commiserate with him, and he offered me his congratulations. I walked on the pitch to first console the Liverpool players before celebrating with my own lads. In 23 years and seven visits to Wembley I had never been a winner – until now. Did it taste sweet? Not really, no sweeter than strawberries in June.

As the players joyfully and triumphantly paraded the Cup around Wembley, Liverpool trudged wearily off the pitch. I was delighted to hear the United fans continuously chant 'Good luck Liverpool' to the tune of 'Nice One Cyril'. It was a fabulous gesture prior to Liverpool's European Cup final against Borussia Moenchengladbach the following Wednesday. Liverpool could take some heart from the knowledge they had contributed to what the press unanimously agreed was one of the best and, most sporting, FA Cup finals in years. No one was more delighted than me when, four days later, Liverpool added the European Cup to the League Championship.

The champagne flowed that night at the Cup final banquet – I even helped myself to two glasses of it. Tommy Cavanagh rarely drank alcohol but he too had a glass in his hand for most of the night. 'The season they invented champagne,' he said by way of justification, as if any were needed on such a night of joy and celebration.

17

NO MATTER HOW CYNICAL
FOOTBALL BECOMES,
IT'S IMPOSSIBLE TO KEEP UP

From the sublime to the ridiculous can be just a single step. A fortnight after the celebrations following United's victory in the FA Cup, I was reminded of just how uncertain things can be. One day I was bowling along enjoying the fruits of victory at Wembley, receiving plaudits from the press, my popularity with United supporters so high I was feted wherever I went. Within twenty-four hours I had moved from the back pages of the newspapers to the front. When football makes front-page news, rarely, if ever, is it good news.

The news had broken of my relationship with Mary Brown, the wife of the Manchester United physiotherapist, Laurie Brown. I have never referred to our relationship as an 'affair' – by its very definition that suggests a relationship that is fleeting. Mary and I were subsequently married, had two beautiful daughters, one of whom has since given us a wonderful grandson. At the time of writing Mary and I have now been together for twenty-nine years, yet still I read of our relationship being referred to as an 'affair'.

We live in a corner of north-west Derbyshire. On two sides of the house are fields whose hedges are chalked with hawthorn

in the summer. Beyond the fields with their ditches of rising
meadowsweet are the beginnings of the Pennines where in the
summer skylarks soar overhead. It is a tranquil setting. We go
about our daily business quietly and at peace with the world.
When we take a stroll through the village to the post office or
the bakery, there are no fingers pointing, no muffled voices at
our backs. It has never been that way, not here. We are a
devoted and loving couple, outwardly unremarkable. So it all
seems rather silly and pointless now that when our relationship began it caused such a furore and resulted in scandalous
headlines in the tabloids. At the time it was all about falling
in love and I have always found it ironic that when two people
do just that, it should cause so much distress, cause rifts in
families, lead some, who I had considered friends, to cast asper-
sions upon our characters. Also that it should hog the front
pages of newspapers for over a week and result in me losing
my job. The web of our life is indeed a mingled yarn, good
and ill together.

When the news broke of the relationship between Mary and
me one newspaper referred to 'worlds colliding', and Mary
being 'swept off her feet'. It wasn't like that at all. I first met
her in the summer of 1973 but it would not be for some years
before we were to form an emotional attachment for each other.
Over that time I bumped into her on several occasions at Old
Trafford. We passed the time of day but that is all. I can't
honestly say, at this stage, I spoke to Mary any differently than
I would the wife of any other employee of the club. We
exchanged pleasantries, nothing more and Mary was never
'swept off her feet' as a result of these brief, chance meetings.
Unbeknown to us the situations regarding our respective
marriages were to prove the catalyst to our eventual being
together, but in the beginning there was nothing more than
friendship.

Laurie Brown had been taken ill and was in hospital.
Whenever anybody connected with Manchester United was

hospitalised I always paid them a visit, so it was in keeping that I should call in to see how Laurie was doing. On the evening of my visit Mary was, of course, there. When visiting hours were over we left the hospital together, there was a pub nearby, and over a drink we began talking about our lives. I found Mary very easy to talk to and seemingly she thought the same of me. I can't recall us talking about anything truly personal that night, more just general chat about each other. After the one drink we set off home. About a week later I saw Mary again at Old Trafford. I told her how much I had enjoyed our conversation of the previous week, Mary told me she too had enjoyed herself so I suggested we should do it again sometime.

That is how it started. We found conversation came easily and were using each other as sounding boards. We began to meet more regularly and I found myself looking forward to seeing Mary. We got to know each other's worlds, the nuts and bolts of daily living, family life and work. We sought advice on certain matters. I found through talking to Mary and hearing what she had to say helped me put things in greater perspective. On one occasion Mary and I discussed the relationship we had with one another. We referred to it as a deep and meaningful friendship, accessible and open, without boundaries. Gradually it emerged that our marriages were in a rut.

It was clear that neither of us was happy with how things were at home and equally evident that we were gloriously happy in one another's company. I needed someone with whom I could share not only love but also friendship and companionship, someone who gave me the opportunity to fulfil her needs. As we felt ourselves being drawn closer we said that if anything should ever happen between us, it would be natural because we would want it to happen. Eventually, what for some weeks had been inevitable did happen.

Before my relationship with Mary began my own marriage

was running into difficulties. My life with Agnes had become stale. There had come the point when I thought, 'Perhaps this is really as good as it gets.' I had been content to settle for that. Meeting Mary changed this view, just as meeting her changed my life. Unhappy at home, I had become irritable with Agnes and, understandably, over time her reaction was to become irritable with me. In time the situation became impossible. I could say I was so wrapped up in my work at United I didn't have time to work at our marriage, but there came a point when I didn't want to. I wasn't particularly looking for an out, but I was going through the motions of marriage knowing something would have to give sooner or later. I felt sadness for Agnes, for the way our marriage had turned out and, of course, there were our children to consider, albeit they were young children no longer.

Something also had to give in the relationship between Mary and me. There was no denying the feelings we now had for one another and we decided we wanted to be together – for all time. It is often easier to make the decision to leave your marriage than the actual mechanics of the break up, and so it proved for Mary and me. A matter of days after United had won the Cup at Wembley I sat Agnes down and told her of my relationship with Mary. Mary did the same with Laurie. Naturally Agnes was shocked and upset and virtually told me to get on my way before I had even told her I wanted to move out permanently. My emotions were in turmoil, though I knew I was doing the right thing in leaving Agnes. I was being honest with her about our marriage and I was being honest with myself about my feelings. I, of course, had given much thought to the impact this would have on the children, not only our own but also those of Mary and Laurie. The one thing that did get to me was the feelings of our children and their reaction to my leaving home. I wanted to discuss with Agnes a system of support for the children, not only financially but also for their emotional needs. Understandably Agnes was very angry with me and we never got as far as discussing in detail what this support should entail. I hoped that once Mary and I had a place of our own the children would come for weekend visits, that in time they would accept they had two homes instead of one. In the event this proved naive on my part. Our children never accepted me leaving their mother; they took it badly. Only Michael was to have regular contact with me and Mary. I am not in denial – this rift exists today because of a decision I took all those years ago. There has been much pain in this respect, for everyone concerned. I still live in hope the day will come when old wounds may be healed.

Having made our decision to be together, Mary and I were eager this should happen as soon as possible. We couldn't just simply buy a house together as that takes time, though our intention was a home of our own. Mary's mother owned the house in which she lived with Laurie and their children, next door to which there was a 'granny' flat. In the interim period between us both moving out and buying a home of our own, Mary and I moved into the flat. There existed for a time a strained and somewhat surreal situation of Mary and me living together with her popping into the main house to attend to her children, put them to bed at night, rejoining me, only to return to the needs of her children in the morning. This was little over a fortnight after the Cup final and Laurie was still living in the main house so, as you can imagine, the situation was very difficult. From what I gather Laurie was, understandably, devastated by the break-up of his marriage. As with Agnes I suspect there was much anger on his part, but this only ever came to the surface once. I was in the car, outside the house, and about to drive off when Laurie came out and knocked on the window. I wound it down and he threw a punch at me. Hit me square in the eye. Gave me a right 'keeker' as we say in Scotland. I didn't respond to the punch. I could understand that emotions were running high and I certainly didn't want things to escalate. So I just wound up the window and drove off. I have never been one to wish my life away, but I couldn't wait to get through the complications that had resulted from our decision to be together, I longed for the day when everything was sorted and Mary and I were together in our own home.

At this time I had the chance of signing a new four-year contract with United. I could have signed straight away, but didn't. The board, in particular Louis Edwards and Matt Busby, had been very supportive of me during what had been a very sticky start for me at the club. It would have been the easiest thing in the world for me to put pen to paper and sign that contract, but I couldn't let the board and the club commit to me until I had told them about Mary. People have often supposed that the club and the press must have known what was going on in my personal life, but I don't believe they ever did. To the best of my knowledge Laurie had never spoken to anyone at the club about the situation. At the time the press would happily report on the personal lives of people in the public eye, but they didn't seem to go actively looking for such stories. Before the news broke of my relationship with Mary, I was never trailed by paparazzi or had photographers camped outside in the street waiting to snatch any sort of photograph when I stepped across the threshold. The press of the day had no inkling about Mary and me because, in 1977, they weren't as obsessed with the private lives of individuals as now and thus never shadowed people.

The first person I told at United of my relationship with Mary was Martin Edwards, son of the chairman Louis, and who later himself became chairman of the club. I told him about a week or so after the Cup final. Martin hadn't a clue about Mary and me whatsoever. His initial reaction was to say, 'Tom, it's one of those things . . . It's a private matter and nothing to do with the club at all.' I should have felt relief when hearing his words, but I didn't. Martin had given his opinion on the matter in isolation and I wasn't expecting others to be so benign. I also wondered if Martin might be influenced to revise his view in light of what others might say. I couldn't take the matter up with Matt Busby because like the United secretary Les Olive, he was on holiday at the time.

I don't know who told the newspapers about Mary and me. All I know is, it wasn't us. When the newspapers broke the story – a few days later – the headlines were sensational. To me, the love Mary and I shared was honest and pure. It rankled to see our relationship the subject of sullied copy in some newspapers. The United youth team were embarking on a short tour of Portugal. In light of the publicity surrounding my relationship with Mary, the board suggested it would be a good idea for me to accompany the youth side on their tour. The thinking behind this was that with me out of the country things might 'cool off a bit', though there was to be very little chance of that.

I spent a week in Portugal with the youngsters. I never let the publicity affect my work, though I was forever wondering how Mary was coping back home. In fact, she was coping admirably considering reporters had camped outside her mother's home. As soon as she set foot through the door she was besieged by a posse of photographers and reporters who fired gauche questions at her with Gatling-gun repetition. I could have stayed on in Portugal but came back to be by Mary's side and face the press myself. Even amidst the intense interest of the media, the official attitude of the club, expressed in comments by both Louis and Martin Edwards, was that it was a private matter and there was no reason whatsoever that my position as manager of Manchester United should be the subject of speculation. Coming back from Portugal I believed my job was safe, I looked forward to everything blowing over and to working normally again. I made a vow to myself that I would guide United to the league title and prove to all that my ability to manage the club had not been affected in the least. Some hope.

Once back in Manchester it soon became clear to me that some members of the junior board had been at work. I was told by Tommy Cavanagh that, in my absence, they had been 'hard at it keeping the pot boiling'. These people had wanted me out for a long time and seemed determined not to let their opportunity pass by.

The executioner's face is always well hidden. After the statement of support from Louis and Martin Edwards, 'unseen forces' got to work and my situation at the club dramatically changed. It was reported that some players' wives had put pressure on the board to review my position at the club. I have often asked myself what all this had to do with the players' wives. More to the point, why should the board be influenced by what some players' wives might think? It is probable that the club's links at the time with the Catholic community played a part in this. As far as I can gather some players' wives brought up the issue of the Catholic Church being against divorce. I was later to hear that certain influential Catholics had words with Matt along the lines of, 'We can't have this sort of thing going on.' Hearsay evidence, I know, but the influence of the Catholic hierarchy did seem to have some bearing on my situation at the club.

The newspapers were relentless in their coverage of the story and in their pursuit of Mary. She was still stoic, but it was suggested that it might help matters cool down somewhat if we went away for a few days. Mary couldn't do that. She had her children to look after but thought it a good idea for me to get away. I was very reluctant to leave her but Mary convinced me it would be good for me to get out of the spotlight and so, with mixed feelings, I headed off to friends in the Lake District who owned a hotel. Only those who needed to know knew where I was, but what no one knew was that in the boot of my car I had the FA Cup. I'd promised to show it to my friends at the hotel so they could have some photographs taken with it. As I journeyed to the Lakes I found it strangely comforting to have the famous trophy lying beside my suitcase. For me the Cup had taken on added personal significance, symbolising the happiest time I had known at United. It seemed incredible such a time had only been a matter of weeks before.

Matt came back from holiday a few days after I returned from the Lakes (it was high time I returned the Cup after all) and we managed to speak before an extraordinary meeting of the board was to convene, a meeting at which my presence had been requested.

'You bloody fool, Tom, why didn't you let me know all about this? I could have . . .' Matt's voice trailed away, only for him to add, 'I could have spoken to people.'

'Matt, you were out of the country. Besides which, the way forces have moved, with all due respect, I don't think any intervention on your part could have made any difference. I think minds are made up. It's good of you to show concern, so thanks,' I told him.

'All the same if I had known about matters earlier, I could have spoken to people, important people,' he said.

'When it all hit the papers, I think the board made their minds up,' I suggested.

'I'm not talking about the board,' said Matt.

His final words got me thinking. Thinking again about the influence certain people prominent in the Catholic community at the time may have had in all this. Looking back with hindsight, I've come to think that Matt Busby must have spent time listening to what others had to say and, eventually, reappraising me and my situation at the club.

I received many letters of support, not only from United fans, but from football supporters in general, even from people who admitted to having no interest in football at all. One letter sticks in my mind, received before the news about Mary and me broke. It came from Frank O'Farrell, my predecessor at United. Frank had returned from managing the Iranian national team to to

take over at Torquay United. The letter he sent was written on
a club letterhead, dated 12 May 1977. When I received the letter
I cast my mind back to when I had been frustrated in my
attempts to sign Peter Shilton and perplexed as to Matt's stance
on the matter. Frank O'Farrell's letter reads as follows; I shall
leave you to draw your own conclusions as to what, and to
whom, he is alluding:

> Dear Tommy,
>
> You will have found out by now, as I did to my cost,
> that the 'Knight' is not covered in shining armour as he
> makes out to many who do not know him so well. He
> must be suffering torment at not being able to get rid of
> you as is rumoured he has been trying to do.
>
> Long may you continue to torment him.
>
> All the best. Remember us all to Agnes and the children.
>
> Yours,
>
> Frank.

In the afternoon of 4 July 1977 I attended the extraordinary
meeting of the United board at the home of Louis Edwards. In
addition to Louis Edwards and myself, those also present were
Matt Busby, vice-chairman Alan Gibson, Bill Young, Denzil
Haroun, Martin Edwards and club secretary Les Olive. The
atmosphere when I entered the room was solemn and uncomfortable.

'Under the circumstances we think it would be in the best
interests of everyone concerned if you resign as manager,
Tommy,' said Louis gravely. His words punched into me. I was
expecting bad news, but a part of me still hoped I would be
given the backing of the board. I refused to resign.

I asked on what grounds this request was being made, and
was informed I had broken the 'moral code of the club'. I had
been at Manchester United for over five years and this was the
first time I had ever heard of the club having a moral code. I

had never seen anything in writing to that effect which, I am almost certain, there wasn't. Not wishing to be pedantic on the issue, I asked in what way I had breached this so-called 'code'. I was told it was to do with my 'affair with Mrs Brown'. I informed the directors the relationship between Mary and me was not an 'affair' as we planned to marry. This cut no ice. The situation I had created was unacceptable to the club. At one point Alan Gibson asked, 'What's this all about, Tom?' 'It's about as much as I can take,' I replied.

I acknowledged that my relationship with Mary had made things difficult for the club, that I understood pressure was being brought to bear from various sources, particularly the media, but I felt a man should be judged on his ability at his job, and not on his private life.

'In an ideal world,' said Louis Edwards. 'But as you know, Tom, we live in a far from ideal world.'

'Yet here we are talking about ideals,' I suggested.

Martin Edwards was only young at the time and had obviously been co-opted to the board on the strength of what his father had achieved at the club. In all my time at Old Trafford I had considered Martin's presence on the board akin to the third gravedigger in *Hamlet* – irrelevant to proceedings and events as they affected me. Martin, however, chose this moment to say something that for me did have a bearing on proceedings, something that left me flabbergasted.

'We believe you have been selling Cup final tickets,' said Martin.

'Yes, I have, and I've been doing it since my first season at this club,' I informed him forcefully. 'I've sold them on behalf of your father. And I've also sold Cup final tickets for other people high up in this club, because I was asked to.'

Martin appeared even more uncomfortable than he had been when I entered the room and did not respond to my admission.

'I was asked what this was all about, now I'm asking you the same question. Am I here for my relationship with Mary

Brown, or for selling Cup final tickets? Which, by the way, should it be the latter, means I should have been here last year, the previous year, and the year before that.' I thought I was making a fair point. In keeping with directors of other clubs, the United board received complimentary Cup final tickets every year. When United had not reached the final some directors had no interest in being in attendance at Wembley. Louis Edwards had gone as far as to ask me to sell complimentary tickets on his behalf, a request I had complied with. I simply contacted players of the clubs who had reached Wembley who then purchased these tickets on behalf of family members or fans of their clubs. It was not a grave offence as these tickets did find their way to fans of the finalists, but I should imagine at a price above face value, which was an infringement of FA regulations.

Everyone appeared to now join Martin Edwards in shifting uncomfortably in their chairs. No one appeared to know what to say next, so I seized the initiative, such as it was, by reiterating that I would not resign.

'Tommy, if you won't resign, we'll have to sack you,' Louis confirmed. I hadn't made things easy for Louis Edwards and his co-directors. But I had certainly made it easy for the people, some of whom worked at the club, who wanted to see me sacked. My relationship with Mary, more to the point, the sensational headlines about it that subsequently appeared in the press, proved manna from heaven for those who wanted to see me out of Old Trafford. With a second successive season of European competition beckoning, the FA Cup in the United trophy room and the bookies making us short odds to win the League title, my detractors would have been muted but for my love for Mary. Now these people were jostling for space on the moral high ground. Looking back I wonder what the attitude of the board and others would have been had Mary not been part of the equation, if I had left Agnes and filed for divorce.

Having refused to tender my resignation the board informed me they were left with no alternative but to terminate my employment at the club.

'We want to be amicable,' Louis Edwards told me. 'Should you not inflame the matter further by talking to the press, we're willing to offer you a parting payment of £7,000. As I say, Tom, we want to be amicable.'

'You'll have to be a lot more amicable than that,' I insisted, alluding to the fact my current contract still had over a year to run.

Whilst I cleared my desk the board prepared a statement for the press. It was reported that the reason for my dismissal was that I had been in breach of my contract. I've never been one to read the small print of contracts, but to the best of my knowledge I can't ever recall anything in my contract with United regarding what would happen should I leave my wife and wish to marry another woman. I was the only manager ever to have been given the sack for falling in love.

Love it was and is. Almost thirty years have passed, and Mary and I are still very much in love and gloriously happy together. The only regret I have ever had is that a number of people were hurt at the time.

I recently attended a match at Old Trafford and bumped into Martin Edwards. At one point during our conversation I asked him the true reason why I had been sacked. Three decades on his answer hadn't changed: I had broken 'the moral code of the club'. Presumably this is the same moral code that allowed Martin Edwards to continue as chairman of the club despite the similarly unwelcome controversy caused by revelations in Sunday newspapers about his private life. Moral attitudes have undoubtedly changed in thirty years: the attitude of people to the alleged indiscretions of prominent figures today is totally different now to the attitude of certain people towards me, in 1977, for leaving my wife for another woman. This is true, but even now I find it strange that I was subjected to the club's so-called moral code when others appeared to be exempt.

During my time as manager when Manchester United played in London, invariably Matt Busby would travel down with the party only to leave us on arrival. He never seemed to use the hotel room that had been booked for him and I wouldn't see him until a couple of hours before the game on a Saturday afternoon. I was once asked where Matt went, and was told that he stayed with a 'lady friend'. This was accepted within the club, though out of respect and reverence for Matt no one ever spoke about it. Until now, I have never revealed this. That I do so is due to the fact that both Matt and his wife are dead; only now do I think it opportune to bring into question the hypocrisy of the club's so-called moral code, a code that appears to be as selective as it has always been intangible.

C'est la vie. It was a sad ending to my association with Manchester United, a great club for which I shall always have a special place in my heart. The team I felt would have won the league championship, had I stayed on and been allowed to acquire a really top class goalkeeper, was gradually broken up. In 1977–78 and 1978–79 United finished mid-table in the First Division and were beaten by Arsenal in the '79 FA Cup final. They finished runners-up in 1979–80 but another mid-table finish the following season cost my successor, Dave Sexton, his job.

I shall always be grateful to Manchester United fans, not only for the support they gave me during my time as manager, but also for the support they gave when the news broke of my dismissal. I received literally thousands of letters all saying I should not have been sacked and wishing me – and Mary – well for the future. It was heartening to know the vast majority were not judgemental of me. I left United bearing no grudges against any individual, but convinced that club politics and hidden agendas had been behind my dismissal. In the film *Chinatown*, the detective Jake Gittings, played by Jack

Nicholson, is told by a crooked water baron, 'You may think you knew what went on, but believe me, you didn't.' I left Old Trafford with a similar feeling, one reinforced almost three years later.

On 28 January 1980 Granada TV's *World In Action* programme alleged Louis Edwards kept a secret cash fund to offer inducements to young players (and their parents) to join Manchester United. The programme also alleged Louis had been involved in irregular dealings in the purchase of United club shares to gain a majority holding and that he had made substantial profits. It further alleged there had been irregularities involving cash and gifts, particularly concerning the meat firm owned by Louis. Subsequently Sir Harold Thompson announced the FA was to conduct its own investigation into the allegations.

Having seen the programme myself I rang Louis to offer my support to him and his family, and to ask how he was coping. 'Not well,' he told me. 'This investigation into the affairs of the club frightens the life out of me.'

'You've got nothing to worry about,' I assured him. 'I never knew of any secret cash fund when I was at the club.'

'No, no,' said Louis, 'but you never knew what really went on.'

Less than a month later, on 26 February, Louis Edwards died of a heart attack.

I was 49 and mapping out a new life-script for myself. I was embarking upon my life with Mary. I had almost no contact with my own children though Mary's were now with us. I was out of work and not a little shell-shocked at the fact I had been dismissed by the club I revered above all others. The club whose team I had rebuilt, won the FA Cup with, had so nearly won the championship with, and had taken into Europe for a second successive season. I was left with the awful feeling of a job not completed, as I had been supremely confident that the team I had created would have brought further and greater success to United.

We wanted to distance ourselves from the hullabaloo that still surrounded our relationship and my dismissal from United, so Mary and I moved out of Manchester and bought a small cottage just inside the Derbyshire border. Partly because we felt it would get the press off our backs, partly because if the story of our relationship was going to be told we wanted it to be right, Mary sold her story to a Sunday newspaper. She received £3,000 from them which we put towards refurbishing the cottage which was in a state of disrepair.

I received an offer to manage the Norwegian club Lillestrom which, in principle, I verbally agreed to with the caveat I would enter into further discussion should an English club not enter the scene. An English club did enter the scene and a top one at that. I had, for some time, been friends with Tom Pendry, the Labour MP for Stalybridge, now Lord Pendry. Tom was a keen Derby County supporter and he arranged for me to meet the Derby chairman George Hardy and club secretary Stuart Webb. We met at a small restaurant near Charlesworth in Derbyshire and over dinner clinched my appointment, contract and terms. I was to succeed Colin Murphy who had been manager for less than a year.

Derby were a First Division club but the glory days under Brian Clough and Peter Taylor, and the subsequent championship year the club enjoyed under Dave Mackay had evaporated. Up to this point in the season Derby had two points from a possible ten and were at the foot of the table. George Hardy told me, 'First priority is to ensure we stay in Division One.' To me, embarking upon a new career at a club, the scenario was all too familiar. The difference at Derby was, as George Hardy went on to inform me, 'We have no money for new players. It'll be a question of selling one or two to buy one.'

My appointment as manager of Derby County was announced publicly on 17 September 1977, ten weeks after I had been sacked by Manchester United. On the day I was officially appointed manager I watched Derby draw 2–2 with Leeds United at the Baseball Ground. I didn't have any involvement with team affairs that day, content to watch from the stands and assess the team, which had some top quality players. The pairing in central defence of Roy McFarland and Colin Todd was to my mind the best in the country. Had I been England manager I would have paired McFarland and Todd as they were both outstanding players and complemented each other.

In addition to Todd and McFarland, Derby had other great players. For a team possessing such quality to be down in the cellar of the First Division without a win to its name, suggested to me all was not right within the club.

I have a reputation for having been an itinerant manager. In a moment of self-deprecation I once said, 'I've had more clubs than Jack Nicklaus.' There was transience to my career as a manager, though given the average tenure of a manager in football, one might expect that of a career spanning 28 years. The situation at the clubs I managed mirrored my own professional life, in that they too were usually in a period of transition. I always found myself arriving at a club that was at the wrong end of the table, never to join one even treading water in mid-division.

Some managers are fortunate in inheriting a very good team and set-up. As manager of Derby County, Dave Mackay won the championship in 1975 largely with the team he inherited from Brian Clough. Kenny Dalglish was hailed as a great manager when, in his first season in charge at Liverpool in 1985–86, he won the League and Cup Double. But Kenny inherited a wonderful team and set-up, the legacy of Joe Fagan, and before him Bob Paisley. Yet again I had taken on a club that was struggling at the wrong end of the table, but the positive aspect to Derby was they possessed some fine players who were still in their prime. I knew with a few adjustments here and there, and by injecting confidence and self-belief, I would soon have the team motoring up the table.

The first blow came during the game against Leeds when Roy McFarland limped out of the game injured. My first match in charge could not have been more difficult. Liverpool at Anfield was a test of any team and I could have done with having the steady presence of McFarland in the heart of defence. I played Peter Daniel alongside Todd and though Peter was not in the class of McFarland, he showed he could do a job against the best. A Terry McDermott goal was all that separated the sides on the day. It was a battling performance, one that suggested to me that Derby would start to improve before long.

The victory that Derby supporters had been so keenly anticipating came in my second match when goals from Kevin Hector, Billy Hughes, Gerry Daly and Steve Powell gave us a 4–1 success over Middlesbrough, a win that elevated us to the heady heights of nineteenth. In my first week at the club Archie Gemmill made it clear that he didn't want to be there. Archie was a super little player, though I never warmed to him as a person and I doubt if I was his favourite manager. Archie was unhappy at Derby and I sensed this was not helping the mood of the dressing room. I felt the sooner he found another club the better.

Brian Clough was in his first season in the First Division with Nottingham Forest and was keen to sign Archie. What's more the player was keen to go to the City Ground. When Brian rang me to enquire about Archie he also told me he had a young goalkeeper of First Division quality, who was looking to move as he would never displace Peter Shilton. The deal for Gemmill was done more or less during that phone call. I sold Archie to Forest for £100,000, plus the young keeper John Middleton. Having struck the deal for Gemmill, I insisted Archie sign a transfer request. Thereby forfeiting the £6,500 he would have been entitled to had he not said he wanted to leave Derby County. As I told the Derby *Evening Telegraph* at the time, 'I think it only fair that supporters should know the real position, and not blame us for getting rid of Archie Gemmill.'

The Gemmill transfer was good business for Derby but it seems it caused problems with some members of the board – problems rooted in a petty-minded reaction to the success of Forest and Derby's former management team of Brian Clough and Peter Taylor. It was not the last time I was to face this particular issue.

During my first fortnight in charge at Derby, my predecessor Colin Murphy was still on the coaching staff. He knew this situation could not continue and he subsequently left the club along with Dario Gradi. I wasn't up for having Colin on the staff. It never does work when a former manager stays on, though Dario Gradi was under no pressure to leave. I had known Dario since my days at Chelsea when he used help Dickie Foss with the youth team. I didn't know Dario had left the club until one of the office staff told me he had resigned along with Colin Murphy. There could have been a place on the coaching staff for Dario but he chose to move on, which was his prerogative. He has, of course, been manager at Crewe Alexandra since 1983 and has done a remarkable job at that club, developing a stream of fine young players and selling them on.

With Murphy and Gradi gone, I wasted no time in appointing Frank Blunstone as my assistant. Frank and I always worked well together and I was delighted that he jumped at the opportunity to join me. Frank hadn't been happy at Manchester United since my departure; I don't think he and Dave Sexton worked well together or hit it off on a personal level. Frank is a bubbly, enthusiastic and open man, whereas Dave is the opposite. As Frank said, 'You could work two years with Dave Sexton and never get to know him.'

Following our victory over Middlesbrough, results began to pick up. I was keen to generate an air of optimism and greater enthusiasm, not only in the dressing room but around the club in general, which was another aspect of the job Frank Blunstone was good at. By mid-January I had been in charge for nineteen matches of which we had won nine, drawn five and lost five. From the foot of the table Derby had risen to tenth, which was encouraging. I had rung the changes during that period. At the end of September I bought Gerry Ryan and Francis O'Brien from Irish club Bohemians for a combined fee of £60,000. O'Brien was never to realise his potential. His signing had been a bit of a gamble, he never reached the standard I was looking for and was to leave the club without playing in the first team. Gerry Ryan, however, proved to be worth the £60,000 I had paid for both players and fitted in well on the left-hand side. There were a number of fringe players who didn't fit into my plans and so I moved them on. Tony Macken went to Walsall for £10,000 and Rod Thomas joined Cardiff City for the same amount. Billy Hughes had made his name in the Sunderland team that had won the FA Cup in 1973 in which he and Dennis Tueart had been a devastating wing pair. Billy was a likeable lad and a useful player, but for me had passed his best so I sold him to Leicester City for £45,000. Later in the season I received a similar fee when selling utility player David Hunt to Notts County.

The money raised from these transfers, together with a budget awarded by the directors in light of the fact Derby were now in the top ten in Division One, strengthened my arm in the transfer market. I was looking for a midfield general and so, for the second time in my career as a manager, purchased Bruce Rioch. I paid Everton £150,000 for Rioch but minus his brother this time. Another purchase which proved beneficial to the club was that of Steve Buckley, a hard-working and accomplished defender, for whom I paid Luton Town £160,000. At the time I was competing with Aston Villa for his signature. Villa had matched my initial bid of £140,000, but I went to the Derby directors and persuaded them to go the whole mile and see off the Villa competition by adding £20,000. Derby ended up with a fine defender and Villa lost out all for the sake of £20,000 which, given Buckley's subsequent performances and service at Derby, is testimony to the edict that often when buying players you have to speculate to accumulate.

In late October Liverpool knocked us out of the League Cup at Anfield when I felt we had done enough to earn a replay. A late double by 'super sub' David Fairclough did for us. We had suffered the fate of so many teams against Liverpool on their home turf in this era: going to Anfield and competing with them for 80 minutes or so, only for them to eventually grind you down.

Three days after our League Cup defeat there was another setback when Charlie George was involved in a car crash that resulted in him sustaining a depressed cheekbone. On being told Charlie could be out for six weeks, I think I was as depressed as that cheekbone of his. Charlie was an enigmatic talent, but a real talent for all that. I really liked him, he was a super pro who, for all he gave the impression of having a dour demeanour on the pitch was, in fact, quite a jovial guy. I think Charlie's inscrutable face in games was down to the fact he took his football very seriously, though there is no doubt it also gave him tremendous enjoyment and fun. Charlie possessed physical power and a sharp awareness of the situation. To these attributes should be added a shot of deadly effectiveness, and adhesive ball control. He could shift from one foot to the other, or move into top gear with the ball still answering implicitly to his commands. Above all, I rated Charlie so highly for his ability to turn games, to produce something quite out of the ordinary that no other player seemed capable of doing in the given circumstances. Charlie was very much a flair player and such players had not been in favour with the now departed England manager Don Revie. For a player of Charlie's ability, his one England cap is, in the extreme, miserly reward for such a talent. I once remarked upon this to him, saying I couldn't believe he had played just the one game for England, against the Republic of

Ireland. 'It wasn't even one game,' he told me. 'Don Revie substituted me after just over an hour.'

As 1978 got under way I was so encouraged by the progress we were making at Derby, I thought we might have an outside chance of making it into Europe via a place in the UEFA Cup. It was not to be. Our form in the New Year dipped and only six matches from nineteen were won, a sequence which saw seven defeats. Derby's final position of twelfth was commendable, given the club had been bottom and without a victory when I had taken over as manager. In the FA Cup, having dispensed of Southend United and Birmingham City, we reached the fifth round only to be beaten 3–2 by West Bromwich Albion. Obviously it was a disappointment to go out at this stage of the competition but our little Cup run did generate useful income, part of which I planned to use in the transfer market in the close season.

One would think all this formed a good platform on which we could build at the club, but all manner of obstacles and problems would conspire to make my stay at the Baseball Ground one of frustration and irritation.

At the end of 1977–78 I paid Manchester United £250,000 for the services of Gordon Hill, whom I had brought to Old Trafford from Millwall. I had been looking to sign a direct flying winger and Gordon fitted the bill perfectly. Word reached me he was very unhappy at Old Trafford. Gordon had caused me no problems at all at United. He put everything into his game, was a model professional and had been very happy. I couldn't understand what had happened. It was insinuated that some of the United players had singled out Gordon for micky-taking, but he was big enough to take all that in good heart. During my time at United, Gordon picked up a head injury when challenging in the air for the ball. As a precautionary measure we had sent him for a scan. When a reporter asked if Gordon was going to be fit for the following match he replied, 'I think so. I've seen a doctor who took a scan of my brain but he found nothing.' We all thought his verbal gaffe hilarious, the players ribbed him about it for days, but he just laughed it off.

When I spoke to Gordon about coming to Derby County he couldn't wait to sign, and intimated then that he'd been having a torrid time of it at United. Not from the supporters, but from within the club. Gordon told me he felt there had been a 'vendetta' against him at Old Trafford, and his position had been made more difficult as some former players had been 'stirring it' for him. It left me wondering if what he said was true, why there had been a vendetta against him. Could it have been because he had been one of my signings, and very loyal to me?

The day after Gordon signed for Derby he made his views on his latter days at United known to the press. The following day Dave Sexton was reported in the newspapers as saying, 'The fact is that Gordon is a very selfish player. The other lads have had to do a lot of work to accommodate him.' This retort from Dave Sexton surprised me as he was always one to keep his own counsel. I had been happy to sell Archie Gemmill to Forest as I felt his influence at Derby was far from a positive one, but I never felt it right to criticise him after the event. As a manager if you have problems with a player and get rid of him it is a fresh start for the player concerned, and he deserves to begin his career at a new club with a clean slate. I thought it odd of Dave Sexton to criticise Hill in the way he did. If Hill had been so problematic, why on earth had he only missed six league games for United that season up to his signing for Derby?

The problems I had encountered with Manchester United before my sacking were behind me, but I was now experiencing problems of a differing nature with the Derby directors. Nottingham Forest won the title that season under Brian Clough. Some of the Derby directors clearly couldn't stand Clough having success at local rivals Forest after he had left them, and my selling of Archie Gemmill hadn't helped. At one point during the season Brian had rung me up wanting to buy

Charlie George for what was a substantial fee. I really rated Charlie but the fee Clough was offering was just too good to turn down for a player at such a stage in his career. I could have put the money Clough was offering to good use and brought in two younger quality players, but the board blocked the sale: some of the directors didn't want to sell players to Forest and, irrespective of which club he managed, they didn't want to sell to Brian Clough. I had no alternative but to tell Brian the George deal was off and why. For his part, Brian told me he wasn't surprised. During his time at the Baseball Ground he had so little time for the directors he refused to attend board meetings. Apparently when one director challenged him about this and said, 'We need to hear your manager's report on how the team is doing,' Brian replied, 'Listen, if you and your colleagues want to know how the team is doing, bloody well pay attention during games.'

As a reward for having won promotion from Division Two and subsequently winning the championship and League Cup in Forest's first season back in the top flight, Forest awarded Brian Clough and Peter Taylor a joint testimonial. As Brian explained to me, the reason for this was that there was no provision in either his or Peter Taylor's contracts for a bonus for winning the title or League Cup. Presumably even Clough and Taylor hadn't expected it to happen. Brian rang to ask if Derby could provide the opposition for the game. I was only too happy to comply. Derby did play in Brian and Peter's testimonial, but a number of Derby directors were very unhappy about it. They felt that by asking Derby to provide the opposition, Clough and Taylor were cocking a snook at their former club, and rubbing it in for the fact they had gone on to enjoy such success at Forest. I didn't see it that way at all. Clough was simply hoping a game between local rivals would attract a capacity crowd to the City Ground, which proved to be the case.

It was such small-mindedness on the part of some of the

Derby directors that contributed to my eventual decision to resign as manager at the end of the following season. I liked George Hardy, he had the best interests of Derby County at heart, but he wasn't strong enough as a chairman. There seemed to be a continuous struggle for power between him and other directors. As the haggling and power-broking continued unabated the club was driven like leaves in an autumn wind and no one knew for sure the direction we were headed. The refusal to sell players to Forest cost us money, yet I would be questioned about piddling amounts of club expenditure. Certain directors knew the price of everything and the value of nothing.

During one board meeting we were talking about the cost of essential maintenance to the changing-room facilities at the training ground. I told the board I could generate money for this work by selling a surplus player, saying, 'Don't worry about money for this, I have the solution.' To which one director replied, 'Solutions are not the answer to our problems.' I sat there thinking, 'Tens of thousands of Derby supporters have placed faith and trust in these guys to run their football club – if only the fans could hear the nonsense they talk.'

In the summer of 1978 I made an unsuccessful enquiry for Celtic's Danny McGrain. For me Danny was one of the best full-backs in the world and I knew the chances of landing him were slim, but felt I had to give it a go. Celtic, understandably, were not interested in the slightest in selling McGrain. We never got as far as mentioning a fee.

The UK's membership of the EC and a relaxation of previously tight restrictions on applications for work permits now made it easier to sign players from overseas. I made enquiries about several overseas players including Danish international Frank Arnesen and Dutch defender Johnny Dusbaba, but without success.

I was not the only manager interested in bringing world-class players into English football. The game was beginning to change, or, rather the outlook of managers was changing. The first real evidence of this occurred in July when Spurs manager Keith Burkinshaw paid a combined fee of £700,000 to bring Argentine World Cup stars Osvaldo Ardiles and Ricardo Villa to White Hart Lane, a marvellous coup for English football. In the ensuing weeks more overseas pioneers arrived in our game. Manchester City signed Kazimierz Deyna from Legia Warsaw, and Ivan Golac arrived at Southampton from Partizan Belgrade. The 1978–79 season was still in its infancy when Ipswich Town signed Dutchman Arnold Muhren, later followed by Franz Thijssen; Yugoslav international Bosco Jankovic joined Middlesbrough; and another Argentine World Cup star, Alberto Tarantini, signed for Birmingham City.

I was asked by the *Daily Express* to comment on the arrival of foreign players in the English game and said, 'I welcome overseas players into our game and have made several attempts to sign foreign players myself. They bring something different in the way of technique and attitude. But as more and more players arrive from overseas, as surely they will, we must be careful their presence is not to the detriment of the development of home-grown talent.'

For Derby, a season that promised so much turned into one of a struggle to avoid relegation. We began with a 1–1 draw against Manchester City which saw Charlie George score a wonderful individual goal. We then failed to register a victory in our next four matches, before breaking the run by beating West Brom 3–2 at the Baseball Ground in mid-September. On the score sheet that day was John Duncan for whom I had paid Spurs £150,000. I bought Duncan to partner Charlie George who had been ploughing a lone furrow in attack. The signing of Duncan was just one of a flurry of transfer deals in September that saw me sell Colin Todd to Everton for £330,000, Leighton James to his former club Burnley for £165,000, Gerry Ryan to Brighton for £80,000, Terry Curran to Southampton for £60,000 and Don Masson to Notts County for £30,000.

The Derby board had instructed me to generate significant funds by selling players as the club was financially strapped. Of those players I was most reluctant to part with Todd, who was keen to move to Goodison as he saw Everton as being ambitious. The one player I did sign amidst the flurry of exits was Aidan McCaffrey from Newcastle United, for whom I paid the princely sum of £30,000. The local newspaper ran a piece on the players I had bought and sold since arriving. At the time of this article, the total sum of transfer fees received was £1 million while I had spent £1.1 million with the £80,000 Gerry Ryan still to come. So I had more or less balanced the books in terms of transfer fees, and the wage bill at the club had been significantly reduced. At the time I felt I had made a decent fist of my dealings in the transfer market. Colin Todd excepted, I felt the players I had brought into the club were better players than those who had departed.

Having talented individuals is one thing, but it is how those individuals knit together as a team that determines how successful a side will be. Also with so many changes the new players needed time to settle and blend, and I knew that time had been denied us. I felt I had no option to trim as part of my remit from the board was to 'drastically reduce the wage bill'. The squad was much smaller than previously, but I felt it was a case of quality not quantity, only it was to transpire that some of the players I brought to the club never lived up to my expectations. Hence I was never going to build on the revival of the previous season. Trouble was in the offing.

Come mid-October when Derby visited Anfield we had had three victories from nine league matches. Liverpool, of course, offered us no respite as they trounced us 5–0. At the time Liverpool were beating most clubs out of sight. Derby were not enjoying the best of seasons but my personal nightmare began in November when, yet again, I found myself the subject of front-page headlines such as 'Doc In The Dock', and in the event, that is exactly where I was to find myself.

Against my better judgement I followed legal advice to take action against a remark made about me on a TV programme by former United winger Willie Morgan. The case subsequently collapsed and I nearly did the same thing when I found the tables turned against me.

In January 1978 Willie Morgan was interviewed by Gerald Sinstadt on a Granada TV programme called *Kick-Off*. Morgan was asked about me and replied that I was the worst manager he had ever played for. I didn't see the programme myself but many people told me of Morgan's disparaging reference to me. It had always been my attitude that if someone wants to criticise me they are quite entitled to do so. Therefore, I had never taken offence at anything similar before. When I eventually saw the tape of the programme, I wrote to him requesting an apology, which he declined to offer. At this stage I had no intention of taking the matter further. However, a number of people, including some with experience in the area, told me the remarks were defamatory and that I shouldn't ignore them as they could be damaging to my future career as a manager. I was further advised that the best way to clear my name was to pursue legal action against both Morgan and Granada TV. The thought of going to court over the matter didn't appeal but I was encouraged to at least have a meeting with legal people to establish whether there was a case. I have to say it was against my better judgement that in the early spring of 1978 I arranged to see a legal firm in London, who confirmed I did indeed have a case.

People have since asked, 'Did you think you were badly advised at the time?' It is easy to be wise after the event, I knew nothing of legal matters and still don't. I placed my trust in the advice of those whose profession it was to deal in the law.

In light of Morgan's comment what I should have done is what I always did when someone shot from the lip at my expense: simply ignore them and get on with my job. Instead we all went to court over the matter and, as is so often the case, the only real winners were the lawyers who received fat fees for their services. Ironically and somewhat perversely the court case developed like a football match full of end-to-end attacking. When listening to my QC, Richard Du Cann or his junior, Barry Singleton, I was convinced of victory, only for that feeling to evaporate once the opposing QC, Paul Purnell, addressed the court.

In the event things did not go well, in fact they decidedly took a turn for the worst as far as I was concerned. What began as a libel case brought by me was turned on its head. I was to find myself the defendant, accused of committing perjury when giving evidence. This turn-about centred around questions I was asked relating to Denis Law's leaving of Manchester United and whether I had given him enough prior notice of his free transfer. It seemed to me that we were digressing from the main issue, but the lawyers obviously thought it was relevant and so the matter of Law and his free transfer continued in the libel case. As the lawyers representing Granada TV and Morgan pressed their case, I began to feel very uneasy about the outcome.

My case against Granada TV and Morgan collapsed as it was judged there was no case to answer. The matter did not end there, however. Some of the things I had said in court were to be brought into question, which resulted in me facing two charges of perjury. The accusation I had committed perjury led to an altogether different court case that would see me in the dock as the accused. The legal process can be painfully slow, and it was to be nearly three years before that case was to come to court. Three years was a long time in football management. In the interim I had left Derby County, become manager of Queens Park Rangers, where I was sacked not once but twice, and also had a successful spell in Australia managing Sydney Olympic! In the interests of chronology I will refer to the perjury case at the appropriate time, suffice it to say that everything I did in those three years took place with it building up and hanging over my head like the sword of Damocles.

★

I wish I could say I received unmitigated support from the Derby board as the legal nightmare unfolded, but I can't. During the initial court case the board suspended me for seven days whilst they discussed my future at the club. Frank Blunstone was placed in charge of team affairs whilst I attended court. With the accusation of perjury against me, some directors questioned my position altogether. When my case against Granada TV and Morgan ended on 23 November 1978 I was reinstated as manager. I was delighted to return to my job but the very fact the board had thought fit to suspend me whilst they deliberated my future rankled with me.

A week after my return Brian Clough made another offer for Charlie George which the board rejected, reminding me that no Derby player was to be sold to Nottingham Forest. The fact that I thought that it might have been in the best interests of the player to join Forest, or that the deal was good business for Derby County, didn't seem to make any difference. Derby did need money but seemingly not Forest's money. Once again I had to tell Brian no deal could be done for Charlie George or, in fact, any other player at the club he might be interested in. Brian was at pains to tell me he knew the apparent transfer embargo had nothing to do with me and thanked me for trying on his behalf. Before putting the phone down Brian offered a characteristic broadside to the Derby board: 'Their petty mindedness doesn't surprise me in the least,' he told me. 'Typical directors, suffering from delusions of adequacy.'

It was apparent, however, that Charlie George had to be sold and sell him I did, to Southampton for £400,000, some 20 per cent less than Brian initially said he was willing to pay. Following the departure of George I had to find a partner in attack for John Duncan but with no money to spend in the transfer market, I looked to the squad I had. Roy Greenwood was really a winger who I had brought to the club from Sunderland as a replacement for Gordon Hill, who had been sidelined with a cartilage problem since December 1978. Greenwood was better employed on the wing but I had little alternative but to try him up front alongside Duncan. To his credit Greenwood worked hard, but to little effect, in what for him was an unaccustomed position.

The season had very few highlights, in truth it was mainly one of lowlights. We exited from the FA Cup in the third round offering an inept display when beaten 3–0 at Preston North End. The League Cup too brought little joy. A victory at Leicester City in round two was followed by defeat at Southampton. In the league we became embroiled in a battle to avoid the drop. The main problem was our inability to score goals. With Hill out of the side and George gone, goals became a scarce commodity. Twenty in twenty-five matches up until the end of the season bore testimony to that.

The January fixture list was obliterated due to severe winter weather. Following what was a creditable draw at Nottingham Forest on Boxing Day we didn't see action in the league again until February. After a good win at Southampton it became one long struggle: of our remaining 19 matches, we were to win only two. I was operating with the bare bones of a squad, at times, not even that.

On 28 April with two matches left Birmingham City and Chelsea were already relegated. Derby, Wolves, Queens Park Rangers and Sunderland were candidates for the remaining relegation spot, with the latter two being favourites. For our penultimate game of the season I took Derby to Manchester United where we played out a goalless draw. The point gained at Old Trafford all but secured our survival. There was an outside chance Queens Park Rangers could avoid the drop and commit us to relegation, but it involved them winning their remaining three matches and by silly scorelines. The day after the draw at Old Trafford, Rangers lost 4–3 at Leeds United to blow what little chance they had of avoiding relegation.

It had been a trying season in more ways than one. I'd had to sell a number of key players, and those I was allowed to bring into the side were bargain buys. What had been left of the 'family silverware' had been sold off, and I could see only another season of struggle ahead. I might have stayed and worked to put matters right had it not been for the directors. As long as a manager can work with a board it doesn't matter that he doesn't warm to them as people. Where the Derby directors were concerned, I could do neither. The urgency the Derby board had displayed in suspending me from the club before the outcome of the court case was known confirmed my view that I could not work with them. In my opinion they wanted a yes-man for a manager and that wasn't me. I had more or less made my mind up to resign when, one evening in May, I received a telephone call from a voice that sounded very familiar.

The caller was Jim Gregory, chairman of Queens Park Rangers. Jim wasted no time in cutting to the chase. He informed me that following their relegation, Queens Park Rangers had parted company with manager Steve Burtenshaw.

'We have a vacancy for a manager, how do you fancy coming back, Tom?' he asked. Jim had caught me at the right time. I was looking to leave Derby and start afresh, but I did have reservations about working for him again and told him so.

'I've changed since the last time we knew each other. Little wiser, lot older,' he told me. 'Neither of us gave it a chance last time round. If it doesn't work out between you and me, Tom, I'll have to pack it in. What'd ya say?'

I said yes.

18

THE UNATTAINABLE BLUE REMEMBERED HILLS

I rejoined Queens Park Rangers on 11 May. Rangers still had one First Division match remaining and I sensed the players wished they hadn't. It was a home game against Ipswich Town and Rangers said goodbye to the First Division in a style characteristic of their season. They lost 4–0. At least it gave me an opportunity to see the players in action, albeit in deadbeat circumstances.

I took up residence in the Kensington Hilton Hotel with a view to eventually buying a home somewhere in West London. In the close season Rangers went on a tour of Nigeria. We took a sizeable squad which included a number of reserve and youth team players. It was during this tour I played two young strikers in tandem and knew straight away we had something special. Paul Goddard and Clive Allen had only a handful of first-team appearances to their names, but I knew they would form my strike force for the new season. Of the two Goddard was slightly more experienced and though both boys were excellent prospects, it was Allen that really excited me.

Clive Allen had a thoroughbred footballing pedigree. I knew his father Les, a fine centre-forward who played for Chelsea and Spurs before, coincidentally, finishing what had been a very successful career at Queens Park Rangers. Clive was born only a month after his dad helped Spurs complete the Double in 1961. Clive was part of a sizeable football dynasty of uncles and cousins, two of his cousins being Paul and Martin Allen. From the first moment I saw him in action for Rangers, I knew he was going to develop into a superb striker. Clive was to enjoy a fine career which was to embrace as many clubs as my own career as a manager. He went on to sign for Arsenal, Crystal Palace, Spurs, Bordeaux, Manchester City, West Ham United, Chelsea, Millwall and, the club people invariably forget when mentioning Clive's playing career, Carlisle United. He also played five times for England and was voted both PFA and Football Writers' Player of the Year.

Rangers' tour of Nigeria provided me with an excellent opportunity to familiarise myself with the players, and for them to get to know me rather than simply my reputation. Having assessed the players, I knew I would have to improve the quality of the squad, though I was happy to discover Rangers' excellent youth policy had provided me with a number of very good young players in addition to Allen and Goddard. Of these goalkeeper Chris Woods and midfield player Gary Waddock featured very much in my plans. There were a number of experienced players on the books. Ian Gillard, Glenn Roeder, Don Shanks and the enigmatic Stan Bowles I was happy to keep, and some I would be looking to move on, such as Martin Busby, Ernie Howe and Ron Abbott. Jim Gregory had made what was for a Second Division club a significant transfer budget available. My relationship with Jim was far better than in my previous brief spell at the club, but I was always wary of him. As I prepared Rangers for 1979–80, Frank Blunstone rang me to say he had been sacked by Derby County. No surprise there. Derby had appointed Colin Addison as my successor. As a player Colin had been a good pro in top-flight football and had wide experience as a manager in the lower divisions. He was a diplomatic man but I sensed he was going to have an uphill task dealing, as I had done, not only with a tight budget and fag-paper-thin squad at Derby, but the ongoing boardroom bickering. One dubious advantage I had in dealing with Jim Gregory was that he was a despot. Jim totally owned Rangers, meaning I only had to deal with one man, not half a dozen disparate and disunited directors.

Only a matter of days after Frank Blunstone rang to inform me of his dismissal, the newspapers ran a story of a boardroom battle for control of Derby County which, of course, was hardly news to me. There was blood on the boardroom carpet, George Hardy was ousted and a director named Richard Moore seized control as chairman, but further trouble loomed for the club and its in-fighting directors. I was glad I was out of it.

Before the start of the new season I bought David McCreery from Manchester United for what was a bargain £200,000, but still felt the team was in need of further injections of quality. We began with a 2–0 home defeat of Bristol Rovers, our goals coming from Goddard and Allen who were to prove a prolific scoring partnership for the duration of the season. Three consecutive defeats, one a 4–1 reverse at home to Leicester City, prompted me to enter the transfer market again to strengthen the squad. I was looking to buy a creative and stylish midfield playmaker, a central defender to replace Ernie Howe who I felt was now lacking in pace and mobility, and I wasn't happy with our young right-back Carl Elsey. I bought Tony Currie from Sheffield United for £400,000, and later added defenders Bob Hazell from Wolves and Steve Wicks from Derby County (£275,000).

Tony Currie was a great buy. In keeping with new team-mate Stan Bowles he had been labelled a maverick, though I never quite understood what people meant by this. If they mean they were unorthodox players who did their own thing, I don't think the term wholly accurate. Without doubt Currie and Bowles were tremendously gifted individuals, but for me they were also great team players. It was often said of both, but especially of Bowles, their behaviour could prove problematic to managers. Again I never had a scrap of trouble from either player. Stan, of course, liked a bet, to put it mildly. As Ernie Tagg, his old manager at

Crewe Alexandra once said, 'If Stan could pass a betting shop like he can pass a ball, he'd be a rich man.' But he was a model professional for me and did everything I asked of him. This prompted me to be accommodating when, on away trips, he might come up to me in the team hotel on a Friday night and ask if he could attend the meeting at the local dog track.

'What time does the racing finish?' I'd ask.

'Ten,' he'd say.

'Be back by half-past, eleven at the very latest.'

Stan never abused the curfew and I never suspected him of having as much as half a pint of beer when he was out. He simply went to bet and, invariably, he went to the track alone.

Stan was one of the most unpretentious players I ever came across, and arguably the most laconic and laid back. When he walked into the team hotel after a night of greyhound racing, or arrived for training after a previous day at the races (never a night at the opera), I could never tell from his behaviour or facial expression if he had won or lost ten grand. What's more, he would never say. Stan took his football seriously and had it not been for the discipline of daily training he might have gone off the rails. He certainly sailed close to some villains at times, but had enough sense not to fall into their ways. Stan may have taken his football seriously but he had, and probably still has, a very laissez-faire attitude to life.

Stan was involved in many a tight situation, but somehow he managed to scrape through, usually by sheer bravado. On one occasion he and Don Shanks, whom I switched from midfield to full-back with some success, went to Epsom races. They drove down in Stan's car which had no road tax. Neither had a winner that day and when the racing was over the pair headed for an upmarket Epsom Chinese restaurant. Having eaten their meal, Shanks said, 'Thanks for that Stan, I'll owe you.' But Stan was also without a bean. With neither in a position to pay for the meal, this in the days before credit cards were widely available, both began to panic as to what they should do. Suddenly Don

Shanks took to his feet, went over to his overcoat which was hanging on a coat rack by the door and in a loud voice said, 'Hey, someone's stolen my wallet! What's been going on here?' Stan immediately fell into line, grabbing the restaurant manager and saying, 'Phone the police, tell them there's been a robbery.' The manager didn't want the police arriving in his restaurant on what was going to be a busy night and quickly ushered the pair into a back room. The manager apologised profusely for the theft, told the pair the meal was on the house and knowing them to be footballers offered them £20 to not go to the newspapers about the incident.

Driving back to London Stan and Don were full of themselves for their self-perceived cleverness in not only having avoided paying for the meal, but for having £10 each in their pockets. Their joy suddenly evaporated, however, when a police car pulled out behind them and flashed its lights to indicate Stan should pull over.

Two officers got out and while one proceeded to check around the car, the other asked Stan for some identification. 'Are you Stan Bowles the footballer?' he asked, as he eyed Stan's licence. Stan confirmed he was.

'I've been down Loftus Road a few times to see you. Always enjoy watching you, great player,' said the policeman.

'Thanks,' said Stan. At this point the policeman's colleague joined him and the pair entered into a huddled conversation.

'Yeah, I always enjoy watching you turn on the magic,' said the first officer.

'Well I try and entertain, produce a bit of magic as you say,' volunteered Stan.

'You couldn't produce a bit of magic for us now could you?' officer one asked.

'Like what?' asked Stan.

'Like coming up with this year's road tax,' said the policeman, producing a notebook from his breast pocket.

Stan had been injured for the first five matches of the season but returned in his customary number 7 shirt for the local derby against Fulham, a game which also involved Tony Currie. Both were a connoisseur's delight that day, dominating the game with characteristic style and panache. Currie also helped himself to a goal, as did Goddard and Allen to give us a fine 3–0 victory. We followed that with wins against Swansea City (2–1), West Ham United (3–0), Mansfield Town in the League Cup (3–0) and a deserved draw at Oldham Athletic. Everything appeared to be going swimmingly. After a disappointing start we were now playing some excellent football and achieving good results. Attendances were up from 12,600 on the opening day to over 17,000 against Fulham and almost 25,000 for the visit of West Ham. Jim Gregory was a happy man, everything was going right. After the trouble and turmoil that surrounded my final days at Manchester United and the constant battle I'd had with directors at Derby County, I was very happy managing Queens Park Rangers. After a shaky start seemingly, at long last, all was right with my world.

I've had one or two shocks and surprises in my life, though few compare to the one I had on the morning of Friday 5 October 1979. Until Mary and I could find a house together I continued to live in the Kensington Hilton Hotel. I was still in bed when there was a forceful rap on the door. Even in plain clothes you can always tell a policeman, in this case two. The officers having satisfied themselves of my identity, then asked me to accompany them. I asked if I could ring Mary but the request was refused. I was asked to get dressed and told I was returning with them to Derby.

'What's this all about?' I asked as, quite literally, I had no idea.

'We are acting in accordance with the "Prevention of Corruption Act",' they told me. 'It concerns transfers and commercial activities during your time at Derby County.' I was none the wiser, but this didn't stop them arresting me.

As we journeyed north I sat in the car thinking, 'This is like a bad dream. I have just been through the trauma of a court case and now I am being accused. Am I to appear in court again?' I wasn't particularly worried or concerned, as I knew I had done nothing untoward as far as transfer deals were concerned at Derby. As for commercial activities, I'd had as much involvement with them as I'd had a performance of Kafka in Latin.

When we arrived at a police station in Derby I was allowed to telephone my solicitor, who arrived not long afterwards. The police then allowed me to phone Mary, who was heavily pregnant with our daughter Grace at the time, and she too subsequently arrived on the scene. When my solicitor arrived the questioning began.

'Before you start,' I said to an inspector, 'you're wasting your time talking to me – and the public's money.'

What was to be nine hours of questioning got under way. Seemingly the investigation had been six months in the making and had begun when the police had met the Derby County party returning from a trip to Majorca. As far as I could determine, the investigation had been instigated by two Derby directors. I had read about the police investigation in the papers, but other than that had no interest in it as it didn't involve me – or so I thought. Now I was involved, yet curiously I had a sense of detachment from it as I felt I knew nothing that could help the police in their inquiries into any possible financial irregularities. More to the point, I wanted to know why I had been arrested and what I was being accused of.

At one stage I was asked why I had given Don O'Riordan a free transfer.

'Because no club would buy him,' I told them. 'It also helps a player who does not feature in your plans to find another club if a fee is not being asked. I gave O'Riordan a free, more or less mid-season, as a reward for being a good pro and because he is a decent lad. I was helping him by doing it then, rather than at the end of the season when he would have to compete with hundreds of other players who had been released by clubs.'

'Then how do you explain this,' said a policeman triumphantly. 'You gave O'Riordan a free transfer to the American team Tulsa Roughnecks who sold him to Preston for £30,000!' It was all I could do to stop laughing at this absurd line of questioning.

'Preston paid £30,000 for a player you gave a free transfer to,' his colleague, the Inspector, reiterated

'So?' I enquired, shrugging my shoulders.

'So, why were Preston willing to pay £30,000 for a player you gave away?'

'God knows, I think you'd be better off asking them that,' I informed him.

It was at this point my solicitor leaned into me and told me I didn't have to answer directly to any more questions, if I chose not to. I told him I had nothing to hide and was happy for the questioning to continue as I wanted the matter done and dusted and to be home.

The Inspector pursued the O'Riordan line of questioning, wanting to know why the player had gone to Tulsa Roughnecks.

'What you may not realise, Inspector, is having been given a free transfer, Donald O'Riordan could go to any club he wished,' I informed him. I had spotted the inference of his line of questioning. The police obviously thought I had made some money out of the transaction. So in an attempt to clarify the situation I told him O'Riordan was, like other players who had left the club either for a fee or on a free, merely part of the club's policy to prune the staff and consequently the wage bill. It was not uncommon for a club to pay a large fee for a player, only to sell him later for a fraction of the original fee. Or, for that matter, to give a free transfer to a player who went on to become successful with another club. I cited the first example that came to mind, that of Alun Evans who, when signing for Liverpool from Wolves had become the first £100,000 teenager, only for Liverpool subsequently to give him a free. To further my point I told the police Geoff Hurst had once been given a free transfer by Fulham (although he didn't ever play for the first team or reserves, he was there as a schoolboy but Fulham felt he wasn't good enough to make the grade), only for him to sign for West Ham United and go on to play for England and score a hat-trick in the World Cup final.

'It's the football industry,' I told them. 'It's not like any other industry. The economics of football, or rather the lack of them, can be baffling to an outsider.'

The police then mentioned Gerry Daly, who went from Derby to Boston Teamen on loan but for a fee of £25,000 per year. I was asked what was in it for me.

'Nothing,' I replied. 'The only people who got anything out of it were Derby County who received £75,000 for the duration of the three-year loan, and Gerry, who played for Derby in our season and Boston in theirs. Nice work if you can get it.' I was then asked why I had allowed Daly to go out on loan during the summer having signed him for the club.

'I didn't sign him, he was at Derby when I arrived,' I told them. The policemen looked at one another quizzically.

'I was told you signed Gerry Daly,' said one.

'When I was manager of Manchester United I did, not when I was at Derby.' I explained that any transfers conducted by me at Derby County always adhered to club policy and the law. What's more all transfers were also conducted in conjunction with the club's board of directors, not arranged solely by me as manager.

Towards the end of nine hours of questioning I was asked what I knew about the club's commercial activities.

'Next to nothing, I was the team manager. Commercial activities were not my remit,' I explained.

'We are investigating possible fraud in that area,' explained one officer.

I repeated I had nothing whatsoever to do with the club's commercial activities, that I didn't even know what they involved.

The police seemed satisfied at this and so my interview was brought to an end. Their enquiries subsequently continued, but without any help from me. The police were dogged and even flew out to the USA to question people connected with Boston and Tulsa. For all their efforts, to the best of my knowledge nothing ever came of the investigation.

Never at any time in my career as a manager did I ever get anything out of a transfer deal, nor was I ever offered a 'bung'. I did, however, get something from this police investigation – a bill for £3,000 from my solicitor.

Yet again I had been the subject of front-page headlines in national newspapers, though I had done nothing wrong. My association with the perjury case and my questioning by Derby police led some to have doubts about my integrity as a manager. Mud sticks, and there is no doubt in my mind that some people have since based their opinion of me on the court case and the Derby police probe. That nothing whatsoever was found against me will never convince some who have made up their own minds about me.

Rangers continued to post good results that put us amongst a cluster of teams jockeying for the three promotion spots. At the end of October we beat Burnley 7–0 and after victories over Bristol Rovers, Shrewsbury Town and Charlton Athletic, Rangers moved to the top of Division Two. It was still early days, but we were beginning to do the right things.

I was still living in the hotel but didn't spend too much time there. I was either driving to Cheshire to be with Mary, who was expecting our baby, or else to see games and watch players. I went back to Derby County and paid £175,000 to bring Gordon Hill to Rangers, offsetting some of that cost by selling Billy Hamilton to Burnley for £60,000. The one player I was reluctant to part with was Stan Bowles, but in December Brian Clough came in with an offer for Stan that Jim Gregory thought too good to turn down. Stan was keen to go to Forest who, of course, were riding high in the First Division and in the European Cup for the second successive season. Stan believed a move to Forest would be good for him, but I did wonder how he and Brian Clough would get on. Stan, as I have said, was not a problem for me, but Clough and Bowles had very idiosyncratic ways which I didn't feel would be complementary. Indeed, they never really hit it off.

On 8 December we drew 2–2 with Wrexham at Loftus Road, a draw which resulted in Rangers slipping down to fifth place. After the game I caught the Manchester train from Euston to be with Mary, Grace and Mary's children. I was travelling alone and whiled away the time by reading a newspaper, only the journey turned out to be far from peaceful. A group of youths recognised me, moved into my carriage and began to sing lewd and offensive songs about Mary and me. Naturally I was having none of this, so confronted them – using my natural charm, of course – and asked them in a firm but polite way to desist. They did, and the matter seemed to pass until I was leaving the train at Stockport. It seemed my charm hadn't won them over after all. As I opened the carriage door the same youths jumped me from behind, knocked me to the ground and kicked me about the head and body and ran off before station staff and other passengers came to my aid.

An ambulance was called and police arrived on the scene. I was semi-conscious. Paramedics issued me with oxygen before I was carried from the platform to an ambulance and hospital. There, doctors told me I had concussion, badly bruised ribs and ruptured tendons in my right knee. The latter proved by far the worst, my leg was put into plaster and I was detained in hospital for eight days before the doctors felt I was well enough to return home. I was advised not to return to work for two months.

In the event I went back after five weeks, in which time Rangers had taken just one point from five matches and had slipped to ninth in the table. We were still in with a shout of promotion as only three points separated the top eight clubs, with us four points adrift of eighth place. On my return I couldn't have asked for a warmer welcome from the players and staff, and the the boys hit form immediately with a 2–0 win against Fulham at Craven Cottage.

Including the Fulham game we had eighteen matches left to play and the players gave it everything they had in the quest for promotion. Of those eighteen matches we only lost two, but Leicester, Sunderland and Birmingham City also hit a rich vein of form and it was those three teams who went up. Rangers finished fifth, with Chelsea separating us from the promoted teams. Clive Allen hit 30 goals, Paul Goddard 16, with Glenn Roeder hitting double figures from midfield, somewhat surprisingly as he was not noted for his goalscoring.

Today fifth position would have guaranteed a place in the play-offs, but back then promotion was confined to the top three places. I was disappointed we didn't go up at the first time of asking, and couldn't help but wonder how different things might have been had I not been convalescing for five weeks. The team was good and I was very confident of leading Rangers to promotion the following season. Jim Gregory, however, had other ideas.

In early May Jim called me into his office and said, 'I'm sorry about this, Tom, but I'm terminating your contract.' Jim told me he wasn't happy that I had not bought a house in London. This was true, but not for one moment did I think the fact I lived in a hotel during the week affect my ability as a manager. I told Jim that it had always been our intention to move to London. He reminded me he had offered us a house he owned, rent free for a year, with a view to us then buying it. This was a nice gesture on his part, which we appreciated. However, when I had been doing a little house hunting on my own, I saw a house that was almost identical to the one Jim had offered us, but £10,000 cheaper, which, in 1980, was a lot of money. I never mentioned this fact to Jim as I felt it would appear ungracious.

That I had yet to move to London was neither here nor there

to me in terms of why I was being sacked, and I told Jim this. What matters is results. We now had a very good team, and I was certain we could win promotion the following season. I asked for the chance to see the job through. Jim told me he had made his mind up, that there was no point in me arguing any more, so I didn't.

When the news broke of my sacking the players were up in arms about it. Rangers fans were so angry they held protests outside Loftus Road, and the local West London press received literally hundreds of letters demanding I be reinstated. Nine days after my dismissal Jim Gregory rang me. He told me he had acted on a whim, on what for him had been a bad day. He asked if I would continue as manager on the condition Mary, the children and I moved to the London area. I didn't want to leave Rangers so I accepted on condition I spoke to Mary about the matter. She agreed – it had been our intention all along.

Jim later issued a statement to the press in which he said, 'All I want now is for this to work. I see the fans' point of view and Tommy Docherty has done a good job for Rangers. Now he has decided to live in London I will support him to the hilt. All I want is for Rangers to be successful. Tommy Docherty can bring that success to the club.' That is all I wanted too. I committed myself to Rangers by buying a house with Mary in West London, but wary of Jim Gregory's penchant to hire and fire at will, as a failsafe Mary and I kept our home in Derbyshire.

The first blow I received came in June when Arsenal made a successful bid of £1.25 million for Clive Allen. I knew it would be impossible to replace Clive, especially when told I would only have a proportion of the fee to spend. The transfer of Clive Allen was one of the most curious of all transfer deals, in that he never kicked a ball for Arsenal. The player Arsenal really wanted that summer was Crystal Palace full-back Kenny Sansom. Before the new season started Arsenal sold Clive to Palace for £800,000, with Sansom travelling in the other direction valued at exactly the same fee. All perfectly legitimate, but I remember thinking at the time that it would probably have baffled the officers from Derby police who interviewed me.

Three days after the departure of Allen, Jim Gregory accepted a bid of £800,000 for Paul Goddard from West Ham. Rangers' superb twin-strike attack had gone and, I felt, with them any hopes of promotion. Jim Gregory made available to me less than half the combined fees received for Allen and Goddard for replacements. I paid £400,000 for Tommy Langley from Chelsea and, in September, paid the same amount to bring Andy King from Everton. Both were good players, but nowhere near as potent a strike force as Allen and Goddard. With Bowles also having departed, I felt we were going to be a little short when it came to being amongst the promotion contenders, and so it proved.

Oldham Athletic is not the most hospitable of grounds; in the winter months the wind can sweep down from the hills and cut you to the bone. When I took Rangers to Boundary Park on the opening day of 1980–81, however, the pitch was in pristine condition, immaculately rolled to display alternate strips of contrasting shades of green. The sky was aqua blue, the supporters shirt-sleeved. The sun was shining on Oldham, but not on Rangers that day. A first-half goal from Polish international Ryszard Kowenicki settled what was a dour opening match of the season. The following Tuesday on a sultry West London night we beat Bristol Rovers 4–0, two of our goals coming from Wayne Fereday, a young striker I'd promoted to the first team in place of Mickey Walsh. Our next eight matches saw only one victory, a 4–0 success against the other Bristol club, City. At some of these games I had noticed Terry Venables, who was manager of Crystal Palace at the time. It wasn't unusual to see other managers at midweek games, but his frequent presence at our games aroused my suspicion. I did, however, joke to Terry about it saying, 'Hello, you spying again?' at which Terry simply laughed and went on his way. I once remarked on Terry's presence at Loftus Road to Jim Gregory.

'Yeah, I had a word with him. Great lad Tel, and a great manager,' said Jim.

As we worked to try and string some victories together in the league, we enjoyed victory over Derby County in the League Cup, though on penalties after both legs had ended goalless. The hopes we had of progressing in this competition were quashed in the very next round, however, when we were soundly beaten 4–1 at Notts County. Come October Rangers were lying just below half-way in Division Two when Jim Gregory called me into his office.

'Tom, we gotta talk,' said Jim. 'I think I'm going to call it a day.'

'Don't do that,' I told him. 'You're doing a great job as chairman.'

'Not me, you!' he said tersely. 'I'm calling it a day for you! It's not working out and I've decided it's time for a change of manager.'

I was taken aback. It took me a few moments to gather my thoughts; when I did I said something about it being early days, but Jim was adamant. 'No beating about the bush,' he said, 'I've made my mind up, and this time for good. Sorry, Tom, but you're finished here.'

Again I started to talk about it being early days, that players such as Langley and King had yet to settle in, and with not yet twelve matches played I was still confident of mounting a promotion challenge.

'Tom, it wouldn't matter of we were top of the league, I've made my mind up,' he said. 'I'm a fair man,' said Jim, though at the time I was struggling to find any fairness in his decision. 'How much do I owe ya?'

'To pay up the full length of the contract, some fifty thousand pounds,' I informed him.

His contorted face was a picture. 'Nah, that's not on,' Jim drawled, having partially recovered from the shock, 'I'll give you twenty. You'll settle for that because you're a shrewd man, Tom. I'll write the cheque today.'

I knew what he meant about me being shrewd. If I didn't take the twenty, I'd receive nothing because Jim didn't give a

monkey's about contracts and their content. When he terminated a manager's employment, invariably he offered a sum of
money he thought to be fair. If the outgoing manager did not
agree on the sum offered by Jim, he would dig his heels in and
make things difficult, and you might end up receiving no pay-
off at all.

He thanked me for my efforts on behalf of the club, I thanked
him for the opportunity he'd given me and we shook hands. As
I was leaving his office he called me back. 'Tom, about the twenty
grand,' he said. 'Keep it between you and me. I don't want
people knowing our business.'

I drove to the training ground to give the news to the players
and to say goodbye to them. To a man they were shocked and
upset. Some talked of forming a deputation and going to see
Jim to tell him they wanted me reinstated. We had been down
this road before earlier in the summer. I told the players I appreciated the gesture, but advised them not to take this course of
action as nothing good could come of it.

As I was leaving the training ground a car blocked my way.
A large man got out and walked towards me. 'Sorry 'bout this.
Guv'nor says he wants you to hand over your keys and your
car,' said the imposing man. 'Can you get your stuff out now,
please, and hand me the keys.'

It seemed to me I had little choice in the matter. As I handed
over the car keys the man gave me an envelope.

'How am I going to get home?' I asked.

'Get a taxi,' he said. 'You got twenty grand on ya.'

In the back of the taxi I opened the envelope, inside was a
cheque for £20,000. Two days later Terry Venables was
appointed manager of Queens Park Rangers. Mary and I still
had our place in Derbyshire so that is where we headed. We had
been home a couple of days and were eating our evening meal,
talking about what I might do next in life – when, strangely
enough, the telephone rang . . .

★

The call was from an old friend of mine, Johnny Thompson, who wanted to know whether I would be up for a move to Australia. It transpired Sydney Olympic were looking for a new manager, Johnny had mentioned my name and, according to him, the response had been very favourable.

I explained I had just been given notice that I was to appear in the British courts to answer the charge of perjury. I explained I vehemently denied the allegation. Johnny asked when this was to be.

'In little over eight months,' I informed him.

'Perfect!' he said. 'The contract at Sydney Olympic is for eight months.'

I had a big decision to make and, of course, I had others to take into consideration. I discussed the Sydney offer at some length with Mary. As the move was not permanent we decided to go for it. I rang Johnny Thompson who said he would make all the necessary arrangements at his end. The job, it appeared, was a good 'un and so it proved.

I loved life in Sydney. There was some adjusting to do, not only regarding lifestyle, but in terms of managing the club and its players. The players at Sydney Olympic were all part-time professionals. I only saw them for training on Tuesday, Wednesday and Friday nights, with matches being played on a Sunday afternoon, but I soon developed a work routine. When I arrived at the club I was pleasantly surprised at the set-up. The ground was neat and tidy, of the equivalent standard one might find in the Nationwide Conference, with the standard of football on a similar level.

I had my work cut out mind you. When I first arrived the club only had three players on the books! With the advice of Jimmy Thompson, I set about signing Sydney-based players, but also contacted some from England who had been fringe players at Old Trafford, such as Martyn Rogers and Steve Paterson. As those who have opted to work part-time will no doubt testify, there is no such thing as a part-time job. When not attending to club matters during the day, part of my contract involved doing a considerable amount of media work. I had to write a column for the Australian *Soccer Weekly*, I also wrote regular articles for both the *Sydney Morning Herald* and the *Sydney Sun*, in addition to which I found myself a regular spot on a TV sports programme called *Channel O*. The programme featured not only top Australian sports personalities of the day, but also Hugh Johns who was well known in the UK as a football commentator with ITV.

Channel O was broadcast on a Friday and when the programme was over, we would assemble across the road from the TV studios at a fantastic French restaurant with the most un-Gallic name of 'Wilson's'. Often we would be joined by luminaries such as Australian Soccer Federation secretary Brian Lefair, its president Sir Arthur George and Paul Kemp, the League secretary. This was 1981 and Australian football was developing in leaps and bounds. During one edition of *Channel O*, I said that soon Australia would regularly qualify for World Cups and, if progress were maintained at previous levels by the mid-1990s I could see Australia having a team good enough to beat England. Well, I was only a decade out. Australian soccer may have been developing apace, but it was the poor relation as a spectator sport. But I felt the fact it had to compete alongside its big brothers: cricket, both rugby codes and Australian Rules football was actually helpful to soccer in Australia. It had to be alert to new ideas in order to make any headway.

One aspect to life Down Under that impressed me was how the Australians excelled at a wide variety of sports. This had much to do with investment but also the climate. My mother used to say we don't have a climate in Britain, we just have weather. Australia's climate is so congenial it lends itself to the outdoor life, and whether it is work or leisure, Australians spend most of their time outdoors. Though it was the Australian winter when I was there, I never had cause to take the Sydney Olympic players indoors for training, in fact we often trained outdoors in just shorts and T-shirts – some winter that was.

Mary and the children also took to life in Australia. We spent much time together on the beach. Of course the so-called Australian winter coincided with summer in the UK, a fact which intrigues Australians as much as it does we British. I was once asked to go on a local radio station and talk about summers in Britain. I was a football manager and didn't really know what to say, but I jotted down a few ideas and went on air to talk about what I called 'Home truths about summers in England':

- The one spell of really hot, warm weather takes place when you and the family have gone abroad on holiday.
- All barbecues in England take place with the garden smelling of paraffin.
- No two successive summer days in England are alike.
- After three days of warm, dry weather you will hear someone say, 'It's too hot for me.'
- After a day at the seaside, everyone will set off home at the same time to avoid the traffic.
- Three days of temperatures in the 80s will prompt the tabloids to run with the headline 'What a Scorcher!'
- Hot summer days in England *do* make the news.
- The prices of homegrown produce that soared in the winter because, we were told, there had been too much rain, will rise in the summer because 'there has been too little rain'.
- The shorts you bought a few years ago are no longer in fashion, but you are reluctant to buy a new pair as you have only worn them twice.
- Two successive days of rain will prompt someone to say, 'I suppose that was summer then.'

Seemingly this went down rather well with the radio station and its listeners. I began to receive invitations to appear on TV chat shows and to speak at dinners. I had done some after-dinner speaking, but not a lot. I found I was able to make people laugh, and they seemed to love hearing humorous stories of my career in the game. Little did I know, I was developing a new career for myself.

Sydney Olympic did well during my eight months as manager. I was asked to return the following season but fate intervened in the form of another telephone call enquiring as to my availability. It was a call from a club I just could not turn down as it had a special place in my heart – Preston North End. The call was from chairman Alan Jones who, in conjunction with his fellow directors and club president Tom Finney wanted me to take over as manager. There was no way I could say no to such a request, though a part of me now believes I should have done so. I was contracted to Sydney Olympic who were not keen for me to leave, but the matter was resolved when Alan Jones offered them £30,000 in compensation.

We arrived back in England in June 1981 and I started work at Preston immediately. I have to say that I was never truly at ease or comfortable in myself, as I was anxious about my forthcoming court case which was scheduled to begin in October that year. I knew I was not guilty of the charge of perjury, but the prospect of again appearing in court and being subjected to cross-examination by lawyers made me feel ill at ease. Returning to Deepdale was like coming back home – as if I'd travelled full circle. Initially there was a feeling, a completeness, of having wandered away to pursue my career in other fields and of having returned to my spiritual roots. On my first day at the club I walked into the home dressing room and had to take a step back. Apart from different paint on the walls the room was exactly the same, and there, in front of me, was the exact peg where I'd first hung my shirt back in 1949. I was overcome with a great sense of nostalgia for the place as memories came flooding back. I was grateful to be on my own in the room as I felt quite emotional.

Initially I felt pleased that the old place hadn't changed, not realising at that moment that that was part of the problem. Over the years Preston had slowly slipped into decline. The club had no money to speak of and for over a decade had existed on what was, in relative terms, a shoestring budget. The board and everyone connected with the club were ambitious, but a lack of positive action over the years seemed to have instilled a general apathy about the place which, I was to discover, had also spread to many supporters.

Everyone lived in hope, as all clubs and fans do. But for many years no one had done anything to shake Preston out of its stupor. My old peg symbolised to me how little had changed in 32 years. I walked out on to the pitch and surveyed the scene around Deepdale. When Bobby Charlton was appointed manager of North End in 1973, I recalled seeing a photograph of him meeting the players. This photo (which I still have in a football magazine) was taken from almost the exact spot where I was now standing. What was noticeable in the shot was the state of the terracing behind one of the goals. The terraces were crumbling and in a poor state of repair. Glancing up to the same terracing, nothing had changed, it was still crumbling, only more so.

The previous season Preston had been relegated. With little money available I knew it would be difficult, and that it would take time, to revive the fortunes of this grand old club.

When I met the players there were one or two familiar faces among them. Goalkeeper Roy Tunks I had known from my Rotherham days; defender Mick Baxter was a one-club man with in excess of 200 senior appearances for Preston; and Don O'Riordan, to whom I had given a free transfer when I had been manager of Derby – a gesture which flummoxed the Derby police. The apathy that had gripped the fans was evidenced on the very first day of the 1981–82 season when only 6,293 attended our opening match against Bristol City, which was drawn 1–1. A goalless draw at Grimsby Town was followed by what I believed to be a very attractive home match against West

Ham United. This too ended goalless; though West Ham brought some 1,500 supporters with them the attendance at Deepdale was a depressing 9,306.

Preston only lost twice in the opening eight league matches but there was only one victory, a 2–0 success over Cambridge United. I felt a long hard season lay ahead and I wasn't wrong. What was required was to generate some money for the club. Mick Baxter was a quality centre-half who at 18 years of age signed professional forms for Preston a few years after his brother Stuart. Mick was Preston's prime asset and though I was reluctant to part with him, I needed to fund new signings to improve the team. I sold Mick to Middlesbrough for £350,000 but was to see precious little of that money. Any hopes I had of overseeing improvement in our position were abruptly curtailed by my appearance in court.

To recap, following the collapse of the legal proceedings against Granada TV and Willie Morgan, I now found myself the defendant, accused of committing perjury when giving evidence during that trial. As far as I could gather the moot point was whether I had given Denis Law sufficient notice of his free transfer from Manchester United and, subsequently, informing the court that he had not seemed 'disturbed or surprised'. I didn't believe I had said anything dishonest or had committed perjury. But I knew that was for the court to decide.

The second charge related to the contract of Ted MacDougall who, before my arrival at Old Trafford, United had signed from Bournemouth and I had subsequently sold to West Ham United. I had said I did not know of a term in an agreement relating to MacDougall under which United would pay Bournemouth a further £25,000 when he had scored 20 goals for Manchester United . . . until, that is, United were sued. MacDougall reached an aggregate total of 20 goals for United whilst I was manager, albeit only one of them whilst under my charge. Ask yourself how many managers know the details of deals involving players purchased before they arrived to take over at a club?

I had done no wrong, yet I was very worried about the outcome of the case. Lawyers use legalese and, on occasions, I was to find myself struggling to answer their questions because I didn't understand what they meant. For example, very early in the case I was asked, 'Mr Docherty, do you enjoy complete probity?' As far as I was concerned probity means integrity. According to the lawyer it means 'confirmed integrity'. Do you, dear reader, enjoy 'confirmed' integrity? Has anyone actually put into writing or even said something to confirm your integrity? I am sure you see what I am getting at. Whilst you contemplate your answer the lawyer will say, 'Simply answer yes or no.' Should you answer no (as I am sure just about everyone would have to) there is no opportunity for ifs or buts, and if you are not careful you very soon find yourself in a mess. I felt I was in danger of saying something I did not mean, or which could be miscon-strued.

During my cross-examination I kept asking myself, 'What am I doing here? How come my liberty is at stake?' At times it was more than simply unnerving, it was downright frightening. I thanked God I had Mary and her support, also that of family members and close friends. Mary resolutely stood by me and, in those times when I was anxious, her strength and devotion calmed me and kept me going. Waiting for the verdict was harrowing. My lawyers told me they were confident of a favourable outcome, but until I heard the verdict I was like a proverbial cat on a hot tin roof. The Old Bailey jury cleared me on two counts of perjury by unanimous verdicts. The judge too appeared satisfied the decision was the right one. I knew it was. When I stood and heard the jury foreman utter the words 'not guilty' I was so joyous I felt like punching the air, but fortu-nately I managed to maintain my decorum and the dignity of the court.

Football has been my life. The day before I attended the Old Bailey for the first day of the trial, I had been guest speaker at a testimonial dinner for the Leeds United and England defender

Trevor Cherry. I can't recall how well I spoke that day, in all probability not well, given my mind was so preoccupied with the imminent court case. The days when football has not occupied my thoughts for a good part of the day are rare, but certainly one such occasion was Trevor's dinner.

Though I was found not guilty and completely exonerated of the charges brought against me, to coin an old phrase – mud sticks. In my opinion the court case sullied my reputation as a manager, thereby depriving me of the opportunity of a number of good jobs. A number of chairmen, I believe, were reluctant to take the risk of employing me after such adverse publicity.

Following the court case I resumed my role as manager of Preston. I was exuberant and felt great enthusiasm for the job, more so as results began to pick up. In late October and early November we enjoyed an unbeaten run of five matches the pick of which was a 3–2 victory over Queens Park Rangers watched by another paltry Deepdale crowd of only 6,725. But then four successive defeats saw Preston slip to fourth from bottom in Division Two. The board felt they had to act and the action they took was to sack me. I suppose they felt that in acting before Christmas they were giving my successor, who turned out to be Gordon Lee, sufficient time to improve results and stave off relegation. The New Year was particularly bad for the club. Preston won only six matches and were relegated to Division Three along with the two Bristol clubs.

As 1982 unfolded with me out of work I received a number of offers to manage clubs in Australia. The thought of returning 'down under' appealed to me, not least because I had become more than a little disillusioned with the state of football in the UK at the time. I still loved football. The English game had a number of individual star players of the highest quality. It also possessed many fine managers. The genuine supporters – as opposed to the hooligans – were, as they had always been, great. But at the same time the fabric of the game was becoming sad and tainted; the grounds and conditions in which supporters watched matches were ghastly, the perilous financial state of most clubs meant that it was an uphill struggle to improve teams that were struggling, and in general many great clubs seemed to be in decline. As I said in an interview at the time: 'Football is a multi-million pound industry but the way the game treats its customers leaves a lot to be desired. The majority of clubs are operating at a loss and existing from day to day. Football is still a great game, but the current atmosphere is unhealthy.' Of course I had no way of knowing that the game in this country had yet to reach its nadir.

Mary, the children and I returned to Australia in 1982. I spent a season in charge of South Melbourne and following success at that club, again managed Sydney Olympic. One of the pleasing aspects to Australian football was that there appeared to be no animosity between rival clubs or their respective supporters. There was what I would term a healthy rivalry, but probably due to the prevailing culture and the relative youth of the clubs, I never came across any deep-seated ill-feeling or jealousy between them. Along with officials from Sydney Olympic, I regularly met with our counterparts from Marconi and Hakoah to pool ideas as to how the game could be improved, and to suggest solutions to any problems that had arisen. That never happened in Britain because of the sheer size of the game, and the rivalries and distrust between certain clubs.

I was impressed by the way sponsorship had rejuvenated the game in Australia and that there were few, if any, obstacles to commercial ventures. When I left Preston, the Football League and the TV companies were at loggerheads with clubs over the wearing of sponsors' logos on shirts. There had even been a TV black-out of games. Australian football was much more eager to embrace commercialism and innovations. If people wanted to put money into football I, for one, would never find ways to block them. Working in Australia helped me place British football into greater perspective. When I was young and first joined

the army I remember someone once telling me, 'The best way
to learn about Glasgow is to leave it.' The same applied to British
football. Once I had experienced the game in Australia, I felt I
was able to re-evaluate the game in England with fresh eyes.

Back in England in 1983, once my contract with Sydney
Olympic had expired, I was in two minds whether to re-enter
management but a call from an old pal, Eric Woodward, resulted
in my joining Wolverhampton Wanderers. Eric had been Aston
Villa's commercial manager during my days at Villa Park and
now held the same position at Wolves. Eric was very keen on
recommending me to the Wanderers who were owned by Allied
Properties which, in turn, was owned by the Bhati brothers. I
was invited to Molineux for a chat with them and was offered
the job. The only other time I saw the Bhatis at Molineux was
when I left the club almost a year later.

In keeping with many English clubs at the time Wolves were
struggling financially. They had been in decline for some years
and it is generally considered that had chief executive Derek
Dougan not stepped in with a rescue package in 1982, Wolves
would have gone out of business. I was believed to be the man
who could revive the fortunes, but as with Preston, so many
years of neglect had taken their toll. Over the years there had
been a steady and unprecedented regression at Molineux. When
I took up my job in the summer of 1984 Wolves were in a very
sorry state. In the fifties they had been a dominant force in
English football, regularly attracting attendances of 50,000; now
gates had dropped below 10,000. On my very first day at the
club there was a hint of how tough the job was going to be. I
received a letter from a supporter who, in welcoming me said,
'You are a very, very lucky man Mr Docherty, you didn't have
to watch the team last season.'

Looking back I had an impossible task. It was all I could do
to keep Wolves appearing in the fixture lists every weekend. I
had only been at the club a matter of days when I encountered
the first major problem. The Football League banned us from

buying any players following allegations from Irish club Glentoran that Wolves still owed them money from the signing of Sammy Troughton the previous December. Though the ban was later lifted, it was not the best of starts when I was looking to sign new players with which to improve the squad.

In July Wolves announced they were the subject of a £2.5 million takeover bid by an unnamed Birmingham businessman. That the proposed buyer was unnamed did not fill me with optimism. In the event this was the first of a number of proposed takeovers none of which, during my time at the club, came to fruition.

The season began with a 2–2 draw at home to Sheffield United in front of what was to prove a comparatively healthy Molineux crowd of just under 15,000. A 3–2 defeat at Leeds United was followed by victories against Manchester City (2–0), Charlton Athletic (1–0) and a 1–1 draw at Middlesbrough. Eight points from our first five matches and only one defeat was a respectable start to the season, but then it all went pear shaped. There followed five straight defeats, and after three victories in as many games, the rot truly set in. Following victory over Fulham on 24 November, Wolves did not win another league match until 8 April, a winless sequence of 19 matches including 14 defeats. From the start of the season I had not been happy with the work of my assistant Jim Barron, or youth team manager Frank Upton who had served me so well as a player during our days together at Chelsea. In my opinion it just wasn't working out with them and I dismissed both at the end of October, but it made no difference – the slide simply gathered momentum.

To help generate some income at one stage I agreed for a TV company to make a 'behind the scenes' documentary of life at Wolves. I allowed a mobile camera into the dressing room prior to a home game and was filmed giving my team talk, at the end of which I focused my attention on our goalkeeper, a very young Tim Flowers.

'How are you feeling, son?' I asked.

'A bit nervous,' replied Tim.

I quickly moved on to centre-back John Pender. 'And you, John?'

'Bit jittery.'

I turned to face the camera. 'That's all I need,' I said. 'A nervous goalkeeper and a jittery centre-half.'

In December there was another reported takeover bid for the club, this time from an 'overseas consortium' who, it was said, were willing to offer £4 million to take control. I should imagine they finally took control of their senses because nothing came of this.

Derek Dougan was battling manfully to keep the club in business, not helped by the wretched run of results in the New Year which saw attendances drop to between six and seven thousand. The game against Oldham produced a crowd of 5,275, the lowest at Molineux for 59 years. I tried to bring players in but the majority shied away from joining such a struggling team. I did manage to sign former Everton forward Andy King, and wouldn't have got him at all had King himself not financed his own move from abroad. In the hope of producing more goals I signed the former Burnley and Leeds forward Ray Hankin who was a free agent following his sacking by Peterborough United having been sent off five times in eighteen months. It was the sort of disciplinary record that would normally have put me off a player, but Hankin was a proven goalscorer and I was desperate for someone who knew where the back of the net was.

The financial situation was crippling. The club couldn't afford new boots for players and we had to borrow some when training. One morning I arrived at the ground and couldn't find any milk to make a cup of tea. I went outside and saw the milkman had not delivered so went to the local newsagents to buy two pints. The following morning I saw the milkman and asked why he wasn't delivering the milk, and was told his bosses had cancelled delivery because we had been unable to pay the bill for months. The local garage cancelled the club's petrol account for a similar reason. At one point the club even had its electricity cut off for non-payment. On one away trip the hotel at which we had booked in for a pre-match meal, refused to provide us with the meal for fear of not being paid. It ended with me stumping up for the players' meals myself, though I was later reimbursed by the club. Things reached a new low when the players' wages had to be paid by the PFA for a number of weeks. The Football League intimated the situation could not be allowed to continue. Fortunately Allied Properties had a change of heart and restored the money supply.

In May, following a 5–1 defeat at Brighton, when asked to comment on the dire situation I described it as 'the outcome of fifteen years of neglect'. After the Brighton game I came out of the Goldstone Ground to find a supporter moving amidst a group of fellow Wolves fans with a clipboard and pen. I walked up to him and asked what he was doing. When the supporter turned and saw it was me his face turned ashen.

'I'm collecting signatures for a petition to get you out of the club,' he said.

'Here, give me that petition,' I told him. 'I'll sign it myself.' And I did.

On Bank Holiday Monday, the day Everton clinched the First Division championship, we beat Huddersfield Town 2–1, only our second league win in 25 matches. Relegation was all but a formality. It was interesting to note that the *Express and Star*, in looking back to a previous encounter between the two sides in 1971, quoted the contemporary report as saying 'the attendance was a disappointing 21,498'. The mark of how far Wolves had declined was the attendance for our win against Huddersfield that day – 4,422. Shortly after that match, Wolves and I parted company. It was stated that I had left the club by 'mutual consent' and for once that was true. The club wanted to get rid of me and I couldn't wait to go.

On 11 May 1985 a 3–0 defeat at Blackburn Rovers relegated Wolves to Division Three. That such a once great club was now to play their football in the lower divisions failed to make news, for on that day football witnessed real tragedy. It was the day of the Bradford fire. Eighteen days later came Heysel.

I told Mary I was 'managed-out'. I had been in football for 38 years, 24 of those as a manager. In all that time I had never applied for a job and, to be honest, I didn't feel like starting now. A number of clubs rang me, but I didn't want to go down a similar road to the one I had trodden with Preston and Wolves, taking on a club that was living hand to mouth, and in constant fear of administrators or liquidators. Becoming manager of such a club, and there were plenty of them around in 1985, was a job for a younger man, someone cutting his managerial teeth who would not mind putting up with and trying to solve a web of problems. Most of which were none of his making and, really, outside the remit of his job.

At this point in my life I felt the desire within me to manage had finally run its course. As a player with Arsenal I had felt a burning desire to manage; it took 28 years for that fire to be extinguished – but in the end it did flicker out.

It wasn't quite the end. I was content to earn a living working in the media, and as an after-dinner speaker, a line of work which by now had really taken off for me. I was, however, persuaded to give management one last shot. It was only in a part-time capacity but I shouldn't even have done that. In 1987 I agreed to become manager of Altrincham of the Vauxhall Conference. The invitation came from 'Alty' chairman Gerry Burman, who was a smashing chairman and a good man to work with. Unfortunately there was a lot of in-fighting on the board which eventually saw Gerry step down. Even in non-league football directors are at each other's throats.

I was very heavily committed to media work at the time but felt I could fulfil my obligations to TV, radio and the press and do a good job for Altrincham. What I couldn't hack was directors with limited experience of football insinuating they knew more about the game than I did. I accepted the job because I still loved a challenge. Those directors were certainly a challenge. When Geoff Lloyd succeeded Gerry he asked to meet me to, as he put it, discuss the future. The first thing Lloyd said was that routines at the club would not be the same under him, and went on to say there was a clash of personalities between us.

'Impossible,' I told him. 'You haven't got one.'

We agreed to disagree. Geoff told me he wanted me to be proactive, so I tendered my resignation.

Not wishing to return to football in any capacity, for the remainder of the 1980s and throughout the '90s I concentrated on my media work and after-dinner speaking. I continued to be heavily involved in the media, particularly radio, until around 2000 when I decided to cut back and concentrate mainly on speaking engagements, a decision which prompted former Manchester United manager Wilf McGuinness, himself a superb after-dinner speaker, to remark, 'Some of Tommy's speeches last longer than the time he spent at some clubs.'

Mary and I moved into a converted barn in a lovely village in north Derbyshire and have continued to be gloriously happy together and, God willing, we shall be for ever more. I haven't retired, I do as much or as little work as I please. I receive offers of work every week and am now in a position where I can cherry pick. Though, just as was the case when I was a manager, money is not all-important to me. I have turned down some lucrative work simply because, for whatever reason, I don't fancy the job. Conversely I will accept work that pays less because I think the job will be fun, or, because I like the people involved.

I often receive invitations to attend games and, the diary willing, always do my best to accept. Some invitations come from people I worked with or for during my time as a manager. For example Doug Ellis has, on several occasions, invited me to be his guest at Villa Park. Without exception I am always warmly greeted by everyone there. Doug is the most congenial host and, invariably, we end up having a good laugh about the old days. Through my old army pal 'Westy', I have become friends with his grandson, David Beckham, and have accepted invitations from David to attend parties and charity dinners. Whenever we meet naturally our conversation is mostly about football, past and present. I still follow football very closely and whenever I am asked to comment on the game today, as ever, I am at pains to be forthright, honest and objective.

Writing this book has been a period of deep reflection for me. I don't regret anything I did in my career. Given I can be compulsive, I have no regrets because whatever decision I took at a certain time, I did so because I believed it to be the right one. When I left Chelsea, a journalist friend, Tony Stratton-Smith, advised me to go away for a time and 'find myself'. I told him life is not about 'finding yourself', it's about developing yourself. All these years on, I still believe that to be true. Throughout my life and career in football, I tried to make the most and best of myself as I developed as a person. There is no tragedy like a wasted life – a life failing of its true destiny. I have had many ups and downs in my life, but feel there is no tragedy to the life I led and certainly not the life I lead now. Nor do I feel my life was wasted. From being a young man I wanted nothing more than to be a footballer then, as my footballing days drew to a close, I wanted to be a manager. I succeeded in those aims, achieved my goals in life and now am blissfully happy with the life Mary and I share. Even now I am often asked for advice by players who are looking to become managers.

The advice I give has more to do with life than simply football and management and it is this – make life happen for you. I feel it certainly happened for me and, lucky me, it is still happening and in the most joyous way. Hallowed Be Thy Game.

DO QUOTE ME:
WHAT THEY SAID ABOUT HIM

Of course Tommy had his weaknesses. For a start he couldn't sew or knit.

BILL SHANKLY

Wherever he goes and whatever he does, they certainly know he has been there. He was a top quality player and a super manager.

SIR TOM FINNEY

I would come back and live in England if the Doc were Prime Minister.

ROD STEWART

When I first made it into the Scotland team, Tommy was an established international. He had a huge personality even then. He was ebullient, effervescent and supremely optimistic, just like the teams he went on to create.

IAN ST JOHN

Typical Scot, may not be sure what he wants, but will fight to the death to get it.

SEAN CONNERY

He was a superb manager. If he had stayed at Manchester United who knows what we would have gone on to achieve, I suspect a lot more success.

LOU MACARI

If Tommy was a manager today he would give Jose Mourinho a run for his money. After the 1976 FA Cup final I was celebrating with Southampton when Tommy telephoned. He said, 'Lawrie, I'm pleased for you and your club. On the day you were deserved winners. Congratulations, enjoy yourselves, you deserve it.' I don't know of another defeated FA Cup final manager who has ever made such a call. He must have been gutted but he was gracious and sporting in defeat.

LAWRIE McMENEMY

He signed me as a kid, played me in the first team at seventeen and made me the youngest captain in the history of Chelsea. I played for seven different managers at Chelsea and he was far and away the best.

RON HARRIS

If the Doc had been a car salesman he would have been a millionaire.

JIM GREGORY (QPR CHAIRMAN)

As a young Celtic professional he sat at the feet of the great European coach, Jimmy Hogan. He always believed defence was 70 per cent of a wing-half's duties and exemplified this belief. As a manager he could be inspirational or chaotic, but his belief in wingers enabled Manchester United to climb out of Division Two and back to the top in English football.

BRIAN GLANVILLE

He used to eat cheats for breakfast. He was the only manager I ever knew who could hold a face-to-face conversation with you and know what was going on twenty yards behind him. He was fantastic as a manager.

TOMMY CAVANAGH

Before a game he always told me the same thing. Go out and enjoy yourself, display your skills and entertain those who have paid hard-earned money to see you play.

CHARLIE COOKE

Tommy was my platoon sergeant. He was one helluva soldier – not some rumbustious hell-raiser – just a bright, dependable, efficient guy you could count on to do what was right when the chips were down.

SYD GRAY (Commanding Officer, British Army – Palestine)

If I had to spend ten years in jail and had to choose a companion, I'd choose Doc. He'd make it seem like one year.

ERIC PURSHOUSE (Former Rotherham United Chairman)

Whenever people criticised Tommy to my face I'd ask them if they knew him. When they said 'No', I'd reply, 'All you know is what you read in the newspapers – he was the finest bloke I ever worked with in the game.'

NEVILLE BRIGGS (Scout)

I remember his Manchester United team particularly well. They played cavalier football and put a smile on the face of supporters in an era when the game was often grim. His team was an extension of himself.

SEAN DOOLEY (Former Editor, Northcliffe Newspapers)

He was a very knowledgeable and jovial manager. That type of person brings something special to the game. Today if a team wins 3–2, the manager says he is concerned about the two goals his team conceded. Tommy wasn't bothered if his

team conceded five as long as they scored six.
GORDON BANKS

Tom was a super manager. My team is Derby County and I helped get him the job as manager. When I was an MP I also spoke on his behalf at his perjury trial. I remember the judge in his summing-up saying, 'His local MP's account must be taken into consideration'. Tommy was quite rightly found not guilty on both counts. When it was all over Tommy thanked me and said, 'No more. I have been in more courts than Bjorn Borg'.
LORD TOM PENDRY (House of Lords)

Tommy upset a lot of players, but which manager hasn't? Every Saturday the reserve team is upset because they are in the reserves.
BRIAN CLOUGH

He was a stylish wing-half and a very good manager. I don't think I ever had a conversation with him without him making me laugh. Doc once said to me, 'Stan, should you ever find yourself being chased by a police dog, don't crawl under a tarpaulin. Run up a little flight of steps, then jump through a hoop of fire – they're trained for that.'
SIR STANLEY MATTHEWS

He could get angry if he felt you weren't putting it in on the field. He once came into the dressing room at half-time and it was like the first twenty minutes of *Saving Private Ryan*.
EDDIE MCCREADIE

He was one of the great managers and a real colourful char-acter. That café of his served good nosh too.
JIMMY GREAVES

I played for him and served under him as a coach. He was great

to work for, an inspirational manager who believed the best form
of defence was attack.

FRANK BLUNSTONE

An agreeable guy who disagreed with everything I did.

GEORGE BEST

He has always been 'boss' to me. When my uncle wrote to him,
Doc gave me a trial at Chelsea and signed me straight away. He
was a tremendous influence on me, in many ways he made me
the player I was.

PETER OSGOOD

Tommy was an excellent defender. He was one of the most difficult opponents I ever encountered.

FERENC PUSKAS

He turned good players into very good players, and the very
good players into greats.

BILLY BREMNER

WHAT HE SAID ABOUT THEM

One of George Best's problems was he was a light sleeper. When it got light he went home and went to sleep.

Football history has been kind to Stan Matthews, largely because he wrote it.

Preston are one of my old clubs, then again most of them are.

Football management is like nuclear war, there is only one winner, the rest are survivors or casualties.

There is a place for the press in football – only they haven't dug it yet.

I promised Rotherham I would take them out of the Second Division and I did – into the Third Division.

I've had more clubs than Jack Nicklaus.

Jim Gregory was a man of whims. One day he could be very generous and give you anything. The next day, if he was a ghost he wouldn't give you a fright.

Roman Abramovich has spent money at Chelsea like Elton John in a flower shop.

DAVID BECKHAM: Alex Ferguson is the best manager I've played for at that level.
DOC: Alex is the only manager you've played for at that level.

No matter how great our triumphs or how tragic our defeats, remember, one billion people in China couldn't care less.

In the end Alan Ball's voice got so high he could only be heard on the pitch during a floodlit game by bats.

I hate that split-screen technique used on SkySport. I don't want to read the football news, that's why I'm watching TV.

Not only should a player never accept an award from a tabloid newspaper, he should try not to do anything that deserves one.

When I watch that antiques programme on TV and see David Dickinson, he strikes me as being living proof the stuff does exactly what it says on the tin.

John Barnes' 'Football Night' is billed as the programme that has 'the whole nation talking'. What we're saying is, 'When is this going to end?'

Vinnie Jones – the only flair was in his nostrils.

Francis Drake went round the world in 1580 – which is over par but not too many strokes when you consider the distance.

I learned a lot about cooking when running my café. For example, there is no such thing as 'a little garlic'.

He was their lone striker and in every sense of the word. He couldn't have been more alone in a game if he had been playing postal chess.

Alex Ferguson is a great manager but not a great man.

I listen to Sven-Goran Eriksson talk about football, I have five cups of coffee but it still doesn't keep me awake.

Ron Atkinson couldn't be here, his hairdresser died – in 1946.

Football is cyclical. At Wolves things went from bad to worse, then the whole process repeated itself.

In football when one door shuts, another will slam in your face.

So they are going to introduce identity cards. Will the Queen have one? Surely she only has to take a five pound note out of her purse.

PR managers at clubs are like nappies. They should be changed regularly and for the same reason.

Because of televising around the world, Jim Watt fought for the world title at two in the morning. What they didn't know was that was to Jim's advantage, everybody fights at two in the morning in Glasgow.

Everybody in Liverpool is getting into this 'City of Culture' thing. I spoke at a dinner there and when I came out, my car was up on four encyclopaedias.

The Romanovs are making as good a job of running Hearts as their namesakes did of running Imperial Russia.

Professionals can sometimes learn from amateurs. The Titanic was built by professionals; Noah was just an amateur boat builder.

MARK RATCLIFFE: You have always been the supreme optimist, Tom. What would you have on your headstone?
DOC: Let's do lunch.

STATISTICS

Thomas Henderson Docherty, born Glasgow 24 August 1928.

Career: St Paul's Boys Guild, Shettleston BG, Shettleston Juniors 1945, served in the Highland Light Infantry July 1946 to 12 July 1948 rising to the rank of Sergeant in Palestine • Celtic 26 July 1948 • Transferred to Preston North End 4 November 1949 (£4,000). Loaned to Third Lanark 12 May 1956 • Transferred to Arsenal 23 August 1958 (£28,000) • Acted as part-time coach to Oxford University and Barnet • Chelsea coach 10 February 1961. Registered as a player 30 August 1961. Appointed Chelsea care-taker-manager 27 September 1961. Became manager 2 January 1962. Loaned to Prague Sydney 1 July 1965. Resigned as Chelsea manager 6 October 1967 • Appointed Rotherham United manager 22 November 1967 • Queens Park Rangers manager 6 November 1968. Left 5 December 1968 • Appointed Aston Villa manager 18 December 1968. Dismissed 19 January 1970 • Coach to Porto February 1970 to June 1971 • Hull City assistant manager 2 July 1971 • Appointed Scotland caretaker manager 12 September 1971. Became manager 1 December 1971 • Appointed Manchester United manager 22 December 1972. Dismissed 4 July 1977 • Appointed Derby County manager 17 September 1977 • Appointed Queens Park Rangers manager 11 May 1979. Dismissed 6 May 1980. Reinstated 15 May 1980. Dismissed 7 October 1980 • Became Sydney Olympic manager December 1980 until 20 June 1981 • Became Preston North End manager 22

June 1981. Dismissed 3 December 1981 • South Melbourne coach July 1982 • Sydney Olympic manager September 1982 until 1 September 1983 • Appointed Wolverhampton Wanderers manager 8 June 1984. Dismissed 4 July 1985 • Altrincham manager 28 September 1987. Resigned 4 February 1988 • Burnley scout 6 June 1989.

Honours:
25 full Scottish caps, 1 goal.
1951 v Wales
1953 v England, Sweden
1954 v Norway, Norway, Austria, Uruguay, Wales, Hungary
1955 v England (1 goal), Austria, Hungary
1956 v Yugoslavia
1957 v England, Spain, Switzerland, West Germany, Spain, Northern Ireland, Switzerland, Wales
1958 v England, Wales, Northern Ireland
1959 v England

Scotland B
1952 v France
1953 v England

Representative matches:
1951 Rest of the UK v Wales
1956 England/Scotland v Ireland/Wales

Honours (as a player):
Preston North End: Football League Division 2 Championship 1950–51, FA Cup (runners-up) 1954.

Honours (as a manager):
Chelsea: Football League Division 2 1962–63 (runners-up), League Cup winners 1965, FA Cup 1967 (runners-up).
Manchester United: Football League Division 2 Championship 1974–75, FA Cup winners 1977.

Season	League		FA Cup		Other cups		Internationals	
	Apps	Goals	Apps	Goals	Apps	Goals	Apps	Goals
CELTIC								
1948–49	9	3	–	–	2	–	–	–
1949–50	–	–	–	–	–	–	–	–
PRESTON NORTH END								
1949–50	15	–	1	–	–	–	–	–
1950–51	42	–	2	–	–	–	–	–
1951–52	42	–	1	–	–	–	1	–
1952–53	41	–	3	–	–	–	2	–
1953–54	26	–	8	–	–	–	4	–
1954–55	39	3	3	–	–	–	5	1
1955–56	41	1	1	–	–	–	–	–
1956–57	37	–	6	–	–	–	6	–
1957–58	40	1	1	–	–	–	4	–
ARSENAL								
1958–59	38	1	4	–	–	–	3	–
1959–60	24	–	3	–	–	–	–	–
1960–61	21	–	–	–	–	–	–	–
CHELSEA								
1961–62	4	–	–	–	–	–	–	–
Totals	420	9	33	–	2	–	25	1

Representative matches 2, Scotland B 2.

INDEX